OUR
EASTERN QUESTION

袁世凱

Yuan Shih K'ai

First President of China, and considered one of the ablest of
Chinese statesmen

OUR
EASTERN QUESTION

AMERICA'S CONTACT WITH THE
ORIENT AND THE TREND OF RE-
LATIONS WITH CHINA AND JAPAN

BY

THOMAS F. MILLARD

AUTHOR OF "THE NEW FAR EAST," "AMERICA AND THE
FAR EASTERN QUESTION," ETC.

ILLUSTRATED WITH
PHOTOGRAPHS AND MAPS

NEW YORK
THE CENTURY CO.
1916

INTRODUCTION

This book is a journalistic summary rather than a literary production. During the period included in its survey I resided in the far East, formerly as correspondent for American publications, and for the last five years as editor of *The China Press* (Shanghai). The design of this work is to extract the more pertinent and significant matters from the tremendous and complex movement of political and economic and sociological forces in the Orient, with intent to expose their directing and controlling elements and tendencies, and with especial attention to their application to America.

The accounts of the revolution in China and its aftermath are of course but imperfect pictures of remarkable events—volumes would be filled to describe them adequately. The effort was to catch the outstanding features and some of the outstanding personalities in their relation to world viewpoint. A great amount of interesting details has perforce been omitted; but those details were in the author's mind when writing, and in formulating the opinions and conclusions expressed.

THOMAS F. MILLARD.

July 1, 1916.

TABLE OF CONTENTS

TABLE OF CONTENTS

LIST OF ILLUSTRATIONS

LIST OF ILLUSTRATIONS

OUR EASTERN QUESTION

OUR EASTERN QUESTION

CHAPTER I

A SHIFT OF POLICIES

Changed conditions—Results of Russo-Japanese War—Japan's accession of power—New factors—Germany's advance—Effects on British policy—Readjustments to meet situation—Effort to sustain *status quo*—The Knox neutralization plan—Principles at stake—The situation in Manchuria—Japan's actions there—The interests of China—Chinchow-Aigun Railway—Basis of Knox plan—International Coöperation desired—Effort to prevent discriminations—Attitude of Great Britain—Diplomatic obstruction at Peking—Position of Russia—Revival of "sphere" idea—What this incident demonstrated.

THE shift of policies and conditions in the far East, which upset the quasi-stability gained by general acceptance of the Hay Doctrine [1] and brought a reversion to dangerous international tendencies there, had its origin in the Russo-Japanese War. This is clear enough now, although, when the war was fought and even for some time after it ended, its effects were but dimly perceived by some governments and hardly at all by the American public. Looking backward, two main factors of the change can be discerned: Japan's accession of power and Germany's advance. The United States, that had acted so importantly in obtaining a basis for stability in the far East, was now to be an unintentional instrument in the disintegration.

Japan's accession of power after the war with Russia affected the far Eastern situation directly; Germany's advance in *Welt-politik* affected it indirectly. Neither Japan's ambi-

[1] Appendix K.

3

tions and new power, nor Germany's progress, alone could have wrought the change. It was their reactions upon other Powers, and especially upon the interests of Great Britain, that gave a new turn to affairs. Japan's success over Russia gave world politics a fresh basis in some important relations. It moderated England's fear of Russia's potency in Asia, which had been a fundamental presumption of Great Britain's Eastern policy for half a century. It brought a new force into Asiatic affairs—Japan. On the other hand, nearer and more obstructive to British commerce and world-influence was the new Germany, pressing for outlets in Africa and Asia Minor. A readjustment of British policy to meet this situation was begun without delay. Russia was placated by admitting her to partnership with England in Persia,[2] and by recognizing her predominating position in central Asia and Mongolia. To offset that, the Anglo-Japanese alliance was revised to include Japan with the defense of India. Japan and Russia were left to compose between themselves their position and attitudes in Manchuria and Mongolia, free of any interference from France and England. This in turn left France and England free to combine to resist Germany, and also, by temporarily securing her far Eastern position, enabled Russia to resume her rôle in Europe in combination with France and England. We need not be concerned here about how these dispositions affected Europe (the great war demonstrated that), but can trace their effects in the far East.

For some time after the conclusion of peace between Japan and Russia there were few surface indications of the changes. There was a period of readjustment when all of the Powers moved cautiously, feeling their ways and each other. The first definite demonstration of the shift was caused by the United States. The interest of America in problems of the far East is a principle of American foreign policy only second to the Monroe Doctrine. John Hay had seen the need to sustain China's autonomy, and his immediate successors to the

[2] Appendix N.

On the right, General Li Yuan Hung, who succeeded Yuan Shih K'ai as President of China. On the left, General Ching Kwan, Tutuh of Szechuen, a prominent progressive

State portfolio had followed his lead. Elihu Root, soon after the Russo-Japanese War, had put Japan once more on record as guaranteeing the Hay Doctrine.[3] Then came the administration of William H. Taft as President of the United States, with P. C. Knox as Secretary of State. Mr. Knox saw the untoward drift of events in Manchuria, and took action that gave the first exposure. By many Mr. Knox has been blamed for forcing the issue then; but a study of his policy and action reveals a sound intention. Mr. Knox failed in his diplomatic efforts for the time, but it is doubtful if that failure worked any real detriment, and it had the advantage of bringing the actual situation nearer to the surface.

Mr. Knox's effort took the form of a proposal to eliminate the causes for international competition and opposition in Manchuria and the whole of China, by providing a basis for international coöperation in accord with the principle of the "open door." Taking Manchuria as a starting-point, his plan was to neutralize existing railways in that region, and for all the Powers that so desired to participate in further development. A review of conditions is necessary to make the Knox plan clear. Railways operating in Manchuria before the Russo-Japanese War had been built by Russia with Russian financing, under an agreement between the Chinese Eastern Railway (Russian company) and China.[4] The lines were an extension of the Siberian Railway across Manchuria to Vladivostok, and an extension southward from Harbin to Port Arthur and Dalny. By the Portsmouth treaty,[5] Russia had ceded to Japan her interests in the railway south of Chang-chun, in central Manchuria. China herself had another railway projected toward Manchuria—the Imperial Railways of North China (now the Peking-Mukden line of the Chinese National Railways). At that time this line extended to Newchwang and to Hsinmintun. There were intimations of British policy, but British subjects in China at that time did not believe that their Government had completely given up its rights under the

[3] Appendix Q. [4] Appendix O. [5] Appendix C.

"open door" in Manchuria to Japan. Some incidents should have enlightened the United States Government, but they did not. The State Department was assuming the *bona fides* of assurances of all the Powers that they would respect the "open door." Mr. Knox must have been dubious of Japan's policy and purposes, but he evidently relied on England. If he erred in his diplomatic calculations, it was in not understanding the extent that Great Britain had shifted her position. Mr. Knox had a clear idea of the state of various foreign interests in China, and he felt that British and American interests there were harmonious as to broad policy. What he apparently failed to comprehend was that, because of conditions affecting British policy in other parts of the world, the British foreign office had deemed it expedient to trade off whatever advantages might come to England by trying to sustain the "open door" in Manchuria. If Mr. Knox did not then understand that, he can be excused, for the great British interests in China and their London connections did not know it, as was demonstrated. Whether, at that time, the British foreign office had decided to drop the "open door" doctrine in the whole of China is not clear, but subsequent events throw some light on this. No doubt there were differences of opinion in the British Government on this point. The trend of policy was unmistakable: to grant Japan and Russia a free hand in Manchuria and Mongolia, in return for certain compensations to England, but to draw the line there if possible. I believe British policy at that time realized the difficulty of preserving Manchuria to China, and for compensations elsewhere was willing to yield British rights and interests in that region to Japan and Russia; but England did not want to go further than she had to, and still thought it was possible to sustain China's autonomy south of the Great Wall. As to the "open door," if it could be preserved, well and good, but if it had to go, then Great Britain had a large "sphere" defined and recognized in understandings with other Powers [6]—indeed, this *quid pro quo* was among

[6] Appendices I, J, U, V.

England's compensations for yielding to Japan. How Japan regarded her part of that obligation, was to appear later.

The Knox "neutralization" plan embodied and exemplified almost completely the principles of the Hay Doctrine on one side, and its opposing hypothesis, and consequently a study of the plan, and the reasons for and manner of its defeat, elucidate what is comprehended in China's struggle to preserve her autonomy, and what the Hay Doctrine was designed for. Undoubtedly Mr. Knox understood these matters, and had in mind in advancing his plan at that time the urgent necessity to check opposing tendencies, and to restore vitality to the Hay Doctrine, rather than merely to support an American project. Some immediate antecedents of the Knox proposal should be explained.

I will not review the commercial campaign of Japan in Manchuria and Korea immediately after the conclusion of peace, which made a mockery of the open door,[7] but will confine discussion to the issue of railways. Soon after the Russo-Japanese War, China prepared to begin development of her Manchurian provinces, which had been backward because of inaccessibility. Railways promise to change this, and to open the comparatively unsettled and fertile regions of the North to be populated and cultivated by Chinese emigrants from densely and over-populated provinces. Furthermore, it may be conceded that China had political considerations also in mind in these arrangements—it would be strange after her experience had she not—and wished by this means to drive a wedge between Japan and Russia, and open a way to preserve the neutrality of Chinese territory. From China's standpoint these purposes are legitimate, and logically cannot be assumed to threaten any valid foreign right or interest. An extension of the Imperial Railways of North China northward to the Amur had been projected for years, and tentatively is marked on modern maps of the Empire. In 1907 China made a con-

---

[7] These events are reviewed fully in the author's "America and the Far Eastern Question" (1909).

tract with a British firm (British and Chinese Corporation, Ltd.) to build an extension of this railway from Hsinmintun to Fakumen. Objection was made by Japan on the ground that this extension would parallel part of the South Manchurian Railway, which Japan secured by the Portsmouth treaty, and she produced in support of her position a *secret* clause of the Yuan-Komura agreement made between Japan and China, concerning Manchuria, in 1905.[8] China denied that she had accepted that secret agreement; but Japan induced England to refuse support to the British firm, and China was compelled to abandon the project. This incident is significant because it is the first definite evidence of England's policy to support her ally in the North even at detriment to British commercial interests. There is no doubt that China, in projecting extensions of her railways in Manchuria, designed to create there a wider international balance of interest, and to this end she desired them to be financed by British and Americans. In the summer of 1908 (August 11), Tang Shao-yi made an agreement with Willard D. Straight, then American consul-general at Mukden, that American capital would be employed in constructing the northern section of a line from Tsitsihar to Aigun, the idea then being that the southern section would be constructed by British interests. The deaths of the Emperor and Empress Dowager, the dismissal of Yuan Shih-k'ai and other events followed, and these projects were held in abeyance. Meanwhile, Mr. Straight had notified his Government of the signing of the memorandum concerning the financing of the northern section of that railway, and soon afterward was himself transferred to the State Department, which he left in 1909 to become agent in China for the American Banking Group which, with the approval of the Government, was organized to finance American participation. The Tsitsihar-Aigun section provided the basis for organizing the American Banking Group, for it was a definite piece

[8] Appendix E.

of business in sight; but events for a time obscured this project by arousing international comment about a similar matter. This was the attempt by China to finance various sections of railways designed to complete the Canton-Hankow and Hankow-Chengtu lines, and which are grouped under the Hukuang loan. This loan had been projected for several years, and in 1909 an agreement was formulated whereby it was to be financed and constructed with British, German, and French capital. At this juncture the American Government reminded China that the Chinese Government specifically had promised that if when it was ready to build these roads it required foreign capital, American interests would have an opportunity to participate. When other foreign interests heard of American intervention, they tried to rush the matter to a conclusion, which brought about some rather sensational moves, including President Taft's personal telegram to the Regent asking that the agreement should not be concluded without American interests being given a chance to participate. As there was no legitimate ground for excluding Americans, the other foreign interests were impelled to assent to their participation, although there was some irritation over the matter. It was agreed to admit Americans, and then followed a period of negotiation about terms. While negotiations concerning the Hukuang loan thus were tied up, the representative of the American Banking Group had been busy about the matter of Manchurian railway extensions. Upon consultation with the Chinese Government, Mr. Straight found that it wished if possible to keep its agreement with British interests about the Fakumen section, although logically it had been abrogated when the project fell through because England would not support it. A result was that the British interests came to an agreement with the American Banking Group by which a consolidation was effected jointly to promote a railway from Chinchow to Aigun, penetrating the same territory which would have been opened by the Fakumen section, but keeping far enough away from the South Manchurian Railway to avoid Japanese objections.

Americans were to finance and British to construct the road.
Semi-official attempts were made to prevent a consolidation of
British and American interests in this project, and to induce
the British contracting firm to join with Japanese interests in
the matter; but the British firm objected to this affiliation on
business grounds, and it also knew that China would rather
not build the road than have it controlled by Japan; moreover,
it was a foregone conclusion that Russia would be alarmed
by such an arrangement. It was thought by China and by the
American Group that its participation would not cause alarm.
On October 2, 1909, a preliminary agreement for construction
and financing of the Chinchow-Aigun Railway was signed at
Mukden by Viceroy Hsi-Liang for China, Willard Straight
for the American Banking Group, and Lord ffrench for Paul-
ing & Company. These negotiations were conducted with
celerity and secrecy, for already diplomatic influence was being
exerted to obstruct them. Japan, ever alert, had made inquiries of the Chinese Government, claiming that if anything
was contemplated she ought to participate. Notwithstanding diplomatic pressure to prevent it, an Imperial edict ratifying the preliminary agreement was issued January 21,
1910.

By procuring an understanding that Americans would have
a part in developing railways and other enterprises in Manchuria, and getting a preliminary agreement with the Chinese
officials in Manchuria to build the Chinchow-Aigun line, Mr.
Straight had made a foundation for the Knox "neutralization" plan by giving American interests a tangible status.
Therefore Mr. Knox, in advancing his proposal, was able to
show that American interests were not playing a selfish game,
by suggesting that other foreign interests would be admitted
to participation in the Chinchow-Aigun project. The attitude
of the United States is expressed in a note to the British Government presented by Ambassador Whitelaw Reid on November 6, 1909; and Sir Edward Grey's reply. The italics are
mine:

Department of State,
Washington, November 6, 1909.

In reply to Sir Edward Grey's inquiries reported in his telegram of October 20, Mr. Reid is instructed to present to the Foreign Office textually the following memorandum:

Now that there has been signed and ratified by an unpublished imperial decree an agreement by which the American and British interests are to coöperate in the financing and construction of the Chinchow-Tsitsihar-Aigun Railroad, the Government of the United States is prepared cordially to coöperate with His Britannic Majesty's Government in diplomatically supporting and facilitating this enterprise, so important alike to the progress and to the commercial development of China. The Government of the United States would be disposed to favor ultimate participation to a proper extent on the part of other interested Powers whose inclusion might be agreeable to China and which are known to support the principle of equality of commercial opportunity and the maintenance of the integrity of the Chinese Empire. However, before the further elaboration of the actual arrangement, the Government of the United States asks His Britannic Majesty's Government to give their consideration to the following alternative and more comprehensive projects: First, perhaps the most effective way to preserve the undisturbed enjoyment by China of all political rights in Manchuria and to promote the development of those provinces under a practical application of the open door and equal commercial opportunity would be to bring the Manchurian highways, the railroads, under an economic, scientific, and *impartial administration* by some plan vesting in China the ownership of the railroads through funds furnished for that purpose by the interested Powers willing to participate. Such loan should be for a period ample to make it reasonably certain that it could be met within the time fixed and should be upon such terms as would make it attractive to bankers and investors. The plan should provide that nationals of the participating Powers should supervise the railroad system during the term of the loan and the governments concerned should enjoy for such period the usual preferences for their nationals and materials upon an equitable basis *inter se.* The execution of such a plan would naturally require the coöperation of China and of Japan and Russia, the reversionary and the concessionaires, respectively, of the existing Manchurian railroads, as well as that of Great Britain and the United States, whose especial interests rest upon the existing contract relative to the Chinchow-Aigun Railroad. The advantages of such a plan to Japan and to Russia are obvious. Both those Powers, desiring in good faith to protect the policy of the open door and equal opportunity in Manchuria and wishing to assure to China unimpaired sovereignty, might well be expected to welcome an opportunity to shift the separate duties, responsibilities, and expenses they have undertaken in the protection of their respective commercial and other interests, for impartial assumption by the combined Powers, including themselves, in proportion to their interests. The Government of the United States has some reason to hope that such a plan might meet favorable consideration on the part of Russia and has reason to believe that American financial participation would be forthcoming. Second, should this suggestion not be found feasible in its entirety, *then the desired end would be approximated, if not attained, by Great Britain and the United States diplomatically supporting the Chinchow-Aigun arrangement and inviting the interested Powers friendly to complete commercial neutralization of Manchuria* to participate in the financing and construction of that line and of such additional lines as future commercial development may demand, and at the same time to supply funds for the purchase by China of such of the existing lines as might be offered for inclusion in this system. The Government of the United States hopes that the principle involved in the foregoing suggestions may commend itself to His Britannic Majesty's Government. That principle finds support in the additional reasons that the communication of some such plan would avoid the irritations likely to be engendered by the uncontrolled direct negotiations of bankers with the Chinese Government, and also that it would create such a community of substantial interest in China as would facilitate a coöperation calculated to simplify the problems of fiscal and monetary reforms now receiving such earnest attention by the Imperial Chinese Government.

American Embassy,
London, November 26, 1909.

Sir: I have the honor to transmit herewith the full text of a reply received this evening from Sir Edward Grey to my note communicating the memorandum contained in your telegram of November 6, 1 P.M. The substance of it is cabled to you simultaneously in my November 26, 6 P.M.   WHITELAW REID.

Foreign Office,
London, November 25, 1909.

Your Excellency:
I have the honor to acknowledge the receipt of your excellency's note of the 9th instant, making certain proposals with a view to

The Chinese Revolution.   Imperial (northern) troops at Hanyang

The Chinese Revolution.   Northern troops at Hankow

preserving the undisturbed enjoyment by China of all political rights in Manchuria and to promoting the development of the Province under a practical application of the policy of the open door and equal commercial opportunity. The first of the proposals made by your excellency is to the effect that the Manchurian highways and the railroad should be brought under an economic and scientific and impartial administration by some plan vesting in China the ownership of railroads through funds furnished for the purpose by the interested Powers willing to participate, and you add that the execution of such a plan would require the coöperation of China and of Japan and Russia, as well as the United States and Great Britain, whose special interests rest upon the existing contract relative to the Chinchow-Aigun Railroad. Your excellency goes on to say that should the above suggestion not be found feasible in its entirety, the desired end would be approximated, if not attained, by Great Britain and the United States diplomatically supporting the Chinchow-Aigun arrangement and inviting interested Powers, friendly to the complete commercial neutrality of Manchuria, to participate in the financing of that line, and of such additional lines as future commercial development may demand, and at the same time to supply funds for the purchase by China of such of the existing lines as might be offered for inclusion in this system. The general principle in the first of your excellency's two suggestions entirely commends itself to His Majesty's Government, so far as the preservation of the open-door policy and equal commercial opportunity are concerned, and would in their opinion be well adapted to securing to China full control in Manchuria. I am, however, of the opinion, that until the pending negotiations on the Hukiang loan have been completed, it would seem undesirable to consider the question of another international loan for China's railway undertakings, and I would suggest, therefore, for the present at any rate, it would be wiser to postpone consideration of the first scheme. As regards the alternative proposal contained in your excellency's note, I observe with satisfaction that the coöperation of interested Powers forms part of the scheme, and I have the honor to suggest, for your excellency's consideration, that as a preliminary step toward attaining this desirable end *the two governments should unite in endeavoring to persuade the Chinese Government to admit the Japanese to participation in the Chinchow-Aigun line,* as being the parties most interested. The question of supplying funds for the purchase by China of existing lines to be connected with the Chinchow-Aigun line could be considered subsequently.

I have, etc.

E. GREY.

Some phrases of this exchange of views between the American and British Governments about the Knox plan are interesting. The American note desires "impartial administration" of railways in Manchuria. That was applicable to a condition in Manchuria which I described with great detail in *America and the Far Eastern Question,* from which book I will quote, pages 210–211: "In all treaties granting to foreign governments or corporations, a right to build and operate railways in China, it is understood that railways must give equal facilities to all foreign nations. It is true that some railway concessions exacted from China at a time when she was particularly helpless and ignorant of such things, are ambiguous in this and other important matters, perhaps purposely so; but this tendency long ago was noted by the diplomacy of the world, and steps were taken, by mutual exchange of views, to guarantee international equity in this. Most observers of events in China will recall John Hay's successful effort to secure definite assurance from Germany that the Shantung Railway will not be operated so as to discriminate against goods of other nations, and the international understanding respecting the open door that resulted from his action. Did not China and foreign nations trading within her borders recognize this principle we might, and probably would, see a German railway in China favoring German products in its tariff rates; a French railway carrying French goods cheaper than British, German, and American; an English railway giving rebates to British shippers while charging a straight rate to their competitors, and so on. Suppose in the United States the Pennsylvania system gave to German goods a lower rate than to British, French, or Austrian; that lines controlled by Mr. Hill were owned by the French Government, which permitted all goods from France to be carried for less than goods originating in England and Germany, or even America. Would not such a condition result in commercial chaos, to say nothing of possibilities for international friction? . . . Nothing can be clearer than that Japan's position as a railway owner and operator in Manchuria is as a corporation, not a government; and as a corporation she is amenable, or should be, to the laws and treaties of China. Any other interpretation of foreign railway franchises there would be tantamount to destruction of China's power to regulate commerce within her domain. Japan may operate railways as a government in Japan . . . but in China she should be required to conduct them as a corporation. When, therefore, Japan announced an intention to permit the transport of Japanese products and goods shipped by Japanese merchants for consumption in Manchuria over a railway in Manchuria free of charges, while other foreign products and traders and the Chinese must pay, it looks like deliberately setting at naught the Hay Agreement." This and other discriminatory uses Japan was making of the South Manchurian Railway was what Mr. Knox meant, no doubt, in trying to secure "impartial administration" of all railways in that part of China.

It is evident that Mr. Knox was not very sanguine that Japan would approve his plan, although the American note states that there was reason to think that Russia might assent; for the note suggests that Great Britain and the United States should, in the event of other Powers refusing to come in, press the Chinchow-Aigun project. Such a course by Great Britain and America, if carried out, would have been almost as effective in neutralizing Manchuria and preserving China's autonomy there as the Knox plan would have done. Sir Edward Grey in his reply approved the principles of all of Mr. Knox's suggestions, but it developed that the British Government was so far committed in other ways that it could not join the United States in pressing the Chinchow-Aigun line. Therefore, when Japan and Russia got together, and decided to oppose the neutralization plan, Great Britain and France were compelled to stand with those Powers and oppose America. This was the hidden snare that Mr. Knox's diplomacy tripped on.

Secretary Knox presented his proposal simultaneously to

Russia and Japan on December 18, 1909. Prior to this it had been laid before the Chinese Government, which was glad to assent, since its acceptance and promulgation would have relieved China of foreign interference in her northern provinces and clarified the whole Eastern situation. The proposal was given publicity by Japan and Russia after they mutually agreed to reject it. While those governments were making a pretense of taking time to consider the proposal (there is evidence that they agreed to reject it within a week after it was received), they began to exert pressure at Peking to prevent issuance of the edict ratifying the Chinchow-Aigun agreement. The Chinchow-Aigun Railway agreement was a factor in the matter, because it gave Americans and English a vested interest in Manchuria. When it was known that an edict would be issued, effort to forestall it by previously announcing the rejection of the neutralization proposal was made, but the rejection came one day late. The legal basis of the neutralization proposal is the vested right of China, by treaties with Japan and Russia, to purchase the Manchurian railways at a fair valuation at the end of a fixed period; so Mr. Knox merely suggested that this recovery be anticipated.

The Knox plan was rejected by Russia on January 22, 1910, and by Japan on January 24, 1910.[9] This action had been preceded by a palpable effort by the Russian and Japanese press to veil the facts with a cloud of false issues. Even statesmen joined in the chorus of misrepresentation. Count Hayashi, then Japanese minister for foreign affairs, talked about "confiscation"; which was an inadvertence when Japan's confiscatory course in Manchuria is remembered. Of course the Knox plan provided for full payment to Russia and Japan for any interests they would surrender. With the rejection of the Knox neutralization plan, which would have included the Chinchow-Aigun Railway, the diplomacy which was actively trying to keep American interests out of China was concentrated on it, and developments came rapidly. The issue raised

[9] Appendix A.

in these negotiations contains the possible genesis of a war which may involve the United States, and so I will elucidate their more important and significant phases. One cannot doubt, when the diplomatic representations are considered in sequence in the light of the existing international alignment in the East, that in this matter Russia, Japan, England, and France acted by mutual agreement under a private understanding between those nations. While fully to comprehend their import requires some explanation, the various representations made in the course of putting the screws upon China and the handcuffs on American diplomacy are illuminating and significant. In all quoted communications the italics are inserted by me for emphasis.

The Japanese Minister to the Wai Wu-pu

January 31, 1910.

Your Excellency:

I formerly had a verbal interview with President Liang Tun-yen on the subject of the Chinchou-Aigun Railway and stated clearly to him the expectation of my Government. I also telegraphed my Government for instructions and have now a reply to the effect that this matter must be considered with extreme caution. My Government is now considering it and cannot hastily formulate its *demands;* but, as I formerly stated in my verbal interview, this is a matter which vitally affects Japan's interests. Before the Chinese Government determines anything, *the consent of my Government must first be obtained.* If the position of my country is ignored and a decision is made *without referring the matter to my Government,* it will be hard to estimate the *seriousness of the trouble* that may be caused in the relations of the two countries. I am therefore instructed to warn the Chinese Government that it must realize the necessity of caution.

With compliments, etc,

IJUIN.

The Russian Minister to the Wai Wu-pu

February 2, 1910.

Your Excellency:

Your Excellency formerly inquired of us verbally as to the view which my Government would take of assisting in the construction of the Chinchou-Aigun Railway. I referred the matter to my Government and now have the following reply:

The Russian Government regards this matter as one of extreme importance and until it has been carefully considered no reply can be made to China.

The Russian Minister is ordered to state clearly what he has already stated to the Wai Wu-pu, viz: that the Russian Government expects that China will not settle any such matter *without first consulting Russia. Otherwise there will be trouble in the relationship between the two countries.*

A necessary despatch, etc.

KOROSTOVETZ.

The Russian Minister to the Wai Wu-pu

February 4, 1910.

Your Excellency:

I have received a note from St. Petersburg regarding the concession to *America* to build the Chinchow-Aigun Railway.

The Russian Minister in America has already received instructions to give Russia's reply concerning the railway *to the American Government* as follows:

Since America has invited Russia to participate in the construction of the Chinchow-Aigun Railway and has consented to Russia's desire to take time for careful consideration of the matter before making a reply, the opinion of Russia is that in not notifying Russia and in not considering that in case Russia did not take a share she would oppose the undertaking America is conscious of having made a mistake and has therefore stopped the loan negotiations. Russia expects that nothing will be settled without first obtaining the consent of Russia.

I now transmit to your excellency the general sense of the above communication and notify your excellency that this matter *must not* be recklessly settled without first having obtained the consent of Russia.

A necessary despatch, etc.

KOROSTOVETZ.

M. Korostovetz took it upon himself, assuming to quote Russia's note to the State Department, to assert that America realized her mistake in not recognizing that she must consult Russia about engaging in enterprises in China, and had quit the negotiations. This caused the Chinese Government to make inquiries, and Henry P. Fletcher, the American Chargé d'Affaires, assured the Wai Wu-pu that the American Government had not so informed Russia.

The Russian Minister to the Prince of Ch'ing

February 8, 1910.

Your Imperial Highness:

I formerly had a verbal interview and also sent notes to the Ministers of Your Highness's Board on the subject of the Chinchow-Aigun Railway. I have now received my Government's instructions in regard to the reply to the American proposition for the neutralization of the Manchurian Railways and the construction of the Chinchow-Aigun Railway in the form of a memorandum, which I forward herewith.

Enclosure. A necessary despatch, etc. KOROSTOVETZ.

Memorandum in Regard to the Chinchou-Aigun Railway.
Transmitted to the Prince of Ch'ing by the
Russian Minister, February 8, 1910.

In respect to the expressed intention of the American Government to build a railway from Chinchow to Aigun, the Russian Government must declare clearly that this road would seriously affect the interests of Russia. This railway when completed would not only connect from the south with the Northern Manchurian Railway, but at Aigun would *reach the actual territories of Russia.* Thus it would affect both *military and political* arrangements and would materially change the relations of the Manchurian Railways *to eastern Mongolia and northern Manchuria.* Therefore this must be inquired into and an acceptable method of procedure must be decided upon, and *it cannot be permitted unless the Russian Government first knows the particulars of the proposed arrangements.* The Russian Government wishes to go into this matter very carefully, and *expects that the plans will first be communicated to it.* After carefully considering the plans the Russian Government will reply as to the construction of the railway, and *will issue a definite pronunciamento as to the conditions on which this railway may be built.*

In regard to all future railways in Manchuria which China may propose to build with borrowed capital, *the Russian Government must be first consulted* and must first consider if the plans have any consequences to *the military and political interests of Russia,* or to the Northern Manchurian Railways, *thereafter determining what must be done* to balance the influence of the arrangements made for the said railways.

In that Note all pretense that Russia's objection is based on possible commercial injury to the Chinese Eastern Railway is dropped, and it clearly is stated that the chief objections are political and strategical. Which is to say, that Russia formally asserted the right to regulate and control railway development within portions of China in the light of Russia's political and strategical interests, and to exclude American participation on these grounds. If language and all the logic of circumstances can make anything clear, it did so in that instance. The fact that this memorandum was sent to Prince Ch'ing instead of to the Wai Wu-pu shows that all possible influences were being brought to bear to bully the latter, for it was well known that Prince Ch'ing took slight interest in foreign affairs and did not keep posted about details. This move evidently was designed to frighten the Court, and bring indirect pressure to bear upon the ministers in the Wai Wu-pu. On February 9, the day after the above memorandum was presented by the Russian Minister, Max Muller, the British Chargé d'Affaires, went to the Wai Wu-pu and discussed the matter with Liang Tun-yen, the Chinese foreign minister. Mr. Muller informed Liang Tun-yen that England feared China was going to be led into serious difficulty by America in this matter, and suggested caution, which was a diplomatic way of giving American diplomacy a backset. He further stated definitely that his Government felt that China should *consult Japan and Russia* about railway development in Manchuria. About that time, also, the French Government came to the assistance of Russia in frightening China, and made representations.

The French Minister to the Wai Wu-pu

February 10, 1910.

Your Excellency:

The French Government with a view to China's welfare intends requesting the Chinese Government not to make any agreement with any other nation regarding the Chinchou-Aigun Railway previous to consulting Russia and Japan regarding the same. Thus international friction in Manchuria will be obviated and the welfare of all nations promoted in Asia.

DE MARGERIE.

What revolution and rebellion means to China. Scenes at Nanking and
Hankow after those cities were burned and looted

The French Minister to the Wai Wu-pu

February 18, 1910.

Your Excellency:

The Government of the French Republic, with the idea that it is in the interest of China to avoid everything which may occasion complications or difficulties in the extreme Orient, and to maintain harmonious relations among the powers *now having interests in Asia*, desires to recommend to the Imperial Chinese Government not to conclude an arrangement on the subject of the railway line between Chinchou and Aigun *without previously having come to an agreement with the Russian Government and the Japanese Government.*

DE MARGERIE.

The Japanese Minister to the Wai Wu-pu

February 14, 1910.

Your Excellency:

The Imperial Government of Japan looks upon the construction of the Chinchou-Aigun Railway as a matter of great importance in its effect upon the prosperity of the South Manchurian Railway. Yet the Chinese Government has for its aim in constructing this railway the development of Manchuria and Mongolia. The Japanese Government takes this into consideration and makes the following propositions with a view to assisting in the construction of the road.

1. Japan will participate in the construction of the Chinchou-Aigun Railway by sharing in the loan, furnishing engineers and railway materials, and participating in the construction work. The rules under which such participation shall take place will be amicably arranged with the powers concerned.

2. In order to connect the Chinchou-Aigun Railway with the South Manchurian Railway, *China will construct a branch line from some station on the Chinchou-Aigun Railway toward the southeast to some station on the South Manchurian Railway.* The location of said line and the point at which it shall connect with the South Manchurian Railway *must* be settled by amicable discussion with the Japanese Government.

It will be observed that the Japanese Government overlooks the important consequences to the South Manchurian Railway which will be caused by the construction of the Chinchow-Aigun Railway, but certainly the reason for assisting in the construction of the Chinchow-Aigun Railway is because the projected line of the railway, starting from Chinchow and passing through Taonan-fu, is at a great distance from the South Manchurian Railway. If the proposed location of the railway is to be materially changed, the Japanese Government will have a concern in this and *will expect to be consulted.*

IJUIN.

Japan thus did not officially oppose the construction of the Chinchow-Aigun Railway, however taking care to assert her right to be consulted as to its location; but she insisted upon participation, and upon terms which were impossible for China to accept without stultifying herself—which was equivalent to obstruction. This proposal by Japan to assist in financing the line and in providing materials illuminates her *bona fides* in advancing the suggestion; for if Japan had got the right to participate in financing the line she would have had to borrow her share of capital to lend it in turn to China. Next followed the Russian counter-proposal.

The Russian Minister to the Wai Wu-pu

March, 4, 1910.

Your Excellency:

The Wai Wu-pu formerly asked the Russian Minister verbally for the views of the Russian Government on the project of China to construct a railway from Chinchow to Aigun. The Russian Minister notified the Russian Foreign Office so that it might take it into consideration. A telegram has been received directing the Russian Minister to state that the Russian Government, having carefully considered the proposal of China to build a railway from Chinchow to Aigun, has concluded that it would result in serious injury both to the *Russian frontier defenses* and to her commercial interests.

In the 25th year of Kuang Hsu (1899) the Chinese Government declared that in constructing all railways northward from Peking capital would be borrowed from no other country than Russia. The Russian Government would not be disposed to insist upon China complying with her former promise in this matter of her borrowing capital for the construction of railways if Russia's *frontier defenses* and profits in respect to the Manchurian Railways were not affected. The Russian railway experts have reported that the Chinchow-Aigun Railway cannot fail to take from the Russian Manchurian Railway profits on transportation to the amount of 5,000,000 rubles annually, and will ruin the property which *China has a right to regain after a period of 29 years,* or which will revert to China free of cost after a period of 73 years.

The Russian Government is of the opinion *that the capitalists concerned in this enterprise* have no other object in making the loan than the obtaining of profit and *that they have no political aims.* If therefore the railway which it is proposed to build from Chinchow to Aigun should be constructed elsewhere, the commercial advantages would be equally great, while Russia would suffer no injury. The foreign capitalists should have no objection to this. In view of the above considerations, the Russian Government now proposes to the Chinese Government that instead of building a railway from Chinchow to Aigun it build a line connecting with the Peking-Mukden Railway from Kalgan to Urga and thence northward to Kiakta on the Russian border. It is understood that China has long had an intention to build this railway, so that China and the foreign nations would be of one mind about this. The difficulty of China which has caused her to hesitate up to the present is that since this railway would not connect with the trans-Siberian Railway it could not be very profitable. The Russian Government would not be averse to establishing such a connection, and would be willing to build a branch road from a station on the railway in the Province of Trans-Baikalia to Kiakta. But in the event of China's building this Kalgan-Kiakta railway she should allow Russian capitalists to be responsible for building the section *from Urga to Kiakta.*

The Russian Government greatly hopes that the Chinese Government will see clearly in this proposal the mutual advantages which would accrue to both countries.

The Russian Government would gladly accede to the wish of the Chinese Government to build a railway in Manchuria with borrowed capital if it did not affect *Russia's frontier defenses* and the profits of her Manchurian Railways. Therefore Russia now brings forward this proposal and trusts that the Chinese Government will show a friendly spirit in helping to carry it out. The American and other Governments concerned have already been notified of the views of Russia.

A necessary despatch, etc. KOROSTOVETZ.

This memorandum was immediately supported by the French Government.

The French Minister to the Wai Wu-pu

March 4, 1910.

Your Excellency:

The Government of the French Republic, desiring to get settled the question of the railways in the north of China originally brought up by the proposal of the *Government of the United States* in connection with the construction of a railway between Chinchow and Aigun, by way of Tsitsihar, believes, however, as it has already made known to the Chinese Government, that this project (Chinchow-Aigun) cannot be realized without the risk of raising certain complications, unless by agreement with the *governments principally interested, notably Russia;* now convinced, besides, of the unfavorable consequences to Russia which the projected railway may have *in relation to her northern frontier* and the commercial interests of the Manchurian Railway, the French Government thinks, with the Imperial Government of Russia, that the interests of the financiers *who have proposed to China* with a purely commercial object a loan for the construction of the Chinchow-Aigun line will be fully satisfied if the Chinese Government should construct, with the aid of the same financiers, the prolongation of the Kalgan Railway toward Urga and Kiakta.

The Government of the French Republic is convinced that this line, the construction of which in an important Chinese region would not give rise to any political question, and, besides, having been fully considered, would likewise offer serious advantages to China.

It [the French Government] would consequently see with particular satisfaction the Imperial Chinese Government accept the propositions which have been submitted in this connection by the Imperial Russian Government.

DE MARGERIE.

Nothing further is required to show that rejection of the Knox plan and obstruction to the Chinchow-Aigun line were entirely lacking in regard for China's wishes and rights, and were contrary to plain provisions of the Portsmouth treaty. British interests in China were surprised and displeased by the attitude of their Government. On June 15, 1910, the matter was brought up in Parliament. Replying to questions, Sir Edward Grey stated the position of the Government as being entirely favorable to the principle of Anglo-American co-operation in the Chinchow-Aigun line, but said the British Government felt bound by the almost forgotten Scott-Muravieff note [10] exchanged between Russia and Great Britain in 1899, when these nations mutually agreed not to attempt

---

[10] Appendix U.

railway exploitation in the Yangtze Valley and north of the Great Wall, respectively. This explanation was interesting because, in the autumn of 1909, Russia made formal request to be admitted to participation in the Hukuang loan, indicating that Russia then regarded the Scott-Muravieff understanding as a dead letter. The understanding had never been formally revoked; but it was presumed to be superseded by general acceptance by all the Powers of the Hay Doctrine. Here we see bi-Power politics at work. If Great Britain retained a right to object to Russian operations in the Yangtze Valley, she logically must not venture outside the Wall. Two courses were possible—to assume that all previous agreements to the contrary were superseded by the Hay agreement, or to cling to the old ''sphere'' idea. Russia adroitly revived the Scott-Muravieff note so as to raise this issue, and since she could not play it both ways, and being also circumscribed by Anglo-Japanese relations, Great Britain fell back on an attempt to conserve an exclusive sphere for herself in the Yangtze Valley.

Germany was asked by some nations to address China in regard to the Chinchow-Aigun Railway in similar terms to those used by Japan, Russia, France, and England; but she declined to do so.

To recapitulate, we find that the following issues affecting the sovereignty of China and the open door principle within her territory were sharply defined by results of Mr. Knox's efforts:

1. The right of China to decide upon the course of railway development within her territory was denied by foreign nations.

2. Certain foreign nations declared that their strategical and political interests must be considered as paramount in planning a railway system within China's territory.

3. Certain foreign nations asserted the right to decide who will finance, construct, and operate railways within China's territory; and to veto arrangements in regard to these matters which China wishes to carry out.

In respect to the United States, this issue was raised:

Foreign nations have asserted the right to interfere in business transactions between American citizens and the Chinese Government, in violation of treaties between the United States and China, and of covenants of those Governments with China and the United States; a doctrine which is susceptible to world-wide application.

With these results, it might be assumed that the effect of the Knox proposal was disastrous to China and to American interests. It is clear, however, that the Knox diplomacy did not create the conditions that caused these results; it only exposed them, and brought them out into the open. This surely was worth doing. And when causes for the slump back to the "sphere" policy are analyzed, Japan appears as the real disintegrator. Had Japan then really wanted and intended to abide by her treaties and agreements, it would have been feasible for Great Britain also to stand by the Hay Doctrine, and that hypothesis would have carried the day.

CHAPTER II

THE REVOLUTION IN CHINA

BEFORE the revised attitude of the Powers, as demonstrated by the Manchuria incident, had time to reformulate on a new basis, a distraction was provided by China herself. This was the revolution of 1911–12.

Although it had been expected and predicted for years and its elements were known to be working throughout the Empire, nevertheless the revolution surprised even those conversant with conditions in the country and its politics. There was nothing in its immediate antecedents to distinguish the situation from scores of previous situations. There was unrest in some provinces, but there always had been unrest. The Government was slowly moving toward reform. A provisional constitution had been proclaimed, and a responsible ministry, with a Privy Council, had in 1911 replaced the Grand Secretariat and Boards. Evidences of a growth of national sentiment, or patriotism, under pressure of events and foreign influences, were apparent in all parts of the Empire. A majority of the dominating middle class, spoken of as gentry and composed of the official and business and propertied elements, were conservative, and seemed to be satisfied with the progress

27

being made. That a strong popular antagonism to the reigning Manchu dynasty existed was known; but this opposition was unorganized and lacked cohesion. There was little noticeable sentiment for a change in the *form* of government. Revolutionary secret societies existed, but were not thought to be formidable. The Peking Government, in taking measures for internal reform, apparently was stimulated more by the necessity of such action to prevent national disintegration under foreign pressure, than by apprehension of internal upheaval. But all the time popular sentiment was focussing its dissatisfaction on the reigning dynasty, which was blamed for all of China's ills and wrongs and humiliations.

A turbulence in the great interior province of Szechuen preceded the revolution, and in a way presaged its motive. The Szechuen trouble had a foreign angle, for it turned on the question of foreign loans, and was an expression of the growing hostility of Chinese to some phases of foreign participation in China's railway development. Intelligent Chinese had begun to understand how China's internal autonomy was being undermined by foreign railway concessions, and by some conditions of foreign loan contracts, and there was a widespread fear that the process would lead to national disintegration and foreign domination. The railways embraced in the Hukuang loan included a line to Szechuen, and the Szechuenese objected to the proposed agreement on several grounds. Some of these objections were reasonable, and some were not; many were founded on misunderstanding and misapprehensions. There was agitation in favor of building the Szechuen line exclusively with native capital, which was impractical. Notwithstanding protests, the Government proceeded with the Hukuang loan, whereupon disorders broke out in Szechuen and the Viceroy was killed. The size and population and wealth of Szechuen, and its inaccessibility, made the task of placating and pacifying it very difficult, and the Government was using the usual combination of diplomacy and threats, when that trouble was submerged by a greater one.

The Chinese Revolution. Sun Yat Sen (seated) and his advisers and staff of the Nanking provisional government

The Chinese Revolution. Seat of the first provisional government established at Wuchang, with Li Yuan Hung as president

On October 10, 1911, troops of the garrison at Wuchang mutinied and the Viceroy, Jui Cheng, was compelled to flee. In a few days the mutineers occupied Wuchang, and also Hanyang on the north bank of the Yangtze River, obtaining supplies, money, and munitions. Even more important was the strategical position thus obtained. The cities of Hankow, Hanyang, and Wuchang lie at the junction of the Han River with the Yangtze—Hankow and Hanyang north of the Yangtze and separated by the Han River, and Wuchang opposite on the south bank of the Yangtze. From Hankow a railway extends north to Peking, and Wuchang is the northern terminus of the uncompleted Canton-Hankow line. Hankow is the principal treaty port of central China, and the head of deep-water navigation on the Yangtze. At Hanyang are the great Hanyehping iron and steel works. On October 13 a provisional Reformed Government was declared at Wuchang, with General Li Yuan Hung, who commanded the mutineers, as President. Huang Hsing was placed in command of the rebels at Hanyang. These two men were destined to figure importantly in subsequent events. The military course of the revolution is interesting here only as it bears on political matters, so a brief review will suffice. Within a few days after the outbreak at Wuchang the Government moved to suppress the rebellion. General Yin Chang, minister of war, was ordered to take command of operations to retake Hanyang and Wuchang. Admirals Sah Cheng-ping and Cheng Yun-Wu were ordered to proceed up the Yangtze River with their squadrons and co-operate with the government land forces. From then until November 27, when the Imperial troops retook Hanyang, severe fighting occurred about Hankow. Meanwhile, the naval forces deposed their commanders and went over to the rebels, and combined land and naval rebel forces took Nanking on December 2. The taking of Nanking placed the country south of the Yangtze in the control of the rebels, for all the southern provinces had declared in favor of the revolution with practically no serious opposition. Except some desultory fighting, the military campaign ended with the fall of Nanking, and the situation thereafter was handled by negotiation.

While these events were happening, conditions at Peking were developing in an extraordinary way. Within a short time after the outbreak at Wuchang it became evident that the Government as then constituted was powerless to handle the situation. The Court was panic-stricken. There are few as curious episodes in history as the immediate recall to power of Yuan Shih K'ai. This able and experienced official had been deposed (and would have been beheaded but for foreign intervention) in January, 1909, after the deaths of the Empress Dowager Tsu Hsi and the Emperor Kwang Hsu, and was living in complete retirement at his native place in Honan province. On October 14 an Imperial edict appointed Yuan Shih K'ai viceroy of the Hukiang provinces (Hupeh and Hunan) and generalissimo of the Imperial forces. With this appointment began the political game, dominated by Yuan, which with a minimum of fighting and bloodshed, finessed the Manchus out of power. It is worthy of note, in that crisis, that Yuan Shih K'ai was considered indispensable by both major political factions, with neither of which he was personally popular. It is not possible for any foreigner to follow with exactness the moves and motives in the subtle game that followed, but the high lights could be discerned. I was in China during that entire period, and had good facilities for comprehending what transpired.

Yuan's astute and politically alert mind responded to the opportunity, but he proceeded with deliberation and care, having in mind Chinese psychology and all the exigencies of the situation. Etiquette demanded the usual show of reluctance and self-depreciation, which gave Yuan time to get into touch with conditions. First, he must know exactly how he would stand with the Government if he returned to Peking; second, he must learn the point of view of the revolutionists and establish communications with them. It is evident that even before he accepted the call to Peking, Yuan sized up the situation in all its bearings and possibilities. He knew it was practically impossible to sustain the old régime; moreover, he did not want to sustain it. During his entire official career Yuan had been known as a progressive, and he was responsible for much that had been accomplished in the way of practical reform. He comprehended (as very few Chinese did) the dangers and complexities of China's foreign contacts, and how these were involved with the internal crisis. He foresaw the difficulties. There is no doubt, taken in retrospect, that when Yuan accepted the call of the Imperial Government and went to Peking, he had a definite program planned, which was designed to oust the old Manchu régime, to unite the country, and to prevent foreign intervention. To fail in any of these things was to fail in all. Unless the Manchu régime was relegated, the country could not be pacified; unless the nation was pacified, foreign intervention was inevitable. Yuan knew that he had not only to contend with internal difficulties, but also would have to resist foreign intrigue striving to disintegrate China. While Yuan seemed to hesitate, conditions grew worse, and he was able to dictate the terms on which he would resume office. On October 27 he was made Premier and an edict conferred powers on him tantamount to a military dictatorship, and on October 30 Yuan left Peking by rail toward Hankow, professedly to take command of the operations in that locality, but really to try to establish communications with Li Yuan Hung, who by then had become the outstanding revolutionary military leader. At the same time General Yin Chang was recalled, although he was conducting the fighting successfully. From then the military operations, on the part of the Imperial troops, became subordinated to political exigencies. Yuan's policy was not to fight unless it was absolutely necessary, after diplomacy had failed. At that time it was announced by the rebels that Yuan's effort to communicate with Li Yuan Hung met with failure, but subsequent events showed that a basis for understanding was broached. The capture of Nanking by the rebels changed the situation materially, and caused Yuan to return to Peking, where he immediately laid plans to open negotiations with the other rebel group. It was afterward alleged that Yuan ordered General Chang Chun to abandon Nanking, to counterbalance the Imperial success in retaking Hanyang.

A complication was created by a dissension between Li Yuan Hung and Huang Hsing. Huang left Hanyang under discreditable circumstances, reflecting on his conduct as commander, and went to Shanghai, where he became a factor in a revolutionary group formed by himself. Shanghai is the commercial and financial center of China, and its influence was strongly felt. Having a personal quarrel with Li Yuan Hung, being jealous of his reputation and popularity, and scheming to displace him as leader of the revolution, Huang Hsing inspired the Shanghai group to object to Li Yuan Hung negotiating with Yuan Shih K'ai, and to deny his right to represent the whole revolutionary party. Li Yuan Hung, always modest and self-effacing, disclaimed intent to usurp authority, and the negotiations were shifted to Shanghai. Tang Shao-yi was appointed a representative of the Imperial Government to confer with representatives of the other party, and negotiations began at Shanghai on December 18, 1911. Dr. Wu Ting-fang was delegated as principal representative of the revolutionists, because of his experience rather than that he was especially identified with the rebellion; indeed, up to that time Dr. Wu had not taken an active part. His selection was the result of a compromise. Huang Hsing is a violent radical, which the leading Chinese of Shanghai soon discovered; and it began to be evident that Huang himself aspired to head the new Government. Li Yuan Hung was the popular idol of the rebellion, and it was known that Li and Huang were enemies. The leaders realized the necessity of maintaining harmony among their party, and a majority wanted to gain the revolution by negotiation if it was possible. On the other hand, Huang Hsing and his personal following were opposed to any compromise, and demanded a military campaign against Peking. In these cir-

cumstances Dr. Wu Ting-fang placed himself at the service of
the Shanghai revolutionists, and, as events proved, he was acting patriotically in the interest of the Chinese nation. So it
was that Tang Shao-yi and Wu Ting-fang, old friends and
former coöfficials, faced each other across a conference table as
representatives of the Imperial Government on one hand and
a rebel party on the other. This was the situation: At Peking
was Yuan Shih K'ai, keeping the Manchu oligarchy under control by adroit intimidation, and also watching the international
aspects; at Wuchang was Li Yuan Hung, the most popular of
rebel military leaders, and the most praiseworthy; at Shanghai
were Tang Shao-yi and Wu Ting-fang, acting as mediators and
moderators. The two opposing extremes were the Manchu
oligarchy, which wanted to retain its position and prerogatives,
and the radicals led by Huang Hsing, who would be satisfied
with nothing less than a complete overturn. In the game that
followed it is probable that less than a dozen men really exerted
influence.

A factor that was to play a part was the so-called National
Council, convened at Nanking in December. The recapture
of Hanyang by the Imperial troops had made Wuchang untenable as a revolutionary capital, so delegates of various
groups assembled at Nanking soon after that city was taken.
A truce preceded the conferences at Shanghai. At the time,
it was remarked that the Imperial troops could have retaken
Wuchang without much difficulty, but Yuan Shih K'ai withheld them. Li Yuan Hung had prepared to evacuate Wuchang, but the truce made it tenable for the time. In this
Yuan's cunning was shown. He feared if he took Wuchang
that the Manchus would recover from their panic, and he would
lose control over them; so the Imperial troops were stopped at
Hanyang, leaving the military situation nicely balanced, which
was what Yuan wanted then.

At the first session of the conference at Shanghai, the revolutionists presented these conditions: (1) the abdication of the
Manchu dynasty, (2) the establishment of a republic, (3)

liberal treatment of the Imperial family. These conditions were transmitted to Peking by Tang Shao-yi, and for nine days no reply was received. Meanwhile several important things occurred at Shanghai. On December 20 the consuls-general of Great Britain, Japan, France, Russia, the United States, and Germany presented a note to the Imperial and revolutionary delegates, expressing a hope that the negotiations would result in a peaceful settlement. This joint action by the Powers was significant, and had considerable influence. A prolongation of the struggle inevitably would create disorder and chaos in the entire country, which would affect foreign interests and security, and might lead to international complications. None of the Powers well could decline to participate in this friendly action, although one of them (Japan) desired a different outcome.

Another important event was the arrival at Shanghai on December 25 of Sun Yat Sen. Sun had long been notorious as a Chinese revolutionary agitator, and had considerable reputation abroad, and prestige among Chinese because of his publications, although he was almost a stranger in China personally. Sun's relation to the revolution was obscure. He was reported to be in England when the revolution started, but he lost no time in getting into the spot-light and claiming a part in it. There was nothing visible in China at the time of the Wuchang outbreak, or immediately prior to it, to show the hand and influence of Sun Yat Sen; and his name did not come into the revolution until the foreign news services began to bring his announcements and manifestos. Very little was known of Sun in China at that time—he was a vague figure, somewhere in the outer world, who was supposed to be working for political liberty in China. Few Chinese of prominence had seen him, and his connections with China were through secret societies and by correspondence, although from time to time there were rumors of visits in person. Nearly two years afterward, in the summer of 1913, I asked Li Yuan Hung about the part Sun Yat Sen had taken in starting the revolution, and

General Li told me that at the time the revolt began he hardly had heard of Sun, and that Sun had no part whatever. Judging from that statement and appearances, Sun came into the situation as an opportunist. When he read in the newspapers of the revolt at Wuchang and its spread, he moved to get into the game, and opened communications with rebel leaders in China, who were glad to have his assistance in gaining sympathy abroad and in influencing the people in China, where Sun's name, if not his deeds, was known. Gathering a few followers, he proceeded to China via Suez, giving out statements, so that his progress was well advertised. At Singapore he was joined by some Japanese, and at Hongkong his entourage received additions. About that time Li Yuan Hung gave an interview, stating that he did not know Sun Yat Sen, and had no relations with him. General Li meant no reflection on Sun; he merely gave a frank answer to a question put by a newspaper correspondent; but it had the effect of putting a slight cloud on Sun's prestige. When he got to Hongkong, Sun's plans and movements were uncertain, for he did not know how he would be received. He stopped there, and communicated with the revolutionists at Shanghai before proceeding. I know of this uncertainty because, at that time, some Chinese prominent in the revolutionary councils asked my opinion of Sun Yat Sen, and what foreigners thought of him, and if his connection with the revolutionary movement would have a good effect abroad. I never had seen Sun, but I replied that I thought his notoriety as a reformer might be used favorably in making a good impression in the United States and England, where people would have a sentimental idea about the revolution and a sympathy with its objects. At that time, most foreign residents in China sympathized with the revolutionists, in principle, because of disgust with the general inertia and inefficiency of the Manchu Government, and they hoped for an improvement to come out of the revolt. This sentiment was especially strong at Shanghai, and consequently the conferences there were conducted in an atmosphere distinctly favorable to the revolutionists. My Chinese friends also asked me if I thought Sun Yat Sen would make a good President of the Chinese Republic, about which I could give no opinion, although from what I had heard of him I regarded Sun as a political visionary.

Sun Yat Sen appeared at an opportune moment. The divergence between Li Yuan Hung and Huang Hsing (which was caused by Li accusing Huang of cowardice and of deserting his troops at Hanyang) had made a division of the revolutionary party in central China, while a third faction was centered at Canton. These differences were repressed and concealed as far as was possible, but they threatened a schism. The so-called National Council at Nanking and the leaders at Shanghai were agreed that, in order effectively to negotiate with the Peking Government, a republican government should be organized. There was practical unanimity on that point, but there was difficulty in selecting a head for the Republic. If either Li Yuan Hung or Huang Hsing was chosen, the other faction would be offended and might split off. Canton was too far to the south to select the President from there. This was the dilemma when Sun Yat Sen reached Hongkong. He seemed to offer a satisfactory compromise. He was aligned with no faction. He never had lived in China, and therefore was identified with no section or political clique. He was known abroad, and his name would help the movement there, and induce the world to take the Republic seriously. Mind, at that time the Republic was merely tentative with the men who were really running things—it might come to that, and it might not. But something had to be set up as against the Peking Imperial Government, as a basis for contention and negotiations, and as a rallying-point for popular appeal. So the way was paved for Sun, and a telegram was sent asking him to come to Shanghai. His arrival there had some unfortunate attendants, his Japanese advisers creating a bad impression, for the Chinese were very suspicious of Japanese influence. It was recognized by Chinese who understood their

Dr. Wu Ting-fang. An eminent diplomat, formerly twice Chinese minister to the United States. In recent years Dr. Wu has been a wise and prudent adviser of his nation

Tang Shao-yi, eminent as a diplomat and official, who was active in compromising China's internal troubles

own country and its politics that Sun Yat Sen was not available to head the Government permanently. For one thing (and that is enough), he professes Christianity. The Chinese are not hostile to Christianity, but they would be uneasy at having a Christian as head of their Government. This does not mean an unworthy prejudice. The feeling is chiefly sentimental and inherited. The United States has liberal institutions, yet it is not yet considered expedient to nominate a Roman Catholic or a Jew for the Presidency. Few Chinese knew what Sun Yat Sen's religion was before he arrived in China, and the issue would not be raised at once on the question of his availability for temporary office. On reaching Shanghai, Sun was immediately invited into a conference with a few revolutionary leaders, and a bargain was struck. The Presidency was to be tendered to him, with a proviso that, in case the negotiations brought about an understanding with Yuan Shih K'ai, Sun would retire in Yuan's favor, when a permanent government was organized. On this understanding, the Presidency was given to Sun. There was a formality of an election by the National Council sitting at Nanking, but that proceeding merely registered the agreement made at Shanghai. This occurred on December 28.

At Peking, Yuan Shih K'ai was getting control by inches, but some of the princes were stubborn and refused to believe the helplessness of the Imperial Government. Yuan's position was very difficult, and required great finesse to prevent a collapse of his power. He had to maintain sufficient strength to hold a military balance with the revolutionists and prevent them from getting the upper hand; he must not strengthen the Government's position too much for fear of losing control over the Court, who were subordinate only to terror; he had to represent to the Court that the revolutionists were very strong and very determined, and that the Government was weak and lacked means for resistance; and he had to maintain relations with the revolutionists favorable to reaching a satisfactory compromise. Yuan's method of handling the Court was clever. When he assumed office he demanded funds for the suppression of the rebellion, knowing that the government treasury was depleted, that foreign loans probably could not be obtained under the circumstances, and that the money would have to be drawn from the savings of the Imperial family. Soon after he went to Peking, Yuan established an understanding with the legations of the leading Powers, and outlined his policy to them. His plan was to subdue the Court by the application, in carefully measured doses, of terror and financial attrition. When funds were spent Yuan demanded more, and when the Imperial family tried to resist a drain which would impoverish them, Yuan would offer his resignation. If the Court tried to raise money by borrowing from foreign bankers, Yuan saw to it that the efforts were frustrated. In that he no doubt was aided by some ministers of foreign Powers, who decided that the best policy was to support Yuan. In that situation, the Powers who wanted to hold China together and to pacify the country soon realized that a definite attitude was needed. Matters could not be permitted to drift. The friendly Powers felt that the Manchu dynasty was doomed; yet what would take its place, was of the utmost importance. A republic might mean improvement and peace; or it might mean anarchy and chaos. Everything depended on bringing some kind of unity among the progressive elements of the country, with a capable head of the new Government. All the leading Chinese officials and politicians were well known to the foreign diplomats, and with practical unanimity Yuan Shih K'ai was selected as the only strong, dependable, and capable man in sight. There was one exception. Japan was very hostile to Yuan for both personal and political reasons. From experience Japan had learned that Yuan was wily, courageous, and incorruptible in matters affecting his country's rights. Yuan had blocked Japan's encroachments and aggressions at every turn when he held office previously. Japan, therefore, would have preferred any one to Yuan as head of the Chinese Government.

Futhermore, Japan did not want the country pacified; she wanted a prolongation of disorder, with the opportunity to disrupt and encroach that condition would provide, and had sprinkled central and south China with Japanese intriguers to work to that end. The friendly Powers did not desire to meddle in China's internal struggle, but the interests at stake were too vast to permit an absolutely negative attitude. The advice given to China at this juncture by foreign nations was, in the main, just and sensible. With that support Yuan was able to prevent the Court from getting funds without his approval, and that gave him control over the northern army, which long had regarded Yuan as its creator and patron.

On December 28 the Empress Dowager issued the following edict:

The telegraphic memorial of Tang Shao-yi transmitted by the Cabinet states that Wu Ting-fang, representative of the People's Army, insists strongly that the wish of the people aims at the establishment of a republican form of government. At the outbreak of disturbances at Wuchang, We acceded to the request of the Tzucheng Yuan in promulgating the nineteen Constitutional articles of good faith, and in taking our oath at the Imperial Ancestral Temple, We hoped that armed conflicts would be suspended at an early date and that We might enjoy with the people the blessings of peace. But simply on account of Our good faith not being well established, the political strife has continued to make its appearance. We consider the problems of the adoption of a constitutional monarchy or of a republic for Our country to have important bearing on Our foreign and domestic affairs. The question could be solved neither by a section of the populace, nor by the Throne alone. There ought to be convoked a National Convention to decide on the question at issue. According to the memorials of the Ministers of State they request a meeting of the princes closely related to Us for considering the question. We have questioned them personally and they have agreed on this step. The Cabinet is ordered to telegraph this idea to Tang Shao-yi, who is to make known the same to the representatives of the People's Army. On the one hand, the Cabinet should speedily and carefully draft election laws by mutual agreement, which are then to be executed for the convocation of a National Assembly at an appointed time. On the other hand, the Cabinet is to consult with Wu

Ting-fang for an agreement to suspend warfare, as a preliminary step, so that the people may be relieved from suffering and the great trouble pacified. We are of the opinion that a Ruler is appointed for the people, who are created by Heaven, and his duty is to act as their shepherd. It is for that one man to nurture the people and not for the people to serve that one man. The Emperor, on ascending to the Throne, is still in his tender age, and We cannot bear to cause suffering to the people and to injure the whole country. We only hope that the decision of the Convention will be based on the interest of the country and the well-being of the people. Heaven hears what the people hear and sees what they see. We wish and sincerely hope that Our patriotic soldiers and subjects will mutually act in accordance with the principles of justice and conjointly seek for the public weal.

On January 1, Sun Yat Sen was installed as President at Nanking, and took this oath: "To overthrow the absolute oligarchic form of the Manchu Government; to consolidate the Republic of China, and to plan and beget blessings for the people. I, Sun Wen, will faithfully obey the popular inclinations of the citizens, be loyal to the nation, and perform my duty in the interest of the public, until the downfall of the absolute oligarchic Government has been accomplished, until the disturbances within the nation have disappeared, and until our Republic has been established as a prominent nation on this earth, duly recognized by all the nations. Then I, Sun Wen, shall relinquish the office of Provisional President. I hereby swear this before the citizens." A republican Cabinet was formed, which included Huang Hsing as minister of war, and Dr. Wu Ting-fang as minister of foreign affairs.

A hitch occurred over the proposal of Peking to submit the question of form of government to a National Convention. The Shanghai revolutionists were disposed to accept the idea, but wanted to create conditions which would have assured a decision in favor of a republic. A proposal to this effect was immediately rejected by Yuan Shih K'ai, who probably wanted to have the convention "fixed" the other way, and as a result Tang Shao-yi resigned as Imperial commissioner on January

2, 1912. This was the first indication of a serious difference
of opinion between Yuan Shih K'ai and the Shanghai leaders.
In a few days after he reached Shanghai, Tang Shao-yi had
come to an agreement with the revolutionary leaders that a
republic was preferable. Tang Shao-yi, Wu Ting-fang, and
the more experienced southern progressives believed that it was
necessary to abolish the monarchy in order to assure genuine
reform. These men had doubts about the practical feasibility
of a republican form of government in China, but they felt
that the name would appeal to the people, and that a change
was required to swing popular thought toward reform and to
convince the people that the old régime actually was abolished.
They felt that promises of reform under the monarchy would
not suffice. Wu Ting-fang and Tang Shao-yi were anxious
equally with Yuan Shih K'ai to pacify the country, but from
their knowledge of sentiment and the situation in central and
south China they believed that this could not be accomplished
unless the monarchy was abolished. To stop short of that
would leave a condition inviting the radical element, led by
Huang Hsing, to start a fresh revolt. Dr. Wu and Tang both
regarded Yuan Shih K'ai as the proper man to head the new
government, but they insisted that he should consent to a republic.

Yuan Shih K'ai had different views. He was as anxious
as the southerners to eliminate the Manchu régime, but he
thought the country could not prosper as a republic, and that
it would be better to retain the monarchy with the infant
Emperor on the throne, while the government was conducted
by a responsible ministry under a constitution. By that
system, the Emperor would be a figurehead. Yuan's idea
approximates the Japanese system. He contended that a real
republic is impossible in China, as things are, and that it would
be a mistake to create a "fake" republic that would soon
destroy itself; and that all practicable reforms could be accomplished under a constitutional monarchy. In that opinion,
Yuan was in accord with a large majority of foreigners who

understood China, and with the foreign ministers at Peking without any exception that I know of. Wu Ting-fang and Tang Shao-yi contended that whether the new government was called a constitutional monarchy, or a republic, probably would make no difference in the administration of affairs, but it nevertheless was true that at that juncture the name meant a great deal, and the republic in name was a concession that must be made to sentiment among the revolutionists. Here was a difference of opinion, as to expediency, among men who wanted to accomplish the same ends. Many revolutionists felt that if the monarchial form was retained, there was a danger of slipping back to the old conditions. While Tang Shao-yi's resignation outwardly indicated a breach with Yuan, it was not really that, but probably was a means employed by Tang to make Yuan understand the strength of his convictions. Tang continued, during the negotiations, to be the real representative of Yuan. The resignation of Tang caused uneasiness, and the foreign Powers took measures to secure order in north China and in the treaty ports if the disorders spread.

At that stage Huang Hsing exerted the malign influence that has usually characterized his part in Chinese affairs, and Sun Yat Sen began to display the weakness that afterward led to unfortunate results. Sun seems, even now, a sincere and patriotic man. He was ignorant of conditions in China, of Chinese politics and problems, and of Chinese popular psychology. His life had been spent in foreign lands. He had but a dim idea of certain forces of foreign intrigue operating inside the mesh of Chinese politics. He had no experience in administration anywhere. Suddenly, as if by a miracle, he had been converted from an exiled wanderer to an office of influence. The Provisional Government at Nanking became the center of the radical elements in Chinese politics, of which the enthusiastic student class formed a noisy part, and which were dominated by Huang Hsing. Huang Hsing was generally regarded as a demagogue and adventurer. He had sprung into prominence suddenly, and had grasped a certain power by the exercise of a forceful personality. He had brought under his influence a number of able men, some of them sincere reformers, and others hoping for preferment. This clique flattered Sun Yat Sen, and obtained a strong influence with him. Under that influence, it was not very difficult to persuade Sun that Yuan Shih K'ai was an unprincipled man, who intended to betray the revolutionists and to sustain the Manchus in power; and at the same time to make Sun believe the flatterers who told him that he should be the President of the permanent Government. Japanese intriguers attached themselves to Sun and the extreme group of reformers. The members of the so-called National Council (many of whom had elected themselves) played at inside politics, having in view place and power in the new Government. Most of these men, including Huang Hsing, felt that their chance of getting office and exerting influence under a government headed by Yuan Shih K'ai was slight. Sun's radical advisers found in the proposal to submit the question of form of government to a National Convention a deep-laid scheme of Yuan to betray the republicans. On January 15, 1912, Sun Yat Sen telegraphed to Yuan Shih K'ai offering him the Presidency, which Yuan of course could not then entertain, for he was in the midst of difficult negotiations to induce the Court to abdicate. Yuan had subdued the Empress Dowager and the senior princes, but some of the younger princes held out. On January 19 Yuan Shih K'ai asked for "leave of absence," an oblique way of frightening the Imperial family. On January 22 Sun Yat Sen sent a long telegram to Wu Ting-fang at Shanghai, virtually repudiating his agreement to resign in favor of Yuan Shih K'ai, and accusing Yuan of duplicity. In effect, he also repudiated Wu Ting-fang as the representative of the Nanking Government in the negotiations.

That put everything in a muddle. Yuan Shih K'ai did not know what to depend on, and he still wanted a constitutional monarchy. At Nanking a clique of radicals about Sun Yat Sen were planning to control affairs and themselves to hold power with Sun as President. At Shanghai Wu Ting-fang and Tang Shao-yi were negotiators virtually repudiated by their principals. At Peking, Yuan was having a hard time keeping the Court intimidated, owing to the revolt of the younger princes. At that juncture the "China Press" gave publicity to Sun Yat Sen's real position, and the causes of the deadlock, which had some effect in damping the radicals. The situation was delicate. So aggressive was the radical faction at Nanking and Shanghai that threats to assassinate Dr. Wu Ting-fang were made, and his residence was constantly guarded by foreign police. On January 17 an attempt was made to assassinate Yuan Shih K'ai in a street at Peking by a bomb, which narrowly failed, and which was attributed to the southern radicals. Some assassinations of prominent officials in the North occurred. The radicals at Nanking were demanding a resumption of hostilities and an advance on Peking, and it appeared that they were receiving financial assistance and promises of military support from an outside quarter. The country was rapidly slipping toward bitter internal strife. At that point representations were made to the sincere progressives at Peking and Shanghai which convinced them that Japan was intriguing to cause civil war by sowing distrust on both sides, and was giving assistance in credits and arms to the Nanking Government. That drove the wiser reformers together. Yuan Shih K'ai decided that he must, against his judgment, yield the form of government to the southern party. Having conceded that, the other difficulties were easier to handle. On January 30 Yuan issued this rejoinder to Sun Yat Sen's accusations: "In regard to the two statements made to the Press by Dr. Sun Wen and the Nanking Provisional Government, Premier Yuan's opinion is to the following effect: It seems throughout the two statements of Dr. Sun Wen that there is misunderstanding and misrepresentation of Premier Yuan's object in view, however much faith he places in Dr. Sun Wen. Whatever is alleged to have transpired between him and Dr. Sun has not been conducted

The Chinese rebellion of 1913. Kiukiang, a port on the Yangtze River, where the first outbreak occurred

Types of rebel soldiers. These troops can be recruited at any time by any who will pay them. When disbanded or unpaid they frequently become brigands and prey on the country

by him either directly in his own name or indirectly by others with his due authorization. The Premier is ready to accept almost any kind of solution as long as peace is gained, and he has no fear as to the security and peace of the country, if they are the fruit of reason, truth, and justice. He has never harbored any ambition to be President of the Chinese Republic, nor has he ever hinted at such intention throughout the negotiations with the revolutionary Government, much less that he should wrangle for the Presidency. His policy has been to maintain the integrity of the whole Empire, to secure unity of the northern and southern sections, to devise speedily the means for the restoration of peace and the cessation of war, and with the support of public opinion to bring about the establishment of order and a really stable government. It is to this end that he has been working since he assumed the duties of Premier. Perhaps this policy has not been understood by the secretaries of Dr. Sun.''

The cause of the monarchy was fast becoming hopeless. The Crown offered Yuan Shih K'ai a marquisate of the first rank, which he declined three times. Yuan advised abdication, bringing to bear all possible influences, including a memorial from the Imperial generals. Other factors contributed to bring the northern and southern progressives together. The obstacles to carrying on the war were almost insuperable. The Nanking Government could talk about a campaign to Peking, but it was without finances to meet ordinary administrative expenses, and could only obtain funds from Japan and a few foreign firms, sources of supply that were being restricted by international pressure. If hostilities were resumed, it was probable that foreign financiers would make loans to the Peking Government, to sustain it. In that situation, neither side had much chance to subdue the other, and prolonged hostilities would tend inevitably to compel some form of foreign intervention. Japan had taken advantage of circumstances to push her interests in the Yangtze Valley, and to send troops to Hankow. Negotiations were resumed in a better atmosphere, and by February 10 terms of abdication agreeable to the revolutionists were formulated. On February 13, 1912, the edicts of abdication were issued, and the passing of the Manchu dynasty was accomplished.

There was a little quibbling by the radicals at Nanking, because of phrases of the edicts conferring on Yuan Shih K'ai the power to organize a republic, but no hitch occurred. On February 13 Yuan Shih K'ai by proclamation announced a republic and assumed the authority to organize it. On February 14 Sun Yat Sen resigned the provisional Presidency in favor of Yuan Shih K'ai.

CHAPTER III

RECONSTRUCTION IN CHINA

Precarious situation of the nation—The financial problem—Dangerous elements—Distrust of Yuan Shih K'ai—Trying to organize the Government—Phases of reconstruction—The attitude of Yuan Shih K'ai—His course analyzed—Foundations for a Republic—The National Council—Yuan's struggle for executive power—The Executive vs. the Parliament —Obstructive tactics—Yuan's efforts at conciliation—The radical faction—The Koumingtang—Sedition at work—Disturbing political tendencies—Yuan's plea for toleration—The new Assembly—Reaction toward conservatism—The rebellion of 1913.

THE revolution in China synchronized with a crisis of the nation's financial affairs. When the revolt started, negotiations were proceeding between the Peking Government and foreign financiers with a view to reforming generally the fiscal system of the Empire, and to provide funds for internal development. The proposed reforms included revision of the revenue system, currency, and loans for railway construction and various administrative requirements. The revolution involved the Government in further financial difficulties. One of its effects was an almost complete stoppage of revenues from the provinces to the central Government. The Government was unable to meet maturing foreign loans and interest. It needed funds to suppress the rebellion and to meet current administrative expenses. The lack of money on both sides was a strong influence in bringing a compromise, and in forcing the Throne to abdicate. Without money, neither faction could go on; and after the Republic was declared its most pressing problem was finance.

The end of hostilities found several hundred thousand troops under arms. The compromise had included an undertaking by the new Government to assume obligations that had been incurred by the revolutionists, and to pay off the revolutionary troops. It was estimated that the revolution had cost taels 230,000,000 (about $160,000,000 gold), besides the complete cessation of internal revenue for several months. An estimate showed that the new Government was facing a probable deficit for its first year of taels 279,000,000 (about $195,000,000 gold). In that estimate a part of the revenue was problematical, and assumed the resumption of taxation processes. The country was in disorder and the people were uneasy. The revolutionary organizations had been maintained principally by enforcing contributions from the prosperous classes. Such government as existed in most parts of the country was based on the power of local military leaders, whose power in turn depended on their ability to hold their troops, which meant to pay them, and to prevent them from being alienated by bribery. If the troops were not paid they would mutiny and riot and loot, and perhaps kill their commanders. Every local dictator needed money, and got it anyhow he could. It was a fine opportunity for intriguing foreign interests and Powers to advance funds to local officials and administrations, and obtain concessions qualifying China's rights; and considerable was done that way, especially by Japan. With those conditions, it was very difficult to resume the customary collections of revenue. Many of the people had paid their taxes to the revolutionists, and would revolt against an attempt to collect from them again. There was much popular uncertainty about the stability of the new Government, and the people were reluctant to pay taxes when at any time a fresh revolution might requisition them again. The presence of bodies of armed men throughout the country, who had composed the revolutionary armies, was a grave danger. These soldiers had hardly any discipline, and they might at any time drift into banditry. Many of the revolutionary commanders were reluctant to disband their troops, for as long as each had an army they could dominate localities, and were political factors. These generals had to be placated by the new Government in some way, their armed followers disbanded, and the local administrations brought under the authority of Peking. Even Yuan Shih K'ai's army was unreliable. A slip anywhere, a misapprehension, lack of tact, a dissatisfied or irreconcilable revolutionist general, might start a new revolt and throw the country into disorder again. A large faction of the revolutionists distrusted and feared Yuan Shih K'ai. Some of them had been Yuan's political antagonists in the past, and others were influenced by reports about him. In those circumstances outward harmony of all the principal popular leaders was absolutely essential. Li Yuan Hung was depended on to keep order in central China. Sun Yat Sen had enough popularity to control the situation in the Yangtze Delta. The Cantonese group had their local leaders, and relied on Tang Shao-yi and Wu Ting-fang, who were both from that section. In forming his first Cabinet Yuan Shih K'ai tried to bring together representatives of all factions. The revolutionists wanted the national capital moved from Peking to Nanking, and Tang Shao-yi made a promise to that effect on behalf of Yuan Shih K'ai. Yuan, however, temporized, and a delegation of southern republicans went to Peking to urge him to go to Nanking. While the delegates were at Peking, on February 29, a division of troops mutinied and looted part of the city. This demonstration of the instability of conditions in the North convinced the southerners that it was better not to move the capital at that time, so the question was dropped and never afterward seriously resumed. The northern army mutinies spread to Paotingfu, Tientsin, and other places, but the Government quickly got control. The whole country was a tinder-box—a spark might cause a blaze.

Yuan Shih K'ai was inaugurated President at Peking on March 10, 1912. General Li Yuan Hung was elected Vice-President. The following day the National Council at Nanking ratified the election of Yuan and adopted a provisional constitution. Yuan issued a manifesto to the people, proclaimed an amnesty, and announced the remission of certain taxes. The selection of a Cabinet required adroit handling. Tang Shao-yi was made Premier, a selection which was satisfactory to the southern republicans. It is believed that both Sun Yat Sen and Wu Ting-fang were offered places in the Cabinet, but they declined. The National Council was still at Nanking, and the Premier went there to confer with it about the Cabinet. The southern party wanted its partizans to have the ministries of war and finance, and Huang Hsing was their candidate for minister of war. Yuan Shih K'ai, however, would not have Huang, and a compromise was affected by making him Resident-General at Nanking. While Tang Shao-yi was at Nanking an agreement was made apportioning the principal offices among the important factions. General Tuan Chi-jui (a Yuan man) was made minister of war. Chen Chi-mei, a radical leader, was nominated minister of commerce and industry. He accepted the post, but did not assume the office. On April 2 the National Council voted to transfer its seat to Peking, thus concentrating all branches of the republican government there. For a while the Council insisted that it should be accompanied to Peking by a guard of southern troops, but it finally receded from that position.

With the concentration of the republican government at Peking began a new phase of national reorganization. The radical republicans had been induced by considerations of national expediency, and by their own necessities, to harmonize outwardly with the northern party, and to consent to the election of Yuan Shih K'ai as President. With some—perhaps a majority—of the former revolutionists the support of Yuan was sincere; but the radical faction had no thought of being contented with conditions as they were. Its leaders took such places and power that fell to them in the division of offices, as a vantage point to obstruct Yuan and eventually to replace him with one of their own group. The task of reorganizing the Government soon developed into a struggle for administrative power by Yuan against the efforts of the radicals to obstruct him.

China's reconstruction has two phases—foreign and internal. The foreign influence was chiefly felt in its relation to finance, which was closely connected with the disputes of Chinese political factions. The internal phase falls into three distinguishable periods, (a) the pre-rebellion period, (b) the rebellion, (c) the post-rebellion period.

Some conditions of the pre-rebellion period that developed were not apparent when the Republic was established, although some of them were suspected. The loyalty of the radicals to the new Government was presumed. Foreigners and Chinese alike felt that everything should be done, and said, to maintain peace and to bring the conservative and radical factions into a semblance of harmony. At the head of the conservatives was Yuan Shih K'ai. Yuan was almost universally regarded as the ablest and most progressive of the experienced senior officials. At that time it was remarked how great was the change in China that suddenly could convert Yuan, who only a few years before had been classed among the radical reformers, to be classed as a conservative. Yuan himself had not changed. He was still, as always, for reform. But Yuan had had much experience, and had gained wisdom therefrom. He knew the practical difficulties in the way of reform. He knew that China is at heart conservative. He knew the materials and conditions out of which reform must be built, and that it could not be a mushroom growth. He knew the country and people could not respond to or assimilate the sudden application of Western political ideals and processes. Yuan understood the psychology of the Chinese masses, he knew the capacity of the official class. He had wanted to retain the monarchial form because he knew that it represented, and would continue to represent for generations, the masses' conception of government. Yuan in his heart believed that it was not possible to have a genuine republic, and he dreaded the task of trying to solve the great practical problems of the nation with an administrative fiction for a Government. Few men have been more decried, and vilified, than Yuan Shih K'ai. Much criticism of him is unjust, founded on a superficial understanding of the conditions and problems he had to deal with. On the face of things, it seemed like treachery for Yuan to accept office from the Manchu Government, after the revolution began, and then use his place to finesse it out of power. Yuan's acts then must be considered in all their bearings. He knew the Manchu régime had to go, that it ought to go. No doubt he reflected deeply when he received in his retirement the summons to Peking. Perhaps he should have been guided by a lofty conception of political honor; and since he could not conscientiously, or successfully, work to uphold the Manchu régime, perhaps he should have declined office. That is what he did do, at first. Then messages began to come to him, from foreign business men, from foreign diplomats, from missionaries, from Chinese, urging him to step into the breach and try to save the country from anarchy and disruption. All recognized that some strong man must come forth, and the demand for Yuan is as high a compliment as ever was paid in a great crisis to a statesman who had been counted down and out. In taking office, probably with no hope, and perhaps with no intention of saving the Manchus, did Yuan betray the Court? His course showed duplicity, but I would not call it treachery. I doubt if anything could have saved the Manchus. I am sure that nothing ought to have saved them. Should Yuan, knowing this, have remained in retirement, and allowed things to take their course? Or should he have thrown himself in, to help make the best of things? Yuan's conduct toward the Court properly should be measured by the possible alternatives. The Manchus were doomed. They had long before signed their own administrative death-warrant. To have put all possible strength into an effort to sustain them could have postponed their downfall a little time, but that is all. Above the rights and interests of a degenerate court were the rights and interests of the nation and people. If extreme

Chinese Red Cross organizations did good work in the revolution and rebellions, on both sides

resistance had been made with such troops as the Peking Government could muster and keep loyal, the end almost certainly would have been the same. Yuan so managed as to give the Court's retirement the appearance of a voluntary abdication, thus saving its dignity, and procured honorable treatment and provision for the Imperial family. Judged by a practical standard, Yuan befriended the Manchus, and stopped a civil war which, if prolonged, would perhaps have ended with the destruction of the nation. He would have saved the monarchy if he could, with the rightful sovereign on the throne. That, however, he could not accomplish.

The situation cannot be comprehended without some knowledge of conditions in China at that time. The so-called nine-year reform program promulgated in 1908 was being carried out almost on the schedule. It aimed to create a constitutional monarchy by 1917. One of the measures designed to prepare the people and country for constitutional government, the provincial assemblies, had been put into effect, with surprising success. The republican form of government rests on a vote of the people. Many think that there is no genuine republicanism without general suffrage. Some are inclined to depreciate constitutional government in Japan as farcical, where about 2 per cent. of the population vote. For a republic there must be some suffrage basis, and election machinery. It is estimated that about 6 per cent. of Chinese are literate, which seems to impose a certain suffrage limitation, although only a small percentage of the literate class in China have any practical idea of the use of the ballot. When the nine-year reform program was commenced, there never had been a political election, in the modern sense, in China. There were no means of ascertaining public opinion, of getting a general vote on any proposition. It would have taken years to devise and put into effect a general election law, and the people could not have been induced to vote if such a law had been enacted. The Chinese masses, in their local affairs, live under the patriarchal form. In each district public opinion is represented by the ideas of a small part of the population, composed of officials, business men, and large property owners. The provincial assemblies were composed of these gentry, who were selected, or "elected" by what Americans call caucuses. Most of the elections were not contested, and contests were perfunctory. The general result was good. The first assemblies were almost wholly composed of leading citizens, and if they did not accomplish very much, they at least sat together and discussed the affairs of their provinces and the Empire. Little radicalism was shown. The assemblies seemed to know their limitations, and proceeded deliberately. In such elections as had been held in China before the Republic, it is doubtful if 10,000 persons took part (about $\frac{1}{35}$ of 1 per cent. of the total population), although many more could have qualified under the regulations. I know of no method by which a better expression of public opinion in an election can be obtained in China now. The inherited ideas of Chinese must be radically changed before they will understand and participate in political elections. In some instances not more than half a dozen men would constitute an election of an assemblyman or member of the Council. Some members of the republican National Council which assembled at Nanking in 1911 had no certificate except their own presumption. A little group in a district would privately agree on a candidate, and elect him. Others appeared at Nanking without any real credentials, claiming to represent some dubious political organizations. I recall a case of two delegates to the Nanking National Council. They claimed to have been elected by a revolutionary society in a western province to go as delegates to Wuchang, where the first provisional revolutionary government was established. When they arrived at Wuchang, Hanyang had been retaken by the Imperial troops, so they continued on to Shanghai. Meanwhile, the revolutionary general they were supposed to represent had been deposed and executed by his own followers. But when the so-called National Council was convened at Nanking, these men were admitted. They probably were as well entitled to sit as most of the other members. The few real leaders of the revolutionists set up the Nanking Council as a figure-head to give a semblance of reality to the republican government. That body elected Sun Yat Sen as President, and adopted a provisional constitution. It was dominated by young Chinese who had received a foreign education, many of whom were only a few years out of school. When its seat was moved to Peking, it and its successors became the center of opposition to Yuan Shih K'ai.

It is not feasible in this brief review to narrate in detail the political factional struggle at Peking from the establishment of the Republic in March, 1912, to the outbreak of the rebellion in the summer of 1913. The line was drawn clearly enough, as between the Presidency, or the executive, and the parliament —the usual demarcation. Yuan Shih K'ai's followers lined up behind the Executive; the opposition became focussed in the parliament, or National Council. That was convenient and logical. The opposition to Yuan had a majority in the Council, and made their fight from there. The issues were almost immaterial, regarded in retrospect, although at that time they seemed important technically. A difference developed about the constitution of the new Government. Yuan Shih K'ai wanted to have a Cabinet drawn from all the political groups (which now began to call themselves parties), thinking in that way to bring leading men of all sections and factions into the Government, consolidating the administration and uniting the country. To this plan the radicals were opposed, basing their opposition on the argument for a party system. They wanted the Cabinet to be composed of members of one party, having a majority in parliament, taking the British system as a precedent. By that plan, Yuan Shih K'ai could have been shorn of authority, and the Government controlled by a party ministry. Yuan would not permit himself to be eliminated like that, so the contest was on. It developed into a test of endurance. In one way the Council had the advantage. The nominal basis for the Government was the provisional constitution adopted in March, 1912, at Nanking. As the Council had itself made that constitution, probably with a view to enhancing its own powers and importance, it usually was able to hold its own in technical arguments with the Executive. One of the first things the Council had to do was to decide who were entitled to seats, for more members appeared at Peking than were authorized seats. When it got organized, the Council became busied with constructing a new constitution, which occupied it when the majority, constituting the Opposition, were not trying to embarrass and obstruct the Executive. Several Cabinet crises occurred in the course of the next few months. The parties in the Council became more and more entangled and at loggerheads. On July 9, 1912, President Yuan issued this appeal to the parties: "After the establishment of the Republic the various parties came into existence. It is an established fact that the political ideas of our people have much developed recently. This is a very different state of affairs from that in existence under the old régime, when the people did not know the value of the suffrage. In all other countries the political parties and the Governments coöperate. There are many parties, but their common aim is to foster whatever is good for their country, without regard to their own proposals. The political parties of our country are newly born. Their leaders are patriots with high ideas and can surely have no selfish motives. Sometimes their opinions differ, but their intentions are good. When the membership of the parties increases, splits and quarrels will occur. The result will be that each party will study its own interests and forget the wants of the country. You must bear in mind that the foundation of the Republic is not strong yet. If there is internal trouble, the State must cease to exist, and then all parties will die out. Therefore, it is necessary that they should give up their own desires, and walk in the same path for the welfare of the country. If the parties continue to maintain their own selfish ways and quarrel with each other without regard to the laws, the proclaimed Republic will cease to exist.

I ask you, was this the reason you overthrew the old régime and established a new State? If so, I am very sorry. You should love and help each other and forget your animosities in order that the Republic may be maintained. I sincerely hope you will listen to my advice."

Notwithstanding the opposition of the Council, and resignations in the Cabinet, Yuan Shih K'ai remained firm in the belief that the time had not come for a party Cabinet, and that the only practicable Government was by a Cabinet composed of the ablest men regardless of party. The President at times nominated members for the Cabinet, and the Council refused or delayed to confirm them. The President issued an appeal to the provincial assemblies, which also were in confusion, asking for harmony. Reorganization proceeded slowly. *Tutuhs* (military governors) governed the provinces in place of viceroys. Sporadic disorders continued. Plots to assassinate the President and the Vice-President, Li Yuan Hung, and to overthrow the Government, were frequent, and some plotters were apprehended and executed, in some cases in an arbitrary manner. The summary execution of General Chang Chen-wu, who was arrested after he attended a dinner at the Wagons-Lits Hotel in Peking, caused a crisis. The Council attempted to impeach the President, but could not carry it. Sun Yat Sen was induced to visit Peking, in an attempt to bring coöperation between the Council and the Executive, but the good effect was only temporary. Sun Yat Sen was received with cordiality by Yuan Shih K'ai, and was entertained profusely during his stay. Just before Sun's visit to Peking, the more important opposition parties were amalgamated into one named the Koumingtang. It seemed for a time that good results would proceed from the meeting of Yuan Shih K'ai and Sun Yat Sen (who had never met before). A position was created for Sun, by making him special railway commissioner, with authority to devise plans for a complete railway system for China. Sun returned to Shanghai, where he opened offices for the National Railway Corporation. In this position Sun had a wonderful opportunity for constructive work beneficial to China. His inherent administrative incapacity soon developed, and his original plans were utterly impractical. However, Sun was sincere in wanting to carry out the work, and employed George Bronson Rea, an American, to draft practical plans.

Yuan Shih K'ai continued to make efforts to reconcile the radical element with the Government. By this time it was evident that the opposition to the President was focussed in a group with headquarters at Shanghai, and led by Huang Hsing and Chen Chi-mei. Between these men and Yuan there was a mutual distrust. Both Huang and Chen had been offerred positions in the Government, but, while professing to support the President, they declined office. Several invitations to visit Peking were extended to them, and it was believed that they hesitated to go for fear of arrest and execution. At length these fears were overcome, and in September, 1912, Huang and Chen visited Peking, where they were well received. Sun Yat Sen also was present, and a national policy was nominally adopted. Huang Hsing and Chen Chi-mei returned to Shanghai, where they lived in the Foreign Settlements. Shanghai had become the headquarters of the radical party. The Foreign Settlements provided peculiar advantages for political intrigue. In the Settlements, Chinese politicians were comparatively immune from the political process of Chinese law, and out of the reach of the Government. A dozen or more vernacular newspapers, organs of the radicals, and one daily newspaper published in English, were established. This press gave a powerful leverage on popular thought in central and south China. It was controlled by the Koumingtang, the party that had a majority in the National Council, and whose leaders were Sun Yat Sen, Huang Hsing, Chen Chi-mei, and others of less reputation. As months passed it became evident that the Koumingtang was antagonistic to the Government. It is hardly possible to discover just when this antagonism ceased to be the legitimate activities of an opposition, and became a conspiracy to overthrow the Government by revolution.

The transition of the objects and purposes of the Koumingtang was gradual. For some months after the Republic was organized with Yuan Shih K'ai as President, the elements opposed to him had the idea that it was possible to eliminate him without resort to arms. They controlled the National Council. But as time passed, Yuan Shih K'ai more and more out-finessed the radicals in the struggle for power between the Executive and parliament. Instead of gaining, the radicals found that they were losing ground. Each battle of wits, and crisis, left them in a slightly worse position. Yuan Shih K'ai was able to make use of the minority in the Council to keep that body deadlocked, and prevent it from making progress in any direction inimical to the Executive power. This caused the Opposition to consolidate their parties into the Koumingtang for more effective management. It also was proposed to consolidate the minority parties in the Council, and moves to accomplish this were made, but failed probably because Yuan Shih K'ai thought the smaller groups could be better used to frustrate the Opposition. In the game of political finesse the Opposition was no match for the veteran politician who was head of the Government. It was realization of this fact that enabled demagogues to swing the Koumingtang toward rebellion. In this they were retarded by the attitude of Sun Yat Sen, who did not then approve any project to resort to arms against Yuan. Nevertheless, Huang Hsing, Chen Chi-mei, and their lieutenants continued secretly to plot rebellion, and to lay plans for a revolt.

Yuan Shih K'ai undoubtedly perceived the drift of politics. He probably was well posted about the plots of the radical clique of revolutionists. He had plenty of evidences of its hatred of himself. Hardly a month passed without one or more attempts on the life of the President. Some of these attempts became public, but many of them were suppressed to prevent the spread of unrest among the people. Yuan no doubt had his agents inside the Koumingtang, and the inner circles of anarchist radicals. He was not beguiled, as events

proved. All the time the President was doing what he could
to consolidate the Government. He was much concerned about
certain disturbing tendencies among the people. The revolution and its aftermath had undermined the foundations of
government. The old standards had been thrown down. The
Emperor, who always had been venerated by the masses as the
political and spiritual father of the people and the fountain-
head of authority, had been deposed, and a new thought was
abroad which denied all previous conceptions of authority and
vested it in the people themselves. This was confusing to the
masses. The people did not understand the Republic, but they
got the idea that it meant that they need not do many things
which formerly were obligatory. Authority, as represented by
the Government, was weakened. The old standards were
partly destroyed, and the new standards as yet were vaguely
comprehended, or not comprehended at all, by the people. On
September 20, 1912, President Yuan Shih K'ai issued the following mandate:

The ex-Resident-General Huang Hsing has in a telegram rightly
pointed out the fact that, owing to the establishment of the Republic
and the sudden influx of new ideas and ideals into China, many
thoughtless and frivolous people have misconstrued the meaning of
the terms republicanism, liberty, and equality. As a result, the well-
established traditions and the fundamental principles of China have
not been well observed. For the purpose of maintaining our standard of morality and the practice of good, ancient traditions, General Huang Hsing urges that the eight cardinal virtues of China—
filial piety, brotherliness, faithfulness, loyalty, politeness, righteous-
ness, honesty, and the sense of shame—should be emphasized and be
brought to the people's mind. Good principles and morality are
the same the world over. The change of a governmental system
should certainly not be taken as a warrant to depart from the well-
established ethical principles of morality. Nowadays, agitated by
the great political changes made in our country, many seekers of
foreign ideas who have failed to grasp the real spirit of Western
sciences and who have simply been impressed by its material progress,
begin to depreciate the great moral principles of our nation which
have been handed down for hundreds of generations. I am well
convinced of the fact that no nation can be called civilized without

A street in Peking. The Chinese capital has been greatly improved in recent years, the main streets being paved, and lighted by electricity

making the eight great virtues as the basis of its government. I, the President, firmly maintain that the great danger of to-day is not in the material weakness of our nation, but in the condition of the human heart. If every person has his heart turned toward good, the country will be set on a firm foundation. May the citizens of the Republic heed this exhortation.

Soon afterward, on September 29, a mandate was issued ordering the suppression of the secret societies that had come into existence in all parts of the country, and which were the centers of political intrigue against the Government. Spurred on by the radical press, various forms of intoleration and persecution were instituted against the former officials and the conservative elements. Compulsory queue-cutting was one form of persecution. One powerful Tutuh issued a proclamation depriving all persons wearing queues of civil rights, and such a bill was introduced in the National Council. In a mandate issued on October 29, 1912, the President rebuked this intoleration, in which he said: "The cutting of queues has a close relationship with the Republic and the Government cannot be indifferent to the question. Compulsory cutting, however, has wrought great harm; and, being warned by the former unpleasant experiences, we should not be too high-handed in this policy. Moreover, the cutting of queues and the right to vote are two different questions." In another mandate, the President said: "When the late dynasty was in power, the officials and gentry in their effort to prohibit revolutionary activities—which was a part of their duty—in many cases took too rigid a view and committed much injustice toward the innocent. Since the Republic has been established and a radical transformation has been initiated, it is altogether fit and proper that the past should be forgotten, and those who have erred should have an opportunity to start anew. It has come to our knowledge that many of these officials and gentry, feeling that harm might be done to them, have deserted their usual residences, and often have to lodge themselves in uncomfortable quarters. We have further observed that many narrow-minded officials who are now in power do not hesitate to use their powers in doing harm to those who have ventured to return to their own places. All these acts are contrary to the principles of a democratic form of government. The executive officials of the various provinces are hereby ordered to stop their molestation of the ex-officials of the late dynasty. Those who are now living away from their usual homes are hereby exhorted to return and enjoy peace.'' In this connection, it should be remembered that former officials of the Empire, with the exception of the few who had taken part in the revolution, constituted the only body of trained and experienced administrators in the country. Yuan Shih K'ai knew these men were needed in the reconstruction, and was making it possible for them to again take part in affairs, while the group of radical and younger politicians who had sprung into prominence with the revolution wanted to exclude the former officials from place in the new Government, and to retain power themselves.

The agitation for a ''second revolution'' began to assume definite form late in 1912, when the radical native press in central and south China openly presented it as a possible alternative to submitting to the alleged autocracy of Yuan Shih K'ai. The National Council had fallen into lethargy, the center of Opposition having been transferred to the Koumingtang headquarters at Shanghai. The President succeeded in pushing a bill through the Council giving the Executive the power to establish martial law, ''in case of war or other extraordinary troubles arising, when it is necessary that either the whole or part of the country should be the scene of military operations.'' A majority of members of the Council were away from Peking, electioneering for the new National Assembly. In February, 1913, Sun Yat Sen visited Japan, where he received much attention. This visit caused much discussion, and suspicions arising from it considerably undermined Sun's popularity in China, where Japan's encroachments caused resentment and alarm, and the undercurrent of Japanese intrigue in China's internal politics was felt more and more. Mutinies and local disorders occurred almost every week in some part of the country, but the Government was able to suppress them. Most of the revolutionary troops had been paid off and disbanded, and Yuan Shih K'ai was gradually putting men in whom he had confidence into the important provincial offices. Yuan was steadily strengthening his position, a fact that caused the Koumingtang to accentuate its campaign against him. Already signs of a conservative reaction were appearing. Some gentry of Hupeh Province petitioned for a restoration of the monarchy, with Yuan as Emperor, but the President responded by ordering the petitioners to be arrested.

An event of great significance was the assassination at Shanghai, on March 21, 1913, of Sung Chiao-jen, a Kouming-tang leader, who was shot at the railway station when he was about to leave for Peking. A connection of Ying Kui-shing, a secret agent of the Government, was established with the crime, which gave occasion for the Koumingtang press to accuse Yuan Shih K'ai of having instigated the murder. From that time the attitude of the Koumingtang was openly hostile toward the President. The new Assembly (parliament) met in April and it soon became evident that it would clash with the Government. The Koumingtang had almost as many seats as all other parties combined, but the Government was stronger than it had been in the previous Council. A number of important matters demanded attention from parliament, but the members found too many things to wrangle about to transact business. Several weeks were consumed before presiding officers could be elected, and the Koumingtang candidates won. The attack on the Government in parliament centered on the foreign loan policy. Everything proposed by the Government was strongly criticized. Many sessions were disorderly, and a few were riotous. It was evident that the stability of the Government depended on the outcome of the struggle between the Executive and the Assembly. Public opinion, which in the first months of the Republic had been with parliament, was veering toward the Executive. The reasons for this change could be discerned. The Assembly was dominated by the younger element, mostly young Chinese who had been educated abroad or in foreign schools in China, and who possessed a fair knowledge of parliamentary forms and procedure. When the Republic was proclaimed, these young men had pushed themselves to the fore in politics by virtue of their presumed knowledge of republican institutions. At public meetings and political conferences, they could talk glibly and confidently about republicanism, while the senior, and wiser, citizens remained silent and gave place to those whose qualifications they then respected. The influence of the Young China element lasted almost unimpaired through the first session of the National Council; but when the new Assembly met a change could be noticed. The older members had by this time discovered that the youngsters had no experience with practical affairs, that their knowledge of republican government was purely theoretical, and that they had little true conception of conditions in China and how to deal with them. The older and more conservative members began to rebel at the assertiveness of the younger group, and to push it back into its correct relative importance. In this shift, the sentiment of the country was with the seniors. Chinese family and social existence for centuries has been based on respect for seniority and the wisdom of age and experience. The people, and the gentry, could not clearly distinguish the merits of the controversies about abstract principles of republican government and measures, over which the contest between the Assembly and the Executive raged. As against the fulminations of the radical press, the public weighed the reasonable, temperate, and conservative mandates and proclamations of the President, to the advantage of the President. The country began to perceive that on one hand was a President trying to pacify the country, and to put its affairs in order, and on the other hand was a parliament that opposed whatever the President proposed. Meanwhile, all the classes which constitute public opinion were

Photo, by Brown Bros.

China's attempt at a republic. A session of the Upper House, or Senate, at Peking

(c) Underwood & Underwood, N. Y.

The United States was the first power to recognize the republic of China. The picture shows President Yuan Shih K'ai receiving the American Legation Staff on that occasion. E. T. Williams, American Chargé d'Affaires, at Yuan Shih K'ai's left

suffering from the disturbed conditions, and wanted a restoration of law and order above all things. The means did not matter so much as the end. Thus in the popular mind the President took shape as wanting to *do things,* while the parliament was always in the attitude of *preventing things from being done.* This was the net result of a year of cross-maneuvering between the Executive and parliament at Peking. Yuan Shih K'ai was slowly but surely getting the country with him.

In that situation, the radical Koumingtang leaders saw themselves and their party facing defeat. There is no doubt that after the assassination of Sung Chiao-jen a majority of the Koumingtang were secretly for revolution, and the radicals succeeded in getting control of the party. Secret preparations for rebellion, with Shanghai as headquarters, were actively carried on. Evidences of foreign intrigue in support of the anti-Government element were numerous. There were shipments of arms to various places, destined for the rebels. The Koumingtang accumulated a war fund. All the Koumingtang leaders were not in favor of revolution, but the extreme radicals, led by Huang Hsing and Chen Chi-mei, carried the party along. By the end of June it was evident that an outbreak was imminent. General Li Yuan Hung, military leader of the revolution, and Vice-President of the Republic, was an important factor. He had never gone to Peking, his presence being necessary to preserve order in central China; so he stayed at Wuchang, and nipped several incipient outbreaks in the bud. One of these plots, which had some features indicating foreign intrigue, was suppressed early in July. It was believed that the plotters of rebellion at Shanghai were making efforts to win the support of Li Yuan Hung, and Koumingtang organs had published reports of his leaning that way. The attitude of Li Yuan Hung was of almost decisive importance, so I decided to go to Wuchang to see him, and if possible to learn his views. I traveled by rail from Shanghai to Nanking, where I took a boat going up the Yangtze River. When the boat reached Kiukiang there was fighting in that vicinity. The rebellion had begun. I proceeded to Hankow, and had a long interview with General Li Yuan Hung at Wuchang. By then he knew of the outbreak, and spoke freely. Among the interesting things he told me, supported by evidence, were that efforts were made to induce him to join the rebels; and that Japanese influence had been officially used to influence him that way, but without avail. He strongly denounced the meddling of Japan and the instigators of the rebellion, and said that Huang Hsing, Sun Yat Sen, and Chen Chi-mei never had been sincere in supporting Yuan Shih K'ai. I returned to Shanghai and published Li Yuan Hung's statements in the "China Press," and they had a great influence upon both Chinese and foreign opinion. A few days after the outbreak near Kiukiang, a manifesto was issued signed by Huang Hsing, Sun Yet Sen, Chen Chi-mei, and other Koumingtang leaders, denouncing Yuan Shih K'ai as a tyrant, demanding his resignation, and announcing the formation of an expedition "for the punishment of Yuan Shih K'ai." Sun Yat Sen afterward repudiated his signature to this manifesto. Sun's relation to the rebellion never has been clearly exposed. His attitude seems to have been undecided. After his visit to Peking, Sun's course (except his visit to Japan) was free from outward association with trouble-making forces and extreme radicals in the Koumingtang; indeed, his influence was to restrain them. The murder of Sung Chiao-jen is said to have destroyed Sun's confidence in Yuan Shih K'ai's good intentions, but he was not ready to promote a new revolution on the insufficient evidence of Yuan's connection with that tragedy. Sun's name was useful to the plotters, and they tried to swing him with them. While Sun was wavering, the radicals decided to act, and did so. The rebels at first tried to give the impression that Li Yuan Hung also favored the rebellion, but the publication of his statement refuted them. Sun Yat Sen did not take an active part in the rebellion, but he permitted himself to become so involved with it that, when it began to subside, he had to flee the country with the other rebel leaders.

I will not give extensive details of the rebellion and its suppression. Yuan Shih K'ai outthought and outmaneuvered his opponents. Li Lieh-chun, former Tutuh of Kiangsi, led the rebel forces in the Kiukiang district. His troops occupied the forts at the entrance to the Po Yang lakes. Nanking went over to the rebels, but attacks on the arsenal at Shanghai failed, because of the spirited defense made by Admiral Tseng Ju-cheng. The government forces gradually got the upper hand, and by September the rebellion collapsed. Early in August Sun Yat Sen, Huang Hsing, and other prominent Koumingtang leaders fled to Japan. Li Lieh-chun also escaped to Japan, being conveyed down the Yangtze by a Japanese gunboat. The outstanding features of the rebellion were: (a) Chinese opinion was with the Government and against reform by revolution; (b) a revulsion of sentiment among foreign residents in China, who had been sympathetic to the younger reformers, but who now perceived the dangers of radicalism, and that the political situation was a choice between Yuan Shih K'ai or chaos; (c) the revelation that Japan was intriguing in a disturbing way in China's internal politics. On October 6 Yuan Shih K'ai was formally elected by the National Assembly under the new constitution, and Li Yuan Hung was elected Vice-President. On November 4 a mandate dissolved the Koumingtang as a seditious organization. The immediate effect of this action was to unseat about half of the members of the Assembly, making a quorum impossible, and leaving the Executive in substantial control of the central government.

CHAPTER IV

RECONSTRUCTION IN CHINA—*Concluded*

External complications—China's financial embarrassment—Basis of foreign loans—Security required—China's peculiar position—The 4-Power banking group—Help to the new Government—Tang Shao-yi's mistake—The Belgian loan—Question of financial monopoly—Wrong impressions—American participation analyzed—Need for regulation—Dangers of former loose methods—International questions—Japan and Russia—6-Power group near disruption—The agreement at Paris—Its underlying principles—China's objections—Foolish agitation—Withdrawal of the American group.

THE chief immediate problem of China's external relations in her reconstruction period was finance, and to understand the situation requires some knowledge of one phase of China's modern evolution.

Up to a recent point in her history China was self-contained and self-sustaining. She was both rich and poor—rich in all kinds of natural resources, poor in her uses of them or failure to use them. In this she may be compared to many settlers of the early generations in America, who owned large tracts of rich lands. Those pioneers extracted from the land what to them was a satisfactory livelihood, taking from nature what nature provided easily and obviously. The settler's land might be underlaid with minerals, but he gave no thought to their value; the materials and facilities for manufacturing might lie conveniently about, but he produced only what was needed for a simple existence. Had not conditions forced change upon him, the settler could have gone on indefinitely as he was. But progress gradually overtook him. Others discovered the value of the minerals under his land, the uses of his water-power and materials. One day he contracted a debt, giving a mortgage on his land. From then the settler was no longer free to be as progressive or as backward as he liked. He had to pay interest on the mortgage. If he was thriftless and fell into arrears and could not make his farm pay, then the mortgagees either had to sell him out, or as trustee had to take over and operate the property to make it profitable.

That in analogy represents the case of China. Up to twenty-five years ago China had no foreign debts of consequence. She was backward and poor, merely scratching an existence off the surface of her immense resources; but she did not know how poor she was, or that there was a way to improve her condition. Even long after foreigners began to tell these things to the Chinese they made little impression, except here and there. The change came to China, when it did come, at the point of a bayonet. The China-Japan War altered China's course, and brought a new factor into her relations with the outside world, by compelling her to borrow to carry on the war, to pay war indemnities, and after the war to remedy the defenseless state which the war demonstrated. That was the beginning. From then China's progress as a borrower was rapid. China's debt is now about £227,000,000 (gold, $1,135,-000,000), and the annual interest charge is about £10,000,000 (gold $50,000,000). It is not a large debt, or excessive, for a nation with China's resources. But that it exists creates a new problem. China no longer can drift along contented in her poverty and inefficiency. Her resources are mortgaged.

There is much in this situation of China, and the way she arrived at it, that deserves study in Western countries. What happened to China may happen to any nation similarly situated, and similarly governed, and dominated by similar ideas. China's civilization is very old, and the Chinese thought it superior and enduring, and that it could be indifferent to outside influences. In her external contacts, China is the supreme example of pacifism—and of nations the least respected now. In her external contacts, China for centuries has shown no aggressive tendencies—and she is the most aggressed upon. China's national debts are due almost entirely to foreign contacts. They fall under four heads: (a) indemnity and war loans, (b) railway loans, (c) general loans, (d) provincial and private loans. The war loans came from China's efforts to defend her prestige and rights, and the indemnities came from her failure to defend them successfully. The railway loans were foisted on China by foreign influence. Foreigners saw the need for railways in China, and the profits, and induced China to permit them to be built. In some cases the railways were projected more in the strategical interest of foreign Powers than in China's interest. The railways are useful and necessary for China's progress and development, and they should have been built. The point I am making is that the first incentive to build them did not come from the Chinese. The railway and general loans, as a whole, have been beneficial to China, for the greater part of them are productive and have gone to create permanent benefits and improvements. Portions of all of them have been diverted improperly, and some of them were squandered; but the main results are good. Moreover, foreigners cannot altogether be blamed for the cupidity and ignorance of Chinese officials that made oblique practices possible, and at times necessary. Given the same combination of conditions and circumstances in any other country, the results would be about the same. China's course is another instance of the degeneracy and powerlessness of inertia.

By getting into debt China created new problems for herself. Her debts fall into two general classes—unsecured and secured. By secured debts, I mean those which have material collateral, like railways, mines, or visible property. China's war loans and indemnities are secured by the credit of the nation, and certain revenues are mortgaged to meet the sinking fund and interest. In building a railway, or opening a mine, or operating a cotton mill, or any similar enterprises that depend for success on scientific construction and management, it has been necessary to have some degree of foreign supervision in the construction and management in order to protect the foreign investors. This is the business side of foreign relations to such enterprises. If a foreign loan to build a railway in China is made, several things are required to make it a business proposition: the railway must be economically and properly constructed, it must be efficiently and economically operated, the revenues must be properly accounted for and applied. Since foreigners lend the capital, the investors must be assured of these things or they will not invest. They must be assured of something else—that the property will have legal and police protection. Capital for these enterprises is obtained by issuing bonds, which reach the investing public through banks that do the underwriting. The individual investor seldom investigates the security back of a bond; he trusts his bankers to do that. If the bankers, in order to gain the profit of brokerage, fail properly to investigate and assure the security back of the investment, they are deceiving their clients and acting dishonestly. Bankers who do that will soon lose standing in the business world; therefore their own interest, as well as the interest of their clients, requires caution, and adherence to certain business principles and conditions. The bankers are only intermediaries between the borrowing Government or corporation, and the investor. The bulk of such bonds go into the possession of comparatively poor people, in small holdings. With investments like those we are considering in China, Governments step in as a check upon the financiers, having in mind international political considerations, and also the protection of investors. For example, the largest investors in foreign securities in the world are the bourgeois and peasantry of France. They will not accept bonds unless they are listed on the bourses, and bonds cannot be listed on the bourses unless the Government permits. Thus the peasant who puts his savings in a foreign bond has first the assurance of his Government, and second the assurance of a banking syndicate in whose knowledge and integrity he

confides. With that he is satisfied; he does not bother about
the other details, nor is it practicable for the average investor
to know or accurately appraise them. It is clear, then, that a
great responsibility lies on both Governments and bankers in
respect to the flotation of such loans. The whole structure of
international credit rests on this foundation. Moreover, this
responsibility of foreign Governments and bankers toward
loans in China extends to safeguarding the interests of China
herself. As between two wholly responsible Powers, or two
fully enlightened and experienced nations, or between subjects
of two such nations, it is assumed that all parties to such
transactions are competent and able to look after their own
interests. In dealings between, let us say, Great Britain and
the United States, or British and Americans, it need not be
presumed that either party is in especial danger of being imposed on, because of its own ignorance about such matters, or
because of invidious pressure. In such a transaction neither
party is under duress or intimidation, and no pressure can be
applied except by persuasion, business considerations, or legal
process. In China's case, she may be and often is subjected
to trickery by unscrupulous lenders, or to duress and intimidation from the Powers, and every large Chinese foreign loan or
indebtedness carries with it a possibility of political complications which may affect not only China but other nations also.

The end of the revolution found China in severe financial
straits. While the struggle was going on, the Powers had opposed loans to either side, since to lend to one side exclusively
(it was legitimate to lend to the Government) would almost assure its success, while to lend to both sides would tend to prolong the civil war. A policy of starving both sides was followed, and this influence had much to do with bringing the compromise. At one time open Japanese loans to the revolutionists
were nearly concluded, but international objections prevented
their consummation; nevertheless, a number of sales of arms
and munitions to the revolutionists were financed by foreign
credits. The republican Government had to assume the ob-

ligations of the Manchu régime, and also the principal obligations made by the revolutionists. The foreign interest and indemnity payments were in arrears, and large amounts were
required for pressing administrative expenses. Before the
revolution the Hukuang and currency loans had brought a
certain international coöperation, and the so-called 4-Power
financial group had been formed, composed of British, French,
German, and American bankers. This group showed willingness to come to the aid of the republican Government, and began to make advances for immediate use, pending the issue of
a large covering loan. These advances were made with an
understanding that the group was to have the financing of the
subsequent big loans. Considerable risk attended these advances. The country was very unsettled, mutinies being frequent, and the new Government was hardly established and by
no means organized. Only the confidence of foreign diplomats and financiers in Yuan Shih K'ai's administrative ability
made it possible for the Government to obtain money. The
basis of these advances is shown by the following letter:

Office of the President,
Peking, March 9, 1912.

To E. G. Hillier, Esq., C.M.G. Agent Hongkong and
Shanghai Banking Corporation; Mons. Casenave,
Manager Banque de L'Indo-Chine; H. Cordes, Esq.,
Deutsch-Asiatische Bank; and Willard D. Straight,
Esq., special representative of the American Group.

Gentlemen:

I am in receipt of your letter of to-day's date informing me that,
having obtained the sanction of your Governments to advance to
the Chinese Provisional Government funds for their urgent requirements, as stated in the letter of the 2nd, March, addressed to you
by the Acting Minister of Finance, your Banks are now prepared
to hold at the disposal of the Chinese Provisional Government,
against the receipts of the Ministry of Finance, the sum of Shanghai
taels one million one hundred thousand (Sh. Tls. 1,100,000), and
I note the arrangement proposed for making this sum available.

It is understood and agreed:

1. That the said advance of Shanghai Tls. 1,100,000 will be treated

in conjunction with the advance of Shanghai Tls. 2,000,000 made in Shanghai to the Chinese Provisional Government on the 28th of February last, and that sterling exchange for the same will be settled by the Banks in Shanghai to-day.

2. That this advance of Shanghai Tls. 1,100,000 as in the case of the previous advance of Shanghai Tls. 2,000,000 above referred to, will be covered by delivery to the banks, as soon as arrangements permit, of sterling Treasury Bills bearing date of the 9th day of March, 1912, and for such amounts as, after being discounted at a rate to be arranged, shall yield the sterling equivalent of the said advance, the said Treasury Bills to be secured, subject to existing charges, upon the revenue of the salt gabelle.

3. That the Banks hold a firm option for the provision of the further monthly requirements of the Chinese Government for the months of March, April, May, June, and possibly July and August, which the Four Groups have already been requested to finance, against the delivery of additional sterling Treasury Bills on terms to be arranged.

4. That in consideration of the assistance rendered by the Groups to China in the present emergency, and of their services in supporting her credit on the foreign markets, the Chinese Government assures to the Groups (provided their terms are equally advantageous with those otherwise obtainable) the firm option of undertaking the comprehensive loan for general reorganization purposes already proposed to them, to be floated as soon as possible, and to be applied in the first instance to the redemption of the sterling Treasury Bills aforesaid.

I hereby confirm the arrangements and conditions above stated, and request you to proceed immediately in accordance therewith.

I am, Gentlemen,

Yours faithfully,

(Signed) YUAN SHIH K'AI.

It was estimated, at that time, that loans amounting to £200,000,000 probably would be required to finance the reconstruction and reorganization programs, and many foreign financiers were anxious to get a part of the business. Several independent syndicates appeared in the field, bidding against the 4-Power group. On March 15, unknown to the members of the quadruple group, Yuan Shih K'ai, acting on advice of the Premier, Tang Shao-yi, signed a contract with a so-called

Belgian syndicate for an immediate advance of £1,000,000, secured on the income and property of the Peking-Kalgan Railway. The 4-Power group at once protested that this loan violated existing agreements and the option given to it to finance the reorganization loans. This protest was upheld by the British, French, German, and American legations; and the British Government further objected because of an agreement by China not to give the Peking-Kalgan Railway as collateral for a foreign loan. The course of Tang Shao-yi in this matter was severely criticized. Immediately after signing the Belgian loan agreement, Tang Shao-yi left Peking and went to Nanking, where he induced the National Council (then sitting there) to confirm the loan. On April 2 Tang Shao-yi signed a further agreement with a member of the Belgian syndicate at Shanghai, and obtained further advances. Meanwhile, negotiations with the 4-Power group were suspended by it until the Belgian loan matter was cleared up.

As this issue raised some important points, it deserves elucidation. Tang Shao-yi's reasons for going outside the 4-Power group had several apparent angles. He claimed to want to prevent any group from having a monopoly of the loan business, which he thought would work to China's disadvantage. That was the reason given publicly, in explaining the matter to the Council, and to the country. Tang Shao-yi assumed the attitude of a patriot protecting his nation from the rapacity of a monopolistic foreign syndicate. This idea, taken up by the radical element of the Council and spread by the radical press, proved popular, and laid the foundations for what developed into a disturbing influence. The facts seem to be that Tang, when acting as Yuan Shih K'ai's representative in the compromise negotiations, had made certain private promises to revolutionary leaders which required funds to meet. Whether these promises were made with Yuan's knowledge is not known definitely. The situation is much the same as promises made by American party managers in behalf of a Presidential candidate—the candidate may know of them, or he may not—but he will be expected to keep them if it is possible. At any rate, the new Government deemed it expedient to fulfil these promises to some extent, and that required money. These expenses were presumed to be those incurred by the Nanking Provisional Government, and to pay off revolutionary troops; but it is probable that some disbursements could not be audited too closely. The 4-Power banking syndicate was working in co-operation with their four Governments; and their dealings with China were predicated on the elimination, as far as was possible, of the old methods of "squeeze" and loose control over disbursements. This attitude was enforced as much in China's interest as in the interest of foreign investors. The four friendly Governments recognized that the former loose method of making foreign loans would create endless complications, and destroy China's credit; and so the advances and loans obtained through the 4-Power syndicate were strictly audited. There probably were items which Tang Shao-yi did not want to submit to foreign auditing, for political reasons, so he went outside the syndicate for a loan under conditions where the use of the funds would not be too closely watched. Being under this necessity, Tang Shao-yi put the best face he could on the matter, and talked about monopoly, and denied that any understanding with the 4-Power group had been violated. This soon proved a short-sighted policy. The terms of the Belgian loan were no better than those offered by the group. The advances obtained from the Belgian syndicate were quickly spent, and the Government needed large additional amounts. The financial influence of the group, combined with the support of the four financial Powers, could practically close the foreign money market to any large Chinese loans.

Tang Shao-yi returned to Peking on April 20 to make his explanations to the group and to the legations of the four Powers. They demanded, before resuming negotiations, that the Belgian loan be canceled, which the Government agreed to do, the group to take up the advances made, amounting to £1,250,000. However, a more serious hitch soon occurred.

The group demanded effective supervision over the security and expenditures of the loans, at which Tang Shao-yi rebelled. It became evident that the negotiations could not be facilitated by Tang, for he had lost the confidence of the bankers, and obdurately refused to meet their views. From then China was represented in the loan negotiations by members of the Ministry of Finance. Tang Shao-yi's attitude on this question eventually drove him out of office and into retirement.

During the next few months politics in China raged about the question of foreign loans. The principles and issues involved in this question are fundamental to China's internal and international situation. On a just and practical solution of them depends her future, her fate as a nation. The question then had two phases in its application to China—effects on her internal reconstruction, and effects on her international position. Tang Shao-yi started out to handle the question chiefly in regard to its relation to internal reconstruction. That was patriotic, and superficially praiseworthy, for China's rights should be considered first by Chinese. But that point of view failed to perceive that the international aspects had the dominating position. China owed money to foreigners that she could not pay. She needed much more money to carry on her internal administration, which could be obtained only from foreigners. She needed still more money for internal improvements and development. China was in the position of a business that is in debt to the banks, has an empty treasury, and cannot go on except by borrowing more capital. If such a business cannot get an extension of credit, and further loans, it must close, or pass into the hands of its creditors. If China failed indefinitely to meet her overdue foreign obligations, she probably would have to submit to a debt commission, and have her revenue system put under foreign management—that is, accept an international receivership. Yuan Shih K'ai's Government was facing this possibility on one hand, and on the other the task of pacifying and reorganizing the country, which could not be done without funds. In that situation, it was inexpedient for the Government to antagonize and arouse the distrust of the leading foreign bankers. Tang Shao-yi apparently was deceived by foreign financiers outside the 4-Power group into believing that China's financial needs could be served independently of it. That was not possible, as events proved. The 4-Power financial syndicate, powerful as it was, was perhaps not of itself unassailable; but combined with its four Governments its position was well-nigh impregnable.

There has been much confusion in the discussion of all phases of this question, in China and in other countries. It has several aspects. There is the relation between the foreign Governments and the foreign banks, as exemplified in the 4-Power grouping. That grouping has been bitterly criticized in England and the United States by British and American bankers who wanted to be included in the British and American groups, and who protested at what they claimed to be a monopoly. The constitution of these national banking groups, and their support by their Governments, is a distinct question by itself, which concerns only the several countries. Let us take the case of the American banking group, and the American Government. That organization and support was a matter of expediency, having in mind what was to be done. America's situation in respect to foreign loans, and especially Chinese loans, is peculiar, as distinguished from Great Britain, France, and Germany, in that American investors have not been accustomed to absorb large amounts of foreign securities. Consequently, when American bankers underwrite a share of Chinese loans, they are doubtful about how American investors will take them. In embarking on this business in China, the American bankers were really pioneering; they had to educate American investors to buy Chinese securities. The outlook was not very promising—almost the contrary—and in taking part the American bankers were influenced by their Government, which had the double object of opening a way to promote American trade in China, and to give the Hay Doctrine some practical foundation of American interest; that is, a wish to aid China and sustain her integrity was included in the purpose of the American Government and the participation of the American bankers. But to be effective, this plan had to be practical, to conform with sound business principles, and to be adjusted to existing conditions. American investors could not be asked to dump their money into China with no prospect of getting it out, or at unusual risk. These conditions were essential: (a) the investment must be sound, (b) it must be attractive, (c) it must yield a fair commission to the underwriters—in short, it must be a straight business proposition. In organizing an American banking group to engage in this business, it manifestly was not possible to include all the leading bankers in the United States. The feasible method would be for a comparatively restricted group, of sufficient prestige to gain the confidence of the other banks and of investors, and with established foreign connections and reputation, to represent the American interest. In the distribution of bonds in America, portions would be allotted to many bankers and banks, as is customary and necessary; but it was impracticable to make each distributor a principal in the loan negotiations. That is why each of the financial Powers decided to support only a selected group of banks in the direct negotiations. Any other plan would lead to confusion. It had been tried in China, with results disastrous to China and damaging to her credit. If every reputable bank or banking house could get the support of its Government in making loans to China a situation would be created whereby loans could be made indiscriminately and without proper supervision, and careless and corrupt Chinese officials could play fast and loose with their nation's credit and its international relations. A study of the process whereby China arrived at her present financial state reveals the dangers of that method. It was out of that experience that the 4-Power governments determined to confine their support at Peking to banks and bankers carefully selected and especially fitted for that part of the work. In respect to American underwriting of Chinese loans, there is this further consideration: It is doubtful if American investors will readily absorb such securities when first offered, in which case the American underwriters either would be left to hold the bonds, or would have to unload them in England or Europe. That cannot be done without the consent of other governments and the coöperation of British and European bankers; and American bankers in the 4-Power group were in the position of claiming a full share of loans, with the privilege of being able to turn back to their British, French, and German partners any bonds that proved to be unsalable in America, to be taken up by the English and European markets.

The ensuing negotiations, which continued for nearly a year, were attended by many interesting developments. These developments had two distinct bearings—relations among the foreign banks and Governments themselves, and questions with China. Japan and Russia became uneasy at some tendencies of the 4-Power activities, and asked to be included in the group. This request was, of course, based on purely political considerations, as Japan and Russia had no free capital for such investments. The question was raised about a provision of the currency loan which allotted £1,500,000 for the promotion of industrial enterprises in Manchuria. Japan and Russia claimed that they should participate in any undertakings in Manchuria, thus injecting the "sphere of influence" complication. This raised an oblique issue, which had to be adjusted before progress could be made. The 4-Power banks, as practical financiers, were disposed to reject the participation of Russia and Japan, which they knew would be fictitious in the financial sense; but the British and French Governments, for the same reasons that had made them support Russia and Japan in opposing the Fakumen and Chinchow-Aigun Railway projects, felt compelled to admit those Powers. The attitudes of Germany and the United States were negative. China ob-

A street in Peking, showing barriers which can be closed to obstruct mobs and rioters. A protection against looting by unruly troops

Scene in the Imperial City at Peking, former residence of the emperors, and where the President lives now

jected to the inclusion of Japan and Russia, knowing their participation to be strategical solely, and based on grounds whose validity China refused to admit. On the face of things, this move by Russia and Japan seemed designed to obstruct the negotiations, and its immediate effect was obstructive. These alternatives were presented: To exclude Russia and Japan, and have them pursue an obstructive policy; or to include them, and in that way make them amenable to influence and regulation by the majority of the group. This latter course was adopted, and on April 19, 1912, it was announced that the Yokohama Specie Bank and the Russo-Asiatic Bank would represent Japanese and Russian interests. Complications were at once made by Russia and Japan, mutually supporting each other. Those Powers wanted a stipulation in the reorganization loan that Russia and Japan must be consulted about any provisions and expenditures in Manchuria, or that those Powers would have the exclusive right to finance and supervise undertakings in Mongolia and Manchuria. The group came near splitting on that point. In May the group bankers began conferences in London, for the purpose of formulating a definite understanding among themselves, and in June the conferences were transferred to Paris. It seemed that an agreement could not be reached within the group, on account of the attitude of Russia. The American representatives, with the approval of the American Government, refused to participate further if any restrictions were placed on China's autonomy and upon the "open door" principle. For a few days it seems that the group would dissolve on this issue, but Russia unexpectedly receded, and an agreement constituting a 6-Power group was signed at Paris on June 20. The conditions of the agreement were not immediately announced, but in September the American group stated in New York its underlying principles, as follows:

1. That the purposes for which the funds were required should be stated by the Chinese Government to the approved groups.

2. That China should adopt a system of audit which would ensure the effective expenditure of the loan funds for the purposes specified.

3. That the Salt Taxes to be hypothecated for the service of this loan should be administered either by the existing Maritime Customs organization, or by a separate service, similar to the Customs, under foreign direction, thus safeguarding the proper administration of the security, despite the possible continuance or recurrence of the unsettled conditions in China.

Tang Shao-yi had resigned the Premiership in June, and left Peking. Meanwhile, the radical leaders and press were conducting a violent agitation against the group syndicate, representing it as a rapacious monopoly aiming, with the consent of Yuan Shih K'ai, to destroy China's autonomy, and subject her internal administration to foreign control. The group had been making advances to the Peking Government, but not as largely and rapidly as it wanted them; and the Government, pressed by its needs, was again trying to obtain money through other agencies. Efforts were made to induce the Governments of the Powers to abandon their support of the group, or to compel the group to modify its terms. These efforts were without avail. Replying, through the British legation at Peking, to a telegram sent to London by the Shanghai Chinese Chamber of Commerce, requesting the British Government to persuade the group to abandon some provisions of its terms, the British Government said: "Sir Edward Grey has authorized me to inform the Chamber of Commerce in reply that so far the action of the groups has met with the entire approval of His Majesty's Government, who, however, cannot urge the Banks to make any loan which does not, in their opinion, offer adequate guarantees for the proper and useful expenditure of the proceeds and satisfactory security for the payment of the principal and interest; and further, that in regard to all questions connected with this loan His Majesty's Government are acting, and will continue to act, in full accord with the other Governments concerned." On July 9 the Minister of Finance, Hsiung Hsi-ling, addressed a letter to the group representatives at Peking, asking for large advances, and stating that unless the group responded the Chinese Government would consider itself free to negotiate elsewhere. Notes were exchanged formally defining the situation. The ministers of the six Powers called on the Premier, Lu Cheng-hsiang, and pointed out that the terms proposed by the group were necessary to satisfy foreign investors and were not imposed from any desire to restrict China. The Minister of Finance resigned, and addressed a telegram to the Provincial Governments, explaining the reasons for the deadlock. His resignation was accepted by the President, but he continued in charge of loan matters as special commissioner. An independent British syndicate entered the field, and the so-called Crisp loan was negotiated for £10,000,000. This brought on a square fight to see if it was possible to finance Chinese loans outside the 6-Power governmental and banking combination. The Crisp syndicate succeeded in floating treasury bills for £500,000 in London on September 19, 1912, and a little later half of the total loan was offered in London. Only £2,000,000 was taken by the public. Although strenuous efforts were made to give this loan the appearance of a success, it soon developed that it was not, and China was driven to resume negotiations with the 6-Power group. The test had been made, and China and the independent bankers had lost. The British investing public would not absorb a loan which was not approved by their Government, and its placing on the European bourses was impossible. As a condition to resuming negotiations, the 6-Power group demanded the cancelation of articles of the Crisp loan contract, that practically nullified it. Subsequently, the Crisp syndicate gave up the fight, and agreed to cancel its agreement for a compensation. The experiment proved costly to China, and futile. On December 27, 1912, the stipulations of a loan agreement were passed by the National Council in secret session; and on April 26, 1913, the Reorganization Loan Agreement was signed.[1]

Before the agreement was signed, however, an unexpected event caused the withdrawal of the American banking group as participants in the loan. This surprising and unfortunate action was caused by a change of policy by the Washington Government, following the inauguration of Mr. Woodrow Wilson as President. With the change of administration, the American group felt that it could not proceed further without knowing the exact attitude of the new Government, and whether the group would continue to receive its support in China. To ascertain this, the group informed the Government that it would withdraw unless it was definitely requested by the Government to participate. It should be remembered that the group was organized in response to a policy of the previous administration, and unless that policy was continued the group's position would be untenable. The Wilson administration declined to request the group to continue its participation in the financing of Chinese loans, on the grounds that the conditions of the reorganization loan touched the independence of China, and by supporting the group the American Government might be led into the necessity of forcible interference in the affairs of China. On March 21 the American banking group announced its withdrawal from the *consortium* at Peking. From the standpoint of American interest and policy in China, this was the most important occurrence since the declaration of the Hay Doctrine, and its significance was obscured both in China and America by misrepresentation and misunderstanding of the facts and conditions. In China the Chinese press acclaimed the action of the American Government, and there was an ebullition of short-sighted pro-American enthusiasm. The withdrawal of the American group and Government was at first hailed as the doom of the 6-Power syndicate, and the restrictive stipulations of the Reorganization Loan; but it soon developed that nothing of consequence was effected. The

[1] Appendix B.

Americans had withdrawn, and that was all. The loan was signed, and on terms satisfactory to the (now 5-Power) group and Governments. There was much talk about independent American loans. Such talk was nonsense, as I, with others, then pointed out. It all along had been doubtful if the most powerful banking group that could be formed in America, with the support of its Government, could float in the United States its allotted quota of Chinese loan bonds. A lesser combination, without government support, and without strong foreign connections, could not then float any considerable amount of Chinese bonds in America. Consider the conditions. For two years the American banking group (comprised of J. P. Morgan & Company; Kuhn, Loeb & Company; the National City Bank of New York; and the First National Bank of New York) had been working in a practical way in China, in London, in Paris, in Berlin, in coöperation with the leading banks of those capitals, and in constant advisement with the diplomatic officials of six Powers, to discover a working method whereby it was feasible to put China on her feet financially, to establish firmly her credit abroad, to aid her in creating a sound internal revenue system, to accommodate these matters with China's intricate international situation and the international balance of power and interest, to preserve the "open door" commercial principle, to create a market for Chinese bonds in the United States on a sound investment basis, and to do all this with a minimum of foreign supervision of China's internal administrative processes. At several stages of the negotiations the American representatives had, by their influence, succeeded in restraining interests that desired to press harsher terms on China, and had qualified forces that were acting on strategical motives which were invidious to China. In any international coöperation, no one Power can have its own way in all things. Coöperation, of necessity, means compromise. There has been a great deal of talk about "independent" American financing in China. Such a thing is not possible at present, except in a small way. Even if conditions in China, and in respect to China's international relations, would permit it, there is now but a small investing public in America receptive to such securities; and if there was a large investing public in America for Chinese bonds, American investors would not be satisfied with less security for their investments than English, French and German investors want. During the time when China was trying to evade the group syndicate and secure independent loans, several attempts were made to procure loans in the United States, without success.

During the entire course of these loan negotiations the opposition to the Government was concentrating its attack on the question of finance, and accusing Yuan Shih K'ai with willingness to betray the country into the clutches of foreign bankers, while at the same time criticizing the Government for failing to make better progress in restoring order and prosperity to the country. Had the Government been suddenly converted, and the Opposition put in power, it would have been compelled to take the same course and accept the same loan terms that were imposed on Yuan Shih K'ai, whose Government resorted to every argument and device before yielding, succumbing only to the inevitable. It was realization of the blatant and irresponsible character of the Opposition, and that its policy was obstructive, and without constructive definiteness, that alienated the solid Chinese elements from the radicals, and snuffed out the rebellion. A majority of intelligent Chinese gradually came to comprehend the difficulties of the Government, and that it required time and patience to reorganize the nation. A wider popular knowledge of the complications of foreign contacts also tended to strengthen the Government. In 1912 a part of Mongolia (apparently by Russian instigation) rebelled, and the rebel faction was recognized by Russia, which used the situation to press her claims to suzerainty over outer Mongolia. This situation was prolonged into 1913, and in the end China had to consent to conditions qualifying her authority in outer Mongolia.[2]

2 Appendix Z.

CHAPTER V

JAPAN'S SEIZURE OF KIAOCHOU

Outbreak of the great war—Dangers to China—Japan's participation —Position of Tsingtau—Efforts to neutralize all leased territory—Diplomatic manœuvering—Japan's precipitate action—Japan's motives— Peculiar conditions in China—Protection of foreigners—An anomalous situation—Japan's ultimatum to Germany—Great Britain's attitude— Effects on British interests—British criticism suppressed—Pretended harmony—Japan's declaration of war.

WITHIN a few days after the outbreak of the great war in Europe, August 4, 1914, there were developments which indicated that China might be involved by the participation of Japan as a belligerent. Students of far Eastern affairs at once perceived that such action by Japan would set forces in motion that would include the fate of China in the course and outcome of the conflict, and which also would involve phases of Western position and prestige in the Orient.

In the period immediately following the declarations that brought Germany, Austria, Russia, France, and Great Britain into the war as belligerents, events moved very swiftly; so swiftly that, beyond doubt, those Governments were to some extent confused and flustered, with a result that affairs not closely related to elements then concentrated in the European situation were for the moment overlooked, or given only casual attention. Nevertheless, intimations that Japan purposed to enter the war were too significant to escape notice. A few days after hostilities commenced, Baron Kato, Japanese minister for foreign affairs, announced in the Diet that Japan was prepared to assume her obligations under the Anglo-Japanese alliance. Since none knew exactly (except the British and

Japanese chancelleries) what the mutual obligations of Great Britain and Japan under this alliance are, Baron Kato's utterance was somewhat cryptic, but it was enough to cause uneasiness at Peking, where the consequences of intervention by Japan were dreaded. What followed is veiled by diplomatic reticence, which may not be broken for years, if ever; but some circumstances and facts are quite clear.

Efforts were made to prevent China from being dragged into the scope of hostilities. The exact origin of these efforts is obscure, for since they failed, no nation or diplomat wishes to assume responsibility. China herself may have taken the initiative, or acted at the friendly suggestion of a foreign diplomat. China simultaneously approached the United States and Japan, these Powers being then neutral and presumably free to respond, with a request that those Governments use their good offices to obtain the consent of all belligerents to preserve the neutrality of all Chinese territory leased to foreign nations. In order to make its application general, and to avoid the appearance of being directed against, or in favor of, any Power or belligerent side, this plan would have included the leased territory of Kiaochou (German), the leased territory including Port Arthur and Dalny (Japanese), the leased territories at Wei-hei-wei and Kowloon (British), and regions occupied by Russia under the Manchurian railway agreements. By this device all territories occupied by belligerents and possible belligerents in China could have been neutralized, any troops and war materials which could not be removed to be interned and their warlike use prevented. It was evident that these possessions were not essential strategically to the military and naval operations, and could have been neutralized without working disadvantage to either belligerent side. Tsingtau was useful as a naval base for Germany, and for the small German squadron which was in the far East when the war started; and to the same extent Wei-hei-wei and Hongkong were useful to the Allies. But it was certain that within a short time the

German squadron would have to quit Tsingtau, or be blockaded in that port. Japan's participation was not necessary to compel that, for a combined Russian, British, and French squadron could have done the work. Foreseeing the inevitable, and that by refusing it would tend to draw Japan in, it is probable that Germany would have consented to neutralize Tsingtau and to withdraw the German squadron, just as it actually was withdrawn. Great Britain would have sustained no appreciable strategical loss by neutralizing Wei-hei-wei, for Hongkong is her central base in Chinese waters and provides ample facilities. The German Asiatic squadron would have put to sea, as it did, and events then would have followed the same course as they took. After the German squadron left Tsingtau that place played no further part in its operations. By accepting this plan, the disposition of Kiaochou after the war would not be affected. If Germany should be decisively defeated in Europe she would have to give up Tsingtau anyhow, if her enemies demand that. Or if Germany should win in Europe, or gain a strategical position there equivalent to tactical success, she would be able to demand restitution of Tsingtau even if it was taken by the Allies during the war. Foreign leased territories in China were only pawns in the war, and could have been eliminated without affecting in the slightest degree the essential strategical zones of operation.

Within a period of ten days after the declarations of war, diplomatic circles at Peking, with of course the consequent reactions at other capitals, were engaged with an effort to find some solution of this situation which would keep China out of the war area. The friendly offices of the United States were enlisted, or an attempt was made to enlist them, and it appears that the United States took some tentative steps toward bringing the Powers into agreement. There were ample basis and precedents for such agreement. It only was necessary to extend to all Chinese territory, including parts under temporary leases to foreign nations, the principle that was actually applied in Peking during the war, and in all the treaty ports in China. For instance, in Peking all the belligerent Powers maintain so-called "legation guards," detachments of troops or marines for the protection of the Legation Quarter, under the terms of the protocol of 1901. Thus it occurs that armed forces of the belligerents continued to stay in Peking, often being only separated by the width of a street, or a compound wall. Theoretically, these troops, in the event of an uprising and attack on the Legations, as in 1900, would combine forces to resist any assault. The Foreign Settlements of Shanghai include residents of all belligerent nations. These settlements, where, in a population of nearly a million Chinese, with several hundreds of thousands more in contiguous Chinese municipalities, are less than twenty thousand foreigners, rely on a volunteer military force for protection against sudden popular revolts and riots. This volunteer force includes companies of different nationalities—British, French, German, American, Japanese, Portuguese, and Chinese. All these organizations were maintained during the Great War, and in the event of disorder were obligated to coöperate in defense of the Settlements. The situation is anomalous, but China's position among the nations constitutes a structure of anomalies. What was done at Peking and in the many treaty ports could have been done with the leased territories.

The interests of every foreign nation, except Japan, and the interests of humanity also, would have been served by such an arrangement. But Japan hastened to block it by interposing the wall of irrevocable events. On August 15 Japan precluded these discussions and efforts by delivering an ultimatum to Germany. On the day before the ultimatum expired, the Japanese minister at Peking called at the Chinese foreign office and tried to reassure China by stating verbally that in case Germany did not comply with the demands of the ultimatum, and Japan was compelled to occupy Kiaochou, that territory would be returned to China after the war. Japan's ultimatum to Germany follows: (My italics)

We consider it highly important and necessary in the present situation to take measures to remove the causes of all disturbances of the peace in the far East, and to safeguard the general interests as contemplated by the agreement of alliance between Japan and Great Britain.

In order to secure a firm and enduring peace in eastern Asia, the establishment of which is the aim of the said agreement, the Imperial Japanese Government sincerely believes it to be its duty to give the advice to the Imperial German Government to carry out the following two propositions:

First—To withdraw immediately from Japanese and Chinese waters German men-of-war and armed vessels of all kinds, and to disarm at once those which cannot be so withdrawn.

Second—To deliver on a date not later than September 15 to the Imperial Japanese authorities, without condition or compensation, the entire leased territory of Kiaochou, *with a view to the eventual restoration of the same to China.*

The Imperial Japanese Government announces at the same time that in the event of not receiving by noon on August 23, 1914, an answer from the Imperial German Government signifying its unconditional acceptance of the above advice offered by the Imperial Japanese Government, Japan will be compelled to take such action as she may deem necessary to meet the situation.

The situation created by Japan's ultimatum to Germany was contemporaneously described by me in the "China Press," dated August 19, 1914, as follows: "No by-product of the war has caused such deep reflections, such profound uneasiness, as the action of Japan regarding Tsingtau. Any one at all conversant with political and racial equilibriums in the far East at once recognizes the disturbing character of this step. What are Japan's reasons for her action? These may be separated into two classes—reasons which Japan officially announces, and her real reasons. Sometimes official reasons given for acts of a Government are also the real reasons; sometimes they are not. Japan's primary official reason for sending her ultimatum to Germany about Tsingtau, according to Count Okuma, is to 'preserve peace.' It was not necessary to state that. To preserve peace always is the chief reason why modern nations go to war, or threaten war. In this instance, it is rather superfluous, for a state of war involving Tsingtau already exists. It also is true that nations already at war with Germany, with their naval and military forces in this part of the world, are capable of putting into effect the war measures required to preserve peace at Tsingtau. We are not much impressed by that reason of Japan—or rather, we are a good deal impressed by the humbug of it. In her ultimatum, Japan does not state that her action is responsive to obligations under the Anglo-Japanese alliance, but this inference can be logically drawn from circumstances, and from much comment and explanation of Japanese statesmen and the Japanese press, which evidently is calculated to give this impression. If Japan really is moving in response to the alliance with Great Britain, then it would follow that her course is approved and welcomed by her ally. Yet there are many intimations that Great Britain does not want Japan in this embroglio. It is fairly certain that British interests in China are not likely to be served, in the long run, by Japan's interference. It is absolutely certain that Japan's interposition is generally resented by British subjects in the far East. From what can be learned of their attitude, and taking conditions into account, France and Russia do not want Japan to take part in the war. China does not want Japan to take over Tsingtau, even under a promise to restore the place to China after the war. The United States of America does not want Japan to seize Tsingtau, or to have the neutrality of China violated. A Reuter telegram from Washington states that the American Government 'regards Japan's promise to restore Kiaochou to China as satisfactory.' From this it appears that Washington has made inquiries about Japan's intentions. It may be that Washington can take satisfaction from Japan's assurance that Kiaochou will be restored to China, but it by no means follows that Washington is satisfied with Japan's course in breaking into this war, and the disturbing reactions it will occasion. Who, then, does want, or has asked Japan to take over the task of occupying Tsingtau? Unless her action is taken at request of some entity, then Japan must be acting on her own initiative. Perhaps an examination of the need for Japan's action, if any exists, may throw light on her incentives and motives. All neutral and most belligerent interests in the far East want to see hostilities confined to Europe, where the issues will be decided; and consequently they will welcome any decent arrangement whereby Tsingtau and the German naval squadron in these waters will be eliminated as belligerent factors. It is quite feasible, as we have previously pointed out, to accomplish this by negotiation and agreement between the belligerents, and between Germany and China. Japan's interference does not make it easier peacefully to neutralize Tsingtau. It makes it more difficult, for the terms and conditions of her ultimatum are so couched as to be provocative of resistance by Germany, as a matter of honor, however hopeless it may be to resist an attack of Japanese naval and military forces. It makes pacific neutralization more difficult because Japan's action arouses strong suspicions of ulterior purpose on her part, and consequently unsettles China and the international balance of power. Japan's ultimatum comes at a time when the Allied naval forces have about negatived activities of the German squadron in Chinese waters, and when, if it should become necessary— negotiations to neutralize Tsingtau by agreement failing— to take the place by force of arms, the Allies themselves are in a position to undertake that task. Where, then, does Japan come in? Where is the need and demand for her action? . . . But it is questionable if anything done by Germans in the far East since this war started really caused Japan's ultimatum to be sent. Such activities provided an excuse. Failing that, another excuse could have been found, if it was wanted. In these cases, the wish is father to the thought. It now is pretty clear that no sooner had this war begun than Japan began to cast about for an excuse to break into it, with a view to improving her position in China. What has happened is the logical sequence of this ambition. Japan has her own present internal political reasons for this aggressive move. It will strengthen the Government at home to grab a valuable possession in China. We wonder if Great Britain was consulted by her ally before this move was made, or did Japan decide and act without giving England a chance to object. We also wonder if there is one person in the world, who is familiar with the conditions, who credits Japan's announced intention to turn Kiaochou back to China. The extent of participation, of opposition or acquiescence, taken by Great Britain, France, and Russia in diplomatic phases of Japan's move probably will not be revealed until long after the war has ended.''

And in the ''China Press,'' dated August 20, 1914, in a leading article discussing Japan's action, I wrote: ''The present war had hardly started when people familiar with conditions in the far East began to remark: 'Here is Japan's opportunity. Europe's hands are tied. What will Japan do?' And the general opinion was that Japan would aggress upon China in some way before the war ended. That opinion was based on two things—a penetration of Japan's ambitions, and certain beliefs about Japan's national character and policy. No one thought of treaties, no one thought of alliances—except to wonder how they would be interpreted to meet the occasion. People in the far East said: 'It is Japan's chance.' Few felt that scruples would prevent her from taking it.''

I insert these quotations to show that the real purposes of Japan were even then obvious to students of far Eastern conditions and politics. I was not alone in these misgivings. They were felt by foreign residents of China almost universally and without regard to nationality, or alignments of belligerent nations, although there were restraints upon expression of them. At the first intimation of Japan's purpose to intervene, evidences of antipathy to such action among British interests in China were plentiful. Suspicion and doubt permeated the British press in China, and there were indications that the British legation at Peking favored general action of the Powers to neutralize Chinese territory during the war. Such attitude of the British legation, and such expression of the British press, were promptly suppressed by outward acquiescence of the British Government in Japan's participation in the war, and the attack on Tsingtau. Deeply as British in China and the far East deplored such a policy, they were constrained by circumstances, with few exceptions, to abstain from public criticism of Japan's course. In this way, the fiction of a harmony of Japan and Great Britain in this matter was created and afterward observed, any inclination of the British press in the far East to criticize being thereafter subjected to the direct and indirect operation of the censorship; indeed, several British editors were disciplined, and one was prosecuted in the British Supreme Court at Shanghai for alleged violations of the special Orders in Council, by condemnation of Japan and Great Britain's toleration of Japan's course.

From the issuance of Japan's ultimatum to Germany to its expiry, the efforts to neutralize Tsingtau were continued in a perfunctory way, but evidently without real prospect of success. Germany understood the situation, and showed willingness to fall in with the neutrality scheme (since it was to her advantage), but knew that nothing she could do would materially change conditions, or prevent Japan from entering China. Therefore, Germany deliberately ignored Japan's ultimatum, permitting it to expire without reply or comment. The time was short for the United States, and other neutral nations, to organize any effective action to obstruct Japan and safeguard China. Great Britain, entering upon a long and precarious war, felt that it was inadvisable to get into friction with Japan at its outset. There are two theories for Great Britain's course at that time. One is that Great Britain initiated Japan's action, by requesting her aid under the alliance. The other theory is that Japan's herself took the initiative, contrary to the real desire of her ally, and by force of circumstances compelled Great Britain to acquiesce with, and officially to sanction, this diplomatic fiction. I believe in the latter theorem. It coincides with all the logic of facts and conditions, with British interests in China, and with an honorable regard for Great Britain's obligations toward China and other nations committed to the "open door" and "integrity of China" policies; and there is plenty of evidence to support it.

But officially, Great Britain stands as having an equal responsibility with Japan, for she yielded to her ally. Nevertheless, in Japan's official pronouncements on entering the war, their phraseology avoided stating that Great Britain asked Japan to come in, while manifestly being designed to give this impression. The Imperial Rescript declaring war follows:

We, by the grace of Heaven, Emperor of Japan, on the throne occupied by the same Dynasty from time immemorial, do hereby make the following proclamation to all Our loyal and brave subjects:

We, hereby, declare war against Germany and We command Our army and navy to carry on hostilities against that Empire with all their strength, and We also command all Our competent authorities to make every effort in pursuance of their respective duties to attain the national aim within the limit of the law of nations.

Since the outbreak of the present war in Europe, the calamitous effect of which We view with grave concern, on Our part, have entertained hopes of preserving the peace of the far East by the maintenance of strict neutrality, but the action of Germany has at length compelled Great Britain, Our ally, to open hostilities on that country, and Germany is at Kiaochou, its leased territory in China, busy with warlike preparations, while her armed vessels, cruising the seas of Eastern Asia, are threatening Our commerce and that of Our ally. The peace of the far East is thus in jeopardy.

Accordingly, Our Government, and that of His Britannic Majesty, after a full and frank communication with each other, agreed to take such measures as may be necessary for the protection of the general interests contemplated by the Agreement of Alliance, and We, on Our part, being desirous to attain that object by peaceful means, commanded Our Government to offer, with sincerity, an advice to the Imperial German Government. By the last day appointed for the purpose, however, Our Government failed to receive an answer accepting their advice.

It is with profound regret that We, in spite of Our ardent devotion to the cause of peace, are thus compelled to declare war, especially at this early period of Our reign and while We are still in mourning for Our lamented Mother.

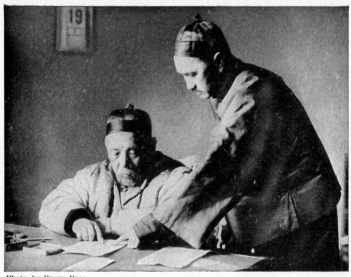

Yuan Shih K'ai at work, with Admiral Tsai Ting-Kan, one of his close
advisers

Yuan Shih K'ai reviewing the President's Guard on a state occasion

It is Our earnest wish that, by the loyalty and valor of Our faithful subjects, peace may soon be restored and the glory of the Empire be enhanced.

In the London "Times' History of the War," pains is taken to point out that "there is no suggestion in the Imperial Rescript that the action of Japan was taken in response to a direct request for assistance from the British Government." Both the British and Japanese Governments tried to avoid a written commitment to that effect, and Great Britain was especially anxious to disclaim responsibility because of her position in China. But Japanese statesmen refused to have it that way, and openly pulled Great Britain in, by the following statement of Baron Kato, minister for foreign affairs, in the Diet, explaining Japan's reasons for entering the war.

Early in August the British Government asked the Imperial Government for assistance under the terms of the Anglo-Japanese Alliance. German men-of-war and armed vessels were prowling around the seas of eastern Asia, menacing our commerce and that of our ally, while Kiaochou was carrying out operations apparently for the purpose of constituting a base for warlike operations in eastern Asia. Grave anxiety was thus felt for the maintenance of peace in the far East.

As all are aware, the agreement and alliance between Japan and Great Britain has for its object the consolidation and maintenance of general peace in eastern Asia and the maintenance of the independence and integrity of China, as well as the principle of equal opportunities for commerce and industry for all nations in that country, and the maintenance and defense respectively of territorial rights and special interests of contracting parties in eastern Asia. Therefore, inasmuch as we were asked by our ally for assistance at a time when commerce in eastern Asia, which Japan and Great Britain regard alike as one of their special interests, is subjected to a constant menace, Japan, who regards that alliance as a guiding principle of her foreign policy, could not but comply to the request to do her part.

Germany's possession of a base for powerful activities in one corner of the far East was not only a serious obstacle to the maintenance of permanent peace, but also threatened the immediate interests of the Japanese Empire. The Japanese Government, therefore, resolved to comply with the British request, and, if necessary, to open hostilities against Germany. After the Imperial sanction had been obtained I communicated this resolution to the British Government, and a full and frank exchange of views between the two Governments followed, and it was finally agreed between them to take such measures as were necessary to protect the general interests contemplated in the agreement and the alliance.

Japan had no desire or inclination to become involved in the present conflict, but she believed she owed it to herself to be faithful to the alliance and to strengthen its foundation by ensuring permanent peace in the East and protecting the special interests of the two Allied Powers. Desiring, however, to solve the situation by pacific means, the Imperial Government, on August 15, gave the following advice to the German Government. [Here the Minister quoted the text of the Japanese ultimatum.] Until the last moment of the time allowed—namely, until August 23—the Imperial Government received no answer, and in consequence the Imperial Rescript declaring war was issued the next day.

From the first intimation of its purpose to enter the war, the Japanese Government began a systematic effort to explain its action in a way to relieve the uneasiness of Western nations and peoples that such action would cause. On the day Japan's ultimatum to Germany was delivered, Count Okuma, the Premier of Japan, sent the following telegram to be distributed to the press in the United States by the East and West Bureau (New York), the Japanese semi-official news service in America: "Japan's proximity to China breeds many absurd rumors; but I declare that Japan acts with a clear conscience, in conformity with justice, and in perfect accord with her ally. Japan has no territorial ambition, and hopes to stand as the protector of peace in the Orient." A few days later, on August 18, Count Okuma gave this further explicit utterance, when addressing a gathering of Japanese business men at Tokio: "Japan's warlike operations will not extend beyond the limits necessary for the attainment of the object of the defense of her own legitimate interests. The Imperial Government will take no such action as could give to a third party any cause for anxiety or uneasiness regarding the safety of their territories or possessions." And on August 24, Count Okuma telegraphed a message to the American people through the "Independent" (New York), as follows: "I gladly seize the opportunity to send, through the medium of the 'Independent,' a message to the people of the United States, who have always been helpful and loyal friends of Japan. It is my desire to convince your people of the sincerity of my Government and of my people in all their utterances and assurances connected with the present regrettable situation in Europe and the far East. Every sense of loyalty and honor oblige Japan to co-operate with Great Britain to clear from these waters the enemies who in the past, the present and the future menace her interests, her trade, her shipping, and her people's lives. The far Eastern situation is not of our seeking. It was ever my desire to maintain peace, as will be amply proved; as President of the Peace Society of Japan I have consistently so endeavored. I have read with admiration the lofty message of President Wilson to his people on the subject of neutrality. We, of Japan, are appreciative of the spirit and motives that prompted the head of your great nation, and we feel confident that his message will meet with a national response

"As Premier of Japan, I have stated and I now again state to the people of America and of the world that Japan has no ulterior motive, no desire to secure more territory, no thought of depriving China or other peoples of anything which they now possess. My Government and my people have given their word and their pledge, which will be as honorably kept as Japan always keeps promises" (My italics).

The fact that Germany had some insular possessions in the Pacific Ocean, coupled with Japan's participation in the war, caused some misgivings in British Australasia, and in the Philippines. Some steps must have been taken to limit Japan's naval activites, for the following announcement of Japan's intentions was made public, as communicated to the State Department by the British foreign office: "It is understood that the action of Japan will not extend to the Pacific beyond the China seas, except as may be necessary to protect Japanese shipping lines in the Pacific, nor in Asiatic waters westward of the China seas, nor in foreign territories except territory in German occupation on the Continent of Asia.'' The measure of trustworthiness of these assurances of Japanese statesmen can be found in Japan's subsequent course. In this manner Japan declared herself in the war, and gave to far Eastern affairs, and to China, a portentous shift.

CHAPTER VI

JAPAN'S AGGRESSIONS IN CHINA

China's efforts to preserve neutrality—Japan's alleged promises regarding Kiaochou—Shooing off the United States—Insufficient protection for foreign interests—Some methods of Japan—Reasons for Japan's moves—Effects in China—Fear of revolutionary activity—Attempts to create a war zone in Shantung—Extending scope of Japanese military operations—British participation—Further encroachments by Japan—Seizure of the Tsinan-Tsingtau Railway—Japan's pretenses exposed—Foreign investments involved—Significant questions raised.

THE significance of Japan's injection into the war as a belligerent was not lost with Governments interested in far Eastern affairs, and uneasiness was immediately shown in some quarters. The United States took notice, notwithstanding the policy of President Wilson's administration to abstain from activity in foreign affairs, and directed a polite inquiry to Japan about her ultimate intentions regarding the leased territory of Kiaochou. When Japan, by sending an ultimatum to Germany, unmistakably indicated an intention to interfere, Baron Kato sought to mitigate the effects of that action among neutral nations, and also with Japan's European allies, by intimating a purpose to turn Kiaochou over to China after Germany had been ejected. In the far East this was generally taken at its true value—as a subterfuge; but it provided an excuse for some diplomatic manoeuvering.

The attack on Tsingtau by a Japanese naval and military force had two phases. Regarded one way, it was merely a drama composed by the hopeless resistance of a few thousands of isolated Germans to an overwhelming army of Orientals. Viewed politically, it intimated an effort of tortuous diplomacy to work out some obscure purpose in the frayed edges of a stupendous European quarrel. Japan's intervention obviously would not stop at temporary occupation of Tsingtau. What it meant, where it tends, are momentous questions to people living in that part of the world. There was a feeling that relief from German belligerent activity promised by Japanese occupation of Tsingtau might be more than counterbalanced by disturbing elements which Japan's action set in motion.

In that connection, the attitude of the United States had an important bearing. The other major Powers already were at war, and there were indications that Italy would join. By being belligerents, the military and naval forces of those nations were not available for foreign police duty in the neutral ports and territory of China, if respect was paid to international law. That left only the United States of nations which have been accustomed to provide warships and troops to perform that duty. In those circumstances, if America did not supply the deficiency, the duty would lapse to the extent that forces of other nations were withdrawn or circumscribed. The only practicable alternative would be for British, Japanese, French, Russian, and Italian troops and warships, after the German and Austrian forces in China were disposed of by capture of Tsingtau, to disregard the neutrality of China, and resume their customary positions and actions there. The United States had ample forces in the Pacific Ocean to fill the deficiency, and there was a general presumption that it would be willing to act unless prevented. Two things might prevent the despatch of American reinforcements to China at that juncture—opposition by China or a foreign Power, or lack of understanding at Washington of the exigencies of the situation. There was small probability that China would object; indeed there were ample indications that she would welcome such action by America. It is difficult to see how a foreign Power would base a legitimate objection, or could make any official objection without affronting America. But a foreign Power might oppose very effectively by raising side issues which, if reflected to Washington by American officials in

China who failed to grasp their significance and values, or who failed to inform their Government of the real situation there, would cause confusion and hesitation at Washington, and result in nothing being done. That something of this nature was attempted, and was in some degree effective, was intimated by events of that period. When China realized the complications that might result from Germany's possession of Tsingtau during the war, and made efforts to prevent them by neutralizing that place, Japan and America were approached. America was well disposed to the suggestion in principle, but it developed that Japan was not. Japan had other designs in the matter, and her method of handling the incident revealed some interesting matters. At that time, the Peking correspondent of the ''North-China Daily News'' (Shanghai), a British newspaper, wrote to that paper as follows:

When this request was made China had no particular desire to preserve Kiaochou to Germany. What she wanted was to be assured that Japan would not have an excuse for operations in China which might be easily developed into activities against the Chinese themselves, and being ignorant of the use of the finesse of diplomacy when blood lust is in the atmosphere, she made the mistake of approaching the Americans to assist in safeguarding her integrity, thereby arousing the suspicions of the Japanese that such a request was directly aimed at the Japanese themselves. And the Japanese had excuse enough for the contention by quoting the statements made from time to time by the Chinese newspapers to the effect that large American naval forces were to be despatched to see to it that China would not suffer at the hands of any evilly disposed persons. Japan, therefore, gave no encouragement to China, and America deemed it prudent to keep off the very tender grass.

How Japan regarded this overture to the United States and the concurrent reports by the Chinese of American activity is evidenced by the circulation in Chinese newspapers supposed to be controlled by Japan, of statements such as the following, which was published in the "Fengtien Daily News" on August 9:

"The Japanese Government has telegraphically informed the British Government that America is sending her fleet to the far East to protect her interests in China, and it is thought that America is using this pretext to assist Germany. Thereupon the British Government replied that they deferred to Japan's desires in the far East, even to the extent of declaring war against America if necessary. The British residents in Japan concurred with the reply of Great Britain."

This message was telegraphed from Tokio, and is certain to be baseless, but the object of serving it up hot to the Chinese is manifest. America was deliberately placed in a wrong light by the energetic imaginativeness of the Chinese newspaper men, and the result has been that she has had to make studied denials of the various reports which have been given circulation. Meantime Japan went about her business of preparing for action and unintentionally, of course, providing groundwork for the structures of the architects of falsehoods, and it was not until the evening of the 16th that the Chinese Government became fully aware of Japanese intent. On that day she notified China of the ultimatum which she had designed for presentation to the war lord at the headquarters of his troops in Germany.

From these and many other evidences discernible to observation trained in knowledge of far Eastern political methods, it became clear that Japan did not want any reinforcement of American military and naval forces in China. For the moment we can leave the Why of that desire aside, and look at Japan's method of impressing her point on China and the United States. The method can be summarized as follows: (a) To cause to be published in Chinese papers controlled by Japan reports that America was sending a fleet to China to assist Germany; (b) then to represent to China that because of uneasiness caused by those reports Japan was unable to participate with America in trying to neutralize Kiaochou by agreement among the belligerents; (c) then to hint in quarters whence it would be carried to American diplomatic officials in the far East that to send any more American warships to China would cause Japan uneasiness and make her suspicious of America's motives; (d) then to reinforce and support this idea by comment in the leading newspapers in Japan; and (e) get it reflected in despatches sent out of Japan and China by news services controlled by Japan, to be published in America and other countries, and (f) deftly to pass the idea to the American ambassador in Tokio to have him pass it along to Washington, and communicate it to American public opinion through the American press.

What were Japan's reasons for that line of action? Her objects relating especially to Kiaochou even then were clear to those familiar with her policy and purposes. But Japan's anxiety to shoo America off, and prevent the United States from responding to its obligation to protect all foreign interests in China in the emergency, were not then quite so clear. Was it really true that Japan would be suspicious of America's motives in sending a small reinforcement to replace forces withdrawn and interned by the belligerents, in order to sustain the usual quota of foreign military and naval strength in China, and would regard it as a move aimed at Japan? Let us look this proposition over. In case of war coming up suddenly between Japan and the United States, American warships in Asiatic waters would be in the same predicament as German ships in the far East were when the Great War started. Unless they had time to make a run for Manila Bay, where they might be safe for a while, they probably would have to intern in a Chinese or a British port. A tyro in naval strategy and tactics knows that if America had a thought of going to war against Japan, she would *withdraw* her naval forces from Chinese waters, not add to them a small reinforcement which would also be sacrificed or tied up as soon as war began, owing to the great numerical superiority of the Japanese navy in that region. So a suspicion of that nature evidently was not Japan's reason for wanting to prevent American, or any other foreign reinforcements in China, and it is amazing that any diplomat or chancellery would be credulous enough to take it seriously, if any did. It was necessary, then, to look elsewhere for the real reasons why Japan at that time tried to forestall the United States from acting upon its plain responsibility in China. And since the reasons were not directly due to Japan's action about Kiaochou, which already was a *fait accompli* diplomatically, they evidently existed in the situation of China as a whole.

In being deeply concerned about Japan's action at Kiaochou, China was not so worried then about the future of Kiaochou as about what Japan's move in that quarter presaged for China's internal political situation and national autonomy. The chief foreign influences that aided and abetted the rebellion of 1913 were fresh in mind, the country to which the chief conspirators fled, and where they found protection and encouragement to continue their agitation and plots. As soon as the Great War started, the exiled Chinese revolutionists in Japan revived their activities. It was reported that some revolutionary leaders had slipped into China, and were working up another rebel organization, and in the Chinese popular mind these disquieting manifestations were associated with Japan. It was known that Japan had mobilized the whole of her standing army, not one tenth of which was required to take Tsingtau. It was felt that, in lieu of other supports, the presence of a larger American naval force would have a quieting effect upon the Chinese people, and in the event of internal trouble starting or being started, such a force would tend to safeguard foreign interests and property and prevent complications. Most people in China, native and foreign, would have felt easier in mind if assured that the United States was prepared and willing to take up that duty. That assurance, however, was not given. At that time Reuter's news agency carried a report to the far Eastern press to the effect that the United States had obtained a promise from Japan that Kiaochou would be restored to China after the war, and that Japan would not take any measures in China outside the leased territory of Kiaochou without consulting the United States. Later events showed that such assurances were not given officially, although the report circulated by Reuter and Japanese news agencies had some effect outside the far East (as it was designed to do), in allaying uneasiness, and suspicion of Japan's motives. That Japan had no thought of abiding by such a policy was soon demonstrated.

Within a few days after declaring war, Japan informed China of her intention to cross Chinese territory outside the leased region of Kiaochou, in order to attack Tsingtau, claiming military necessity. Germany promptly protested to China against this violation of China's neutrality, and, in turn, China protested to Japan. These protests were perfunctory, for by then China realized that efforts by her to maintain genuine neutrality would be unsupported by any Power, and that she could not resist Japan alone. On Germany's part, the protest to China was in the nature of saving a diplomatic exception, to be raised at some future time. On China's part, her protest also had in mind the technical requirements of the situation, vis-a-vis Germany, but more particularly it was a move to try to limit Japan's military operations to the smallest possible area. China therefore suggested that a definite "war zone" be set apart, within which Japan would confine her operations against Tsingtau; and in support of this proposal China cited the instance, during the Russo-Japanese War, of limiting the war zone in Chinese territory to the part of Manchuria lying east of the Liao River, when the good offices of the United States were exerted to secure the assent of Russia and Japan, and the recognition of other Powers. Japan first evaded, then rejected, China's desire to establish a definite and restricted war zone in Shantung. Her reasons for that refusal are found in her subsequent moves. China, however, went through the formality of declaring a zone. On September 2, 1914, Japanese troops began to land at points in Shantung Province, from where they advanced overland to besiege Tsingtau. Bodies of Japanese troops made detours, occupying important cities and towns in the province wide of a direct line of march. Wherever they went, the Japanese assumed control of the country, means of communication, posts, and telegraphs; and subjected the Chinese population to many hardships, depriva-

tions, and indignities, which were observed and reported
by American and British missionaries in that region.[1] Tsingtau is connected with the interior of Shantung Province by a
railway, built by German capital principally, and constructed
under German supervision. This railway extends to Tsinan-fu,
capital of Shantung, where it makes a connection with the
Tientsin-Pukou Railway running north and south. The Japanese soon reached a point on the Tsinan-Tsingtau Railway
west of Tsingtau, thereby cutting German communications.
During this time Great Britain was considering the situation
caused by Japan's operations in China, and had decided to
participate in them. It was evident that in doing this Great
Britain was acting on political considerations, since the few
troops she supplied were not needed. Japanese felt this, and
deeply resented the presence of British troops with the expe-
ditionary force, making their situation as unpleasant as was
possible without open insult. The British force was landed
at Laoshan Bay, *inside the German leased territory,* on September 23, thus, as the ''London Times'' said, ''avoiding the
breach of neutrality alleged by the Chinese against the Japanese.'' The ''Times'' (History of the War) also makes this
comment: ''The distance which separated Laoshan Bay
from Tsingtau was so much shorter, and presented so much
less of difficulty than the Japanese had to encounter in their
preliminary advances, that the British really arrived on the
scene just as the Japanese were finishing their first engagement in force.'' In other words, the Japanese took round-
about routes, violating China's neutrality, without having a
real military necessity to do so.

Further encroachments by Japanese forces on Chinese territory and Chinese and foreign vested interests quickly followed.
No surprise was felt, among persons familiar with conditions,
when the Japanese army seized the whole length of the
Tsinan-Tsingtau Railway. It was a logical development in the
line of Japan's real object in engaging in the war. In seizing

[1] Appendix T.

this railway Japan advanced an explanation, which in effect was that it was made necessary by military exigencies. That excuse served as well as another. It is of a piece with reasons given for Japan's participation in the war, and her original violation of China's neutrality. Viewed broadly, it did not then matter much what excuses Japan gave for her course in Shantung. They are interesting chiefly for light they throw upon her ultimate intentions and purposes, and the workings of her diplomacy; and since Great Britain was coöperating with Japan under the terms of an alliance between those nations, those events may in a way be taken as sign-posts of future policy toward China by more than one Power. This possibility makes it interesting to analyze the explanations Japan gave at that time. In connection with her seizure of the whole line of the Tsinan-Tsingtau Railway, nine tenths of which lies exclusively in Chinese territory and outside the German leasehold, Japan advanced these propositions:

(a) That because the railway was constructed under a concession to a company composed principally of Germans and financed principally by German capital, it takes on German nationality, and therefore becomes liable to seizure by an enemy in war, although lying in the territory of a neutral nation.

(b) That because at one end the railway terminates in territory leased to Germany, it thereby becomes German property over its whole length, and can be considered as enemy property in international law.

(c) That because, before arrival of Japanese troops in Shantung (or interruption by flood) the railway carried ordinary traffic between Tsinan-fu and Tsingtau, and among this traffic were Germans who now form part of the garrison of Tsingtau, and certain supplies now useful in the defense of that place, the Japanese military authorities are justified in considering those occurrences a violation of neutrality.

(d) That this railway "constitutes an indivisible part of the leased territory of Tsingtau."

(e) That Japan is entitled, in view of the foregoing circumstances, to seize and operate the railway without referring the matter to the Chinese Government.

If these propositions are conceded, and become a part of recognized international law (or of a special international law applying to China), then it is evident that many conditions relating to business and property there will be seriously affected. I take it that this railway does not differ materially in its legal and property status from other railways in China built under generally similar conditions; and that principles that apply to China's position in this question and to property rights involved, also will apply to other railway lines in China which were financed by foreign capital, under the countenance of other foreign Governments, and of which there is a certain degree of foreign management and supervision. Therefore, if conditions were reversed, and Germany had the military power to do so, she might consider herself justified in taking control over British-built and British-operated lines in China without consulting China's wishes in the matter, and without regard to the interests of investors.

When, as result of war or other causes, a change takes place in the sovereignty of a territory, such property that belongs to the Government becomes property of the succeeding Government. But all private property must under the practice of civilized nations be respected. It is not liable to confiscation, or diversion, except by civil legal process. If her opponents overcome Germany in Europe, and take over the Government of the whole country, the new Government would assume control and direction over any railways owned by the present German Government; but privately owned railways would be entitled to all the legal safeguards usually thrown about property. Privately owned railways in Germany, and in all countries, are not the exclusive property of nationals of the countries where they operate. The railways of the United States of America are owned all over the world, through distribution of American railway shares and bonds.

The same is true, to a large extent, of railways in China. Chinese own outright but a small part of railways now operating in that country. Some railways in China involve foreign property rights to the extent that bonds issued as liens upon them are owned by foreigners. Those bonds may be underwritten by a German, or a British, syndicate which gets the contract to finance and construct the line: but once the bonds are out in the open financial market, they become in a sense international property, for in the course of transfers and sales they change ownership. So may British be interested in a property sense in the Tsinan-Tsingtau Railway, while Germans may be so interested in railway lines in China called British in the diplomatic differential sense, which were financed by British banks, and which are operated under British supervision. It is a new idea whereby foreign investments in the railways of any country may, in war, be considered enemy property by a belligerent and treated as such: and when this doctrine is extended to foreign investments in railways *lying in a neutral country* all accepted principles are overturned. If Japan's action in Shantung becomes a precedent, then the whole legal basis of such investments is shaken.

Japan's contention that because, prior to Japan's entering the war, and perhaps for a short time subsequently, German reservists not in uniform traveled over the Tsinan-Tsingtau line, and supplies useful in the defense of Tsingtau were carried in the course of ordinary traffic, that the railway forfeited its neutral character, is preposterous. In the first place, it is not a violation of neutrality for a railway anywhere to carry such passengers under the circumstances that existed, and to haul such supplies at any time. Japan set out to make some international law specially suitable for her use in China, and to enforce her own definitions and interpretations of neutrality and contraband. Even if the Tsinan-Tsingtau railway had actually carried, after the declaration of war by Japan against Germany, arms and munitions of war to Tsingtau, it would not be a violation of neutrality. There is nothing unlawful in a neutral selling arms and munitions of war to belligerents in time of war, or for railways to transport such articles to their destination. Except on the high seas, the rule of contraband does not apply, for articles recognized as being absolutely contraband in all circumstances of war, are free of transport and sale within any neutral territory.

Now if the Tsinan-Tsingtau Railway forfeited its neutral character by accepting as paying passengers German subjects who were traveling to Tsingtau with intent to join the garrison there, and by accepting for shipment goods of a contraband character for that destination, then any other railway in China or elsewhere that during war did the same things for any belligerents also forfeited its neutral character. Yet there is not a railway in China, and very few railways in the world, that have not done these things in wars. Suppose that Japan would give a further extension of the principle she applied to the Tsinan-Tsingtau Railway, and reason that the northern part of the Tientsin-Pukou Railway also was financed and constructed by Germans and is operated in some degree under German supervision, and that it in war did (as it undoubtedly did) the same things the Tsinan-Tsingtau line has done, and would take charge of the so-called German part of the Tientsin-Pukou Railway. It would be as reasonable, and as justifiable, as her seizure of the Tsinan-Tsingtau line is. Japan's contention that it was necessary for military reasons for her to seize the entire line to Tsinan-fu is a transparent subterfuge. An interruption of traffic at one point is enough to prevent use of the railway to supply Tsingtau. By taking over the whole line, Japan could not alter or mitigate whatever help it had already been toward the defense of Tsingtau. That was done, and finished. There was no violation of neutrality in doing it. Seizing the line afterward could not affect in the slightest degree whatever defense the Germans in Tsingtau were able to make; nor could it be of any military advantage to Japan, unless she intended to do, conversely, exactly what she com-

Scenes at Tsingtau, the handsome city built by Germany at Kiaochou
Bay, in German leased territory

plained about, and use the line outside the so-called war zone for her own military purposes.

From this it appears that Japan's seizure of the entire Tsinan-Tsingtau Railway was not a necessary military measure, as was pretended, but was a *political* move. The seeming acquiescence of Great Britain with that move gives it additional importance. Does Great Britain regard the Canton-Kowloon Railway (extending from British leased territory opposite Hongkong) as also constituting, in Japan's phraseology, "an indivisible part" of Great Britain 's Kowloon leasehold? These considerations make this question very significant to China; and also significant to all foreign investments existing in China now, and those which may hope to get a legitimate foothold in China hereafter.

CHAPTER VII

JAPAN'S AGGRESSIONS IN CHINA—*Continued*

Extending Japan's power over Shantung province—Usurping China's authority—A familiar process—Seizure of private property—The principles involved—Effects on the United States—Secret undermining of treaties—Dropping the mask—Japan's implied promises repudiated —Menace to peace of the far East—Dr. Charles W. Eliot's views— Future causes of war—The logic of Japan's policy—Dangerous forces set in motion.

TSINGTAU was occupied by the Japanese on November 16, 1914. In the series of official functions preceding and including the surrender of the city and port, British participation was nominal only; indeed, there was a manifest disposition by the Japanese to slight and keep the British in the background. The outward official attitudes were punctiliously correct on both sides, but beneath the surface was a strong irritation, which found expression in petty frictions. The Japanese understood that the presence of British with the expedition was due to political considerations, designed as a check upon Japan; while the British knew that Japan wanted a free hand, and resented any intention or effort to circumscribe her liberty of action in Shantung.

With the surrender of Tsingtau, and removal of its garrison to Japan as prisoners of war, Germany's military power and serious offensive capacity in the far East terminated. Japan showed no signs of retiring from Tsingtau and Chinese territory outside the German leasehold. On the contrary, she proceeded systematically to establish her authority in the places already occupied, and to extend it over Shantung Province. Garrisons were stationed along the Tsinan-Tsingtau Railway, and at Tsinan-fu, the capital of the province; at

Lungkow, Wei-shien, and other important points.   By a gradual and at times subtle process, Chinese police, communication
and other local administrative functions were negatived and
usurped, after the system which had been employed and per-
fected in Korea and Manchuria.[1]   An influx of a low class
of Japanese immigration, to which the Chinese population was
more or less subordinated, followed on the heels of the Japanese
military.   A year after the occupation, an official report
showed 16,000 Japanese in the city of Tsingtau.   Hardly had
the Japanese flag been raised over Tsingtau when the process
whereby Korea and southern Manchuria were brought under
Japanese rule, and subjected to exploitation in favor of Japanese immigrants, began to operate energetically.   German public and private property was confiscated, and much other foreign and Chinese property held vexatiously.   The Chinese, and
foreign residents of China, saw the drift of things.   I wrote in
the "China Press," dated November 24, 1914:   "In discussing
eventualities of Japan's eviction of Germany from Shantung,
in consort with Great Britain, the consequent violations of
China's neutrality, and the Japanese occupation of parts of
that province which has resulted, the subject has several
phases, of which we now take two—effects upon China, and
effects upon nations other than Japan and Great Britain.
To us, this question is chiefly interesting in its relations to
the United States, and China: for the principal nations
allied with Japan and England against Germany can be
presumed to be satisfied, or at least acquiescent with their actions in Shantung.   With those nations, a presumption reasonably lies that they were consulted in advance, and assented
to the course taken.   From that, it might follow that they
also can be expected to assent to whatever intentions Japan
and Great Britain have about their future policies in Shantung,
and toward the general position of China, that are interlocked

[1] Detailed accounts of the operation of this process are given in the
author's previous books, "The New Far East," and "America and the
Far Eastern Question."

therewith.   But these presumptions cannot be taken regarding China and the United States.   We know that China objected to the course taken by Japan, in many instances, but has been powerless to defend her neutrality, and to prevent encroachments.   We do not know exactly what the official position of the United States has been: but that it displayed official interest in the matter was shown by the fact that Japan took pains (or was asked) to explain her purpose and ultimate intentions to Washington—which brought out a statement that Japan will restore Kiaochou to China, and that she will not use her military occupation of the leased territory of Kiaochou and her temporary control of the province to extend her own interests by discrimination against the interests of other foreign nations. . . . Perhaps this is a good place, in the argument, to state our own views about these matters.   Here goes: (a) *That Japan has no intention of ever abandoning the hold she has gained in Shantung, unless some kind of compulsion is put upon her to require it.*   (b) *That Japan has no intention of respecting the commercial principle of the open door in Shantung, any more than she has respected it in Manchuria and Korea, unless compulsion in some form is put upon her.* . . . These opinions have not been carelessly formed, and are not stated lightly.   They amount to a deep conviction (the result of fourteen years of observation and study of events and policies in the far East) which can be reversed in only one way—by future events demonstrating to the contrary.   They cannot be shaken by any treaty citations, or by any amount of official disclaimers, and pronouncements of intent and purpose.   We know quite well what the treaty stipulations, regarding China, of all the Powers are.   Most of them have been adopted, and printed in the record, for a good many years. And for a good many years we have been witnessing the cold, hard facts which have, in regard to some Powers, reduced those treaty promises to 'scraps of paper.'   For a good many years we have, a little at a time, been discovering by specific instances of unmistakable import that the published terms of treaties respecting China, regarding the 'open door' and 'territorial integrity' doctrines, are merely for publication, while the real policies and intentions of some of the Powers are expressed in secret agreements among them.   A good deal of this can be specifically proven, and the rest follows by deduction from the definite proofs. Just now we are merely recording an opinion, as a premise to certain other phases of this argument. . . . Now it is well known that the United States favors the 'open door' and 'territorial integrity' doctrines toward China; and the American Government in successive administrations has labored to define those doctrines, and to assure their practice by all the Powers, and by China. If, then, anything is transpiring which threatens and is designed to undermine those doctrines, and to reduce the treaties and agreements which make a part of the accepted Law of Nations, to inanition, we assume that the United States has an interest in the matter, and that China also has. If Japan's actions and policy in Shantung (and in other parts of China) have the secret support of Great Britain, and do tend to invalidate those doctrines, then it is probable that such actions do contain causes of dissension between Great Britain and Japan, and China; and between Great Britain and Japan, and the United States.   Any treaty, and international doctrine having general consent, can be, and often properly may be altered, or abrogated.   But there is a right way to do this, and a wrong way.   The right way is for the nations concerned, or any of them, to come out openly, and state their point of view. The wrong way is for some nations to intrigue secretly between themselves, and make mutual compacts contrary to the published treaties, and invidious to their principles, without informing other nations whose interests are also bound up in the published treaties, and which rely on all the signatory Powers to adhere to the treaties. If something like that has taken place, or is taking place now regarding the 'open door' and 'territorial integrity' doctrines respecting China, it should be made public. If it is assumed that all the interested

Powers, and China too, have secretly decided to relegate those doctrines, and to revert hereafter to the 'sphere of influence' theory, then the issue would be fair as between the Governments. But it would not serve any general interest to keep the new compacts secret, for commerce and industry and material development must proceed on what is known about policies, and Law. Therefore, if the 'open door' and 'territorial integrity' doctrines have been relegated by mutual consent of all the signatory Powers, and China, the fact should be published. On the contrary, if only some of the signatory Powers have secretly agreed to knife these doctrines, what Americans call the 'double-cross' is being 'put over' on somebody. If all the signatory Powers have secretly agreed to relegate the doctrines, without China's knowledge and consent, then it is China alone that is being 'double-crossed.' If the United States is cognizant of, and a party to, relegation of the doctrines, without China's consent, then America is assisting in playing a 'bunco game' on China. If the United States is not apprised of the doctrines being abandoned by other Powers, and that this is taking place, and it is taking place, then the Powers so doing are 'double-crossing' the United States. And if the United States is being 'double-crossed' there should be no delay, in the interest of America, in exposing the duplicity. Some may say: 'Well, even so. It is better to keep quiet about it anyhow, for fear of ruffling certain susceptibilities. America has not sufficient at stake to warrant raising a row, and possibly to cause friction with Japan and Great Britain.' Let us consider that. The matter can be looked at two ways—as to material interests involved, and as to principles involved. For the moment, we can exclude China's point of view, on the theory that no foreign nation justly can be called upon to make sacrifices to save China. At present, the material interests of America in China are not large, nor very important in comparison with the total activities of the American nation, and the total of foreign trade and investments in China. The future prospects are—

here even imagination halts. In principle, America is entitled to a fair chance to participate in whatever the future development of China may hold for foreign commerce and finance. In looking forward to that chance, America does not seek to displace other foreign interests and trade already established. She does want to have the door held open for her to enter when she is ready, and can enter, on equal terms of competition. American statesmen also have believed, and presumably do still believe, that this policy coincides with the interest and security of China as a nation. The relations and policies of all the Powers toward China are defined in treaties, and agreements, that are published, and thereby become a part of recognized international law, which the nations are supposed to respect and live up to. Now treaties and agreements respecting China are of two kinds—those between foreign nations and China, and those among foreign nations concerning China. It can be granted, or assumed, that China, as a theoretically independent nation, has a right at any time to alter her treaties, without asking the consent (although she may consider the interests) of other nations than the ones negotiated with. If Great Britain and China wanted to make a new treaty, as between themselves, they have a right to do so, although they are obligated to inform other nations about it. If China would make a commercial treaty with Japan, abrogating, in effect, the most-favored-nation clauses in her commercial treaties with America, the United States might be disgruntled, but hardly could justly make a belligerent issue out of it, for she possesses the power of commercial retaliation. It is one thing for any Power, or Powers, acting with the consent of China, to make new treaties with her superseding old ones. It is another thing for any Power, or Powers, without China's consent, to supersede their treaties with her by other treaties, or with interpretations of existing treaties with which she does not assent. And it is still another thing for a Power, or Powers, to supersede treaties existing between the United States and China, *without the consent of the United States, or of China.* If any

Powers have, among themselves, and in secret, superseded the 'open door' and 'territorial integrity' doctrines, which are assented to or guaranteed by all published treaties and agreements, they have, in effect, not only abrogated their own agreements with China, but also have reduced treaties between the United States and China to 'scraps of paper.' That is the issue, the principle, which is involved in action of Japan, and Great Britain, in respect to Shantung, as it affects the United States. The vital question to America is not solely whether other Powers should be allowed to violate their obligations regarding China, to the incidental detriment of American interests, as between themselves and China: but also is whether any nation, or combination of nations, shall be permitted, at *their* pleasure, to tear up treaties existing *between the United States and China,* and contrary to the wishes of both the United States and China. If other nations have the right to do that to America's treaties with China, and American rights in China under those treaties, then they have the right to do it with America's treaties with any other nation, and American rights in other countries. And what will be the eventual position, in the world, of a nation that permits, or tolerates or is *compelled to submit to that?* We have, so far, left the moralities of the question out. But that the question has moralities, is a good thing to remember in these days when so much stress is being laid upon treaties as the basis for international Justice, and Peace. And, if anything of the kind is going on, or is being contemplated, the time to call attention to, and to throw light upon it, is now: without waiting until it may be carried beyond possibility of reversal."

By then (the end of 1914) the Japanese Government had to some extent adjusted its vision to the perspective of the European War, and certain conditions in the far East influenced by it. It already was apparent that the war would not be quickly decided, or ended; and that before its conclusion both belligerent sides would be called on to put forth their utmost of strength and resources, which meant that for the time their activities

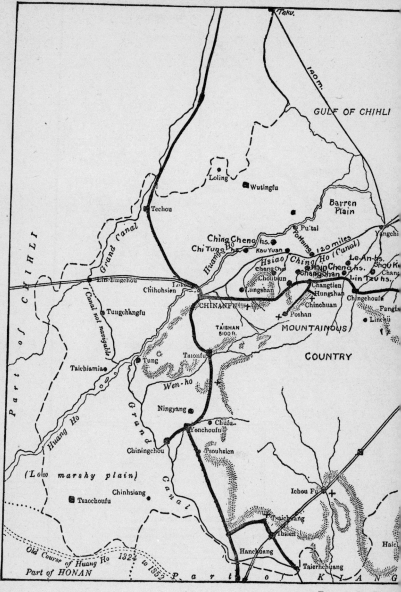

From the Far Easter[n]

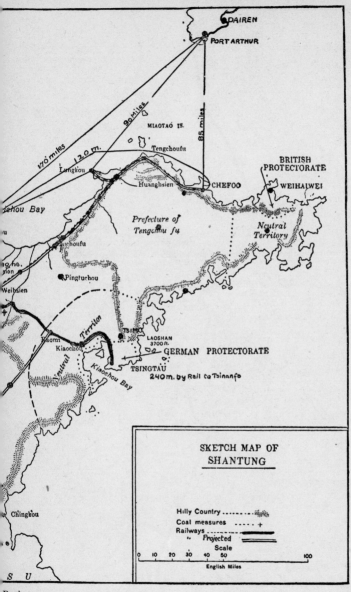

DAIREN

PORT ARTHUR

170 miles

120 m.

90 miles

85 miles

MIAOTAO IS.

Tengchoufu

Lungkou

Huanghsien

CHEFOO

BRITISH PROTECTORATE

WEIHAIWEI

...chou Bay

...u

Prefecture of Tengchu fu

Neutral Territory

...choufu

...ho.

...sion

Weihsien

Pingtuchou

TSIMO

LAOSHAN 3700 ft.

GERMAN PROTECTORATE

Kiaomi

Neutral Territory

Kiaochou

Kiaochou Bay

TSINGTAU

240 m. by Rail to Tsinanfo

Chingkou

S U

SKETCH MAP OF SHANTUNG

Hilly Country ....
Coal measures ..... +
Railways ....
" Projected
Scale

0 10 20 30 40 50   100
English Miles

and power in other parts of the world, and especially in China, would be limited. Japan therefore perceived that for a while, at least, she would have a comparatively free hand in China. She expected some diplomatic opposition from the United States, but her recent experience with America in the Fukien incident and other matters caused her to believe that it would be perfunctory. She acted promptly. First, it was necessary to establish a claim of preferential status in Shantung, and to possession of Kiaochou. This required that the mask be dropped to some extent, and especially that Japan's implied intention to restore Kiaochou to China be repudiated, it having served its purpose to quiet suspicions and allay foreign criticism until the occupation was accomplished.

Early in December, 1914, Baron Kato took the occasion of an interpellation in the Diet, to shift Japan's position in respect to Kiaochou. The proposition is included in the following questions and answers, published in the Japan press:

QUESTIONS

(a) Whether Kiaochou will be returned to China?

(b) Whether the Imperial Government of Japan were pledged to China, or to any other Power, in the matter of the final diposition of Kiaochou?

(c) Whether the clause in the ultimatum referring to the final restitution of Kiaochou to China did not bind the action of Japan?

BARON KATO'S REPLIES

(a) The question regarding the future of Kiaochou was, at present, unanswerable.

(b) Japan had never committed herself to any foreign Power on this point.

(c) The purpose of the ultimatum to Germany was to take Kiaochou from Germany and so to restore peace in the Orient. Restitution after a campaign was not thought of and was not referred to in the ultimatum.

That is plain enough. Baron Kato states that Japan attacked Tsingtau to put Germany out at a time when Germany could make no effective resistance. Japan never committed herself to any foreign Power, or to China, about her future intentions toward Kiaochou. Early restitution to China was not seriously considered. About the future of Kiaochou no decision had been reached. That was dropping the mask with a vengeance, but few persons in the far East were surprised. From the moment that Japan entered the war, because of the manner and obvious purposes of her actions, those purposes and actions revealed not a genuine wish to preserve peace in the far East, but in themselves constituted a grave menace to the peace of the far East. At that time, on December 11, 1914, I wrote in the "China Press": "One is justified, with the horrors of this terrible war before us, in being deeply concerned with anything that menaces peace anywhere. We are especially concerned in this case because the peace of China is menaced. We are further deeply concerned because we believe that Japan's acts have put into motion forces which seriously menace the peace of the United States of America, and its peaceable relations with Great Britain, and other nations with whom America is on friendly terms, and with whom she desires to remain friendly. This is why we have made some analyses of these events and policies, and have tried to keep the topic to the fore. In our opinion, a shift has taken place, in respect to China, not of the policy of Japan, for that never has altered except conditionally, and her moves in Shantung to-day are logical expressions of it—but of the policies of Great Britain and other Powers which formerly have served to check predatory acts at China's expense, and to maintain with the United States the 'open door' and 'territorial integrity' doctrines.''

In 1913, Dr. Charles W. Eliot, president emeritus of Harvard University, visited the far East on a commission from the Carnegie Peace Foundation, to investigate conditions in that part of the world which bear upon peace and war, and to make recommendations favoring the preservation of peace, based on his inquiries and observations. In Dr. Eliot's comprehensive report, he wrote:

THE CAUSES OF WAR HAVE CHANGED

Advocacy of these slow-acting means of preventing wars in the East implies that within the superintended areas the probable causes of international war have changed within fifty years. Dynastic and religious wars, and wars in support of despotic government are no longer probable; and racial antipathies are held in check by the superintending European powers in all the countries to which that superintendence extends. Thus, the Pax Britannica has practically put an end to the racial and religious warfare which from time to time dislocated the Asiatic countries over which British influence now extends. Small outbreaks of racial antipathy or religious fanaticism occur locally; but these are insignificant exceptions to the prevailing tranquility. The fighting Great Britain has done to establish and maintain this quieting influence has been fighting on a small scale compared with that which went on among European nations during the nineteenth century, or among Oriental peoples in many earlier centuries, and the Pax Britannica has therefore been a great contribution to the peace of the world.

It is not only in the East that the probable causes of international war have lately changed. All over the world, it is reasonable to suppose that wars for dynastic motives will occur no more, and that religious motives for warfare will hereafter be incidental or secondary instead of primary. It is also reasonable to believe that wars in support of absolute monarchs and despotic government will hence forth be unknown, so general is the worldwide movement towards constitutional government and free institutions—a movement from fifty to three hundred and fifty years old among the different nations of the West, but comparatively recent in the East.

THE FUTURE CAUSES OF WAR

What, then, will be the probable causes of international war in the future?

The causes of war in the future are likely to be national distrusts, dislikes, and apprehensions, which have been nursed in ignorance, and fed on rumors, suspicions, and conjectures propagated by unscrupulous newsmongers, until suddenly developed by some untoward event into active hatred, or widespread alarm which easily passes into panic. While the Eastern peoples—far and near—will have some causes of their own for war, because in some instances neither their geographical limits nor their governmental institutions are as yet settled, among the Western peoples the most probable future causes of war, in addition to national antipathies, will be clashing commercial or industrial interests, contests for new markets and fresh opportunities for profitable investments of capital, and possibly, extensive migrations of laborers. All modern governments, in which life, liberty, and property are secured by public law, desire to extend the commerce and trade of their people, to develop their home industries by procuring markets for their products in foreign lands, to obtain in comparatively unoccupied or undeveloped parts of the earth opportunities for the profitable employment of their accumulated capital, and to gain room for a possible surplus of population in the future. Eastern and Western peoples alike feel the desire for a large, strong governmental unit, too formidable to be attacked from without, too cohesive to be disintegrated from within. Both East and West exhibit the modern irrepressible objection to alien rule, especially when such rule, like that of the Manchus or the Turks, produces poverty and desolation, denies liberty, and prevents progress.

Several Western nations which have the saving, or accumulating habit, are eager to make loans to remote and comparatively poor nations which are in great need of money to pay for costly public works of transportation, conservancy, public health, and public security. In making such loans the bankers of each Western nation expect the support and protection of their own government. As security for such loans the borrowing government, national, provincial or municipal, pledges some of its resources; and if the expected interest or dividend is not paid, the lender forecloses. Hence serious international complications. In this lending business the Western powers come into competition with each other, and stimulated by mutual jealousies, engage in aggressive operations against the Oriental peoples, who have been as a rule helpless in their hands, until Japan adopted and improved on the Western military organization and methods of fighting, and succeeded for a short time in borrowing the money needed to pay the heavy costs of a modern warfare.

As I interpret Dr. Eliot's conclusions (which, it should be remembered, are directed especially to conditions in the far East), he rates among the chief future causes for wars in that part of the world, (a) frictions and collisions among Oriental nations due to clash of interests and ambitions, and possible *aggressions upon each other,* and (b) antagonisms that may develop from commercial and financial competitions there of foreign nations. I hold it to be self-evident, that both of those stated causes for future wars in the far East distinctly express, in different terms, what are included in the "territorial integrity" and "open door" doctrines relating to China, in so far as those causes have any expression in present conditions, and policies of Governments. If, therefore, those recognized doctrines are being insidiously undermined, and are in danger of being overthrown, it is evident that a fresh and far-reaching cause for war in the far East, which scarcely can fail to involve several foreign nations by seriously affecting their interests and rights, was set in motion by Japan's acts in Shantung.

CHAPTER VIII

JAPAN'S AGGRESSIONS IN CHINA—*Continued*

The demands in twenty-one articles—Japan's deceit—Lulling suspicion while planning new move—Presentation of the demands—Unusual method employed—Interview between Yuan Shih K'ai and the Japanese minister—A dramatic scene—Japan's implied threats—Japan's policy transparent—Her course in Shantung—China's serious predicament—Her isolation—Position and obligations of America—Possible checks on Japan—Japan's efforts at secrecy—Diplomatic evasions—Suppression of publicity—The light turned on.

HAVING established her virtual control over Shantung Province, Japan proceeded with little delay toward accomplishing her further designs in China. Preliminary to the next move, the Japanese Government tried by various devices to lull other Powers, and China, into a feeling of security, and to prevent any knowledge of Japan's plans from getting out. Among these devices one was to entrust foreigners who live in China, and have frequently shown friendship for that nation, with special messages to the Chinese Government, giving assurances of Japan's friendly purposes. Count Okuma, Premier of Japan, himself sent such a message privately to Yuan Shih K'ai. At the time this message was delivered, the Japanese Government was preparing to deliver the *coup* which it hoped would bring China practically under Japan's suzerainty.

On January 18, 1915, Japan presented her now famous demands on China, in twenty-one articles. The time was opportunely chosen, in respect to some matters. It was most important to Japan that close secrecy be observed, in order to prevent other nations (including Japan's allies) from knowing what was going on. There are intimations that Japan really thought, at that time, that it was feasible so to intimidate China that Japan's demands would be conceded, and the question closed, without other interested Powers realizing the significance of events. Japan chose a time to broach this matter, when representatives of several important news services and papers were absent from Peking in Japan, including the correspondents of the Associated Press, Reuter and "The Times" (London). Follows a translation of Japan's demands, as originally presented:

I

The Japanese Government and the Chinese Government being desirous of maintaining the general peace in eastern Asia and further strengthening the friendly relations and good neighborhood existing between the two nations agree to the following articles:

Article 1. The Chinese Government engages to give full assent to all matters upon which the Japanese Government may hereafter agree with the German Government relating to the disposition of all rights, interests, and concessions, which Germany by virtue of treaties or otherwise, possesses in relation to the Province of Shantung.

Article 2. The Chinese Government engages that within the Province of Shantung and along its coast, no territory or island will be ceded or leased to a third Power under any pretext.

Article 3. The Chinese Government consents to Japan's building a railway from Chefoo or Lungkou to join the Kiaochou-Tsinanfu Railway.

Article 4. The Chinese Government engages, in the interest of trade and for the residence of foreigners, to open by herself as soon as possible certain important cities and towns in the Province of Shantung as commercial ports. What places shall be opened are to be jointly decided upon in a separate agreement.

II

The Japanese Government and the Chinese Government, since the Chinese Government has always acknowledged the special position enjoyed by Japan in south Manchuria and eastern inner Mongolia, agree to the following articles:

Article 1. The two contracting parties mutually agree that the term of lease of Port Arthur and Dalny and the term of lease of the South Manchurian Railway and the Antung-Mukden Railway shall be extended to the period of 99 years.

Article 2. Japanese subjects in south Manchuria and eastern inner Mongolia shall have the right to lease or own land required either for erecting suitable buildings for trade and manufacture or for farming.

Article 3. Japanese subjects shall be free to reside and travel in south Manchuria and eastern inner Mongolia and to engage in business and in manufacture of any kind whatsoever.

Article 4. The Chinese Government agrees to grant to Japanese subjects the right of opening the mines in south Manchuria and eastern Mongolia. As regards what mines are to be opened, they shall be decided upon jointly.

Article 5. The Chinese Government agrees that in respect of the (two) cases mentioned herein below the Japanese Government's consent shall be first obtained before action is taken:

(*a*) Whenever permission is granted to the subject of a third Power to build a railway or to make a loan with a third Power for the purpose of building a railway in south Manchuria and eastern inner Mongolia.

(*b*) Whenever a loan is to be made with a third Power pledging the local taxes of south Manchuria and eastern inner Mongolia as security.

Article 6. The Chinese Government agrees that if the Chinese Government employs political, financial or military advisers or instructors in south Manchuria or eastern Mongolia, the Japanese Government shall first be consulted.

Article 7. The Chinese Government agrees that the control and management of the Kirin-Changchun Railway shall be handed over to the Japanese Government for a term of 99 years dating from the signing of this agreement.

III

The Japanese Government and the Chinese Government, seeing that Japanese financiers and the Hanyehping Company, have close relations with each other at present and desiring that the common interests of the two nations shall be advanced, agree to the following articles:

Article 1. The two contracting parties mutually agree that when the opportune moment arrives the Hanyehping Company shall be made a joint concern of the two nations and they further agree that without the previous consent of Japan, China shall not by her own

Japanese troops landing to attack Tsingtau

Japanese troops used the Tsinan-Tsingtau Railway in their operations

act dispose of the rights and property of whatsoever nature of the said company nor cause the said company to dispose freely of the same.

Article 2.   The Chinese Government agrees that all mines in the neighborhood of those owned by the Hanyehping Company shall not be permitted, without the consent of the said company, to be worked by other persons outside of the said company; and further agrees that if it is desired to carry out any undertaking which, it is apprehended, may directly or indirectly affect the interests of the said company, the consent of the said company shall first be obtained.

IV

The Japanese Government and the Chinese Government with the object of effectively preserving the territorial integrity of China agree to the following special article:

The Chinese Government engages not to cede or lease to a third Power any harbor or bay or island along the coast of China.

V

Article 1.   The Chinese Central Government shall employ influential Japanese as advisers in political, financial, and military affairs.

Article 2.   Japanese hospitals, churches and schools in the interior of China shall be granted the right of owning land.

Article 3.   Inasmuch as the Japanese Government and the Chinese Government have had many cases of dispute between Japanese and Chinese police which caused no little misunderstanding, it is for this reason necessary that the police departments of important places (in China) shall be jointly administered by Japanese and Chinese or that the police departments of these places shall employ numerous Japanese, so that they may at the same time help to plan for the improvement of the Chinese Police Service.

Article 4.   China shall purchase from Japan a fixed amount of munitions of war (say 50 per cent. or more of what is needed by the Chinese Government) or that there shall be established in China a Sino-Japanese jointly worked arsenal.   Japanese technical experts are to be employed and Japanese material to be purchased.

Article 5.   China agrees to grant to Japan the right of constructing a railway connecting Wuchang with Kiukiang and Nanchang, another line between Nanchang and Hangchow, and another between Nanchang and Chaochou.

Article 6.   If China needs foreign capital to work mines, build

railways and construct harbor-works (including dock-yards) in the
Province of Fukien, Japan shall be first consulted.

Article 7.   China agrees that Japanese subjects shall have the
right of missionary propaganda in China.

The manner of presenting these demands was unusual, and
significant.   Instead of being communicated through the Japanese minister to the Wai Chiao-pu (Chinese foreign office),
as is customary, the Japanese minister, Mr. Hioki, formally
requested an interview with Yuan Shih K'ai.   The request
was granted in due course.   I have good information that, in
granting an interview to Mr. Hioki, Yuan Shih K'ai and his
counselors had no premonition of what was coming.   In so far
as they had any idea about the purposes of Mr. Hioki, it was
thought that some matters relating to Shantung might be discussed, or perhaps the Japanese minister wished to convey personally to the President the pleasant assurances of Japan's
consideration and friendship which Count Okuma previously
had conveyed through mutual friends, or perhaps Mr. Hioki's
call was socially diplomatic.   On the morning of the day
appointed, January 18, the Japanese legation sent direct to
the President a copy of the demands, which were hurriedly
translated, and the gist of them told to the President just
before he received the Japanese minister.   The interview was
most dramatic in its element of suspense, according to details
recounted by one who was present.   After the usual formalities, the Japanese minister preceded the presentation of the
demands by some remarks.   He began by stating his Government's deep concern about China's welfare, a concern which
prompted it to give "friendly advice" to China at critical
times.   He said that, with these motives, Japan wished to
"advise" China in certain particulars, which were defined in
a memorandum, which he read.   I am informed that during
the reading of the demands, the true meaning of which he
began to comprehend, Yuan Shih K'ai sat with an expression-
less face, and made no interruption.   When Mr. Hioki had
finished, the President gravely said that he would read and

consider the advice carefully. Beyond that, he made no comment. Mr. Hioki then made some extended remarks, in the course of which he said that his Government considered it very desirable in order to prevent "complications," that neither the Chinese nor Japanese Governments, nor officials, would give out any information about this advice which Japan had given to China, until the two Governments had settled the questions between themselves. Mr. Hioki further said that it was the earnest desire of his Government that an agreement between China and Japan on the questions presented should be concluded without delay, in order to prevent "outside complications." Mr. Hioki further said that if China failed to meet Japan's advice in a satisfactory manner, and caused delay in adjusting the questions, it might not be possible for Japan to continue to restrain the activities of the Chinese revolutionists then sojourning in Japan. With the usual perfunctory polite exchanges, the interview ended.

A less experienced, strong, and astute statesman than Yuan Shih K'ai might well have been stunned, and cowed, by Japan's demands and the manner of their presentation. In general scope and character the demands, if conceded, would amount to the establishment of a Japanese suzerainty over China; and with that contingency imminent, the Chinese Government was strictly warned by Japan not to communicate her situation to other Powers, and not to give the matter publicity in any form. In short, Japan put the sword at China's throat, and intended to impose star-chamber proceedings until China's assent was procured. To accomplish this Japan used her widespread control and influence over international publicity relating to far Eastern affairs to prevent news about her demands from getting out, and after it began to leak, to obscure the truth by denials and evasions. But by that time Japan's general course in China was leaving unmistakable imprints. Some time after the fall of Tsingtau, China notified Japan of China's wish to abolish the so-called "war zone" in Shantung Province, since the alleged need for its creation had passed by the extinction of Germany's armed force in the far East. This proposal of China caused an outburst in the Japanese press, which assumed a menacing tone toward China. After a short visit to Peking, early in January, 1915, I wrote in the "China Press" on January 27 (at that time the twenty-one demands, although presented on January 18, were not known to me): "It is not possible any longer for candid friends of China, who are not mental and moral invertebrates, to practise any form of self-deception that will obscure the fact that Japan is taking advantage of conditions caused by the Great War to push her occupation of Chinese territory, and her exclusive commercial position in this country, to the limit. As to this limit, it is obvious that Japan sets none for herself. She will go as far as she can. If there is a limit to her aggressions, it must be fixed by some form of interposition, done, or instigated, by nations that are powerful enough, and which can control forces, to put compulsion upon Japan. In considering what nations possess these qualifications, singly or in coöperation, we must analyze conditions as they are now, and as they may develop during and out of the war. The situation is peculiar in this: the nation whose inherent right, and duty, is to repulse Japan's aggressions—China—is at present incapable of doing it alone. If China were strong, even mediumly strong, there would be no such situation as that which exists. Thus, other peoples cannot notice too often, for their own security and liberty, this practical demonstration of the peril that goes with political impotency and military helplessness. Yet China has a part to play in obstructing Japan—a part that may make or mar any efforts in her behalf that other Powers may make now, or later. China's part is to refrain from acts calculated to, and likely to provide Japan with excuses for taking the high hand with her, and of pressing the crown of thorns on China's brow. Not that moderation on China's part will cause Japan to lack excuses. If China gives no openings, Japan will create excuses for herself, as she has done already in Shantung. Indeed, it is reasonably safe to say that whatever China does,

in the way of protest, and of effort to maintain her rights, will
be taken by Japan as some kind of impropriety, and offense.
An example of this is just now provided by the way Japan has
taken China's abolition of the so-called 'war zone' in Shantung. Can anything be more unreasonable, and bare-faced,
than Japan's attitude? Recall the circumstances. When
Japan, rejecting proposals which would have assured the
neutrality of Tsingtau during the war without recourse to
fighting, determined to attack that place by invading China's
territory, China was advised (by her *Japanese* legal adviser,
Dr. Ariga) to define part of the Province of Shantung, across
which the Japanese troops would march, as a 'war zone';
which she did under protest. Germany also protested at that
action, as a violation of China's neutrality—for it enabled
the Japanese to attack Tsingtau more advantageously than
they could have done otherwise. It was a violation of
neutrality—a double violation—first of China's territory by
Japan, then by China herself in allowing a 'war zone.' Japan
immediately proceeded to violate China's neutrality further,
by extending against China's protest the 'war zone' to include
the greater part of Shantung Province, and seized the Shantung Railway over its entire length, on pretexts so transparent
as to disgust impartial people. Tsingtau, after a siege, was
taken. The last vestige of German military and naval power
in the far East has been eliminated, and there is no prospect
whatever that it can again be a factor in the war. Therefore,
China has attempted to restrict the Japanese military occupation to the territory which was leased to Germany, by abolishing the 'war zone' as being no longer necessary. Is that unreasonable? Japan seems to think so, and contends that she
ought to have been consulted. Why should Japan be consulted? Her *military* position is in no way impaired by this
move. Is it not curious that, a few months ago, both Germany and Japan regarded the existence of this 'war zone' as
facilitating an attack on Tsingtau: in fact, Japan contended
that Tsingtau could not be conveniently attacked except by

crossing China's territory. Now Japan is in possession of Tsingtau, and the whole of the German leased territory: yet she apparently now assumes that the 'war zone' is necessary to the *defense* of the place. And, in common sense, with what attack is Tsingtau now threatened? Yet, we are told that China's effort to regain control over her violated and occupied territory, by a perfectly legitimate action, is an 'insult' to Japan, which must be redressed by China acceding to fresh demands of Japan, of exclusive concessions for railways and mines, not only over the whole of Shantung, but in other provinces of China as well. Is there an intelligent person, of any Western nationality, who has resided long enough in the far East to be informed of conditions here, and who now has any faith in the *bona fides* of Japan's actions in Shantung, and the rectitude of her intentions there? Nearly three months have passed since Tsingtau surrendered, and Japan, to 'secure the peace of the far East,' acting in coöperation with Great Britain and presumably in accord with France and Russia, took over entire control of the place. She had assured the world (a promise since repudiated as 'unauthorized') that she would administer the port, and the railway, in harmony with the 'open door' commercial doctrine, as Germany had done. She made other promises to respect the 'integrity of China.' So far, Japan has kept none of these promises. While merchants of other nations are shut out of Tsingtau, or so handicapped in business operations there as to be practically suppressed, Japanese commercial interests are having the run of the port, and the whole of Shantung Province, just as they did under Japanese occupation in Manchuria, and are usurping special preferential privileges calculated to undermine competitors just as they have done in Manchuria. The commercial world of the far East is by now perfectly familiar with these methods of Japan, and knows what to expect as a result of them. Japan gives excuses, of course. She is adept at excuses, and the invention of pretexts. Who believes them? This is certain— Japan's credit, among intelligent persons in the far East, for carrying out promises of fair trade in territories where she exercises administrative control, is absolutely bankrupt. They are now received with cynicism, or with disgust, and with swelling indignation. And her professions of intention to respect China's territorial integrity, and administrative autonomy, are no more credited than her trade policy. Korea and Manchuria remind us. It follows, therefore, that any moderation of attitude and policy in China need not be expected from Japan voluntarily. It must be brought about, if that is possible, by applying to her some form of compulsion. We have seen that China cannot herself supply any appreciable part of this compulsion. Her familiar weapon against foreign injustice—the boycott—cannot help her in this case. If it is attempted, it almost certainly will be taken as an affront, and provide an excuse to put the screws on China further. The devices which China, in the past, has used to forestall similar encroachments, by obtaining diplomatic support of other Powers, are not available now, because of the war. It is injurious to British, and all other Western interests in China, for Japan to proceed as she is doing. But it is plain that Great Britain's hands are tied, and that even her presumed ability to influence her ally has been deprived of vitality. Coolly, insolently, almost truculently, Japan goes on her course, to take advantage of this war in Europe to entrench herself so strongly in China, that it will be very difficult, and perhaps impossible, to dislodge her afterward. She does not hesitate, nor delay, but strikes while the iron is hot. Will she 'get away with it'? Is it possible to stop her? In casting about for any possible succor, and support for China in this vital crisis, and for means to secure her against such aggressions in the future, until she can protect herself, the situation is dubious, but not absolutely hopeless. For the time, Great Britain is out of it. For the time, France also is out of it. For the time, Germany is out of it. Russia's influence probably will be negative, during the next few years. There is no doubt that Russia and Japan have made a trade, whereby they will not interfere with or oppose each other within certain limitations. As long as Japan does not encroach upon, and interfere with, Russia's paramount position in northern Manchuria and Mongolia, it is a matter of indifference to Russia how much Japan cuts into British influence and interests elsewhere in China. One of the curious phases of these developments, is that in respect to Japan's encroachments, her ally Great Britain is the chief sufferer next to China. Yet Great Britain seems to have gotten in a position, by being mixed up in the war, where she cannot protest—where she even has to pretend satisfaction with whatever Japan does to undermine her position in the Yangtsze and to cripple British interests in general. Of the great Powers vitally interested in the balance of power in the Pacific, which depends on a balance among Oriental as well as Western nations, and turns upon the fate of China, the United States remains. What, if anything, can the United States do under the circumstances? What the United States can do is one thing. What the United States will do may be quite another. What the United States can and will do should depend on what she ought to do. And she ought to do what is right, without hesitation, or timidity, or fear. Among actions which the United States might take, but which would be drastic and perhaps unwise, would be to intervene actively in China's behalf, backing her position with force, if necessary. Ample justification, in the diplomatic sense, for such a course, can be found in existing agreements and treaties respecting China, between the United States and other nations, particularly Japan, and in America's present and future stake in the issues created. But we feel safe in assuming that the United States will not take that course, especially while Mr. Wilson and Mr. Bryan direct the foreign affairs of the Government. China, therefore, should not place any dependence upon support from America that would, if opposed, call for the exercise of force. If China does not already realize this, it should be impressed upon her statesmen. Japan knows it, without doubt, and that is why she is moving with callous disregard of her agreements. Japan evidently is confident that she can, for a long time yet, play the California question off against any move by America to support China: just as she is using her support of Great Britain in this war, under the alliance, to suppress British outward irritation with Japan's policy here, and as a further check upon America. Let us consider what, if any, pacific compulsions might be put upon Japan, by an initiative taken by the United States. What wires can America pull, that will exert power in Japan, directly and indirectly? One pacific force that can touch Japan is finance. Another pacific force that can touch Japan is diplomacy, by working to bring about an international situation, and international action, which will drive Japan, from necessity, into a more reasonable course. Alone, entirely on her own resources, Japan cannot successfully prosecute an aggressive and predatory policy in China, or anywhere, if opposed seriously. She is enabled to do this now chiefly because of the strength she derives, and obliquely manages to extract from, the alliance with Great Britain. Deprived of that strength, Japan would lose weight in other directions, and could be put in a position where she could not pursue her ambition to dominate China—a supremacy, by the way, now openly asserted by the Japanese press. Can the Anglo-Japanese alliance be broken? Not at this moment. But it already is apparent that, in the situation that is likely to follow the Great War, the alliance will lose its vital essence—community of interest. Many students of world affairs have long thought that Great Britain was paying more for the alliance than it is worth to her. If Great Britain can be convinced of that, the alliance is doomed, for it obviously contains many embarrassments. By so convincing Great Britain, perhaps by offering equalizations and compensations, American diplomacy may save China. For, deprived of the financial support which Great Britain and the United States can give, and which hardly can be secured elsewhere in the lean years to follow the Great War, when all the Powers must raise vast sums for reconstruction and restoration, Japan cannot support a military and naval program sufficient to make headway against the opposition of other Powers. Mind, we do not for a moment presume that Japan would be surprised by such a development. Indeed, we believe that she expects it, and has anticipated it by steadily laying the foundations for an alliance with Russia in the East. Japanese diplomacy has its well defined objects, and will not be easily baffled. It will trade any way, with any Power, to gain a step toward its goal. When the Great War ends, the situation it creates will require an international Congress to adjust; and that Congress provides a suitable opportunity for the United States to exert pressure in favor of China. The United States should insist on being represented in the Congress, with a voice in the settlement of questions that directly affect her interests, and the peace of the world. China is entitled to representation, as a nation which has been vicariously involved. Before that Congress, the United States should vigorously press for recognition of China's rights, and for justice for her and all the weaker nations. It could be proposed that China's case be submitted to an international Court of Arbitration, or to the Hague Tribunal; and if Japan, or any Powers, objected to that course, it would be conclusive proof of ulterior motives, and purposes. In such a case, it would be very difficult for Great Britain to refuse to support the United States and China on moral grounds, and her interest would lie the same way. Germany would assent, as would Austria no doubt: and also Italy and lesser nations. France would have no reason of her own for objecting, unless her relations with Russia have tied her up. Indeed, it would be very difficult for any nation that pretends to enlightenment, and justice in its dealings, to refuse China a fair trial at the Court of Nations. And if China does get a fair trial, she will win her case. Here is something, then, for genuine friends of China to work for, to create a sentiment in America that will induce the United States to use its power and influence to this end; and to try

to secure support for the idea among British. China is almost
inhibited from pleading her own case before the bar of world
opinion. Her press is silenced by indirect intimidation.
Even her Government finds its feeble protests twisted into
'insults' to her aggressor. Her friends, and lovers of justice
the world over, must speak for her. By the time a Congress
meets to tie up the loose threads of this war, civilization
probably will have enough of violence, and tricky diplomacy,
and intrigue, to suffice for a while, and, having their results
before them, may be willing, and anxious, to get international
affairs established on a basis of justice and equity for the
weak as well as the strong. In such a chance, lies the
hope of China—almost her only hope, in fact. The menace
of Japan's predatory ambitions must be met, and quelled.
The Congress will provide an opportunity to accomplish
this peacefully, by laying foundations, and formulating covenants, which will provide a basis for practical forces to work
on. If it is not checked by peaceful means, Japan's policy
will either work out the subjugation of China to her rule,
with all that that means to the future of the world, and the
security of Western civilization, or its course will have to be
turned by Western arms.''

I insert my comments written while those events were
transpiring, rather than similar comments written after time
has given some perspective on them, because they show that
perspective was not required to reveal the true character of
Japan's course in China. It was transparent to competent
critics as it unfolded, even before it unfolded. If ever coming
events cast their shadows before them, the portent to China
of Japan's entrance to the Great War illustrates that maxim.
Moreover, it is pertinent to show that the situation in the far
East caused by Japan was being kept before the United
States Government, with its interests and obligations and
responsibilities plainly charted. When I wrote, as just quoted,
I did not then know of the presentation of Japan's twenty-
one demands; but that Japan would take measures to secure

herself in complete domination of the whole of China was plainly indicated by what already had happened. One plainly saw the next move coming, without being able to guess exactly the form it would take, or when it would be made.

Late in January, 1915, information of Japan's new demands began to leak out. The first publication about them, I believe, was by the acting Peking correspondent of the "China Press," W. E. Giles, a British subject; who telegraphed the news to a newspaper in the United States. About the same time W. H. Donald, also British, acting correspondent of the Associated Press, telegraphed the news to America, but the Associated Press feared to give it out in the face of official contradictions. The facts stated by Mr. Giles and Mr. Donald were substantially accurate, although not then complete; but they were immediately denied by Japanese news agencies and propagandists in America and China. Nevertheless, further information soon brought complete confirmation. It is a curious feature of Japan's attitude to these matters, that her Government conceived it to be possible to carry through an issue overturning a complicated international balance of power and interest, and subtly transferring the sovereignty of the oldest nation, and one of the largest, without it attracting notice, or being detected. Here is what happened. The Chinese Government was at first rather stunned by Japan's demands, and took a little time to reflect about the best course to pursue. Japan's insistence on secrecy, which had been coupled with an implied menace, made caution necessary. It is believed that the information was first slipped quietly and "unofficially," by the Chinese, to a legation in Peking of a neutral nation, with a hint that if it got around among the diplomatic corps and newspaper correspondents it would do China no harm. Of course, in those circumstances, the news soon did get around, and created a sensation. At first, the news was received incredulously, and especially at the legations of Japan's allies. It is said that the British minister at first refused to credit the reports. The reports persisted, however, and this gave cause for some of the legations to make official inquiries of China; whereupon the Wai Chiao-pu (Chinese Foreign Office), with a show of reticence and reluctance, gradually admitted the facts, and provided the foreign diplomats with copies of the demands.

The fat was then in the fire; but for some time the Japanese Government persisted in denying the truth, pursuing a course whose mendacity and duplicity have few parallels in history. The British, American, Russian, French, and other legations at Peking immediately comprehended the immense importance of the matter, and telegraphed the full text of Japan's demands to their Governments. It followed, then, that at London, Washington, Petrograd, Paris, *et al.*, the foreign offices made inquiries of the Japanese ambassadors there, and also made inquiries at Tokio through their own ambassadors. Without known exception, the Japanese Government and its ambassadors officially denied the correctness of the news; and similar denials were simultaneously given out through Japan-controlled and other news agencies, and through Japan's foreign propagandists. Several leading newspapers in Japan were disciplined for publishing reports about the demands, and comment about them in newspapers was forbidden in Japan.

The following letter to his paper from the regular Peking correspondent of the "North-China Daily News" (Shanghai), the leading British newspaper published in China, which was printed in its issue of February 4, 1915, is very interesting:

To the Editor of the "North China Daily News."

Sir.—When Reuter's agent telegraphs from Tokio, as he did on January 28, that "the information originating at Peking and elsewhere purporting to outline the basis of negotiations between Japan and China is absolutely without foundation," he states what is probably unknown to him to be an absolute misrepresentation of facts.

In the next breath, however, he admits that the "highest authority," who is his informant, confesses that "conversations and negotiations" are proceeding between Tokio and Peking, but that they do not "injure the territorial integrity of China, and do not affect and do not injure the properties and interests of other Powers."

This matter is too large and too grave to be permitted to be dismissed in such an equivocal *dementi* as that issued by the Japanese authorities through their special news bureau.

On January 18 the Japanese minister in Peking waited upon the President personally to explain the attitude of his Government towards China, and to bring home to the President the fact that Japan required the Chinese Government to effect an important change in its policy in favor of the former country. Prior to the visit of the Japanese minister there had been sent to the President a set of twenty-one articles acceptance of which was demanded. They embraced special privileges, railway and mining rights in eastern Mongolia, Manchuria, Shantung, the Yangtze Valley, and Fukien provinces.

The Japanese minister, it is reliably stated, explained to the President that the Japanese Government submitted the articles for acceptance as the simplest way of allaying antagonistic feeling towards China in Japan. A large section of the people of Japan, Mr. Hioki is said to have indicated, were opposed to the President, and unless the demands made could be accepted the relations between the two countries would be imperiled. He warned the President that rebel agents were still very active in Japan in fomenting another revolution against the Chinese Government, and while the Japanese Government had no sympathy with the rebels, yet, if the President should decline to agree to the terms, it would find itself unable to restrain them. Nor could the Japanese Government tell what would happen should the rebels be permitted to go unrestrained.

The Japanese minister urged that it was in the best interests of the President and the Government of China that the demands be accepted, and he is said to have declared that should the demands be refused Japan would be compelled to present harsher and more serious ones. And he enjoined the strictest secrecy. It was in the best interests of both countries, he is stated to have said, that no disclosure be made to any Power. It was suspected in Japan, he added, that China always followed a policy of befriending distant nations and showing hostility to her immediate neighbor, and especially were Great Britain and America always taken as China's sponsors, a fact which was a source of feeling in Japan.

In conclusion, the minister is said to have expressed it as his sincere advice that none of the terms be divulged to any one.

The above are the only reasons given by Japan as justification for the demands made, and since it is impossible, apparently, for anything so important to remain long a secret in China or anywhere else, the minister's interview with the President soon became public property.

While high officials have steadfastly refused to divulge the details of the demands, it can now be said with surety that they are of such a nature as seriously to effect the interests of other Powers concerned in the development of China. They may not violate the territorial integrity of the country, but, if granted, they will ultimately give Japan a dominant voice in many provinces and also in the internal administration of the Government.

Of the demands this much is known. In eastern Mongolia, railway and mining rights and special privileges are requested which would give Japan the power to prevent any other nationals acquiring any similar rights in the territory.

In Manchuria she strives to secure a voice in the local administration and desires a hold upon commercial and industrial development which will close the door in that territory more effectively than is now the case.

In Shantung, Japan desires to inherit in full the whole of the railway and mining privileges hitherto held by Germany, and in addition seeks other special rights which will make the province a private domain for Japanese enterprise. Among other things she demands the right to build a railway from Lungkow to Weihsien on the ground that it is analogous to the Antung-Mukden line in its relation to Port Arthur at the time of the Russo-Japanese War. Critics may well ask, what of Chifu?

In the Yangtze Valley, she seeks what would be tantamount to a monopoly of the iron and coal deposits, requiring a firm title over the Hanyang works and the deposits that they live upon, as well as the chief ones of Kiangsi and Anhui provinces. More important, she asks for railway privileges which would enable her to attract from the Hankow region to the Fukien seaboard, traffic which otherwise would be carried on lines now being built with British capital. In short, she would secure a foothold in the Yangtze Valley such as would frustrate the long-cherished desires of British statesmen and seriously challenge British commercial activities.

In Fukien she seeks to be paramount in all things of importance, and from that province she desires to extend railways to Kwangtung as well as to Kiangsi Province.

In China, in general, she aims at obtaining a dominant voice in important departments of internal administration thereby establishing herself as the mentor of the nation and placing it beyond the power of any other country to take any vital part in the regeneration and development of China.

Broadly speaking the above desires are well within the extent of the demands asked. So far details are not available, but if other Powers remain passive they will eventually find that all their past hopes and ambitions to participate in the development of this vast market will be shattered.

The Chinese officials are dumbfounded by the extent and nature of the demands; they are astounded at the procedure of Japan, and humiliated that they are too weak to resist. Above all, they are grievously distressed that they find themselves practically isolated and unable to ascertain the views of any of the great nations who have professed friendship for China, and who have large interests in their country.

Negotiations have not yet taken place with regard to the demands, but they begin on Tuesday, and unless other nations wake up they will find concession after concession being granted until Japan will have secured such a hold throughout the country that it will be impossible to oust her when they will have leisure to ascertain what they have lost.

I am, etc.,

YOUR PEKING CORRESPONDENT.

Peking, January 29.

Devices and subterfuges could not serve for long. The British minister at Peking directly inquired of the Japanese minister there about the demands, and the Japanese minister, after evasions, admitted that a memoramdum had been presented to China, but asserted that only eleven points were raised, and that these did not infringe upon China's political autonomy, or the rights of other foreign nations. For a short while Japan played this pretext to gain time. Through the Japanese embassies at London, Washington, Paris, and Petrograd, the falsehood of the eleven proposals to China was sedulously propagated. Meanwhile, correspondents of foreign newspapers who had been away from Peking when Japan presented her demands, hurried back to Peking, and began telegraphing the full details to their newspapers, thus supporting and confirming the news already sent. But by then the Japanese Government had got such a start with its denials and evasions that in many cases the true reports of the Peking correspondents were not credited by their own newspapers,

Chinese coolies in Shantung pressed into service of the Japanese army

Japanese Buddhist priests with the Japanese army in Shantung

which hesitated to publish them. This caused two prominent Peking correspondents to offer their resignations, which served to impress on editors the seriousness of the situation. A little later, the mails brought to Washington, and to European capitals, full official reports from the legations at Peking. Japan's plan to rush the demands through, and coerce China in secret, was thus frustrated, and attention attracted to the negotiations.

CHAPTER IX

JAPAN'S AGGRESSIONS IN CHINA—*Concluded*

The "fake" demands in eleven articles—Japan's devious course—
Analysis of the original demands in twenty-one articles—Questions
relating to Germany's possessions and rights—China's neutral attitude—
Some principles involved—Strategical considerations involving China—
Infringements of other foreign rights—A slap at America—The blow at
British interests—Significance of Group V—Insidious destruction of
China's sovereignty—The revised demands—Japan's ultimatum—Ameri-
can influence in China's behalf—Reasons for China's course—Protest by
the United States.

BEFORE analyzing Japan's demands in twenty-one
articles, it is interesting to consider the subterfuge
by which she tried to delude other nations, including
and *especially her allies*, about the extent and character of
those demands. When it was first reported that the demands
had been presented at Peking, Japan took refuge behind a
general denial, describing the reports as "rumors." Then
when that attitude was rendered untenable, by the facts
gradually coming out, Japan's next evasion was to admit that
certain questions had been raised with China, but solely for
the purpose of friendly discussion, and they were not being
pressed. When asked by other Powers for more definite information, Japan handed them a memorandum of eleven
articles, embracing matters under discussion with China.
These articles were published in the "Times" (London), as
coming from the Japanese embassy at London, which ridiculed
the reports that Japan had presented oppressive demands.
The eleven articles follow:

I.—In relation to the Province of Shantung.

1.—Engagement on the part of China to consent to all matters that
may be agreed upon between Japan and Germany with regard to the

disposition of all rights, interests and concessions, which in virtue of treaties or otherwise Germany possesses in relation to the Province of Shantung.

2.—Engagement not to alienate or lease upon any pretext the Province of Shantung or any portion thereof and any island lying near the coast of the said province.

3.—Grant to Japan the right of construction of a railway connecting Chifu or Lungkow and the Tsinan-Kiaochou railway.

4.—Addition of open marts in the Province of Shantung.

II.—In relation to south Manchuria and eastern inner Mongolia.

1.—Extension of the terms of the lease of Kwangtung, the South Manchuria Railway, and the Antung-Mukden Railway.

2.—(A). Acquisition by the Japanese of the right of residence and ownership of land.

(B). Grant to Japan of the mining rights of mines specified by Japan.

3.—Obligation on the part of China to obtain in advance the consent of Japan if she grants railway concessions to any third Power, or procures the supply of capital from any Power for railway construction or a loan from any other Power on the security of any duties or taxes.

4.—Obligation on the part of China to consult Japan before employing advisers or tutors regarding political, financial or military matters.

5.—Transfer of the management and control of the Kirin-Changchun Railway to Japan.

III.—Agreement in principle that, at an opportune moment in the future, the Hanyehping Company should be placed under Japanese and Chinese coöperation.

IV.—Engagement in accordance with the principle of the maintenance of the territorial integrity of China, not to alienate or lease any ports and bays on, or any island near, the coast of China.

This "fake" series of demands was not presented to the other interested Powers until about one month after the real demands had been delivered to China. A résumé of Japan's method during that period is illuminating, given chronologically.

(a) Presentation of demands in *twenty-one* articles, coupled with a strong admonition to China that both haste and secrecy were insisted on by Japan.

(b) Continuous pressure on China to force her to concede the demands *en bloc*, without discussion.

(c) Repeated warnings to China not to inform other Powers of the negotiations, even confidentially.

(d) First publications of news about the demands were categorically and officially denied by Japan.

(e) Newspapers in Japan were warned by the Government not to publish or discuss news about the demands.

(f) Japan's diplomatic representatives abroad were instructed to deny and discredit news about the demands.

(g) The Japanese minister at Peking denied to inquiries of other legations that any demands had been made.

(h) When copies of the original demands, procured from the Chinese Government, were received by other foreign Governments, Japan still denied the twenty-one demands, and presented a list of eleven articles, omitting the most objectionable matters.

Japan's original demands were divided into five groups, each group referring to a particular subject. Group I dealt with the province of Shantung, Group II with southern Manchuria and inner Mongolia, Group III with the Hanyang iron works and mining rights in central China, Group IV with China's coast and coastal islands, Group V with various matters relating to China's internal administrative functions and special privileges for Japan in China.

The essence of Group I was that Japan wanted China to agree that Japan might inherit all of Germany's concessions and property in the Kiaochou leased territory, and in the whole of Shantung Province, with some additional special privileges. As to rights which Germany had in Kiaochou and Shantung when the Great War started, these depended to some extent on the outcome of that war. While Japan had for the time dispossessed Germany, Germany's possessions and rights in China would have to go into the melting pot of the peace set-

Tsingtau terminal of the Tsinan-Tsingtau Railway

Tsinan-fu station of the Tsinan-Tsingtau Railway. This railway was seized by Japan

tlement. For instance, if the peace negotiations should find Germany in possession of territory and other assets of her enemies in Europe, thereby making the peace settlement a general adjustment and trading of holdings, it might be necessary to restore Kiaochou to Germany as an offset to concessions by Germany in Europe and elsewhere. From the day Japan entered the war, she clearly aimed to retain Kiaochou for herself, and also to claim for herself and to extend Germany's tentative "sphere of influence" in Shantung. But Japan's ability to accomplish this was to some extent dependent on the course of her European allies, and their success or non-success in the war. To share in the spoils of war it usually is necessary to be on the winning side, and to be able to dictate terms to some extent. Japan recognized that the war might end in a military stale-mate, under conditions whereby the Allies, in exchange for their own territory then occupied by the Central Alliance, would have to restore some German possessions occupied by them. Japan for some time evaded giving assent to the mutual Allied pact that none of them would agree to a separate peace, and that all would coöperate in making the peace terms; but she finally did so, under pressure. Therefore, Japan foresaw a possibility that her European allies, in making peace, might want to restore the *status quo ante bellum* in China, that Germany might insist on that, and that the Powers would have a legal and moral right, under Japan's own original declarations, to insist on her vacation of Kiaochou. Japan furthermore knows that some of her allies would in their own interest prefer to have Germany at Kiaochou than to have Japan there. With those contingencies in view, Japan was trying to manœuver so as to establish herself in sole and complete possession of Kiaochou, and also to take advantage of circumstances to wring from China a written consent to have Japan replace Germany there, and to further extensions of Japanese privileges in Shantung.

In respect to Germany's leased territory of Kiaochou, China's position was technically clear. China had declared her neu-

trality in the war, and had observed it so far as she was able
to. The situation was similar to that of the Russian leased
territory of Liaotung (Port Arthur) in the Russo-Japanese
War. When Russia abdicated her leasehold in favor of Japan,
China assented, although reluctantly, because the strategical
relation of Port Arthur in Russia's possession to China herself
differed materially from its possession by Japan. So, too, possession by Japan of the Kiaochou leasehold, and a Japanese
"sphere" in Shantung, makes a very different situation for
China herself and for other Powers than Germany's presence
there. When China, under various forms of compulsion and
persuasion, granted portions of her territory in lease to foreign Governments, she consoled herself somewhat by the fact
that, by scattering these concessions among the Powers, she
was creating a balance of power and interest among them which
tended, as conditions were then, to protect China against further
aggressions from any of them. China's representations, after
the Russo-Japanese War, that she should be consulted about
any transfers of her own leased territory, was rejected by
Japan, and China had not the power to make her contention,
which is reasonable, respected. With that experience in mind,
China preferred to assume a detached and neutral attitude
toward the ultimate disposition of the Kiaochou leasehold.
China would have preferred not to commit herself at all, on
that point; but, under menace, it was not worth while for China
to refuse, in advance, to assent to any disposition of Kiaochou
made in the peace settlement.

The articles of Group I granting to Japan additional privileges and concessions in Shantung, outside the Kiaochou leased
territory, had another complexion. In some of these matters
Japan's demand for a preferential position, or "sphere," in
Shantung Province as a whole infringes upon projects and
rights of other foreigners, and upon the "open door" policy
of equal opportunity. One of Japan's demands in this group
evidently was obliquely aimed at the United States of America
—the article asking that China will not cede or lease to a *third*

Power (meaning any Power except Japan) any territory or island in Shantung or on its coast. For many years the American Asiatic squadron has used Chifu as a base for summer practice, and several times a project for the United States to lease that port for a naval base and coaling station has been mooted. China's objection to demands of the character made by Japan is that such provisions circumscribe her right to do as she likes with her own territory, and to that extent qualify her sovereignty.

Group II relates to Manchuria and inner Mongolia. While the articles of this group are in complete contravention of principles of the "open door," are a violation of Japan's treaties and agreements with other Powers, and subordinate Chinese administration in those regions to Japan's authority, these things were already *de facto;* and Japan's demands were that China should formally accede to and extend conditions that existed, but which never had been officially assented to by China. By the demands included in Group II, Japan was merely getting China's formal sanction to Japan's régime of usurpation in Manchuria. Issues involved in Group II had slight relation to the Great War, and were of slight interest to any Powers except the United States and Germany, since Russia, France, and Great Britain had previously assented to Japan's assumption of an exclusive position in Manchuria. Japan was taking advantage of the war in Europe to clear up the Manchurian questions to her satisfaction.

Group III related to Japanese interest in the Hanyang iron works, dubiously acquired during the revolution, with a very important and significant addition. Article 2 stipulates that no mines in "the neighborhood" of mines owned by the Hanyephing Company shall be permitted to be worked by persons outside that company; and further "that if it is desired to carry out *any undertaking* which, it is apprehended, may *directly or indirectly* affect the interests of the said company, the consent of said company shall first be obtained." The "blanket" character of that provision is apparent. By consenting to it, China would have first to consult Japan before undertaking, *either herself or with foreign coöperation*, any mining operations in the Yangtze Valley and western China, or any activities whatever which might be construed by Japan to "directly or indirectly affect the interests of said company." Since the Hanyehping Company makes many products, and has a charter to engage in numerous and widespread enterprises, that article could be made to inhibit all important industrial and financial undertakings in central and western China, whether initiated by Chinese or foreigners, except under conditions dictated by Japan. For many years Great Britain has claimed, and has safeguarded, or tried to safeguard in agreements with China and with other nations, an especial "sphere of influence" embracing the Yangtze Valley, Szechuen Province, and Kwangtung. At one time, when proceeding on the premise that an "open door" in the whole Empire was more advantageous to British interests than any restricted "sphere," however ample and desirable, Great Britain was at considerable pains to bring other Powers to accept that hypothesis; and later, when the trend of events was to revert to the "sphere" status, Great Britain endeavored definitely to outline her own and the spheres which she conceded to other Powers, in response to a reciprocal attitude from them. That Great Britain's position and her predominating vested interests in central China and Kwangtung would be respected, and that she in turn would respect Japan's position in south Manchuria, Russia's position in north Manchuria and Mongolia, France's position in Yunnan, and Germany's position in Shantung, was clearly demonstrated in agreements and by various acts.[1] Now Japan, while Great Britain was engaged in a European war that taxed her resources and engrossed her attention, seized the opportunity surreptitiously to undermine her ally's "sphere" in China, and to substitute therefor a Japanese domination of that region.

Group IV extends to the whole coastline of China the restric-

[1] Appendix I, J, U, V.

tions applied to Shantung in Group I, thereby asserting a claim by Japan of a right to restrict China's disposition of her own maritime territory.

In Group V of the original demands, Japan made conditions which, in effect, would reduce China to a vassal of Japan, by making her relation to Japan almost identical to the existing relation between Great Britain and Egypt, and to Japan's relation to Korea before the annexation. China must employ "influential Japanese as advisers in political, financial, and military affairs." "The police departments of important places in China shall be jointly administered by Japanese and Chinese," or Japanese shall direct the police departments of such important places. China must purchase a majority of her war munitions from Japan, and accept Japanese coöperation in the management of China's own arsenals. China must first consult Japan before obtaining foreign capital to open and work mines, or to build railways and harbor works in Fukien Province. Japan shall get the right to construct railways in central China in direct violation of existing agreements for similar concessions between China and Great Britain, a plain encroachment on the British "sphere." Japanese shall have the right to own land anywhere in China, to conduct schools, and also churches and hospitals; in other words, Japanese shall have in China equal religious and civil rights with Chinese, coupled with extra-territoriality and quasi-suzerainty. Japanese shall have the right to conduct religious propaganda anywhere in China. The sweeping character of these provisions is clear. Existing treaty conditions which establish the position of foreigners in China are abolished for Japanese, which means that unless these rights are extended to all foreigners, Japanese will have preferred position; and if these rights are extended to all foreigners, coupled with extra-territoriality, then China's administrative autonomy over *all* her territory will be circumscribed. These provisions reproduce, in principle, the method employed to establish Japan's authority in Korea, and gradually to absorb the administrative functions of the Korean Government, by subjecting it to the compulsory "advice" of Japanese advisers. By this oblique method, China's finances and police power would be taken over by degrees, as was done in Korea, and is taking place in Manchuria.

Now note that, in the "fake" demands, or "advice" in eleven articles, which Japan for a while pretended were the only representations she had made to China, the whole of Group V was omitted, as also was the article in Group III giving the Hanyehping Company a monopoly in central China; and other provisions of the original demands were changed to be apparently innocuous, or less objectionable to other Powers.

Japan immediately followed up her presentation on January 18 of twenty-one demands, by pressing China to accede to them *en bloc* without debate. Japan insisted on prompt action, and so conferences were commenced at Peking between the Japanese minister and the Wai Chiao-pu, represented by Lou Tseng-Tsiang, the Chinese minister for foreign affairs. The first conference was held on February 2, when the Japanese minister insisted that daily conferences be held thereafter until a settlement was reached. To that China dissented, and under strong pressure agreed to hold conferences twice a week. Japan's menacing attitude, brought out at the first conference, probably caused the Chinese confidentially to inform some of the other foreign legations what was going on. The subsequent course of negotiations is illuminated in the official statement afterward published by the Chinese Government.[1] Although taken by surprise, and being unwilling to settle such important questions at such a time, China did not adopt dilatory tactics in the negotiations until toward their end, when it had become apparent that Japan intended to press her advantage to the limit. However, Japan employed bludgeoning tactics all through the negotiations. She reinforced her military forces in Shantung and Manchuria, and made strategical dispositions unmistakably directed against China. To Japan's surprise, China was obstinate on some points, and Japan in

[2] Appendix R.

turn began to feel the reactions caused by exposure to all the Powers of her duplicity. Consequently, Japan consented to some modification of her original twenty-one demands, and on April 26, 1915, presented revised demands in three groups and twenty-four articles. These revised demands follow:

GROUP I

The Japanese Government and the Chinese Government, being desirous of maintaining the general peace in Eastern Asia and further strengthening the friendly relations and good neighborhood existing between the two nations, agree to the following articles:

Article 1. The Chinese Government engages to give full assent to all matters upon which the Japanese Government may hereafter agree with the German Government, relating to the disposition of all rights, interests, and concessions, which Germany, by virtue of treaties or otherwise, possesses in relation to the Province of Shantung.

Article 2. (Changed into an exchange of notes.)[3] The Chinese Government declares that within the Province of Shantung and along its coast no territory or island will be ceded or leased to any Power under any pretext.

Article 3. The Chinese Government consents that as regards the railway to be built by China herself from Chefoo or Lungkow, to connect with the Kiaochow-Tsinanfu Railway, if Germany is willing to abandon the privilege of financing the Chefoo-Weihsien line, China will approach Japanese capitalists to negotiate for a loan.

Article 4. The Chinese Government engages, in the interest of trade and for the residence of foreigners, to open by China herself as soon as possible certain suitable places in the Province of Shantung as commercial ports.

(Supplementary exchange of notes.)[3]

The places which ought to be opened are to be chosen, and the regulations are to be drafted, by the Chinese Government, but the Japanese minister must be consulted before making a decision.

GROUP II

The Japanese Government and the Chinese Government, with a view to developing their economic relations in south Manchuria and eastern inner Mongolia, agree to the following articles:

Article 1. The two contracting Powers mutually agree that the

[3] Appendix S.

term of lease of Port Arthur and Dalny and the term of the South Manchurian Railway and the Antung-Mukden Railway, shall be extended to 99 years.

(Supplementary exchange of notes.)[3]

The term of lease of Port Arthur and Dalny shall expire in the 86th year of the Republic or 1997. The date for restoring the South Manchurian Railway to China shall fall due in the 91st year of the Republic or 2002. Article 12 in the original South Manchurian Railway Agreement that it may be redeemed by China after 36 years after the traffic is opened is hereby canceled. The term of the Antung-Mukden Railway shall expire in the 96th year of the Republic or 2007.

Article 2. Japanese subjects in south Manchuria may lease or purchase the necessary land for erecting suitable buildings for trade and manufacture or for prosecuting agricultural enterprises.

Article 3. Japanese subjects shall be free to reside and travel in south Manchuria and to engage in business and manufacture of any kind whatsoever.

Article 3a. The Japanese subjects referred to in the preceding two articles, besides being required to register with the local authorities passports which they must procure under the existing regulations, shall also submit to police laws and ordinances and tax regulations, which are approved by the Japanese consul. Civil and criminal cases in which the defendants are Japanese shall be tried and adjudicated by the Japanese consul; those in which the defendants are Chinese shall be tried and adjudicated by Chinese authorities. In either case an officer can be deputed to the court to attend the proceedings. But mixed civil cases between Chinese and Japanese relating to land shall be tried and adjudicated by delegates of both nations conjointly, in accordance with Chinese law and local usage. When the judicial system in the said region is completely reformed, all civil and criminal cases concerning Japanese subjects shall be tried entirely by Chinese law courts.

Article 4. (Changed to an exchange of notes.)[3]

The Chinese Government agrees that Japanese subjects shall be permitted forthwith to investigate, select, and then prospect for and open mines at the following places in south Manchuria, apart from those mining areas in which mines are being prospected for or worked; until the mining ordinance is definitely settled, methods at present in force shall be followed:

[3] Appendix S.

Hungshan mines in Shantung province, seized by Japan

Fangtse mines in Shantung province, seized by Japan

Province of Feng-tien

LOCALITY	DISTRICT	MINERAL
Niu Hsin T'ai	Pen-hsi	Coal
Tien Shih Fu Kou	Pen-hsi	do.
Sha Sung Kang	Hai-lung	do.
T'ieh Ch'ang	T'ung-hua	do.
Nuan Ti T'ang	Chin	do.
An Shan Chan region	From Liao-yang to Pen-hsi	Iron

Province of Kirin (Southern Portion)

Sha Sung Kang	Ho-lung	C. & I.
Kang Yao	Chi-lin	
	(Kirin)	Coal
Chia P'i Kou	Hua-tien	Gold

Article 5. (Changed to an exchange of notes.)[3]
The Chinese Government declares that China will hereafter provide funds for building railways in south Manchuria; if foreign capital is required the Chinese Government agrees to negotiate for a loan with Japanese capitalists first.

Article 5a. (Changed to an exchange of notes.)[3]
The Chinese Government agrees that hereafter, when a foreign loan is to be made on the security of the taxes of south Manchuria (not including customs and salt revenue on the security of which loans have already been made by the Central Government), it will negotiate for the loan with Japanese capitalists first.

Article 6. (Changed to an exchange of notes.)[3]
The Chinese Government declares that hereafter if foreign advisers or instructors on political, financial, military, or police matters are to be employed in south Manchuria, Japanese will be employed first.

Article 7. The Chinese Government agrees speedily to make a fundamental revision of the Kirin-Changchun Railway Loan Agreement, taking as a standard the provisions in railway loan agreements made heretofore between China and foreign financiers. If, in future, more advantageous terms than those in existing railway loan agreements are granted to foreign financiers, in connection with railway loans, the above agreement shall again be revised in accordance with Japan's wishes.

[3] Appendix S.

Chinese Counter-Proposal to Article 7

All existing treaties between China and Japan relating to Manchuria shall, except where otherwise provided for by this convention, remain in force.

Matters Relating to Eastern Inner Mongolia

1. The Chinese Government agrees that hereafter when a foreign loan is to be made on the security of the taxes of eastern inner Mongolia, China must negotiate with the Japanese Government first.

2. The Chinese Government agrees that China will herself provide funds for building the railways in eastern inner Mongolia; if foreign capital is required, she must negotiate with the Japanese Government first.

3. The Chinese Government agrees, in the interest of trade and for the residence of foreigners, to open by China herself, as soon as possible, certain places suitable in eastern inner Mongolia as commercial ports. The places which ought to be opened are to be chosen, and the regulations are to be drafted, by the Chinese Government, but the Japanese minister must be consulted before making a decision.

4. In the event of Japanese and Chinese desiring jointly to undertake agricultural enterprises and industries incidental thereto, the Chinese Government shall give its permission.

GROUP III

The relations between Japan and the Hanyehping Company being very intimate, if the interested party of the said company comes to an agreement with the Japanese capitalists for coöperation, the Chinese Government shall forthwith give its consent thereto. The Chinese Government further agrees that, without the consent of the Japanese capitalists, China will not convert the company into a state enterprise, nor confiscate it, nor cause it to borrow and use foreign capital other than Japanese.

Article IV

China to give a pronouncement by herself in accordance with the following principle:

No bay, harbor, or island along the coast of China may be ceded or leased to any Power.

NOTES TO BE EXCHANGED

A

As regards the right of financing a railway from Wuchang to connect with the Kiukiang-Nanchang line, the Nanchang-Hangchow

Railway, and the Nanchang-Chaochow Railway, if it is clearly ascertained that other Powers have no objection, China shall grant the said right to Japan.

B

As regards the right of financing a railway from Wuchang to connect with the Kiukiang-Nanchang Railway, a railway from Nanchang to Hangchow and another from Nanchang to Chaochow, the Chinese Government shall not *grant* the said right to any *foreign Power* before Japan comes to an understanding with the other Power which is heretofore *interested* therein.

NOTES TO BE EXCHANGED

The Chinese Government agrees that no nation whatever is to be permitted to construct, on the coast of Fukien Province, a dockyard, a coaling station for military use, or a naval base; nor to be authorized to set up any other military establishment. The Chinese Government further agrees not to use foreign capital for setting up the above-mentioned construction or establishment.

Mr. Lu, the Minister of Foreign Affairs, stated as follows:

1. The Chinese Government shall, whenever, in future, it considers this step necessary, engage numerous Japanese advisers.

2. Whenever, in future, Japanese subjects desire to lease or purchase land in the interior of China for establishing schools or hospitals, the Chinese Government shall forthwith give its consent thereto.

3. When a suitable opportunity arises in future, the Chinese Government will send military officers to Japan to negotiate with Japanese military authorities the matter of purchasing arms or that of establishing a joint arsenal.

Mr. Hioki, the Japanese minister, stated as follows:

As relates to the question of the right of missionary propaganda, the same shall be taken up again for negotiation in future.

These amended demands were concessions more to phraseology than spirit, by making it easier for China to accept them; the pill was coated a little. In respect to Manchuria, Mongolia, and Shantung, Japan still insisted on her demands in principle. Article 2 of Group III of the original demands, which was designed to give Japan a practical monopoly in central and western China, and would have superseded the British "sphere" in the Yangtze Valley by a Japanese "sphere" there, was dropped. Group V also was omitted; but an exchange of notes was insisted on, by which China will consent to certain matters, if such steps should become necessary. By this time the real character of Japan's policy was fully exposed, and foreign influences, and some developments of the Great War, were injected into the situation as restraining influences upon her. Nevertheless, she continued to press China steadily, culminating in an ultimatum delivered at Peking on May 7, 1915, in the following terms:

The Imperial Japanese Government hereby again offer their advice and hope that the Chinese Government, upon this advice, will give a satisfactory reply by six o'clock P. M. on the ninth day of May. It is hereby declared that if no satisfactory reply is received before or at the specified time the Imperial Japanese Government will take such steps as they may deem necessary.

Under this menace, China yielded, and on May 8 accepted the Japanese ultimatum and an agreement based on the revised demands of Japan.

In the latter stages of the negotiations, the United States of America exerted some influence in behalf of China, which helped to induce Japan to defer pressure as to the original Group V. The course of the American Government in approaching that action illustrates the hypothesis which dominated the State Department in respect to such questions during the incumbency of W. J. Bryan as secretary of state. As soon as the meaning of Japan's original demands was comprehended in China, American business interests, already made uneasy by the course of events in Manchuria and Shantung, made efforts to induce the State Department to protest against the violation of the "open door" policy, but without apparent success, although the department showed an interest by making some pertinent inquiries of Japan and China. It was activity by American missionaries in China that brought the State Department (or rather Mr. Bryan, for his subordinates understood the situation) to the point of trying to do something to restrain Japan. American missionaries in China, having the example of Korea before them, saw that

Japan's domination of China would impede and perhaps destroy their work and activities there; and they also were deeply concerned about the moral injustice to China. Very strong representations were made to the State Department [4] by American missionaries, just at a time, in April, when Japan was insisting that China accede to her demands *en bloc;* and these representations induced Mr. Bryan to remonstrate with the Japanese ambassador at Washington, and to urge upon him the serious consequences that might follow if Japan drove China to extremity. The exact measure of these representations in influencing Japan's course at that time is, of course, doubtful, but there is reason to assume that they had some weight.

In the official statement of the Chinese Government regarding these negotiations with Japan this language occurs, in concluding:

It is plain that the Chinese Government proceeded to the fullest extent of possible concession in view of the strong national sentiment manifested by the people throughout the whole period of the negotiations. All that the Chinese Government strove to maintain was China's plenary sovereignty, the treaty rights of foreign Powers in China, and the principle of equal opportunity. . . . In considering the nature of the course they should take in reference to the ultimatum, the Chinese Government was influenced by its desire to preserve the Chinese people, as well as a large number of foreign residents in China, from unnecessary suffering, and also to prevent the interests of friendly Powers from being imperiled. For these reasons the Chinese Government was constrained to comply in full with the ultimatum, but, in complying, the Chinese Government disclaims any desire to associate itself with any revision which may thus be affected in the various conventions and agreements concluded between other Powers, with respect to the maintenance of China's territorial independence and integrity, the preservation of the *status quo,* and the principle of equal opportunity for the commerce and industry of all nations in China.

That statement comes as near to reflecting truth as any combination of words and phrases could. I have in previous

[4] Appendix W.

chapters sketched the general internal condition of China at
that time, to whose complications were added those caused by
the Great War. The Chinese Government was charged with
a triple responsibility—to preserve its own neutrality, to maintain neutrality among belligerents, and to safeguard without
discrimination all foreign interests in China in a period when
many of those interests were handicaped in protecting themselves. Moreover, the Chinese Government, after Japan's demands became known, was confronted with a serious internal
political difficulty. Chinese popular sentiment was aroused to
a hitherto unknown extent by Japan's aggressions, and demanded that the Peking Government should reject them. The
Peking Government had, therefore, to meet Japan's menacing
diplomacy, and at the same time so to conduct affairs as to
prevent popular indignation among Chinese from flaming up
in an attempt to overthrow the Government. In this connection, Mr. Hioki's verbal statements to Yuan Shih K'ai, when
presenting the original demands in January, are interesting.
Mr. Hioki then said, if China did not promptly comply with
Japan's demands, that Japan might be unable to restrain the
activities of the group of Chinese revolutionists then sojourning in Japan—or, in other words, Japan threatened to instigate another internal revolution in China. Yuan Shih K'ai's
dilemma is obvious. If he rejected Japan's demands, Japan
would use military force to obtain them, which China could not
resist successfully. If he accepted Japan's demands, even in
part, the Chinese radical party opposing the Government
would accuse Yuan of betraying his country, and perhaps
would succeed in starting another rebellion on that issue, especially if the revolutionists received financial and other assistance from Japan. If he decided to resist Japan, and make
such a fight as was possible, the whole country would be
plunged into disorder, and such progress as had been made
toward reconstruction would be thrown back, while all foreign residents and interests in the country would be imperiled. In these circumstances, Yuan chose the wiser course.

He conceded what he must, and saved such exceptions as he could, hoping that China's case would get a hearing before civilization later.

Of the Powers directly concerned about the fate of China, only the United States is definitely known to have then made any protest in regard to the "agreement" thus wrung from China by Japan. On May 16, 1915, the following note from the American Government was delivered to the Chinese Government by the American minister at Peking:

In view of the circumstances of the negotiations which have taken place or which are now pending between the Government of China and the Government of Japan and the agreements which have been reached and as a result thereof, the Government of the United States has the honor to notify the Government of the Chinese Republic that it cannot recognize any agreement or undertaking which has been entered into, or which may be entered into between the Governments of China and Japan impairing the treaty rights of the United States and its citizens in China, the political or territorial integrity of the Republic of China, or the international policy, commonly known as the open door policy.

An identical note was handed to the Japanese Government through the American embassy at Tokio.

CHAPTER X

CHINA'S STRUGGLE FOR STABILITY

A peaceful interim—Disturbing undercurrents—Weakness of the Republic—Yuan Shih K'ai's position and attitude—Revival of the monarchy—Internal and external factors—Japan's influence—Her policy outlined—Memorial of the Black Dragon Society—Its significance—Proposal to incite rebellion—A "defensive alliance" of Japan and China—Its terms—Japan and the Chinese revolutionists—Alleged seditious agreements—Japan's "advice" to Yuan Shih K'ai—Yuan's acceptance of the Crown—Playing the game against Japan—Revolt against the monarchy movement—Its course and incentives—The country in disorder—Yuan's renunciation and death—Distrust of Japan—True function of Young China—Order vs. anarchy.

CHINA was comparatively peaceful when the Great War commenced. The Central Government was getting the whole country well under its authority and control. Internal reforms were making noticeable headway. The primary problem, finance, was in a way to be solved. The reorganized Salt Gabelle, under the able direction of Sir Richard Dane, a British subject, was more than fulfilling expectations in the production of revenue. The Government had adopted a budget system, and there was more intelligence and economy in administration than ever before. The cultivation and sale of opium were being steadily suppressed. An amnesty was extended to those who took part in the rebellion of 1913, except a few of its leaders who had taken refuge abroad and who continued to agitate against the Government. The country seemed to be settling down to a period of reform and progress.

But while conditions superficially were promising, there were disturbing internal undercurrents. There was much in the method whereby Yuan Shih K'ai had consolidated his

The Hanyehping Iron Works at Hanyang, China, which Japan has secured control of by coercing China

power that caused dissatisfaction among an influential element of Chinese. China, in fact, was divided in sentiment politically. A decided popular reaction against the Republic was noticeable (the word "popular" as applied to political thought in China should be taken as applying to not more than 2 per cent. of the total population—the masses are ignorant and indifferent). Extreme radicalism of some revolutionary leaders, coupled with visionary overenthusiasm of the Young China element, had been distasteful to the innate conservatism of the people. The Republic had struggled along, but it had not been satisfactory to any considerable political faction or party; in fact, the Government had only become workable after its republican features were practically annulled. I never have met a foreigner whom I consider competent to give an authoritative opinion who, after the experiences of the years following the revolution, believed a republic to be a form of government suitable for China. The essentials of real republicanism do not exist in China. They cannot be created within a century; and until they are created, no matter what the government is named, it will be, and must be, oligarchic. If that is true, a monarchy is more adjustable to the political status and more acceptable to the genius of the Chinese. It is more workable. It tends to concentrate authority, and helps to focus the fealty of the masses. Under either a so-called republic, or a monarchy, China will be governed by the same class, in much the same way. With a strong monarch, the power of the Executive will enhance; with a weak monarch the Parliament, or the political entity which stands for a Parliament, will dominate. Write President for Emperor, and the same principles apply. The only substantial difference is this: an emperor stands with the masses as the temporal and spiritual head of the nation, by divine right; while a president is merely an official who holds power temporarily, and thereby loses prestige. Every election carries a danger of revolution. Students of modern Japan recognize the strength which popular veneration of the Emperor gives to the Japanese Government, yet the Emperor has little to say about affairs of state. An oligarchy nominally elected by about 2 per cent. of the population governs Japan, and governs efficiently by standards applicable to the Orient now. The Chinese masses understand the monarchical idea and are accustomed to it. It fits in with their life and habits of thought. It makes for stability, and stability is what China needs more than anything else at this stage of her evolution. At the time of the revolution most foreigners in China, who understand China in some measure, sympathized with the reformers, and regarded the Republic favorably if a little skeptically. But the conduct of the progressive, or radical faction, during the reconstruction period after the revolution and culminating in the foolish rebellion of 1913, caused many to doubt its capacity to guide the nation safely through the crisis. Among the progressives were many very able and patriotic young Chinese, but their youth and inexperience made them susceptible to the influence of demagogues, who arrayed many of them against the Government and against the deep-lying conservatism of the country. A reaction was inevitable, and when it came it swung logically toward a restoration of the monarchy.

An outstanding figure in the development of this reaction was Yuan Shih K'ai. Always skeptical about the practicability of the Republic, and having accepted it against his convictions, Yuan undoubtedly was strongly confirmed in those opinions by the course of events in the reconstruction period. He found it impossible to work with the extreme progressive element, and with its parliament; and it was natural that his experiences would swing him toward the other extreme, and to a belief that an autocracy was China's only hope. In that, I believe Yuan was somewhat in error; but the circumstances must be considered in judging him. Yuan is blamed for secretiveness, for cutting himself off from outside ideas and influences, and with seeing China only through the eyes of a small group who constituted his immediate entourage. Yet much of this position and attitude was compulsory. Every day since he took the Presidency, Yuan has been in danger of assassination—he dared not travel about the country, he hardly dared to leave his residence, and even his food must be carefully watched. The utmost circumspection must be exercised about the persons admitted to his presence. This condition is not due especially to anything Yuan did, it does not apply particularly to his personality. It goes with the office. Following the primary failure to win over Yuan to the revolutionary movement, in 1911, even while he was working at Peking to dethrone the Manchus, efforts to assassinate him began, and continued constantly thereafter. Assassination is a commonplace of Oriental politics, and often is retaliatory. There have been more than one hundred prominent political assassinations in China during and since the revolution. It is fruitless to blame one faction or party for this condition, but it is pertinent to mention that it was first invoked, as applying to present-day Chinese politics, by the radicals. Dr. Wu Ting-fang remarked sadly in 1912: "I 'm afraid China will see thirty years of assassination." Yuan Shih K'ai's successor will inherit the disabilities and dangers of his position.

Yuan believed in the monarchical form of government for China on grounds of principle and expediency. His original attitude was not dictated by personal ambition, for he had tried to preserve the reigning dynasty. Yet it was natural and logical, when conditions showed a drift toward restoration of the monarchy, that Yuan would entertain the thought of taking the throne himself. To what extent this ambition influenced his course none but Yuan himself knew positively. In reorganizing the Government, and bringing its jangling elements into a semblance of order, Yuan had been compelled to put himself outwardly in opposition to certain sincere reformers, and to do some things that smacked of dictatorship. Finding that he could not get the machinery of pseudo-republicanism to work, he had to disregard or evade its provisions, and to subordinate its protagonists in distributing the important offices. This meant temporary elimination of many able young Chinese who had been swept in with the radical movement, and created a strong faction opposed to the continuance of Yuan in power, among whom the extreme radical leaders could work to incite another revolution.

The proposal to restore the monarchy, brought forward in the summer of 1915, was a logical development of China's internal situation; but its controlling influences seem to have been foreign, and were a reflection of the further influence of Japan's aggressions on Chinese politics. Internally, China was almost ready to restore the monarchy, although many intelligent Chinese opposed the change. But there was the danger of foreign complications. This danger existed either way: it took one form if the monarchy was restored, and it took another form if the monarchy was not restored. In their more menacing aspects, these two forms of danger merged into one entity—Japan.

A study of Japan's attitude and course in relation to the proposal to restore the monarchy in China discloses their guiding purpose. Japan's attitude toward China's form of government is complex. Japan is opposed, on fundamental grounds, to a republic in China. A successful republic in China will eventually subvert Japan's present form of government, and with that change Japan's present imperial policy would decline. Prince Yamagata once remarked that a strong emperor is what is needed to rejuvenate China, and to enable her to surpass Japan. Japan, therefore, does not want a strong emperor in China. Still less does Japan want a successful republic there. Japan wants a weak and incapable China; and a weak China under a weak emperor, subject to Japan's influence, would be the ideal state. One of the most lucid expositions of Japan's attitude toward these questions that I have seen is contained in a report and memorial of the Japanese Hei Lung Hui (or Black Dragon Society), an organization of Japanese in China. This report was made late in 1914, or early in 1915, and parts of it were published. I obtained through semi-official sources a copy of this report, from which I will quote. The report has a preamble setting forth certain arguments concerning the Great War in Europe and its effects upon Japan, which concludes with these words: "It is therefore our first important duty at this moment to enquire of our Government what course is to be adopted to face the general situation after the war? What preparations are being made to meet the combined pressure of the Allies upon China? What policy has been followed to solve the Chinese question? When the European War is terminated and peace is restored, we are not concerned so much with the question whether it be the Dual Monarchies or the Triple Entente which emerge victorious, but whether, in anticipation of the future expansion of European influence in the continents of Europe and Asia, the Imperial Japanese Government should or should not hesitate to employ force to check the movement before this occurrence. Now is the most opportune time for Japan quickly to solve the Chinese question. Such an opportunity will not occur for hundreds of years to come. Not only is it Japan's divine duty to act now, but present conditions in China favor the execution of such a plan. We should by all means decide and act at once. If our authorities do not avail themselves of this rare opportunity, great difficulty will surely be encountered in future in settlement of the Chinese question. Japan will be isolated from the European Powers after the war, and will be regarded by them with envy and jealousy, just as Germany is now regarded. Is it not then a vital necessity for Japan to solve at this very moment the Chinese question?" Follows the greater part of the memorial (my italics):

THE CHINESE QUESTION AND THE
DEFENSIVE ALLIANCE

It is a very important matter of policy whether the Japanese Government, in obedience to its divine mission shall solve the Chinese question in a heroic manner *by making China voluntarily rely upon Japan or by forcing her to a position where she is obliged to rely upon Japan.* To force China to such a position there is nothing else for the Imperial Japanese Government to do but to take advantage of the present opportunity to *seize the reigns of political and financial power* and to enter by all means into a defensive alliance with her under secret terms as enumerated below:

The Secret Terms of the Defensive Alliance

The Imperial Japanese Government, with due respect for the sovereignty and integrity of China, and with the object and hope of maintaining the peace of the far East, undertakes to share the responsibility of coöperating with China to guard her against internal trouble and foreign invasion, and China shall accord to Japan special facilities in the matter of China's national defense, or the protection of Japan's special rights and privileges, and for these objects the following treaty of alliance is entered into between the two contracting parties:

1. When there is internal trouble in China or when she is at war with another nation or nations, Japan shall send her army to render assistance, to assume the responsibility of guarding Chinese territory, and to maintain peace and order in China.

2. China agrees to recognize Japan's privileged position in South Manchuria and Inner Mongolia, and to cede the sovereign rights of these regions to Japan to enable her to carry out a scheme of local defense on a permanent basis.

3. After the Japanese occupation of Kiaochou, Japan shall acquire all the rights and privileges hitherto enjoyed by the Germans in regard to railways, mines, and all other interests, and after peace and order is restored in Tsingtao, the place shall be handed back to China to be opened as an international treaty port.

4. For the maritime defense of China and Japan, China shall lease strategic harbors along the coast of the Fukien Province to Japan to be converted into naval bases, and grant to Japan in the said province all railway and mining rights.

5. For the reorganization of the Chinese army, China shall entrust the training and drilling of the army to Japan.

6. For the unification of China's firearms and munitions of war,

China shall adopt firearms of Japanese pattern, and at the same time establish arsenals (with the help of Japan) in different strategic points.

7. With the object of creating and maintaining a Chinese Navy, China shall entrust the training of her navy to Japan.

8. With the object of reorganizing her finances and improving the methods of taxation, China shall entrust the work to Japan, and the latter shall elect competent financial experts who shall act as first class advisors to the Chinese Government.

9. China shall engage Japanese educational experts as educational advisors, and extensively establish schools in different parts of the country to teach Japanese, so as to raise the educational standard of the country.

10. China shall first consult with and obtain the consent of Japan before she can enter into an agreement with another power for making loans, the leasing of territory, or the cession of the same.

From the date of the signing of this defensive alliance, Japan and China shall work together hand-in-hand. Japan will assume the responsibility of safeguarding Chinese territory and maintaining the peace and order in China. This will relieve China of all future anxieties and enable her to proceed energetically with her reforms, and, with a sense of territorial security, she may wait for her national development and regeneration. Even after the present European War is over and peace is restored China will absolutely have nothing to fear in the future of having pressure brought against her by the foreign powers. It is only thus that permanent peace can be secured in the far East.

But before concluding this defensive alliance, two points must first be ascertained and settled. (1) Its bearing on the Chinese Government. (2) Its bearing on those Powers having intimate relations with and great interests in China.

In considering its effect on the Chinese Government, Japan *must try to foresee whether the position of China's present ruler, Yuan Shih K'ai, shall be permanent or not;* whether the present Government's policy will enjoy the confidence of a large section of the Chinese people; *whether Yuan Shih K'ai will readily agree to the Japanese Government's proposal to enter into a treaty of alliance with us.* These are points to which we are bound to give a thorough consideration. Judging by the attitude hitherto adopted by Yuan Shih K'ai, we know he has always resorted to the policy of expediency in his diplomatic dealings, and although he may now outwardly show a friendliness toward us, he will in fact rely upon the influence of the different Powers as the easiest check against us, *and refuse to accede to our demands.*   Take for a single instance, his conduct toward us since the Imperial Government declared war against Germany, and his action will then be clear to all.   Whether we can rely upon the ordinary friendly methods of diplomacy to gain our object or not, it does not require much wisdom to decide.   After the gigantic struggle in Europe is over, leaving aside America which will not press for advantages, China will not be able to obtain any loans from the other Powers.   *With a depleted treasury, without means to pay the officials and the army, with local bandits inciting the poverty-stricken populace to trouble, with the revolutionists waiting for opportunities to rise, should an insurrection actually occur while no outside assistance can be rendered to quell it, we are certain it will be impossible for Yuan Shih K'ai, single-handed, to restore order and consolidate the country.   The result will be that the nation will be cut up into many parts beyond all hope of remedy.*   That this state of affairs will come is not difficult to foresee.   When this occurs, shall we uphold Yuan's Government and assist him to suppress the internal insurrection *with the certain assurance that we could influence him to agree to our demands, or shall we help the revolutionists to achieve a success and realize our object through them?*   This question must be definitely decided upon this very moment, so that we may put it into practical execution.   If we do not look into the future fate of China, but go blindly to uphold Yuan's Government, to enter into a defensive alliance with China, hoping thus to secure a complete realization of our object by assisting him to suppress the revolutionists, it is obviously a wrong policy.   Why?   Because the majority of the Chinese people have lost all faith in the tottering Yuan Shih K'ai, who is discredited and attacked by the whole nation for having sold his country.   If Japan gives Yuan the support, his Government, though in a very precarious state, may possibly avoid destruction.   Yuan Shih K'ai belongs to that school of politicians who are fond of employing craftiness and cunning.   He may be friendly to us for a time, but he will certainly abandon us and again befriend the other Powers when the European War is at an end.   Judging by his past, we have no doubt as to what he will do in the future.   For Japan to ignore the general sentiment of the Chinese people and support Yuan Shih K'ai with the hope that we can settle with him the Chinese question, is a blunder indeed.   Therefore, in order to secure the permanent peace of the far East, instead of supporting a Chinese Government which can neither be long continued in power nor assist in the attainment of our object, we should rather support the 400,000,000 Chinese people to renovate their corrupt Government, to change its present form, to maintain peace and order in the land, and to usher into China a

Courtesy, of The New York "Times"

Liang Shao-yi. One of the most astute of Chinese politicians, who exercised great influence during Yuan Shih K'ai's presidency

Photo, by International Film Service, Inc.

Sun Pao-chi. Minister of Foreign Affairs in Yuan Shih K'ai's government

new era of prosperity, so that China and Japan may in fact as well as in name be brought into the most intimate and vital relations with each other. China's era of prosperity is based on a Chino-Japanese alliance, and this alliance is the fundamental power for the repelling of the foreign aggression that is to be directed against the far East at the conclusion of the European War. This alliance is also the foundation stone of the peace of the world. Japan therefore should take this as the last warning and immediately solve this question. *Since the Imperial Japanese Government has considered it imperative to support the Chinese people, we should induce the Chinese revolutionists, the Imperialists, and other Chinese malcontents to create trouble all over China.* The whole country will be thrown into disorder and Yuan's Government will consequently be overthrown. *We shall then select a man* from amongst the most influential and most noted of the 400,000,000 of Chinese and help him to organize a new form of government and to consolidate the whole country. In the meantime our army must assist in the restoration of peace and order in the country, and in the protection of the lives and properties of the people, so that they may gladly tender their allegiance to the new Government which will then naturally confide in and rely upon Japan. It is after the accomplishment of only these things that we shall without difficulty gain our object by the conclusion of a defensive alliance with China.

For us to incite the Chinese revolutionists and malcontents to rise in China, we consider the present to be the most opportune moment. The reason why these men cannot now carry on an active campaign is because they are insufficiently provided with funds. *If the Imperial Government can take advantage of this fact to make them a loan and instruct them to rise simultaneously, great commotion and disorder will surely prevail all over China. We can then intervene and easily adjust matters.*

The progress of the European War warns Japan with greater urgency of the imperative necessity of solving this most vital of questions. The Imperial Government cannot be considered as embarking on a rash project. This opportunity will not repeat itself for our benefit. We must avail ourselves of this chance and under no circumstances to hesitate. *Why should we wait for the spontaneous uprising of the revolutionists and malcontents? Why should we not think out and lay down a plan beforehand? When we examine into the form of government in China, we must ask whether the existing Republic is well suited to the national temperament and well adapted to the thoughts and aspirations of the Chinese people.* From the time the Republic of China was established up to the present moment, if what it has passed through is to be compared to what it ought to be in the matter of administration and unification, we find disappointment everywhere. Even the revolutionists themselves, the very ones who first advocated the republican form of government, acknowledge that they have made a mistake. *The retention of the republican form of government in China will be a great future obstacle in the way of a Chino-Japanese alliance.* And why must it be so? Because, in a republic the fundamental principles of government as well as the social and moral aims of the people are distinctly different from that of a constitutional monarchy. Their laws and administration also conflict. If Japan acts as a guide to China and China models herself after Japan, it will only then be possible for the two nations to solve by mutual effort the far East question without differences and disagreements. Therefore to start from the foundation for the purpose of reconstructing the Chinese Government, of establishing a Chino-Japanese alliance, of maintaining the permanent peace of the far East, and of realizing the consummation of Japan's Imperial policy, *we must take advantage of the present opportunity to alter China's republican form of government into a constitutional monarchy which shall necessarily be identical, in all its details, to the constitutional monarchy of Japan, and to no other.* This is really the key and first principle to be firmly held for the actual reconstruction of the form of government in China. *If China changes her republican form of government to that of a constitutional monarchy, shall we, in the selection of a new ruler, restore the Emperor Hsuan T'ung to his throne, or choose the most capable man from the monarchists, or select the most worthy member from among the revolutionists?* We think, however, that it is advisable at present to leave this question to the exigency of the future when the matter is brought up for decision. *But we must not lose sight of the fact that to actually put into execution this policy of a Chino-Japanese alliance and the transformation of the Republic of China into a constitutional monarchy is, in reality, the fundamental principle to be adopted for the reconstruction of China.*

We shall now consider the bearing of this defensive alliance on the other Powers. Needless to say, Japan and China will in no way impair the rights and interests already acquired by the Powers. At this moment it is of paramount importance for Japan to come to a special understanding with Russia to define our respective spheres of influence in Manchuria and Mongolia so that the two countries may coöperate with each other in the future. This means that Japan, after the acquisition of sovereign rights in South Manchuria and Inner Mongolia, will work together with Russia after her acquisition of sovereign rights in North Manchuria and Outer Mongolia, to maintain the status quo, and endeavor by every effort to protect the peace of the far East. Russia, since the outbreak of the European War, has not only laid aside all ill feelings against Japan, but has adopted the same attitude as her allies and shown warm friendship for us. No matter how we regard the Manchurian and Mongolian questions in the future, she is anxious that we find some way of settlement. Therefore we need not doubt but that Russia, in her attitude toward this Chinese question, will be able to come to an understanding with us for mutual coöperation.

The British sphere of influence and interest in China is centered in Tibet and the Yangtze Valley. Therefore if Japan can come to some satisfactory arrangement with China in regard to Tibet and also give certain privileges to Great Britain in the Yangtze Valley, with an assurance to protect those privileges, no matter how powerful Great Britain might be, she will surely not oppose Japan's policy in regard to this Chinese question. While this present European War is going on, Great Britain has even asked Japan to render her assistance. That her strength will certainly not enable her to oppose us in the future need not be doubted in the least.

Since Great Britain and Russia will not oppose Japan's policy toward China, it can readily be seen what attitude France will adopt in regard to the subject. What Japan must now reckon with is America. But America in her attitude toward us regarding our policy toward China has already declared the principle of maintaining China's territorial integrity and equal opportunity, and will be satisfied if we do not impair America's already acquired rights and privileges. We think America will also have no cause for complaint. Nevertheless, America has in the East a naval force which can be fairly relied upon, though not sufficiently strong to be feared. Therefore in Japan's attitude toward America there is nothing really for us to be afraid of.

While nominally put forth as a spontaneous memorial of Japanese living in China, this report apparently was prepared by agents who had been detailed to study internal conditions there. It reveals itself as the work of no ordinary minds, and is obviously the product of trained political thinkers familiar with world politics. The proposed plan first creates the fiction of an ''alliance'' between China and Japan, whereby the sovereignty of China is turned over to Japan, much like the sovereignty of Korea was transferred.

The monarchy in China is to be restored, but the throne must be occupied by a man who is amenable to Japanese suggestion. If Yuan Shih K'ai would agree to such a course, then Japan might support him; but if he would not submit to Japan's terms, then he must be overthrown by means of a rebellion incited against him in the name of republicanism. When this rebellion has overthrown Yuan, one of its leaders controlled by Japan will be selected to head the Government, and after an interval will be made Emperor. This report and various other documents and information showing the activities of Japanese political intriguers in China came into the possession of the Chinese Government while the negotiations about Japan's demands were taking place at Peking. By then it had become evident that the Japanese Government was following the lines outlined by this memorial in pressing its demands. I am now taking the matter in its relations to the question of the monarchy. With Japan, the first question was whether Yuan Shih K'ai could be induced to fall in with Japan's plan. In his interview with President Yuan when first presenting the demands, Mr. Hioki had pointedly intimated to Yuan that Japan might be unable to "restrain" the Chinese revolutionists unless Yuan was more amenable to Japan's policy, and this possibility was thereafter kept privately in the purview of the negotiations. It was a matter for the Chinese Government seriously to reflect upon. That some of the rebel leaders were cajoled by Japan and given reserved support, was known to the Chinese Government, which also knew that Japanese agents were working to undermine the loyalty of officials in the central and southern provinces. From time to time evidences of these activities were discovered. Sun Yat Sen, Chen Chi-mei, and Huang Hsing were accorded asylum by Japan. Following are agreements alleged to have been made in 1914:

Published April 18, 1915.

(TRANSLATION)

Secret Agreement made between Sun Wen (Sun Yat Sen) and the Japanese.

In order to preserve the peace in the far East, it is necessary for China and Japan to enter into an offensive and defensive alliance whereby in case of war with any other nation or nations Japan shall supply the military force while China shall be responsible for the finances. It is impossible for the present Chinese Government to work hand in hand with the Japanese Government, nor does the Japanese Government desire to coöperate with the former. Consequently Japanese politicians and merchants who have the peace of the far East at heart are anxious to assist China in her reconstruction. For this object the following agreement is entered into by the two parties:

1. Before an uprising is started, Terao, Okura, Tseji Karoku, and their associates shall provide the necessary funds, weapons, and military force, but the funds so provided must not exceed 1,500,000 yen and rifles not to exceed 100,000 pieces.

2. Before the uprising takes place the loan shall be temporarily secured by 10,000,000 yen worth of bonds to be issued by Sun Wen (Sun Yat Sen). It shall, however, be secured afterwards by all the movable properties of the occupied territory. (See Article 14 of this agreement.)

3. The funds from the present loan and military force to be provided are for operations in the provinces south of the Yellow River, viz.: Yunnan, Kweichow, Hunan, Hupeh, Szechuen, Kiangsi, Anhuei, Kiangsu, Chekiang, Fukien, Kuangsi and Kuangtung. If it is intended to invade the northern provinces north of the Yellow River, Tseji Karoku and his associates shall participate with the revolutionists in all deliberations connected with such operations.

4. The Japanese volunteer force shall be allowed from the date of their enrolment active service pay in accordance with the regulations of the Japanese army. After the occupation of a place, the two parties will settle the mode of rewarding the meritorious and compensating the family of the killed, adopting the most generous practice in vogue in China and Japan. In the case of the killed, compensation for each soldier shall, at the least, be more than 1,000 yen.

5. Wherever the revolutionary army might be located the Japanese military officers accompanying these expeditions shall have the right to advise a continuation or cessation of operations.

6. After the revolutionary army has occupied a region and strengthened its defenses, all industrial undertakings and railway con-

struction and the like, not mentioned in the treaties with other foreign Powers shall be worked with joint capital together with the Japanese.

7. On the establishment of a new Government in China, all Japan's demands on China shall be recognized by the new Government as settled and binding.

8. All Japanese military officers holding the rank of captain or higher ranks engaged by the Chinese revolutionary army shall have the privilege of being continued in their employment without a limit as to date and shall have the right to ask to be thus employed.

9. The loan shall be paid over in three instalments. The first instalment will be 400,000 yen, the second instalment . . . yen, and the third instalment . . . yen. After the first instalment is paid over, Okura, who advances the loan, shall have the right to appoint men to surpervise the expenditure of the money.

10. The Japanese shall undertake to deliver all arms and ammunition in the districts of Jih Chao and Haichow. (In Shantung and Kiangsu, South of Kiaochow.)

11. The payment of the first instalment of the loan shall be made not later than three days after the signing of this agreement.

12. All the employed Japanese military officers and Japanese volunteers are in duty bound to obey the orders of the commander of the revolutionary army.

13. The commander of the revolutionary army shall have the right to send back to Japan those Japanese military officers and Japanese volunteers who disobey his orders, and their passage money shall not be paid if such decision meets with the approval of three or more of the Japanese who accompany the revolutionary force.

14. All the commissariat departments in the occupied territory must employ Japanese experts to coöperate in their management.

15. This agreement takes effect immediately it is signed by the two parties.

The forgoing fifteen articles have been discussed several times between the two parties and signed by them in February. The first instalment of 400,000 yen has been paid according to the terms of this agreement.

Published April 20, 1915.

(TRANSLATION)

Loan Agreement made between the Revolutionary Party represented by Chang Yao Ching and his Associates of the first part, and Kawasaki Kulanoske of the second part.

1. The Europe and Asia Trading Company undertakes to raise a loan of 500,000 yen. After the agreement is signed and sealed by

the contracting parties, the Japanese Central Bank shall hand over $\frac{3}{10}$ of the loan as the first instalment. When Chang Yao Ching and his associates arrive at their proper destination, the sum of 150,000 yen shall be paid over as the second instalment. When final arrangements are made the third and last instalment of 200,000 yen shall be paid.

2. When money is to be paid out, the Europe and Asia Trading Company shall appoint supervisors. Responsible individuals of the contracting parties shall jointly affix their seals (to the checks) before money is drawn for expenditure.

3. The Europe and Asia Trading Company shall secure a volunteer force of 150 men, only retired officers of the Japanese army to be eligible.

4. On leaving Japan the traveling expenses and personal effects of the volunteers shall be borne by themselves. After reaching China, Chang Yao Ching and his associates shall give the volunteers the pay of officers of the subordinate grade according to the established regulations of the Japanese army.

5. If a volunteer is wounded while on duty, Chang Yao Ching and his associates shall pay him a provisional compensation of not exceeding 1,000 yen. When wounded seriously a provisional compensation of 5,000 yen shall be paid. When wounded to the extent of mutilation a compensation of 50,000 yen shall be paid as well as a life pension in accordance with the rules of the Japanese army. If a volunteer meets with an accident, thus losing his life, an indemnity of 50,000 yen shall be paid to his family.

6. If a volunteer is not qualified for duty, Chang Yao Ching and his associates shall have the power to dismiss him. All volunteers are subject to the orders of Chang Yao Ching and his associates and to their command in the battle fields.

7. When volunteers are required to attack a certain selected place it shall be their duty to do so. But the necessary expenses for the undertaking shall be determined beforehand by both parties after investigating into existing conditions.

8. The volunteer force shall be organized after the model of the Japanese army. Two Japanese officers recommended by the Europe and Asia Trading Company shall be employed.

9. The Europe and Asia Trading Company shall have the power to dispose of the public properties in the places occupied by the volunteer force.

10. The Europe and Asia Trading Company shall have the first preference for working the mines in places occupied and protected by the volunteer force.

The usual fictions are preserved in these arrangements—a Japanese company, or several firms jointly, acting in its business capacity, engages to finance political enterprises in China, to be recompensed by certain concessions and privileges. I do not vouch for the authenticity of these documents, but I obtained them from semi-official sources, and there is much circumstantial evidence to show that they truly represent arrangements that did take place, and plans that were being formulated. These matters were contemporaneous with the negotiations at Peking, and the application of Japan's pressure on Yuan Shih K'ai to compel him to submit to the demands; that is, while Japan was bullying the Peking Government, she was privately instigating a sentiment against it in central and south China based on Yuan's yielding to concessions which Japan herself was forcibly wringing from him. Yuan knew all the time what was going on, yet he was powerless to act otherwise, except to resist Japan by force. Japan's next move is profoundly interesting. A few weeks after China yielded to Japan's ultimatum, and the "agreement" was signed, in May, 1915, an official of the Japanese Government personally made a proposition to Yuan Shih K'ai to restore the monarchy under Japan's protection. I have been told the name of this emissary, but withhold it. His proposal took the form of "advice" to Yuan that the monarchy should be restored with Yuan as Emperor, Japan to lend support on the lines set out by the report and memorial of the so-called Black Dragon Society, and Yuan to acquiesce in Japan's policy of "protection" to China. One can imagine the feelings with which Yuan listened to this "advice." He knew that to accept it probably would secure him on the throne of China as long as he played Japan's game; but he also believed that China's existence as a nation would pass in the process. Furthermore, he believed that if he refused Japan probably would instigate a revolution to overthrow him, using one of her Chinese puppets first to become President, then to restore the monarchy. It was a difficult position, and Yuan, always

Chang Chien
Minister of Commerce and Agriculture

Liang Tun-yen
Minister of Communications

Chang Cheng-hsiang
Minister of Justice

Hsu Shih Chang
Secretary of State

Prominent Officials in China's Reconstruction Period

crafty, temporized. He pretended to take Japan's "advice" into consideration, and probably permitted the news to "leak" to some of the foreign legations, with a view to forestalling Japan. As to the restoration of the monarchy, *per se,* nearly every Power favors it, for reasons making for China's stability that I have outlined. But there was the danger, almost the certainty, that to make the change at that time would give an excuse for another rebellion which would be taken advantage of by Japan. The matter drifted, Yuan postponing a decision as long as he could. Meanwhile, some efforts were made to make a diversion and to secure China's stability during the Great War, of which the proposal for China to join the Allied Entente was noteworthy. Japan's opposition defeated that plan. Yuan Shih K'ai's motives in what followed must have been very complex even to himself. It fairly may be assumed that he wanted to be Emperor, and also that he believed a restoration of the monarchy would be better for the country. He had been privately "advised" by Japan to restore the monarchy. He knew that advice was conditional on the new Emperor playing Japan's game, which Yuan had no thought of doing; but the situation presented an alternative which would appeal strongly to Oriental politicians—the possibility of seeming to act on Japan's "advice," and making the shift, thus consolidating and strengthening the Government, and dealing with Japan's policy afterward. There were, in this process, the usual motives of men about Yuan who hoped to gain place and power with him as Emperor, but these were minor influences. The plan to restore the monarchy was launched with extreme caution, as was necessary. Yuan quietly sounded leading officials in all parts of the country, and a majority seemed favorably disposed to the change. Meanwhile, Yuan was watching Japan, and Japan was watching him. Yuan must have known the risks he ran; but he also probably thought that he would have a rebellion on his hands either course he took. He was careful to observe certain formalities, and the pretense of seeking to ascertain the wishes of the people. The form of submitting the question to the people was gone through with, and when that response was favorable to the monarchy, Yuan accepted conditionally and with a display of reluctance. Yuan felt able to handle the situation in China if there was no foreign interference.

Two theories are held about Japan's course. One is that Japan up to a point believed that it had gained an influence over Yuan and intended to assent to him becoming Emperor. The other is that Japan, in giving confidential advice to Yuan to restore the monarchy, merely wanted to induce him to take that course, in order to provide a favorable condition for fomenting another rebellion. In any event, when the monarchy movement got so far, and Yuan (after delay and careful consideration) had accepted the throne, the rebellion was sprung. It began in December, 1915, in Yunnan Province, and it is interesting to note that for some time before it started the Japanese press had predicted that it would begin there, and that the announcement of its beginning was published in Japan before the outbreak occurred. Before it became evident that there would be serious internal opposition to Yuan assuming the throne, several of the Powers (October, 1915) advised the Chinese Government to postpone the change. Japan, curiously enough, publicly joined in this advice, on the ground that to make the change would disturb China. It is difficult, in these events, to distinguish Japan's real purposes as developed by her secret diplomacy from her official attitude as shown by the Government's public utterances and acts. Officially, Japan deprecated the proposed restoration of the monarchy and advised China against it because it might cause internal turbulence. Unofficially, Japan advised Yuan Shih K'ai to restore the monarchy, and moved obliquely to stimulate the internal turbulence she professed to dread. The United States did not join in advising China about her course at that juncture, an attitude which was correct technically.

The rebellion developed momentum, and moved similarly to

the one of 1913, displaying the same general characteristics. Although some of the outlying provinces were the points of revolutionary activity, the Foreign Settlements of Shanghai soon became a focus of intrigue. A very good picture of some workings of the rebellion is given in a report of the Captain-Superintendent of Police of the Shanghai Foreign Settlements (K. J. McEuen), published April 20, 1916:

Wild rumors have been circulated as to the local situation, and the general uneasiness has not been decreased by the uncontrollable out-pourings of the Chinese rebel organs. So Shanghai finds itself at the moment of writing in a position similar to that of 1911 and 1913. Trade is at a standstill, and there have been signs, which have not yet passed, of considerable danger to peace and good order. The rebel leaders, with the money they have in hand, have been active in trying to buy over the soldiers of the garrison and with their aid to carry out an attack on the Chinese Government's establishments, but they have not succeeded owing to the watchfulness of the military authorities, who are thoroughly on their guard and well posted on the subject of rebel arrangements. The latter days of March and the first week of April saw the situation in the South develop rapidly and culminate in the Kwangtung Province declaring independence and throwing in its lot with Kweichow, Yunnan, and Kwangsi. Thus the four southernmost provinces of China have cut themselves aloof from all control from the Central Government and have placed themselves under the guidance of their various military leaders, who seem to be acting independently and without any apparent unity of purpose. It was confidently prophesied that the secession of Hunan, Kiangsi, and Fukien would follow next, so that the defection of the Chekiang Province on the morning of April 12, before any move had been made by these three provinces, was thought to be a premature step forced on by the anticipated arrival of northern troops in Chekiang. Up to this point Shanghai was able calmly to look upon the squabble without any grave fears of being actively involved, and in full anticipation that the Central Government would soon restore order. So soon, however, as the important Province of Kwangtung rebelled and Chekiang followed suit, Shanghai became directly affected. The interruption of communication with Hangchow, the imminent danger of collision with hostile troops at a point not thirty-five miles away from Shanghai, and the presence of a large number of rebels with unsavory reputations with their disreputable followers, have caused unusual restlessness among local residents. Special attention has been given to the presence of bad characters who by their recent arrival have led to a considerable increase in crime. During the closing months of 1915 and the opening weeks of 1916, when rumors of projected insurrection have been rife in Shanghai, a great number of unemployed persons from the north of this province and the region beyond drifted hither. Many of them were discharged soldiers who had served in this locality before in regiments of the Vanguard and the Dare-to-Die type, others were simply agricultural laborers who were out of work during the winter months and who were lured southward by stories of wealth to be gained without working for it. There were several persons of importance residing near the Settlement who were actively opposing the monarchical movement, and being joined by a few others who had come from the north and from over the sea and elsewhere, an attempt was made to pay, and, in some measure, keep under their control a number of men who might form the nucleus of a force which they believed they would be able to raise in the future. The scheme only partially succeeded because, as usual, the funds ran out, and the men, as has sometimes happened before, were thrown on their own resources. Some were armed and most of them were ready to do anything to obtain money, with the result that the police have had to deal with more robbery. As always happens when any plot of this description is on foot, the Settlement is invaded by swarms of government detectives who usually bring in their train a great number of satellites, some of whom are persons of somewhat dark reputation. They, too, are often unpaid. The heads are fairly liberally supplied with money, but it does not always reach their subordinates; and the latter, who have plenty of time on their hands, are apt to supplement their income by extortion and robbery whilst waiting for their salaries, or for the portion of a reward which the kidnapping of a member of the Kuomingtang may bring. That the tables are sometimes turned on these men is evident from the murder of one of their number by a former officer of the revolutionary army in a house in Cemetery Road on January 30, 1916. They have not been entirely unsuccessful in carrying out part of the work with which they have been entrusted, as may be seen from the carrying off to Peking of a resident of the French Concession who was lured to the International Settlement boundary on the evening of March 6 and betrayed into their hands by a relative. For his arrest, a heavy reward is reported to have been paid. As a rule, these men, as well as the men who circle around those they seek to arrest, are in a chronic state of indigence, and it is not astonishing that there is an increase of crime to be recorded in the Settlement when it is open to invasion on all sides from bands of this description. Robberies are not likely to diminish very much in number, nor is tranquillity likely to reign in the Settlement whilst the districts around are seething with political strife. There is another crowd of persons who are almost as dangerous as the armed robber although they do not descend to his methods. They adopt others which in intent are every whit as criminal, viz., the writing of letters to members of the wealthy class of Shanghai Chinese, pleading sometimes that they are stranded, and cannot get home, sometimes that they wish to depart to the war in the Southwest, taking with them the funds to carry it on, and demanding anything between 10,000 and 100,000 dollars. There is usually in the letter a hint about bombs or bullets if the money is not forthcoming. Chen Chi-mei is again in evidence soliciting the wherewithal to stir up strife in this locality as well as in others, and professing to be anxious that would-be subscribers should not be misled into mistaking what he calls a political loan for a private contribution. Money has undoubtedly been contributed, and contributed liberally in Shanghai to further the object of the rebellion, but it appears to have been given mostly by those who believe that political changes are imminent and who deem it well to have a connection with all parties.

Here were the same elements and conditions at work that were observed during the revolution and the former rebellion— enforced money contributions, intimidation, kidnapping, assassination, bribery, banditry—a general lapse toward anarchy. As before, funds played an important part. When it became evident that the disorder was spreading, Chen Chi-mei went from Japan to Shanghai and resumed his former tactics, until he in turn was assassinated. Huang Hsing left the United States for China, but stopped in Japan, from where he circulated manifestos protesting against foreign loans to the Peking Government. Sun Yat Sen expressed sympathy with the rebellion, which rallied to it all the men and factions opposed to Yuan Shih K'ai. The Government set out to suppress the rebellion, but it soon developed that it could not control its own officials and troops. Authority crumbled, except in the north. Tutuhs would not recognize the authority of the Government, generals would not follow orders, and soldiers would not obey their officers. As it lost control over some provinces, the Government found its revenue reduced, and lacked funds to subdue the rebellion. Its efforts to borrow abroad were hampered by the international situation, and by the opposition of the rebels. It appeared that the rebellion was receiving financial support and arms from Japanese sources, and the Japanese Government intimated where its sympathies were by withholding Japan's quota of the Salt revenue periodically releasable under the Quintuple Loan agreement. In these circumstances, Yuan Shih K'ai realized that an immediate reversion was all that could save the situation, if that could. He therefore issued, in March, 1916, a mandate renouncing the throne and announcing a continuation of the Republic. Yuan had not assumed the crown, so the act was one of rejection rather than of reversal. In this interesting mandate, Yuan said, in part:

Disturbances rapidly followed one another and, therefore, fearing that disaster might befall us at any day, all who had the welfare of the country at heart advocated the reinstitution of a monarchical system in order to end all strife for power and to inaugurate a *régime* of peace. Suggestions in this sense have unceasingly been made to me since the first Revolution, and each time a sharp rebuke has been administered to those making the suggestion. The situation last year, however, became so different that it was impossible to prevent the spread of such ideas.

The mandate then recounts the history of the monarchical movement culminating in the unanimous vote in favor of a monarchy and the election of Yuan Shih K'ai as Emperor. Continuing, it says:

Nevertheless it continued to be my conviction that this sudden elevation to a great seat would be a violation of my oath and compromise my good faith. I therefore declined in order to make clear the view which I always held. The Lifayuan, however, stated firmly that the oath of the Chief Executive rested on a peculiar sanction which should be observed or discarded according to the will of the people. Therefore there was no excuse for me to decline the offer. I, therefore, took refuge behind the excuse of preparations in order that the desire of the people might be satisfied, but I took no steps actually to carry out the program, and when trouble arose in Yunnan and Kweichow a mandate was issued announcing the postponement of the measure and forbidding the further presentation of petitions praying for the enthronement. I then hastened the convocation of the Lifayuan in order to secure the views of that body, hoping thus to return to the original state of affairs.

The mandate then describes Yuan Shih K'ai's retirement to private life and his return to public service as a result of the first Revolution. It says:

Reluctantly I came out of my retirement and endeavored to prop up the tottering structure. I cared for nothing but the salvation of the country. A perusal of our history reveals in a vivid manner the sad fate of the descendants of the ancient kings and emperors. What then could have prompted me to aspire to the throne? Yet, while the representatives of the people were not willing to believe in the sincerity of my refusal, a section of the people appear to have suspected me of harboring a desire to gain more power and privileges. Such a difference of thought resulted in an exceedingly dangerous situation. As my sincerity has not been such as to win the hearts of the people my judgment has not been sound enough to appraise every man. I, myself, am alone to blame for my lack of virtue. The people have been thrown into misery and soldiers made to bear hardships; further, the people have been cast into a panic, and commerce has rapidly declined. When I search my heart, sorrow fills it. I am therefore not unwilling to suppress myself in order to yield to others. I am still of opinion that the petitions designating me as Emperor, submitted through the Lifayuan, are not suited to the demands of the time, and my official acceptance to the throne made on December 11, 1915, is hereby canceled. Petitions received from the provinces and the administrative areas are all hereby returned through the State Department to the Lifayuan and to the petitioners for destruction, and all preparation in connection with the monarchy are to cease immediately. Those who advocated a monarchy have been prompted by a desire to strengthen the foundation of the country. Those who oppose it have done so in order to express their political views. It may, therefore, be presumed that they will not go to the extreme and so endanger the country. They should, therefore, all hearken to the voice of their own conscience, sacrifice all prejudices and with one mind and purpose unite in an effort to save the situation, so that the glorious descendants of our sacred continent may be spared the horror of internal strife. In brief, I now confess that all the faults of the country are the result of my own faults. Now that the acceptance of the throne has been canceled every man will be responsible if he further disturb the peace. I, the Great President, being charged with the duty of ruling the whole country, cannot remain idle while the country is racing to perdition. At the present moment homesteads are in misery, discipline has been disregarded, administration neglected and real talents have not been given a chance. When I think of conditions I awake in the night with the thought, "How can we stand as a nation if such a state of affairs be allowed to continue?" Hereafter all officials should get rid of their corrupt habits and endeavor to achieve merits. They should work with might and main in their duties, whether introducing reforms or abolishing old corruptions. Let all not be satisfied with empty words. They should uphold as the main principle of their administrative policy that which only in reality counts. Reward or punishment will be dealt out promptly. Let all generals, officials, soldiers, and the people act in accordance with this ideal.

After this renunciation, the question was whether the influences which were working to disrupt China would succeed in keeping the rebellion alive, or whether the more sensible Chinese, as they did in 1911, and again in 1913, would realize the situation and compromise their political differences. In some quarters, Yuan's renunciation of the throne was taken as a confession of weakness, and his political opponents were encouraged to continue and extend their obstruction, and to demand his retirement from official life. The major motives and influences at work were plain. Chinese were divided into several groups. The great mass were indifferent. Of the politically intelligent section, there were two principal groups—the Yuan Shih K'ai faction, and the opposition to him. Of the opposition, some were animated by sincere and patriotic motives, and some were acting solely from personal ambitions. The "Japan Chronicle" expressed, on March 30, 1916, this view:

Indeed, so far as the European Powers were concerned, they staked everything on the political good sense of the Chinese people. They knew that the disturbances likely to follow the proclamation of Yuan as Emperor were less serious than those likely to follow

General L. Chang, leader in China's fight against
opium

China's fight against opium. Ceremony of destroying paraphernalia
for smoking

his disappearance from the headship of the State, yet they calculated that the Chinese people would retain him in the Presidentship notwithstanding his frustrated plan to seize the crown, in spite of this demonstration that he was the helpless puppet of the legations, and although in demonstrating their power over him the legations had publicly advertised that they would give him no support against his opponents. On the whole, this faith in the commonsense of the Chinese people has been justified, but it would hardly have been so had it not been for the deep distrust of the Chinese in the intentions of Japan. Such is this distrust that a great many Chinese politicians who would like to turn the President out of office altogether would almost rather have him Emperor than give Japan any pretext for intervention. Others, such as Dr. Sun Yat Sen, appear to regard Japanese intervention as the lesser evil. Unfortunately, though it is easy enough to show that Japan loyally fulfils the obligations entailed by her international contracts, those who suspect Japan of ambitions in China inconsistent with a proper respect for the integrity of that country, have plenty of materials from which to construct their case. The demands made on China in the early part of last year, especially Group V, had all the appearance of being pressed at a time which was considered suitable only because the European Powers were not in a position to express any very emphatic opinion. The more recent "advice" to the President also seemed so obviously designed to throw China into the turmoil which it was professedly trying to avoid that people naturally considered who among the advisers would be likely to gain an advantage from it. Then, again, the large number of Japanese who are always found busily occupied in Chinese revolutionary movements create a certain amount of suspicion against their country. The other day a foreign office authority, interviewed by the "Yorodzu," expressed no doubt on the subject of the report that there were between seventy and eighty Japanese fighting with the Yunnan insurgents, and he even went so far as to maintain that these individuals, who were reported to be deserting the losing side had the rights of "neutrals" if they happened to be caught by the Chinese Government authorities. The idea that a foreigner can take part in a revolutionary disturbance and claim, if he is caught, to be a "neutral," is a fantastic conception of neutrality; and if the Government of Japan claims extra-territorial inviolability for the persons of its subjects who may be taken prisoner in a mutiny or arrested for having conspired and fought against the Government, the Chinese would have very good grounds for believing that Japanese were actively engaged in disrupting China under the ægis of their Government, and that their Government was interested in the promotion of such disturbances. That the troublesome Japanese in China are free lances out of control of their own Government, is not likely to be believed. Finally, if the good intentions of the Japanese Government are not appreciated abroad, it is in no small degree because a press over which the Government has very complete control maintains an unrestricted volume of output of abuse of China and of demands that Japan should seize the opportunity which now presents itself of practically annexing the country. It may not be advisable to suppress the free expression of opinion—though no such compunction is exhibited as a general rule—but at least cabinet ministers might have been expected strongly to protest against the tone of a large number of newspapers which continually urge Japan to repudiate her treaties, to defy justice and morality, and to make a Japanese province of China.

Following his renunciation of the throne, Yuan Shih K'ai made moves calculated to placate the Chinese republicans. He nominated a new cabinet, headed by Tuan Chi-jui, and including some progressives; and announced that a policy permitting of greater parliamentary power in the Government would be pursued. At the same time he ordered the suspension of military operations against the rebels, and set in motion arrangements to affect a compromise. Conferences were begun between representatives of the Government and the so-called "independent" provinces. The main issue was whether Yuan should remain as President, or whether he would resign. Apropos the situation, the "North-China Daily News" (Shanghai) said on April 27, 1916:

Were political campaigns conducted in China as they are in the West, with no greater reality of violence than the empty vituperation of posters and platforms, we know well that not one per cent. of China's population would care a fig which side was in power. Unhappily, in China, any change in government must be paid for by the multitude with life, limb, and prosperity. We get a good picture from our Kashing correspondent of what revolution means to the average man: "The fear is that retreating soldiers would begin the looting; then the victors, following, would plunder more extensively; after them, the local rascals would finish up what was left." Such is the experience of ages. To-day we receive from our Tai-kuhsien correspondent another side of the same story. Shensi as yet has taken little or no part in the political agitations of the rest of China. But bandits supply all the necessary excitement. Five years ago the eviction of the Manchus gave them their chance and they have ever since traded on it with impunity. Lastly, let us refer to the effort made by the gentry and merchants of Wenchow to form a municipal council in order to coöperate with the officials, if possible, in preserving public order. Give us only peace, is the unending cry from one side of China to the other. But politicians have been too busy, with their own notions of what China wants, to harken. . . . In certain hands, those for example of the late Admiral Tseng, the new army has proved both efficient and valuable; the discipline and smartness of the handful of troops who defended the Arsenal in 1913 were a revelation to most of us. Yet, as a whole, it can hardly be denied that the army generally has been the most dangerous factor in all recent revolutions. Too often kept for weeks in arrears of their pay through the dishonesty of their leaders, fully conscious by now of their own power and demoralized by lack of occupation, the army is and knows itself to be the prize for which both sides in any political controversy will compete, each striving to outbid the other in bribery. That the soldiers' terms should tend to become more and more extravagant is, in such circumstances, not surprising. A few days ago we were told that the soldiers at Wuhu demanded tls. 30,000 as the price of not looting, because Nanking was reported to have declared its independence; when that report proved untrue, they asked for tls. 10,000 as compensation for their disappointment.

In view of what had happened, the following utterance of Count Okuma, published in the "Asahi," is very interesting:

President Yuan Shih-k'ai has been caught in a trap set by himself, and his trickery has met its fate in the failure of his monarchical scheme. The Japanese Government, acting in concert with friendly Powers, has served on the Peking Government several warnings, being persuaded that the introduction of a monarchy would provoke disturbances, but President Yuan Shih-k'ai failed to appreciate this advice and set it at nought until he was obliged to declare the abandonment of the scheme. The Mandate abandoning the monarchy ought to have been issued much earlier, for the revolutionists, who were originally opposed to the monarchial régime, have come to entertain strong personal feeling against the President. A resourceful statesman, President Yuan is now trying to utilize both Hsu Shih-chang and Tuan Chi-jui, whom he once dismissed from posts of responsibility, to mediate between the North and the South. Granting that they consent to this step, it will be very difficult to say how far they are likely to succeed in their efforts, especially when it is remembered that a strong anti-Yuan sentiment pervades the whole of China. If President Yuan is really solicitous, the course to pursue in the present circumstances will be to retire from the Presidency. Some people appear to be under the impression that China lacks another statesman to replace President Yuan, and that, therefore, the situation would be complicated by his resignation, but I do not endorse this view. I think peace and order would be restored in China immediately President Yuan resigned, and that it would be easy to find a successor.

By then the Japanese Government, from being uneasy lest Yuan should become Emperor after it had failed to influence him, had become equally uneasy lest the revolutionists should fail to force Yuan's resignation as President. Shifts in the Tokio Cabinet indicated a resumption of a "forward policy" in China, and the Japanese press was almost unanimous in urging that course. Notwithstanding untoward incidents due to the disturbed conditions, none of the Powers except Japan showed disposition to aggravate the situation by meddling or threatening to intervene. It was inevitable (as had been foreseen) that the presence of thousands of Japanese in the interior, and the occupation of Chinese territory by Japanese troops, would provoke some anti-Japanese demonstrations among the people. Collisions occurred at several places, and especially in Shantung.

The argument about whether Yuan Shih K'ai should resign was ended, unexpectedly, by his death on June 6, 1916, in rather mysterious circumstances. Li Yuan Hung, the Vice President, at once succeeded to the Presidency. In some ways the death of Yuan cleared the political atmosphere. It deprived the rebel leaders of what had been their chief open reason for opposition to the Government; if they were irreconcilable thereafter it would indicate clearly that a desire for power, not principle, animated them. As a man and patriot, Li Yuan Hung is esteemed and respected; but as an administrator his experience is small, and his qualifications are little known. He is believed to be at heart as strongly antagonistic to Japan's policy as Yuan Shih K'ai was; but he is not expected to show that statesman's cunning and courage in resisting pressure.

In considering China's internal national problem, most foreign authorities can see only two probable alternatives—the organization of a strong central government under one dominating personality, or disintegration. The dominating personality need not be the President. Support of Yuan Shih K'ai was due to two reasons—he was the man in office, and it was doubtful if any change would bring improvement, while it might cause disaster. Yuan Shih K'ai's government should not be judged by comparing it with an approximately ideal administration; it should be judged by comparison with probable alternatives. The men who have during and since the revolution been prominent as radical leaders and agitators have not acted in a way to warrant confidence in their ability to handle the situation any better than Yuan did. Young China has fretted under Yuan's conservatism and so-called reactionary tendencies; but Yuan showed that he wanted to use the younger Chinese in the Government by giving many of them important offices. It is to the Young China element that China must look for regeneration, if there is to be regeneration, but the day when Young China can be entrusted exclusively with the direction of the nation has not yet arrived. The sincere progressives can play a very important part in carefully swinging the nation toward reform, by doing the work that is assigned to them by their seniors in the Government, and waiting upon orderly advancement. Young China's day will come, if the nation endures, and it may not be far distant.

Meanwhile, is China to be made into another Mexico by the undisciplined ambitions of her politicians? The real issue is between Government and anarchy, with foreign intervention stalking visibly in the background.

CHAPTER XI

INTERNATIONAL PUBLICITY AND THE FAR EAST

International influences of publicity—Conditions in the far East—News services operating there—National propagandas—Objections to the system—A British service—A German service—The Japan National News Service—How they work—Effects upon the United States—Indirect intimidation of newspapers—Handicaps on American interests—News "faked" and perverted—Japan's propaganda in China and America—Japan's censorship—Anti-American agitation in Japan—Some illustrations—A unique incident—Use of Pacifist organizations—The American Peace Society of Japan—The Japan Peace Society—Effects of these efforts.

NO factor that enters into international affairs and influences relations between nations, is of more importance than publicity. Certain reactions of the Great War in the United States drew the attention of Americans forcibly to this condition, by demonstrating the use and misuse of publicity by foreign Governments to sway public opinion. Although such methods have been for a long time extensively used by Governments to shape opinion about international affairs, in favor of, or against certain nations, it is only very recently that Americans and the American press have begun to comprehend how such publicity affects American interests and national security. In no part of the world are conditions which attend publicity of greater significance to the United States than those existing in the far East. I have written on this topic frequently in commenting on events transpiring in that region, and some of that comment elucidates the subject as well as anything that I can write now. There are three general news telegram services now operating to and from the far East: Reuter (British), Ostasiatische Lloyd and its connections (German), and the Koksai (Japan National

News Agency). A few newspapers, particularly some of the great Japanese dailies, receive telegrams from their foreign correspondents on important matters, and from time to time some foreign newspapers in the far East get limited special services; but the bulk of news published in the far East that is transmitted by telegraph comes through the three agencies mentioned. The same three services also carry the greater part of news telegrams sent out of the far East for publication in Europe; although certain London and American papers have special correspondents in Japan and China, and American news agencies also have correspondents in those countries who send important news. No regular American news telegram service is delivered in China, and very little news by telegraph comes to Japan from America except to the vernacular press. Something of the effects of these conditions I will show. On September 3, 1914, a British parliamentary paper was issued, giving a report by Sir William Edward Goschen, who had been British ambassador at Berlin before the war, about a German organization to obtain favorable publicity for Germany and German interests in foreign countries, and showing that one of the methods to be used was for German commercial and financial interests to dispose their advertising patronage only with publications that would print German news. On February 1, 1914, the Koksai had taken over the functions previously performed in Japan by Reuter under an arrangement which amounts to this: Reuter for certain compensations got out of Japan in favor of the Japan National News Agency, which receives direct and indirect support from the Government to an extent that competition with it in Japan is expensive and difficult. Reuter entered into a contract by which it distributes abroad news from Japan supplied by the Koksai, and also supplies the Koksai with a general news service from abroad. Thus in respect to news out of Japan, Reuter became merely a distributing agent for the Koksai. News from Japan, therefore, delivered anywhere in the world by Reuter does

not originate with Reuter, but with the Koksai, Reuter acting only as a transmittor.

This explanation will probably make the following comments
lucid. Apropos the parliamentary paper on Sir William Edward Goschen's report, and the "Times" (London) comment
on it, which was published in the "China Press," I wrote in
that newspaper on October 3, 1914, as follows: "Now the fact
of the organization of this German publicity scheme was published early in the present year in this and various newspapers
throughout the world—that is, many months before this war
began, and before the war was thought of, so far as the public
knew. At that time aspects of the German publicity plan were
commented on by the press, and especially in England, where
its significance was better appreciated. A brief résumé of the
plan was published in the far East, and attracted notice because
of its analogies with the deal then just made between Reuter
and the Koksai, or Japan National News Agency. When Reuter turned over its service in and out of Japan to a news
agency indirectly supported by the Japanese Government,
the British press showed little uneasiness. Allowing for unavoidable variations, this German publicity scheme is merely
another Koksai. Evidently the Germans were unable to 'hook
up' with Reuter like the Koksai did, for in those matters Reuter
is influenced by British imperial political considerations; but
the Germans apparently had established a connection with
Havas, the principal French agency. In our opinion, such
publicity schemes operated under quasi-government control
are contrary to correct journalistic principles, and are inimical
to civilization, but we will not now attempt to demonstrate the
argument. When Reuter made its agreement with the Koksai,
this newspaper exposed the matter fully, but the greater part
of the British press at home and in the Orient kept silent. The
reason for that silence, we take it, is that for half a century or
so Reuter has been fulfilling the same function in principle,
and almost the same function as to method, for the British Gov-

Chou Hsueh-hsi, Minister of Finance in Yuan Shih K'ai's government

Photo, by International Film Service, Inc.

General Tuan Chi Jui, leader of Military Party in China. Premier and Minister of War in 1916

ernment and British interests that the Koksai is now fulfilling
for the Japanese Government and Japanese interests and which
this German scheme was designed to do for the German Government and German interests. The German scheme, as its
private method was exposed by Sir Edward Goschen, may be
somewhat lacking in finesse, but its principles, objects, and
basis of organization are almost identical with those of the
Koksai with which Reuter now coöperates, and with principles
and objects that have since its inception been a guiding precept
of the policy of Reuter. That being true—and it is true—
one hardly can stomach the Pharisaical moral shivers of the
British press about it. It is a little curious, too, that the matter should have been revived and given world publicity by the
British Government just at a time when it served a purpose
in reflecting upon news about the war derived from German
sources, and upon newspapers disposed to give German viewpoint fair representation in their columns. Our attention became directed many years ago, in the course of journalistic
work abroad, to the system by which Great Britain for so long
almost controlled the process of collecting, transmitting, and
distributing news of international interest; and the reactions
of that system upon other nations, and especially upon the
United States, made a deep impression. Until quite recent
times Great Britain has had nearly a monopoly of this form
of political and commercial propaganda, and it has been a
tremendous factor in advancing her imperial interests. None
can blame the British for having the wit to see the advantages of this system, and the intelligence to utilize it. But
when other nations begin to adopt the system, and apply it
to boosting their own game (or, conversely, to obstruct England's game), it smacks of hypocrisy for the British press to
call the process immoral. That the system is immoral we
are quite willing to concede—indeed, we have devoted some
effort trying to demonstrate its immoralities, and the insidious
detriments it can and does inject into international relations.
But the system is not moral and proper as used by one nation

and its allies, and immoral and improper when adopted by other nations. If it is invidious and wrong in one case, it is invidious and wrong in all cases. The system should be broken down, and it will be broken down. Governments will not abandon it as long as it is effective as a leverage upon international thought. But it can exert such leverage only by the toleration and aid of the press. When journalistic ethics abjures the system, it will go, for without connivance of the press it will become a useless thing."

Following that publication, several British residents of China wrote to the "China Press" criticizing my comments, to which I replied in the issue of that paper of October 7, 1914: "Our correspondent calls upon us to produce 'proofs' of our assertion that Reuter performs a similar function for British international policy and British interests to that performed by the Koksai for Japan, and which the proposed German scheme is designed to perform for Germany. Now what does he mean by 'proofs'—what will he accept as 'proofs'? Apparently he is convinced that the accounts given about the organization and purposes and methods of the Koksai, and the German scheme, may be taken as 'proofs.' . . . When the Koksai was organized, an effort was made to keep the circumstances of its organization secret, and when they were published, denials concerning some of its features were made by the Japanese Government and by the Japanese semi-official press for the obvious purpose of obscuring the relation of the Japanese Government to it. In short, Governments do not want their relations with news services to be generally known, for such knowledge impairs effective use of them for political purposes. Yet as the facts came out piecemeal, the connection of the Japanese Government with the Koksai, although oblique, became apparent. Now as to the relations of Reuter to British political propaganda, through association with the British Government, the same conditions apply. In Reuter's case, the relation has existed a long time, and has gone through many modifications in the course of half a century. In the sense of being able to produce any categorical evidence about the basis of relations between Reuter and the British Government, we cannot do that now. In journalistic circles, Reuter long has been presumed to receive official support in the indirect form of cheap telegraph rates, and other special concessions. These assertions have been made by British news services trying to compete in certain fields with Reuter, and which claimed that they could not do so because of preferential treatment accorded to Reuter. In one way and another, in the course of many years, information of this character has been published. We have no means of collating it at this moment. But entirely disregarding such evidence, the fact that Reuter does function as we have asserted is found *in the service itself*. The circumstantial proof of this is so overwhelming that no reasonable mind can remain unconvinced provided opportunity is given to review it, and to analyze it. It is not feasible to present this proof in an article, or in twenty articles, or in a hundred articles. It is spread thickly over the published record of the service in ways that no trained newspaper man can overlook, if he reflects at all about origins of news, and political import back of the news. Our correspondent must not think that we mean to allege that all of the news carried by this kind of news services is biased as to political viewpoint. Such a course would soon make the service valueless. Regarding news without special political bearing—which includes the greater part of news in ordinary times—Reuter is impartial, and handles the news 'straight,' as newspaper men say. But in emergency, or at special occasion, these services fulfil the function of keeping a certain viewpoint to the fore; and of obscuring, minimizing, or suppressing altogether the opposite or contrary viewpoints. Indeed, one of the most effective ways of serving political ends is by suppressing news. In fulfilling a political function, a news service does not have to misrepresent the facts. The propaganda is manufactured and provided by the Governments, which put it out in ways whereby the function of a news service becomes merely narration. The services only give it publicity. By long practice, the use of Reuter as a propagandist for British imperial policy and British commercial interests—which march hand in hand—has been refined into a finished subtlety, which completely escapes the average newspaper reader, but which trained journalists, especially those with international experience, instantly detect. It is only when a news service thus subtly 'colored' has a comparative or actual monopoly of news distribution in any field that it becomes severely invidious to interests other than those it supports. Thus it is difficult for Reuter or any news service, appreciably to influence the English home press, or the press of continental Europe—or to influence it injuriously—about events in near-by localities, for the press in those places has other sources of information which represent different viewpoints. But since the development of modern news dissemination, in which Reuter was a pioneer, England has been able, by coöperation of Reuter and control over cable telegraph communications, to give the news of world policies and events published in a large part of the world's area the 'coloring' she desired, whenever she desired it to be 'colored.' Conversely, by concentrating news obtained through Reuter in London, editing it there, and reissuing it for publication in Europe and America through continental and American news services, a virtual censorship over a considerable volume of important news was obtained. This is a subject about which the writer claims to possess expert knowledge, gained from professional experience, and by tracing ramifications of the system through thousands of actual instances. For a long time Reuter, and consequently Great Britain's, ability to give a desired turning to the view of certain events and policies held by a large part of humanity, passed without notice and without question, and without its significance even being suspected except by a few especially inquisitive and astute persons. But with pressure of other nations and nationalities into outer channels of world trade and politics, came first comprehension of Reuter's political and economic functions, then realization of their reactions upon other national interests; and finally a desire to offset, counteract, or at least to neutralize those reactions to the extent that they are detrimental to competing interests and ambitions, or to imitate the method to promote other national interests and ambitions. The Koksai and the proposed German scheme are expressions of this desire. When it realized that to try and compete with the Koksai in Japan would be financially profitless, and learning that because of the alliance a working agreement with the Japanese service would not be inimical to British interests for the time, Reuter agreed, *with the approval of the foreign offices of both Governments,* to coöperate. The German scheme also planned to coöperate with Reuter, but there political considerations seem to have intervened. On a purely business basis, to work in agreement with the German proposed service would be a more profitable arrangement for Reuter than its deal with the Koksai appears to be. After these explanations, we will revert to features of the proposed German service which the 'Times' and other English newspapers have criticized harshly. The German scheme, as outlined by the report of Sir Edward Goschen, may be divided into two elements. One function is to prepare and transmit for publication abroad news favorable to German policy and German interests. Under the circumstances, that is legitimate, and it is legitimate for any Government openly to give financial or other aid to such an enterprise. One form of encouragement was to reduce cable rates in favor of the service, a practice that the British Government is alleged to have used to help Reuter. The other function was to bring pressure to bear upon foreign newspapers to have them publish the German service, by a judicious distribution of advertising patronage of German firms, which was to be controlled by a 'pool,' and withheld from papers that would not publish the German news service, and give it fair place and presentation in comparison with news from other sources. This latter phase, we presume, is the part of the scheme which Sir Edward Goschen characterized as 'preparing the ground for a vast system of international blackmail.' We agree that this proposed association of advertising patronage with official political propaganda is highly objectionable—but is it different from what is a fairly common practice in most countries, including England and her dependencies? On its face, it seems to be better organized than is usual, which means that it stands more naked to scrutiny as to its purposes and morals. But is Reuter free from such associations? We have to go back only a short time to when the establishment of an advertising department of Reuter, and the prospectus issued by it, was so vigorously condemned by part of the English press, notably the 'Times,' that it seems to have been abandoned—although we are not sure of it. That this form of pressure is applied, or attempted to be applied to influence newspapers in favor of British policy has recently been strikingly brought within the experience of the 'China Press.' When this war began we realized that newspapers would suffer from it along with all other business, by loss of advertising revenue. Those who read Mr. F. A. McKenzie's interesting London letter published yesterday will see how newspapers in England have suffered. We expected to lose advertising, and have lost it because of stoppage of business by the war. We did not expect, however, to lose advertising because of the neutral attitude of the paper. Yet we have lost advertising for that reason—British advertising. Soon after the war began, when it became evident that this paper would not follow, in its editorial policy, the 'leads' provided by Reuter's news service and by the British press in general, but would give both sides equally fair representation in its news columns, and consideration in its criticisms, a systematic effort was instituted to injure this paper, and to cause it to lose whatever revenue could be alienated by accusing it of being anti-British. After the campaign had continued for a while, its reactions upon our advertising revenue began to be felt. Several British firms have withdrawn their patronage, stating that while the presumed business value of the advertising, based on circulation, was unimpaired, they could not withstand the pressure that was being applied to them. We do not wish to intimate that all advertising that has been stopped, was stopped for political reasons. We are quite sure that this is not the case, that some of the falling-off is from the same causes from which the London newspapers are suffering. We are equally sure that advertising has been withdrawn on account of political influence. Now we ask our correspondent if that, in principle, is not what the proposed German service is accused of planning to do in a systematic way? Indeed, the British theory in this instance seems to go far beyond the alleged German method, which only aims to procure publication of a German news service, by seeming to require not only publication of British news services, but editorial advocacy also. . . . Now we are going a little further, and will try to show why as an American newspaper published in China, the 'China Press' is concerned about this question of international publicity, as demonstrated by the functions in the far East of Reuter and the Koksai, and their relations to each other. Without touching deeply upon delicate matters, it will, we think, be granted that the United States as a Pacific Ocean Power has a fundamental interest in the fate of China, and in phases of the policy of Japan. Japan is allied with Great Britain, and recent events have caused much speculation about what that alliance comprehends, and as a consequence speculations must arise about how the United States may be affected by these developments. By its connections in London with American press services, Reuter becomes a principal source of information for news published in the United States about events in the far East. Reuter's service from Japan is *entirely* supplied by the Koksai. The relation of this coincidence to public knowledge and opinion in America about the policy, attitude, and intentions of Japan, and about the course of events in China, is obvious. The time has come when the American press, and Americans, must carefully scrutinize the origins of their world news. To be misinformed is to be misguided, and to be misguided about foreign affairs, with civilization in its present state, may bring not only detriments, but an actual peril to the American nation.''

In the ''China Press'' of October 13, 1914, I wrote: ''Compensations to civilization from this war must arise from its psychological reactions upon humanity, and in that the press plays an important part. It is gratifying, therefore, to notice that out of certain conditions relating to publicity during the war is springing a new popular consciousness about the press, and about publicity concerning matters of great public import. This is bound to be beneficial, for the more people know about publicity, the functions it is presumed to perform and the functions it does perform, the easier it is for the press to fulfil its higher functions and its true purposes. That is why we have welcomed the discussion in this newspaper of certain relations that exist between Governments and the press—or rather, with publicity as a whole, for the press is only one form of publicity. A few days ago we printed a letter from Mr. M. J. Cox, local manager of Reuter's Telegram Company, in which he controverted and disputed some assertions and arguments we had made concerning the connection of Reuter with British propaganda. . . . In continuing this discussion, we will go beyond matters touched upon by Mr. Cox; but first we will take up some points advanced by him. He enters into some explanations relating to the business side of Reuter service in the far East, with a view to showing that it exists solely as a business concern, and consequently is independent of any connection with the British Government. We have not contended that Reuter is now dependent upon official support for existence as a news service, neither have we wished to imply that it is slavishly subordinated to official political viewpoint. What we do contend is that Reuter services do give widespread publicity to British official viewpoint; that because it (or any well-conducted news service) could perform this function, it did in the past (and probably does) receive help from the British Government in getting organized and extending its organization; and that by the fact of that assistance and its present

Count Okuma, Premier of Japan, and Countess Okuma, with Dr. and Mrs. David Starr Jordan. Japan's influence with pacifist organizations in America has been exerted to retard defensive measures by the United States and to propagate a false idea of Japan's policy in America

organization, it enjoys something of the nature of a monopoly of news dissemination and distribution in certain fields. By Mr. Cox's showing, it is possible for Reuter to deliver a news service in China at a comparatively low cost—a cost far below that of bringing any other news service, or of a similar service to a single newspaper. The chief item of expense of such a news service is telegraph tolls, and if Reuter receives any assistance in the financial sense it probably applies to that item, by reduction or rebate of tolls. To understand the situation as it exists to-day, one must go back to the origins of certain things—to the time when the telegraph was invented, when the world began to be linked together by cables, and when the news possibilities of this development began to be appreciated. In those days and out of those conditions Reuter was born. The originator, de Reuter, was a German, but he went to live in England because, from circumstances, he found more encouragement there to carry out his ideas, from the fact of Great Britain's position in the world and her imperial policy, which required the extension of cable communications. The importance of keeping Great Britain in touch in a news sense with the outlying world, and with her colonies and dependencies, and conversely, to keep them in touch with England, was realized by the British Government, which found means to make it feasible for Reuter to undertake this function. In those circumstances, for a Government to give preferential treatment, in the form of low telegraph tolls or any other indirect encouragement, would be, it seems to us, entirely legitimate; and if in return, or by way of compensation, a news service would agree to transmit for publication certain official matter, and certain news which the Government desired to have widely published, it would seem to be equally legitimate. Baron de Reuter, the elder, actually promoted a number of cable telegraph companies, and was instrumental in the promotion of others. We never have had any idea that the British Government pays over so much a month, or year, to subsidize Reuter. If a Government wanted to subsidize a news service, it would not use a method so clumsy as that. Such expenditure would appear in budgets and, as Mr. Cox says, would be the subject of inquiries in Parliaments. No! if a Government wanted to subsidize (or assist is a better word) a news service, the assistance would be given in the form of a transaction for value received on both sides—or, if secrecy was desired, most Governments have a fund which can be drawn upon without making any public accounting for its disbursements. We do not wish to intimate that Reuter gets support by that method, for it has long since passed the point where it needs such support; but other news services and publicity propaganda do receive support from such funds. Nor is such support entirely illegitimate. Let us consider the matter. We will not trace further the origins of Reuter and the means (partly business acumen and skill, and partly official encouragement) by which it has been brought to its present status, but will take this status as it exists to-day. Whatever view may be taken as to how Reuter is able to do it, and is induced to do it, the fact remains that Reuter does function as we have stated—that when occasion requires it does give a coloring to the news carried by it, in favor of British official viewpoint.

"Let us, in demonstrating this, get away from this war, where the one-sidedness of the various news services is apparent. Take, for instance, the argument between Great Britain and the United States about the Panama Canal tolls. In the course of a good deal of news about that subject, brought to this part of the world during the many months it was to the fore, Reuter almost invariably carried nothing except what presented the British viewpoint favorably. If a British official statement was made in Parliament, Reuter would let us know about it; but contrary arguments raised in Congress were almost entirely ignored, or presented in a depreciatory way. If a symposium of American press opinion was cabled, it would be composed of comment favoring the British viewpoint. We could multiply this example by thousands. Among people who read the news intelligently these things are common knowledge. How, in broader political matters, this coloring is communicated to Reuter we do not know—it may be by arrangement between Reuter and the Government, or it may be by the power of mental suggestion conveyed in various subtle ways. That it is done is certain, and, as we wrote previously, the proof of it is in the published record of the service back through the decades of its existence.

"Now suppose that other Governments take note of this matter, and of the function which Reuter performs in relation to British Imperial policy, and discover in many affairs of importance that they (the other Governments) are being obstructed by such a condition, and want to get equal or fair representation in world-wide publicity. How will they go about it? It has not been feasible for the press of itself to change all these conditions. As Mr. Cox points out, most newspapers served by Reuter in the foreign field are British newspapers, published to serve communities largely British in interest and sympathies, which accounts for the news being chiefly British. We know that many British newspapers have at times been very dissatisfied with the Reuter service, and have sought for ways and means to replace it, but without success for these reasons: Most newspapers in the foreign field cannot afford much expense for telegraph news, and must get what they print cheaply to be able to afford it at all. By reason of its organization and connections, and the help it has had in the past Reuter now can supply a service more cheaply than any opposition service (British or otherwise) can. Thus a condition has been created that, in effect, gives Reuter a practical monopoly, by debarring opposition. In this situation, it is not necessary for the British Government, in case it desires to influence Reuter, to subsidize it now; for it would be easy for the Government to establish ways and means that would allow opposition services to compete with Reuter, and this gives it a leverage on Reuter. Some may say: 'But that would not apply to other Governments, and to other than British news services. Why don't they break into the game?'

Let us take conditions as they are—as they have grown, so to speak. What chance would an American service, let us say, have to compete with Reuter in this field? There is only one daily newspaper in China edited by Americans and sympathetically to America—the 'China Press.' Apart from Manila papers, and the 'Japan Advertiser,' there is none other in this part of the world, or east of Suez. An American news service to the press east of Suez would, under present conditions, cost probably twice or three times as much as Reuter now delivers an equal service (in amount) for. To start an American service would therefore require a large outlay to get it established and recognized, and entail a period of financial loss. If it was started, would the newspapers subscribe to it? We have shown that most newspapers east of Suez cannot afford two services, and that nearly all of them are British papers, or papers edited by British subjects. By all the newspapers, or all that can afford any service, taking Reuter, the cost of it is distributed so that it does not fall heavily on any one paper. If an American service was offered to these papers, what would the editors say? Some would say truthfully: 'We can't afford it.' Others would say: 'We are taking Reuter's service, and can't afford two. We are not satisfied entirely with Reuter, but we are a British newspaper and can't cut it out for a foreign news service. Our readers would not like that.' The end would be that the American news service could get probably not more than two or three subscribers east of Suez, which would make it impossible as a business proposition. There would be only one way for an American service to get a foothold, and that would be for some entity to supply the deficit between the cost of delivering the service, and the revenue which could be obtained for it. Under conditions as they exist in the world now, the only entity that can and will make up such a deficiency is a Government. So we see how government support, in some form, is necessary if German, American or any other national interests, political and commercial, are now to get equal pub-

Part of the buildings and grounds of Peking University, an American
school. Christian mission work and influence are threatened by
Japan's policy in China

licity in telegraph news published throughout the world.
Japan took a leaf out of England's (or Reuter's) book, and
organized the Koksai. Reuter sized up the situation in Japan,
and decided that rather than have to compete with the Koksai
outside of Japan, and in Japan, it would make a deal with
it—which was done. There is no way existing whereby the
American Government can promote publicity, except by official
utterance; for the Government has no appropriation that can
be used for that purpose, and such practices are contrary to
American custom and ideas. Yet something must be done to
equalize this matter, in respect to the United States, unless
American policy and interests are to continue to suffer detriments and dangers which present conditions create. . . . As
pointed an instance as one could wish for, to demonstrate the
pernicious influence of political motives upon international
news services, is found in a Reuter telegram dated at Tokio,
and published in the local newspapers last Sunday and Mon-
day. This telegram recounts a systematic effort in Japan to
arouse 'intense feeling against America in Japan by means of
publications in the Japanese press.' The method employed
was to publish alleged interviews with American public men
making them express sentiments hostile to Japan, and giving
the idea that the United States expects war with Japan about
Japan's actions in China. Along toward the end of the despatch is found its chief purpose, or 'kick,' in an intimation
that the spurious information was provided to the Japanese
press by Germans, the idea being that Germany is trying to
stir up bitter feeling between Japan and the United States.
It is hard to conceive a more poisonous news telegram than that
one. Veiled behind its information about anti-American propaganda in the Japanese press, are a number of suggestions
bearing directly on Japan's national policy and contemporary
expressions of that policy. This discovery by the Koksai (for
Reuter is only the transmitter of the telegram) of a propaganda in Japan to arouse feeling against America, and to instil
among the people an idea that there is a conflict of national

interests between Japan and the United States that will lead
to war, is interesting coming just now. This propaganda has
been going on for years, following the general course adopted
to stir up anti-Russian sentiment a dozen or so years ago as a
precedent to the Russo-Japanese War, and even has appeared
in school instruction. It is winked at, even subtly instigated
by the Government, which could have stopped it instantly
had it wanted to. The propaganda recently has begun to
attract attention outside of Japan, and consequently no longer
can be carried on *sub rosa*. Now some news about it is given
out for publication broadcast, for the purpose of conveying
the following intimations, which are cleverly insinuated in the
Koksai-Reuter despatch: (a) That the anti-American propaganda in Japan is instigated by Germany. (b) That the Japanese people are becoming hostile toward America because they
fear that America will interpose in behalf of China, to obstruct
Japan's policy in China. (c) That efforts made to prevent
Japan from carrying on as she likes in China are likely to
embroil any nation making such efforts in China's behalf with
Japan. (d) That representations and publications exposing
Japan's actions in China now, in connection with her interference in the European War, tend to embroil the United States
and Japan, and therefore that (e) The United States should
be very cautious about how it tries to advise and assist China
in resisting Japan's aggressions, and that (f) China by opposing Japan's repeated and progressive violations of her neutrality, is trying to involve the United States in war with
Japan, and (g) That efforts made by the United States to
protect China's integrity in this case, amount to action in favor
of Germany, and consequently is interfering in the war. That
is a pretty good lump of politics to encompass in a short news
telegram, without mentioning any of the chief matters directly.
Reuter will sprinkle it through the press, English and vernacular, east of Suez, and carry it to London, where it will be
picked up by American correspondents and services and passed
along. That is the system we object to in the existing rela-

tions of theoretically impartial news services to international intelligence.''

Applications of European publicity propaganda in the United States were pretty thoroughly exposed during the course of the Great War. The ramifications of Japan's propaganda, in the far East and in America, are not less significant and interesting. Japan's organized propaganda which relates to the United States includes the following:

In China. From ten to twenty Chinese vernacular newspapers, and several Japanese and English newspapers; close and continuous telegraph news connections; a thorough system of espionage; numerous political intriguers, or *provocateurs*.

In Japan. A system of press control which gives the Government power to regulate Japanese public opinion about important political questions; a semi-official news agency which serves newspapers in Japan with foreign news, and which dispenses news in foreign countries; various organizations of Japanese, and foreigners, through which propaganda designed to reach America is disseminated, and important foreign visitors are imbued with Japan's point of view, and prevented from getting contrary information.

In the United States. News services and publications through which Japan's point of view is distributed, and opposite arguments and facts disputed; various American organizations which directly and indirectly serve the same purposes.

Even in peace a strict press censorship is enforced in Japan, which especially applies to news and comments which touch Japan's foreign relations. On September 16, 1914, what is called a ''super-censorship'' was put into effect. Of this super-censorship the ''Japan Financial and Economic Monthly'' of October, 1914, said: ''As to the method of procedure, it was provided that the despatches or news or comments which have reference to foreign policy cannot be published without first submitting them to the approval of the Foreign Ministry.'' This regulation should be remembered in reading utterances of the Japanese press which I quote in this book. Japanese public opinion about foreign affairs is, therefore, nearly what the Government wants it to be, and any general trend of publicity in Japan, which extends over a period of time and sustains an evident continuity, must be taken as being permitted, if not actually inspired, by the Government. For several years before the war against Russia, the Japanese vernacular press conducted a systematic and steady campaign to arouse popular indignation and hostility to Russia. For about five years, now, there has been a similar campaign in the Japanese vernacular press against the United States. On this matter I will quote the Japan correspondent of the "Morning Post" (London), printed in that newspaper on April 4, 1915 (my italics).

For some time now the vernacular press of Japan has been engaged in an agitation of grievances against the United States. The tendency *was strongly in evidence before the outbreak of war in Europe;* on the commencement of Japan's hostilities with Germany, it grew more virulent, as it was thought that America was going to favor Germany, but that position hastily proving untenable, there was and is a reversal to repeating accusations of discriminations and injustice in regard to the treatment of Japanese in California. At one time the attitude of the vernacular press became so alarming that Americans in Japan could not refrain from appealing to the authorities to impose some restraint on so unwonted an outburst; and after this there was some abatement of the tirade; but complaint against alleged American injustice to Japanese still continues in force, and the time has come to ask what it means.

One thing certain is that the American method of remedying the situation has proved futile. This has consisted chiefly in sending men of importance on deputations to Japan to tell the people how friendly Americans are towards Japan. The Japanese have little confidence in talk, and are seldom or never influenced by it. With them speech is silver, but action is golden. As the visitor usually knows little or nothing about the genius of Japanese civilization he probably says as many things which displease as please his hearers. It is an almost impossible task for him to recommend his own civilization and its democratic institutions without indirectly condemning those of the people he is addressing. In many cases the good he does is wholly incommensurate with the time, trouble and expense taken. This is well suggested by the "Kokumin," a leading Tokio daily, when it says: "We doubt if relations between the two nations can in any way be improved by merely shaking hands and exchanging cordial compliments." The paper then goes on to warn these American deputations that friendship between the two countries cannot be permanent so long as Japanese do not receive in the United States treatment equal to that accorded Europeans.

What seems lamentably lacking in the Japanese press is a desire to face the facts of the case and state the whole truth. By this attitude the weight of opprobrium is placed on the United States, and Japan is given a clean bill. America cannot thus continue to be held up before the people of Japan to apprehension and resentment without greatly prejudicing relations between the two countries.

A majority of the leading vernacular publications in Japan are owned or influenced by leading statesmen, officials, and corporations, and consequently are presumed to reflect their views about national questions. For a long time what was published about foreign countries in the Japanese press attracted little attention among foreigners, who had not then come to realize the significance of such comments; but within the last fews years this has changed. Nowadays, when it is desired to put into circulation any particularly damaging, untrue, and libelous report about a foreign nation or Government, the usual method is to employ one of Japan's numerous publications abroad. If publicity is wanted in the far East, some publication in China frequently is used. For instance, soon after Japan declared war against Germany, a report was published in the "Fengtien Daily News" on August 9, 1914, that an American fleet had been despatched to the far East to protect China against Japan. Japan's vernacular organs in China spread this report, and caused some excitement among Chinese. The report was telegraphed to Tokio, and for a while it served as a topic for bitter editorial criticism of the United States. When denial was made by the United States, the Japanese press had to drop the matter; and it then sidestepped responsibility by charging the origin of the report to Germany. The facts seem to be that the report originated

in Japan, with the purpose of using it for all it was worth to
stir up popular feeling there against America, then accuse
Germany of inciting it; thus making it serve the various purposes of further stimulating Japanese resentment against America, rousing American resentment against Germany, and warning Chinese against alleged German and American intrigues. I
could give scores of similar recent instances, a noteworthy one
being the publication in Japanese newspapers of an alleged
speech made at Peking by Admiral Cowles, then commanding
the American Asiatic squadron, warning China against Japan.
Admiral Cowles made no such statement. One feature of this
anti-American agitation in Japan is, I believe, unique. It
dates from the Portsmouth treaty, when, as is popularly believed, President Roosevelt took part in securing peace between
Japan and Russia. Behind the scenes it was well understood
that the Japanese Government was anxious for peace at that
time, although assuming the attitude of victors, and that Mr.
Roosevelt's activity was in the nature of coming to Japan's assistance diplomatically, although not so partizanly intended.
But the peace terms were very disappointing to the Japanese
people, who had been led by their press and Government to
expect something different; and a consequence was that the
meddling of the United States was blamed for robbing Japan
of substantial fruits of victory. The Japanese Government
knew the truth, yet, with ample means and opportunity to do
so, it did not counteract this popular impression, which obtains
to this day, nourished among other sources for the prevailing
dislike of America among Japanese.

Another form of propaganda which Japan finds very useful
is conducted through Americans in the employ of the Japanese
Government, through American organizations in Japan, and
organizations in America that have actual or sentimental associations with Japan. Most Americans who consciously or un-
consciously lend themselves to this practice are animated by
sincere motives, I do not doubt; but the method should be
ventilated and its effects exposed. As an apt instance I will

take the American Peace Society of Japan. This society is one of the innumerable offshoots of the pacifist movement. I don't know its exact origin, and it is hardly worth while to investigate here; but apparently it sprang from a suggestion that such an organization might serve to reduce irritations between Japan and the United States by (I am heartily sick of this phrase, which accompanies nearly all propaganda designed to prevent people in America from learning the truth about Japan, but it fits here) "clearing away misconceptions." About certain activities of the American Peace Society of Japan, I will quote the "Japan Chronicle" (British) of December 21, 1915. The editor was discussing the annual meeting and report of the Society.

In this connection we note that the American Peace Society of Japan has appointed a committee to prepare a resolution appealing to the American people to withstand the forces which, if unchecked, will further tend toward the development of militarism. The protest will have widespread sympathy, but it will not solve the question as to what steps the United States must take to protect the shores of America against possible hostile action. It is, however, with the relations between Japan and the United States that the American Peace Society is most concerned. It says: "We have still to be even more vigilant to see that we are not misunderstood here, and that our fellow countrymen at home do not misjudge Japan." Both of these are worthy objects, but the policy of the society would seem to be represented by Dr. S. L. Gulick, who is, we observe, a member of the committee, and whose method is confined to justifying the policy of Japan. At its annual meeting the society endorsed a resolution appealing to the Congress of the United States to adopt an immigration policy based on the just and equitable treatment of all races. Nothing could be more correct. Yet the resistance of California to the immigration of Asiatics has some reason behind it as well as unreason, exactly as is the case with the Japanese objection to the unrestricted immigration of Chinese labor into this country. The American Peace Society would, it seems to us, be doing a good work if it endeavored to explain the valid reason of the American objection to cheap labor by citing the objections naturally felt in Japan to the incursion of cheap labor from China. . . . The barrier in America against Asiatic immigration and in Japan against Chinese immigration may fall as soon as the standards of living in the different countries begin to approximate.

We observe that the president in the course of his speech severely censured an unnamed American resident in Japan for continually furnishing "misinformation" to American papers, giving as an example "pretending to give them an accurate translation of an unimportant Japanese book with a high-sounding title purporting to have the approval of the leading men in Government circles in Japan." . . . The fact remains that the book to which we understand reference is made, like "The Next War," which has recently been summarized in our columns, does represent a strong body of opinion in this country, and has a large circulation. . . . Clearly there is some incongruity in the American Peace Society of Japan deploring the increase of armaments in the United States while being absolutely silent on the expansion of the Japanese army this year by two divisions, and the impending program for the enlargement of the Japanese navy. . . . It is curious, indeed, that even the Japan Peace Society, which numbers Japanese as well as foreigners among its members, and has as its president Count Okuma, never seems to consider it essential to oppose the expansion of armaments in Japan or to deprecate the chauvinism so often exhibited in Japanese newspapers and public statements. So far as we have observed, the Japan Peace Society has never passed a single resolution against the enlargement of the Japanese army or the increase of the navy, nor has it uttered a word in depreciation of the hostile action which the Government is often urged to take against China. It seems to be chiefly concerned in the attitude of other countries toward Japan, especially of America, the dangers of militarism and armaments in this country being wholly ignored. Again, the Japan Society of America, also concerned in the maintenance of good relations between Japan and the United States, some time ago published a "Symposium of Papers by Political Leaders and Representative Citizens of Japan on the Relations Between Japan and the United States." Some of the declarations in that book are of the most chauvinistic nature. Mr. Takekoshi, a journalist and M.P., says that "Korea exists now for Japan, from the viewpoint of Imperial policy," and demands the development of Manchuria also. Another prominent journalist in an article entitled "Centripetal Mikadoism," shows himself a flamboyant Imperialist. The Japanese editor of the book tilts against American missionaries in Japan. . . . If it is incumbent on the American Peace Society of Japan to censure a particular American for translating into English a Japanese jingo publication, why should not such writing as that referred to above, prepared for American consumption, be equally condemned? A peace society in Japan which concentrates all its attention on menaces to peace abroad while ignoring those at its own doors may be adopting a very prudent policy, but it is not contributing much to the cause of international good will.

It is increasingly evident that organizations like the American Peace Society of Japan and similar societies in America, such as the Japan Society, under the guise of working for peace and better understanding, are being used by Japan to propagate an insidious form of mendacity—the mendacity of suppression. The actions and work of these societies have no effect upon the policy of Japan, or to make the Japanese masses understand American viewpoint, or to check the rapid development of Japan's militarism, or toward repressing Japan's remarkable naval and military preparations. The only noticeable influence they have exerted is deterrently upon the policy of the United States, and to retard naval and military preparedness by America, by a continuous and systematic obscuring and misrepresentation of facts about Japan which show the aggressive ideals and purposes and preparations of that nation. The "Far East" (Tokio) in its issue of July 17, 1915, said: "It must not be forgotten that to-day the peace movement, so well represented in Japan, is a heavily subsidized movement led by men who are paid for the work they do. But while in Japan there is a Government absolutely indifferent to the efforts of the pacifists, in America their views have seriously influenced the administration." And in its issue of July 24, 1915, the "Far East" said: "According to the Tokio papers, the Japan Peace Association, of which Count Okuma is the president, and the American Peace Society in Japan have a scheme under consideration to establish an organ for the publication of various communications exchanged between Japan and America for the purpose of acquainting the people of each country with the conditions of the other with a view of allaying the anti-Japanese sentiments prevalent in America. According to the scheme, the agency will be established with a capital of yen 500,000, borne equally by the two parties," etc. In the purposes of this scheme nothing was said about allaying anti-American agitation in Japan, which was then in full swing. Any who are acquainted with conditions know that such a plan could be financed, on the Japanese side, only by the Government. On the American side, it might be supported out of some of the various funds, and "foundations" that work for peace. The chief practical effects of this propaganda are to prevent *Americans* from comprehending the difficulties and dangers involved in relations with Japan, and to obstruct the provision of means to meet them.

CHAPTER XII

JAPAN'S MODERN WORLD POLICY

Basis of Japan's diplomacy—Key to her world policy—Its major objectives—Wars fought to secure them—The China-Japan War—Results to Japan—The Russo-Japanese War—Its results to Japan—Development of a new phase—The emigration issue with America—New situation created—The deadlock and its outlook—The Great War—Japan and her allies—Looking for compensations—Japan's military strength—Plan to isolate the United States—Rapprochement with Russia—Directed at America—Putting on the soft-pedal—Japan's cards—Cards in America's hand—Japan waiting on events.

IN an article published in "Shin Nijon" (May, 1915), Count Okuma wrote: "Diplomacy, to be really effective and successful, must be backed up by sufficient national strength. It is only ten or fifteen years since Japanese diplomacy began to carry weight with foreign countries, and it began from the time that Western Powers commenced to recognize Japan's military strength."

That utterance of the Premier of Japan has a two-edged significance—it defines authoritatively the period within which Japan's world policy was born, in the modern diplomatic sense; and it shows that Japan's leading statesmen frankly recognize that the nation's military and naval strength constitutes its sole practical title to a seat at the great council of nations. On that point Japan has no illusions. Her leaders are not deceived about the source of a nation's diplomatic influence; they know whence is derived the driving-power behind Japan's expansion and growth of international prestige. They know, too, that they must depend on that same driving-power to carry forward Japan's policies hereafter.

Since the world policy of Japan, in so far as it has progressed, was and still is predicated on military and naval force, it is evident that in the key to that policy lies much of interest to nations that have irritating contacts with her. Use of the sword, or threat to use it, has brought almost every national advantage dependent on foreign relations, as Japan reckons advantage, that has accrued to the nation since it emerged from its cocoon of isolation. No wonder, then, that Japan believes in the sword as a fundamental factor in her national rise, and trusts chiefly to it for the attainment of still wider ambitions. And in this belief, Japan is correct; for her wider ambitions are of a character that they can be gained only by the sword— by its use in war, or by using it to intimidate, or by getting its trade value in some politico-military balance of power. What are Japan's wider ambitions? In a true answer to this question lies one of America's most pressing and important international problems.

Japan's national ambitions, as they have developed within the fifteen-year period indicated by Count Okuma in the quotation given, have only two main branches, although each branch has collateral issues. These main branches are:

1. To obtain the hegemony of eastern Asia and the Pacific Ocean.

2. To open a way for Japanese immigration to the Western Hemisphere.

By way of pursuing the first and primary object, Japan has fought two wars within twenty years, and is now (1916) participating in a third war. Her war against China (1894) was something of a disappointment in its immediate results, for the European Powers coerced her to abandon Port Arthur and to respect the independence of Korea, and to accept in lieu thereof a money indemnity. Her war against Russia (1904–5) more than recouped those repulses, for out of it Japan has annexed Korea, occupied south Manchuria and inner Mongolia, and regained Port Arthur. Ten years later came the great European War, which presented an unexpected opportunity for Japan. Japan never has been for long discouraged by rebuffs. She bided her time, and never abandoned her ultimate purpose. She acquiesced with what grace she could assume in the outcome of her war with China, when compelled to yield to a combination of Powers. "I was not strong enough," Japan figuratively said to herself, "but wait." She had, however, shown enough military strength in that war to get an alliance with Great Britain in the far East, whose foreign policy then was to obstruct Russia everywhere; and so another ten years found Japan able to attack Russia, which Power was then her immediate obstacle.

The second main branch of Japan's world policy grew out of certain developments of her partial success in the primary one. Japan's rise and modernization had caused economic and sociological changes within her own boundaries, and among the fruits of these changes was a great acceleration of increase of population. These phenomena had been observed before the Russo-Japanese War, but at that time a theory was widely entertained that Asia would provide a suitable field for Japanese colonization, while at the same time Japanese domination of China politically and commercially might enable Japan to develop and regulate her own industries, and in that way take care of her swelling millions. Japan now sees that, for a long time to come, Japanese industry cannot forge ahead in the markets of China, in competition with Western products, except by having exclusive preferential facilities and position there; and while so retarded, Japan's home industries do not expand as was hoped. Moreover, one powerful factor apparently was then overlooked, or underestimated—an impulse of Japanese across the Pacific rather than to the mainland of Asia, and the new contacts that would bring.

In both main branches of Japan's world policy, the United States always has taken an important place. America's fundamental interest in the fate of China is perfectly understood by the statesmen of Japan, even if it is but vaguely comprehended by most Americans. American statesmen of a past period had consistently recognized this condition, and it eventually was made a cardinal principle of American foreign policy as formulated by the Hay Doctrine. But Japanese statesmen knew the uncertain nature of the foreign policy of the United States, and the vitiating effects of extreme pacifist doctrines upon it; and they hoped by degrees to undermine the Hay Doctrine, and establish Japan's paramountcy in China, without coming to strife with America. That was the thesis of Japan's conception of the relation of the United States to her world policy up to a few years ago, when the failure of Japanese colonization in Asia was perceived at Tokio, and was followed by a realization that Japan's complete ambitions could not be accomplished without a field for expansion on the Western Hemisphere.

The full effects of these developments were not at once comprehended at Tokio. This is shown in discussions by the Japanese press, and utterances of eminent Japanese statesmen, extending over a period of years. It is only quite recently that the ultimate meaning to Japan of this new condition has been faced, and the national diplomacy and strength shaped to meet the situation. In doing this, the secondary object of Japan's world policy has been given priority of the primary object—not priority of purpose, but of accomplishment. In other words, Japanese statesmanship has come to believe that, in the order of doing, establishment of the undisputed equality of Japanese on the Western Hemisphere should take precedence of Japan's completion of her domination of China, and is a necessary antecedent to her full domination of China. Just as it was necessary, in turn, for Japan to demonstrate her military superiority over China, and then her superiority over Russia in the far East, as steps toward her goal, so it is next necessary for Japan to demonstrate her military superiority over the United States in the far East. Having in the period following the war with Russia consolidated her enhanced international position, and made good her gains, Japan bent her energy to preparing for the next move. The emigration question with America had drifted up obliquely, and rather unexpectedly; but it did not take the Japanese Government long to realize that until that and its connected issues are disposed of, in a manner favorable to Japan, and Japan has given a practical demonstration of her power to enforce her policies in China as against America, the position which Japan has gained in the far East will not be secure, and her freedom of movement and scope in the sphere she has marked for her own will be dangerously circumscribed.

That the Japanese Government recognized this condition before the great European War commenced, is shown conclusively by its action in May, 1914, in officially closing the diplomatic correspondence with the United States relating to the immigration questions, and unmistakably announcing that while it seemed useless to prolong the negotiations then, Japan was by no means satisfied and would reopen the question at a convenient time. It was Japan that then caused publication of the status of this question, as is revealed by official correspondence between the Governments; [1] yet that tremendously significant action hardly caused a ripple of interest in America where, under Mr. Bryan's administration of the State Department, the soft-pedal was put on the incident and the American public kept partly in the dark. That theory of dealing with the nation's irritating foreign affairs had full sway during Mr. Bryan's administration, his belief apparently being that public discussion of such matters tended to increase friction. The method has also, it may be pointed out, the convenience of temporarily concealing incompetence of the State Department in the conduct of foreign affairs, and its mistakes, and any sacrifices of national interests from its errors or timidity. On the other hand, the Japanese Government, contrary to its usual course, gave its action wide publicity in Japan, and some language used in the Diet was almost menacing toward America. On January 21, 1915, replying to an interpellation in the Japanese Diet, Baron Kato, minister for foreign affairs, said: "The Imperial Government have found the replies of the American Government not at all satis-

[1] Appendix X.

factory and recognizes the necessity of elaborating other plans for the solution of the pending questions. As regards the nature of these plans, the time to report them has not, to our regret, arrived.'' That is remarkably plain language for a responsible minister to use. Baron Kato plainly intimated that diplomacy had failed to obtain satisfaction from the United States, and consequently ''other plans'' must be adopted to obtain satisfaction for Japan, but ''to our regret'' these plans were not ready to put into operation. Usually in international disputes, it is understood that when diplomacy fails to adjust them there is but one other resource, unless one side recedes —a resort to force. This is recognized by many prominent Japanese publicists as applying to the existing Japan-America situation. In a lecture delivered at Tokio in September, 1915, Mr. Ryuji Nagashima, son-in-law of Marquis Katsura, said: ''If Japan desires to solve the question with America fundamentally, the only way would be to resort to war.''

Soon after Japan broke off negotiations with America on the emigration question, came the tremendous diversion of the Great War, which for the time distracted Japan's attention from America and concentrated it on the opportunity opened in China. Within eight months after war commenced, Japan was in possession of all its ''spoils'' that had changed hands in the far East and the north Pacific Ocean. She promised to restore Kiaochou to China, but that was promptly repudiated when the course of events showed Japan how completely she had the whiphand in that region. As none except ignorant persons and a pro-Japanese pacifist group in America ever had credited Japan's promises about restoring Kiaochou, this caused no new complication.

At that point, Japan paused and again took stock of the situation. She had entered the war as an opportunist, and that thought still controlled her policy. Meanwhile, there had been suggestions that Japan would extend her participation to the extent of sending troops to fight for the Allies in Europe. This project was mentioned in the Diet, in Parliament, and in

Hackett Medical College for women at Canton, an American school. Students playing basket-ball

David Gregg Hospital at Canton, an American mission

the French Chamber of Deputies, where it took the form of a proposal to compensate Japan by ceding to her a part of French Indo-China. This proposal obtained some favor; but it was nipped in the bud by the French Government, which is believed to have taken the position that at that time France was doing her utmost to sustain the war, and that not until all her allies had done the same would the time be opportune to discuss any cessions of French territory. Japan also was not especially attracted by that proposal, although to replace France and French influence in Asia and southern China is included in the scope of her tentative ambitions. Japan had entered the war for her own advantage exclusively, and her every move would be influenced by no other consideration. At that point, Japanese statesmen deliberated, and tried to figure out what else Japan could get out of the war. There were certain things her allies could offer—or promise. Some of those things Japan knew that she did not care much about. Other things she does care about, but she was not sure that the Allies could deliver the goods, except on paper. The only tangible asset to Japan which the Allies could reasonably promise is a free scope for Japan in China, and their confirmation of what Japan has seized there—except? Except what? The Allies might secretly agree that in the event of Japan going to war against the United States they would not take sides against her. In considering a possible war with the United States, the neutrality of Europe is all that Japan hopes or expects to get. Japan has no doubt whatever of her ability to defeat the United States in a war between these nations now, if not wholly at least sufficiently to secure part of what she wants, and to advance another step toward her ultimate object. Japan's war experiences have taught her not to expect to gain everything by a single war; she must advance a step at a time. In a war against the United States at this period, Japan would not expect to gain too much. She would be satisfied with stripping America of its Pacific possessions, giving the Hay Doctrine in China its final *coup*, and forcing open a free path for Japanese colonization in Central and South Americas. Japan is confident, as between Japan and the United States, that she can accomplish those things. It should be understood that, in this question, it is not the Americans' estimate of themselves that is conclusive, but it is *Japan's estimate of herself and America* that will determine her attitude and course. Japan's estimate of her own superior strength in comparison with America has much expert foreign support. Writing in 1915 about the military and strategical situation in the far East, the military correspondent of the London "Times" stated:

The supreme advantage possessed by Japan as a military Power is that, thanks to national service, her home territory is unassailable, not only by any single enemy, but by any reasonable or unreasonable combination of enemies. Her navy is sufficiently formidable to deter any Power except England from the idea of attacking her in her home waters, and her two fighting services in combination, joined with her geographical position, assure her a dominant position in the far East. Nothing but the military regeneration of China or the United States seems likely to deprive her of this privileged position, and to talk to a Japanese of such possibilities only provokes a smile.

Japan is already twice as powerful as when she challenged Russia in arms. She intends to be thrice as powerful, and nothing but an internal cataclysm or some internal convulsion, of which there is yet no symptom, or scarcely one, can prevent her from becoming so. The weight of her numbers, the excellence of her organization, the adequacy of her armament, the skill of her staff, the science of her officers, and the splendid spirit which animates not only the army and navy, but the whole nation, have no exact counterpart, whether in the Old World or the New. Were these mighty forces ever employed upon aggressive war, Japan would shake Asia to her foundations.

Thus not Japan only, but English and European military experts also, class the United States with China in military impotency, not exactly in present comparative strength and potentialities, but in respect to those factors and the inner forces and tendencies of national existence. Japan's military and naval staffs are confident that if a situation can be brought about depriving the United States of aid and moral

support from Europe, and freeing Japan from outside interference or menace, she will in a few years be in a position
safely to challenge America at arms.

This contingency provided Japan's chief reason for making
a new agreement or understanding with Russia, in 1916.   The
exact terms and conditions of this agreement are still a diplomatic secret between Japan and Russia, there being indications that even the Powers allied with them in the war were not
fully informed.   Some loose ends of the contacts of Russia
and Japan in Manchuria and inner Mongolia are elucidated, by
way of giving a reason for the negotiations.   But there is
no doubt that other and far more important considerations
were involved, including Japan's part in supplying Russia
with war munitions and similar functions.   This broader intent and scope of the understanding was plainly revealed by
evidently inspired comments, at that time, of the Japanese and
Russian press, and from other critical sources.   The "Morning Post" (London) published on February 2, 1915, an analysis of this rapprochement from its special correspondent at
Tokio, which among other things said: "The Japanese press
is full of the subject of the proposed Russo-Japanese alliance.
A very significant aspect of the alliance proposed is that it is
not merely for mutual protection in the far East, but *is aimed
particularly at a third party*.   Such is the assertion of the
Japanese vernacular press.   Who the third party is need not
now be guessed, though such a diversion would be easy."   The
"Japan Monthly" a little later commented thus: "Leading
Japanese papers and publicists continue warmly to advocate
an alliance with Russia . . . Mr. Shimada, Japan's leading
orator says: 'There is no reason why Japan should not enter
into an alliance with Russia.'   As the alliance should not only
be for protection of mutual interests, *but have a third party as
its objective*, it might be better, thinks Mr. Shimada, to hold
it in abeyance for the present, so as to avoid creating misapprehension."   In less responsible quarters there was no pretense of concealing the identity of the "third party" against

which, in Japanese minds, the proposed alliance is directed
—the United States. For about two months in the first part
of 1915 the vernacular press in Japan was filled with this kind
of comment and criticism, which also had reflections in the
Russian press. Then, suddenly, the official muffler was put
upon such comment in Japan by the censorship; which meant
that the Japanese Government, having given publicity freedom to implant in the popular mind the desired ideas, realized
the expediency of putting a restraint on the discussion before
it excited too much uneasiness and suspicion in America. The
tone of these criticisms was attracting attention in England
too. From that time, a more reticent policy was pursued regarding the Russo-Japanese rapprochement, in both those
countries. Russia also realized that a spectacular rapprochement with Japan, coupled with interpretations which were
given to it in Japan, might react adversely on relations between
Russia and the United States. While it can be assumed that
Russia is indifferent, or at least will not worry if Japan should
give America a set-back in China and the Pacific, Russia has
no compelling reason for desiring that to happen. Russia
faces the probable necessity or desirability, after the war, of
revising her commerce and finance to throw off the influence
of Germany, and in that eventuality friendly relations with
America are important, perhaps essential. Probably it was
this contingency that caused the Duma, some months later,
to utter an implied warning to Japan that the new rapprochement, whatever its terms, must not be construed to involve
Russia in frictions between Japan and the United States, or
as arraying Russia against the United States. It is interesting
to note that that position of Russia was made public, doubtless
for the impression it would make in America, after the American financial and commercial world had begun to notice certain aspects of Russo-Japanese relations and their possible application to America. While the soft-pedal was put on frank
discussion of certain phases of the new rapprochement in
Japan and Russia, the work of formulating the rapprochement

in those countries proceeded. Russia sent late in 1915 the Grand Duke Mikhailovitch as a special envoy to Japan, where he was received with unusual honors. Japanese press comment and criticism on that occasion, having been cautioned, were restrained, but the Japanese populace placed the construction on the visit for which the previous publicity had prepared them.

Whatever ideas about this matter may thus have been inculcated with the Japanese middle and lower classes, it is probable that the Japanese Government expects no belligerent help from Russia in the event of war between Japan and the United States; but Japan does want to feel, and perhaps now does feel, that Russia will not take such an occasion to attack Japan in Manchuria. With that possibility pending, Japan could not risk war with America. Until very recently Japan has felt confident that the United States would remain indefinitely under the influence of the extreme pacifists, and that America will not seriously and adequately face its position in the world, and provide the military and naval forces to protect it. But in events of the years 1915–16 are portents which qualify that view and which, joined with other doubtful elements produced by the Great War, give Japan pause. If it is assumed that Japan succeeds in trading with her allies of the Great War (in so far as those Powers can influence events) to have a free hand in China, and makes a division of spoils with Russia in the far East that relieves Japan for the next decade of fear of Russia, how would the situation stand as between Japan and the United States? In bringing her belligerent allies into line, Japan had these diplomatic cards:

(a) Russia's need for munitions.

(b) Russia will have a period of exhaustion after the war, during which she will like to safeguard her position in the far East by agreement with Japan.

(c) Russia's resentment toward America because of America's sympathy with Japan in the war of 1904, and forgetfulness of Russia's long-standing friendship for America.

(d)   The possibility that the Allies might need Japan's further help to defeat or offset Germany.

(e)   The belief strongly held among statesmen of the European Powers that the United States, because of its form of government, stage of national development, the influence of pacifism and other theories inconsistent with the practical administration of world affairs, will exert only a negligible power in international politics during the next quarter or half century, and perhaps permanently.

As opposed to those cards held by Japan (this assumes, of course that these other cards will be played, for the best hand cannot take a pot if it is laid down), the United States within the same period would have:

(f)   The fundamental interests of Great Britain and France, and all the neutral nations of Europe, are opposed to the policy of Japan in China.

(g)   China herself is opposed to Japan's policy, which menaces China's sovereignty.

(h)   Need of the Allies in Europe for munitions and financial assistance from America during the war, and for commercial and financial relations after the war.

(i)   Great Britain's integral parts—Canada, Australasia, and South Africa—are strongly hostile to Japan's paramountcy in the Pacific for the same racial and economic reasons that cause friction between Japan and the United States.

(j)   In all fundamental human and political issues contained in this problem, the interests of the white races and nations of Europe and South America coincide with the interests of the United States and China, rather than with the policy of Japan.

(k)   Japan's movement across the Pacific, if successful, will constitute a direct menace to the Central and South American nations.

(l)   Japan's financial and economic weakness subjects her to pressure that can be applied by America directly and indirectly.

(m) Russia's need after the Great War to have closer and more extensive commercial and financial relations with America.

So after Japan had forced her way into the Great War to the extent of seizing what she coveted that was within easy reach, she stopped and waited upon events. With the war tending toward a stale-mate, and a situation so complex as perhaps to deadlock Europe's far Eastern diplomacy for many years, Japan turned attention to her own ultimate objectives, and thought about the war only as it might affect them. And squarely across the path of these objectives lies the policy of the United States, which nation seems ordained by circumstances and by Japan's purpose to receive the next buffet, if America does not timidly stand aside and thereby purchase a temporary respite.

When a nation meditates an aggression or assault on another nation, it does not advertise such intention unduly. Some plain hints usually are given in favor of obtaining the object without war, and if these are ignored or misunderstood, the effort thereafter until time for the first blow to be struck is to lull suspicion and alarm, and to retard preparation by the expected enemy.

CHAPTER XIII

JAPAN AND GREAT BRITAIN

The three alliances—Their meanings analyzed—Great Britain's objects—Japan's objects—The alliances in perspective—Demonstration of events—Secret internal modifications—Application to the United States—Possibilities involved—The balance of compensations—Japan's free hand in Manchuria—Japan's disregard of British "sphere" —A turning point—Japan's aggression in China—British criticism of Japan's acts—A collision of interests—Japanese criticism of England— Further causes of friction—Japan and India—The warnings to China— Japan's irritation under British restraint.

OF external factors which influence the world policy of Japan, her relations with Great Britain probably are the most important at this stage. Technically, these relations hinge on the Anglo-Japanese alliance. Like many another treaty between nations, this alliance cannot be fully defined by its published text. There have been three alliances—the first signed in 1902, which was superseded by one signed in 1905, which in turn was amended in 1911.[1] It is interesting to quote the preamble of the first alliance (my italics).

The Governments of Great Britain and Japan, actuated solely by a desire to maintain the *status quo* and general peace in the extreme East, being moreover specially interested *in maintaining the independence and territorial integrity of the Empire of China and the Empire of Korea, and in securing equal opportunities in those countries for the commerce and industry of all nations,* hereby agree as follows:

The first alliance was preparatory to and in expectation of the Russo-Japanese War about preponderance of interest and influence between those nations in Korea and Manchuria.

[1] Appendix L.

Let us now set out the preamble of the second, and also existing agreement:

The Governments of Great Britain and Japan, being desirous of replacing the agreement concluded between them on the 30th January, 1902, by fresh stipulations, have agreed upon the following articles, which have for their object:

(a)   The consolidation and maintenance of the general peace in the regions of eastern Asia and India:

(b)   The preservation of the common interests of all Powers in China by insuring the independence and integrity of the Chinese Empire and the principle of equal opportunity for the commerce and industry of all nations in China:

(c)   The maintenance of the territorial rights of the high contracting parties in the regions of eastern Asia and of India, and the defense of their special interests in the said regions.

The situation had changed somewhat between 1902 and 1905. Japan had defeated Russia, and was in occupation of Korea and southern Manchuria. So the guarantee of Korea's independence which the first alliance contained was dropped, and a clause substituted by which Japan's right to do as she pleased there was recognized by Great Britain. The similar clause relating to China, and maintenance of the "open door" there, was retained. India also was included, for the first time, in the scope of the agreement.

The only satisfactory way of estimating the true meaning of an alliance between nations is to discover, if possible, what each of the parties wanted, and hoped to gain or secure by it. It cannot be presumed that Japan and Great Britain made an alliance, mutually obligating themselves to go to war in certain circumstances, without having strong reasons and objects for so doing. Those reasons may be differentiated as (a) Great Britain's reasons, and (b) Japan's reasons. These may be examined separately.

The primary cause for Great Britain making an alliance with Japan was the rise of Germany's commercial power into a formidable competitor with British trade, and the consequent development of a German navy, which unbalanced the naval and military situation of Europe as it affected England, and made England want to be able to concentrate her navy in home waters without thereby exposing her interests elsewhere. The deal with Japan accomplished that, and made possible the series of diplomatic manœuvers that eventually created the Triple Entente. Perhaps a desire to check Russia's progress in the far East also influenced England. Unless Great Britain had those objects, it is hard to discover any reasons which impelled her to tie up with Japan. Great Britain wanted to be free to readjust her relations in Europe to meet the rise of Germany. At that time, Great Britain also wanted to preserve China, and the "open door" doctrine there—but that was a secondary consideration, as events have proven. The phraseology of the first alliance gave preservation of the independence of Korea as one of its objects. That undoubtedly was humbug, and was inserted then because Japan intended to make the "independence of Korea" her ostensible reason for going to war against Russia. The seizure of Korea having been accomplished, this pretense was omitted from the revised alliance, for it was no longer needed—in fact, it then stood in Japan's way. The primary cause of Japan making the alliance was her determination to possess Korea, and to extend her influence and power in China. To do those things, Japan knew she must first fight and defeat Russia. The alliance with Great Britain enabled her to finance a war, and assured Japan that no other Powers would interfere.

After the publication of the second alliance, none who was posted about far Eastern affairs and diplomacy had any doubt that Japan would annex Korea—as she did. Many still thought, however, that the terms of the alliance respecting China would hold good. Events soon qualified that belief. We have the following sequence of events which reveal, at least in part, the meaning of the alliance:

1. Annexation of Korea by Japan.
2. The Fakumen and Chinchou-Aigun Railway schemes (British-American enterprises) which demonstrated that Great

Britain was committed to support Japan's paramount position in Manchuria, and her violation of the open door and integrity of China policies there.

3. The revelation, by confidential warnings to British interests and oblique representations to the United States, that Great Britain is committed to recognize and help protect Japan's paramount position in Fukien Province, and contiguous territory, and that Japan asserts such paramount position.

4. Demonstration that Great Britain is in some degree committed to support Japan's actions and policy in enforcing in Shantung Province a similar policy to that she has pursued in Manchuria.

From this it appears that the Alliance has undergone a process of secret internal modification, to suit events, until in what seemed to be its most essential features it has almost entirely gotten away from its published terms. Therefore, the published terms of the alliance can no longer be relied upon to express the meaning of the instrument, and we are driven to try to grasp that by analysis.

The first Anglo-Japanese alliance attracted little notice in America, and caused practically no apprehension. It did not seem to apply to or affect the United States, and in its guarantees of the independence of China and Korea, and the "open door" in those countries, it was in complete harmony with the American policy, as expressed by the Hay doctrine. It was welcomed as providing a further assurance of the Hay doctrine. At that time, Japan's military and naval efficiency, and her predatory ambitions, were hardly suspected in America. The second alliance did attract some attention in America, where its abandonment of Korea was noticed, and caused some misgivings as to dependence to be placed on its announced motives. When friction between Japan and the United States developed out of the California questions, it began to strike some Americans that in case of trouble between the United States and Japan, the alliance might apply. This uneasiness

led to qualifications designed to reassure America, and to make
it appear that the alliance would not bind Great Britain to
aid Japan in a war with the United States. But notwithstanding that, ever since then the alliance has been regarded with
growing distrust in America. Even before the Great War
came, to give a striking revelation of its unsuspected scope, it
was borne upon the United States Government that the alliance
did have a bearing upon the relations of the United States and
Japan, and the relations of the United States and Great Britain.
That came about in connection with the controversy between
Great Britain and America about administration of the Panama
Canal, which question was diplomatically given a connection
with the Japanese immigration issue in California. About the
same time the United States learned, in connection with the so-
called steel loan to China, that Japan claimed paramount position in Fukien and vicinity, and that she was tacitly supported
by Great Britain. Coming after the Manchuria railway incidents, that gave America another jar, and further circumscribed the application of the "open door" clause of the alliance in China.

These matters conclusively showed that the Anglo-Japanese
alliance does apply to the United States, in some circumstances. How far it does apply is still uncertain, but the fact
that it applies at all, compels the United States to look at its
relations with both those nations in a new light. It has become evident that the published terms of the alliance provide
scarcely more than a clue to its real scope and meaning. It
further is evident that its meaning is as obscure as meanings of
some European agreements were that played a part in plung-
ing the world into war. The Anglo-Japanese alliance is a real
treaty—we have concrete and indisputable evidence of this—
but those on the outside are compelled more or less to guess
at its meaning, and its scope. Taking its possible application
to the United States, it is clear that it revolutionizes hypoth-
eses that heretofore have guided America's plans and preparations for national defense and security. Those plans un-

doubtedly have included the possibility of a hostile collision
with any principal nations. But in respect to Japan and
Great Britain, plans for the defense and security of America have taken those nations separately. In a war between
the United States and Great Britain alone, Americans have
felt able to defend their country and its interests. The British navy is greatly superior in numbers to the American
navy, but as things were, Americans felt no uneasiness therefrom, for lacking a large military force, the British navy could
not inflict serious damage upon American territory, nor
threaten it with invasion: while Canada would be exposed to
invasion from the States. Moreover, by concentrating her
entire navy upon America, Great Britain would expose herself
in other directions. It always has been understood by American military and naval experts, that if the whole British navy
should be free to act against America, and had the coöperation
of a large military force, that America would be vulnerable, and
would be compelled to take new and greater measures for security and defense. For years, British writers have been
pointing out the possible danger to America consequent with
the growth of a German navy, because it could make the German army effective over-seas. European or Asiatic armies
that cannot be transported over-seas cannot invade America,
and armies cannot cross the seas for this purpose as long as
the American navy is superior to the navy of a nation it is at
war with. The principle is that America need not feel menaced
by either a superior naval or military power, but the two in
combination will make her feel uneasy and unsafe, as long as
she remains isolated and unsupported by any alliances. In a
war between the United States and Japan alone, Americans
have felt able to defend their main territories and interests,
for if the American navy has decisive superiority over the
Japanese navy, the superiority in numbers of the Japanese
army causes no alarm. But if there is a possibility of Great
Britain and Japan combining against the United States on an
issue which may arise between the United States and either of

those Powers, the whole situation is altered. In such a case, the superior Japanese army would supplement the superior British navy, and an invasion of America would be made feasible.

These considerations give America a deep concern with Anglo-Japanese relations in all their bearings. One cannot say just what Great Britain expected to pay, by way of compensation to Japan, when the first alliance was made. At that time it is probable, judging by subsequent developments, that Great Britain did not fully grasp Japan's ambitions or latent strength. There is no doubt that Great Britain expected Japan to annex Korea; and British interests in Korea, which were not extensive, had to take chances under Japanese rule in that country. Great Britain also became financial sponsor for Japan, and made it possible for Japan to go to war against Russia; but in doing that Great Britain was serving her own political advantage (as she then saw it) of checking Russia; while British financing of Japan also served to promote British trade interests in Japan, and to give British influence a leading position there. On that basis, the balance of compensations seemed fair, and Great Britain thought she was getting as much as she was giving. It was not long, however, before events showed that Japan did not intend to be contented with those compensations. She steadily pushed her position in south Manchuria. The process whereby Great Britain was induced to recognize Japan's paramount position in Manchuria, to the sacrifice of British interests in those regions, is somewhat obscure. That major British interests in the far East were not previously informed of this understanding with Japan is explicitly demonstrated by the course of the Fakumen and Chinchow-Aigun Railway projects. Great Britain's compensations for these further concessions to Japan, at the expense of British rights and prospects under the "open door," and of China's autonomy and integrity (which, by the way, was assured in the amended alliance), are not clear. British in China strongly objected to the policy of abandoning an equal position in Manchuria, but their Government gave them no satisfaction except alleged "imperial requirements." At that time it was generally assumed in the far East that in return for assenting to Japan's paramountcy in Manchuria, Japan had agreed to respect Great Britain's paramount position in the Yangtze Valley and south China. Both Japan and Great Britain, in agreements between themselves and with other Powers, had covenanted to respect the "open door" doctrine in the whole of China, and therefore they had no legal or moral right secretly to conclude arrangements that would invalidate that policy in its application to other nations. But if Great Britain's compensations were included in such a trade, actual or implied, it soon developed that Japan had no intention of respecting the British "sphere." There were evidences of this before the Great War; but it was not until Japan presented her extraordinary demands upon China, in 1915, that the full measure of her scheme to undermine British interests and position there was exposed. This action by Japan brought Anglo-Japanese relations to another turning-point, by setting the policy and interests of the two nations in almost complete opposition of purpose and interests in the far East.

Realization of this fact caused an outbreak of criticism in both countries, which the exigencies of their belligerent alliance in war could not suppress. Almost without important exception, leading British newspapers in the far East depreciated Japan's aggressions in China; and the press in England also was outspoken. The following editorial comment of the "Nation" (London), May 8, 1915, very well summarizes informed British opinion, and the strain put by Japan on the Anglo-Japanese alliance (my italics):

A neutral spectator who watched the present crisis between Japan and China from an Alpine height or a Scandinavian fiord would find in it an interesting illustration of modern Imperialism. On the one hand, he would note that the valiant little island Power, over-populated, *too rapidly industrialized, and taxed beyond the limits of endurance, has elected to invest half her revenues in armaments. It is, he would presume, a capital outlay, and its only economic justification must be conquest.* China presents herself as the predestined field. She has begun to reform herself, and after a republican revolution, is passing through a phase of consolidation and strong government. The dying Empire is always vulnerable at such a moment, for if time should be allowed it to recover, it may presently be too strong for conquest. The absorption of all the rival Powers in the European War makes the predestined moment. It will mean, our neutral would reflect, a period of violence, exploitation, and wrong, but in the end the probability is that the Chinese will profit by the unwelcome lesson in modern methods. It is a risky business to galvanize sleeping giants, and the spectator who likes to see poetic justice may be invited to wait for a generation. That would be an adequate commentary for a detached onlooker. But we are the ally of Japan, and shared military operations at Kiaochou in which this crisis originated. We have ourselves a great trade in China. Above all, we have joined with Japan in a guarantee of China's integrity and independence. If we could afford, on the ground that the world is wide, to overlook the inroad which our ally is making on our economic opportunities, can we as easily waive the point of honor?

It is not easy to state the case behind these Japanese claims. It might be urged that Japan rendered China a service by ejecting the Germans from Kiaochou. It was a service which China did not ask for; it was a minor military operation, undertaken in fulfilment of Japan's alliance with us, and the utmost that could fairly be claimed from China would be that she should pay some part of the expenses of the undertaking, if it is clear that she will profit by it. It is, however, quite uncertain whether Japan does propose to restore Kiaochou to her, and at the best the restoration will be partial. The payment (if that is the justification of these claims) is to be made in kind, and it amounts to concessions and political privileges to a total which exceeds by immeasurable ratio the value of Kiaochou. China would gladly cede Kiaochou and all it contains to Japan, if by so doing she could be quit of these demands. The immense list of railway concessions, mining monopolies, and privileges for colonists is sufficiently serious. All Powers, to our thinking, abuse their prestige when they use diplomacy to press such claims. But when Japan goes on, in spite of the partial compliance of China, to enforce her demands in their entirety by an ultimatum backed by 60,000 troops already on Chinese soil the procedure surpasses the worst European precedents, and becomes merely predatory. The case is aggravated when it is realized that these demands amount to an exclusive Japanese monopoly over the immense provinces of Manchuria, eastern Mongolia, and Fukien, and to a privileged position only a little less absolute in parts of Shantung and the Yangtze Valley. If Germany (let us say) had put forward such claims in Turkey and China, there would have been no need of the Serajevo incident to make a European war. The climax of these demands is the general claim that Japanese advisers shall be appointed for the "political, financial, and military affairs" of China. A proposal of that kind would raise the gravest international questions if China herself had spontaneously asked for these advisers. When it is enforced at the bayonet point, it is little less than the proclamation of a general Japanese suzerainty over China.

To address moral exhortations to Japan would be to show a want of humor. She knows quite well what she is doing. She has, at the moment, an unchallengeable military ascendancy in the far East, and she is using it as "real Politik" dictates. We assume that the Foreign Office has used plain language in recording its view of these transactions. If Japan elects to disregard a frank statement, she may speculate with perfect safety on the fact that we are too deeply involved in Europe to give effect to our opinion. There, for the time being, the matter must rest. But it ought also to be made clear that the affairs of China cannot be excepted from the general settlements after the war. One ally can no more remove them from the consideration of the Congress than one ally could claim to dispose of Turkey. It ought to be clearly understood that we are in no way bound to recognize any concessions, economic or political, which Japan may extort from China by force. China may at the last moment decide to yield to overwhelming force, and may be compelled to accept the Japanese demands as a whole. That would probably be for the moment the best provisional solution, for if Japan should actually proceed to the use of force, she is likely to raise rather than to lower her claims. In the long run, if China requires "advice" or control it must come from an international concert, while the only way to check the devastating rivalry for railway concessions is to amalgamate foreign capital in an international syndicate. These are the vast issues of the future. In the meanwhile, what is at stake is primarily Japan's moral standing in the world. *It will not have escaped the intelligence of Japanese statesmen that alliances can hardly survive the destruction of their basis,* and that an ally who elects to plow her own furrow while her partner is engaged in a life-and-death struggle, renounces by her own act the ties of comradeship. For our part, we refuse to regard the aggrandizement of Japan as an accomplished fact, whatever her military position may be. This modern financial Imperialism cannot be carried on without capital, and the future of China will not have been decided until Japan has tested her standing in the money markets of London and New York.

Japan's aggressions in China during the war had revealed a purpose on her part to proceed without regard to the interests of Great Britain, and the terms of the alliance; and it was evident that such a proceeding by Japan deprived the alliance of all advantages to Great Britain except such as might be derived strategically, outside the far East. With Great Britain, then, the value of the alliance now and hereafter will depend on striking such a balance. If Great Britain insists that her ally will respect the terms of the alliance in China, then its advantages to Japan become doubtful. It is not surprising, therefore, that criticism of the alliance by Japanese should follow the manifest disposition of the British press to regard Japan's course in China as a betrayal of Great Britain, and to side with China on moral grounds. Several popular Japanese vernacular newspapers took up the argument, and gave prominence to articles berating the alliance, which displayed a deep-rooted sentiment opposed to a continuation of it, and hostile to England. This anti-British propaganda became so virulent that the Government repudiated it, and put some limitations on it through the censorship, but not until its effects had reached the people. While it would be very interesting to quote extensively from the Japanese press and publicists on this question, the criticisms are well summarized by the "Japan Chronicle," the leading British newspaper published in Japan, and which under the editorship of Robert Young has established and preserved at all times an independent and unshackled viewpoint. The "Chronicle" republished freely the Japanese press comments from time to time, notwithstanding attempts to suppress their circulation outside of Japan. The following is from the "Chronicle" of February 3, 1916:

As our readers are aware, during the last two months there have appeared in various Japanese newspapers a number of articles attacking Great Britain and the Anglo-Japanese alliance in unmeasured terms. The British have been credited with every undesirable quality, from cupidity to cowardice. Many of these articles have appeared in the "Yamato," a Tokio paper, under the general heading of "Japan's Message to England," and some of these articles—probably less than a quarter of the whole number—have been reproduced or referred to in our columns. We note that the "Seoul Press" does not approve of the publicity given to these articles. The "Seoul Press" says:

"We regret to note that the 'Japan Chronicle' continues to publish in its columns translations of diatribes on Great Britain published by the 'Yamato Shimbun,' of Tokio. The editor, who has a very good knowledge of things Japanese, ought to be well aware that utterances of the 'Yamato' are by no means representative of Japanese sentiment and have never been taken seriously. It is a third-rate journal and is read chiefly by lower-class people. The very foolish anti-British articles published by it should be entirely ignored. When, however, the 'Chronicle' takes trouble to give them prominence in its columns, we are afraid that our contemporary is only helping the cause of the enemy, who is doing everything possible to estrange the Allies. Every country contains among its people some malcontents, whose delight it is to throw mud on existing conditions and things. Japan has no lack of abusers among Britishers, especially among those living in China. We are careful, however, not to take seriously whatever they say against us in the press and on the rostrum, believing that a great majority of the British people are our sincere allies and friends."

We quite appreciate the moderate tone in which exception is taken to the reproduction of these articles, but the "Seoul Press" misses the point completely. Granting for the sake of argument that the "Yamato" is a third-rate journal, read by third-rate people, and that its utterances are never taken seriously, the articles we have quoted from its columns were not written by third-rate publicists. Attacks on Great Britain written for a gutter press by gutter scribes for gutter readers could, we admit, be regarded as of comparatively little consequence, though not at all conducive to the continuance of friendly international relations. But the writers who have been expressing their views on Anglo-Japanese relations in the "Yamato" are by no means men without education, position, and influence, and it is therefore only right, in the interests of those attacked, that they should know what is being said about them. The editor of the "Yamato" started the ball rolling with a series of articles from his own pen. Mr. Matsui is a journalist of considerable ability and experience in his profession but, even assuming the contrary, those who have continued the "Messages to England" are men whose views cannot be described in the "Seoul Press" phrase as "by no means repre-

sentative of Japanese sentiment" and who "have never been taken
seriously." We find Professor Tatebe, of the Imperial University of
Tokio, expressing the view that Britain is lacking in high ideals, that
she stands for selfishness and disloyalty, and that British troops are
lacking in military courage:

"The coöperation of General Barnardiston of the British army and
his 'brave' soldiers in the attack on Tsingtau has proved that for the
Japanese army to mix with such an army as the British would be like
mixing alcohol with saké."

If the editor of the "Seoul Press" knows anything of Japanese sentiment, he must know that the most disparaging things have been said
about the British troops engaged in the Tsingtau operations even by
official guides appointed to take Japanese visitors round the forts at
Tsingtau—and cynical innuendoes have been thrown about in the Diet
itself. Other university professors have written on precisely the
same lines as Mr. Tatebe, one describing the British as a race of
"long-sleeves," a Chinese expression of contempt for people unable or
unwilling to fight, while another, a LL.D., complained that the Anglo-
Japanese treaty was used by Britain as a club, that Britain controlled
Japan's diplomacy, and that it was for Japan to hold out a "protecting hand" to the people of India. We have seen, too, the remarks
of a Japanese general whose name was withheld, but whose sneers at
the British army were most offensive. Then there were the uncompli-
mentary remarks by Mr. Shimada, whose position in Japanese public
life corresponds with that of the Speaker in the House of Commons,
and whose opinions cannot, at any rate, be lightly dismissed as representing the "third-rate" or "lower class" section of the people. More
recently we have seen what Mr. Kodera, a well-known member of the
Diet, thinks of Anglo-Japanese relations. He considers the alliance
harmful and disadvantageous to Japan, of no benefit but a great burden, not only dead in spirit but dangerous in operation, while it is
used by the British to interfere with the development of Japanese interests in China. Mr. Kodera is a member of the Diet, a millionaire,
a graduate of American universities and has studied law and politics
in—Germany and Austria. He sits in the House of Representatives
as one of the members for Hyogo Prefecture, in which is situated the
premier port of Japan—Kobe,—a city he represents indirectly in the
legislative chamber. It is absurd to suggest that the opinions of such
men as those we have mentioned should be regarded as "by no means
representative of Japanese sentiment." Obviously they must be
representative of a section of Japanese sentiment—possibly not large,
possibly not influential, but certainly neither third-rate nor lower
class. We are of opinion that when signed articles of the character

Canton Christian College, an American school

Part of buildings and grounds of St. John's University, Shanghai, an American mission

of those we have quoted are published, they deserve some attention, if only with the object of showing where their arguments are weak and unconvincing. Criticism of the Anglo-Japanese alliance *per se* cannot be properly objected to; it is as proper for Japanese journalists to express their opinions of the treaty as it is for British journalists—though this scarcely seems an opportune time for such a discussion, with both nations allied in arms against a common enemy. Criticism of British methods of conducting the war cannot be objected to if made in sober language; there is still evident the same old "muddle through somehow" policy in regard to administrative affairs for which Britain has been so long notorious, and it must be allowed that our Japanese friends are as free to criticize and comment upon such aspects of British national affairs as may seem worthy of attention. But what Great Britain and her subjects in this country are entitled to take exception to is the ungenerous and bitter tone of the attacks made, the inability to realize that a treaty is a reciprocal arrangement which necessitates giving as well as taking, and the careless manner in which the most serious assertions are made for which it would be impossible to find proofs to satisfy an impartial judge. British residents in this country, bearing in mind the repeated assurances of cabinet ministers of continued Anglo-Japanese friendship, and bearing in mind the valuable assistance Japan has given her ally in this war, thus confirming those assurances, find it difficult to understand the motives of such men as have joined in the attacks made through the "Yamato." The Tokio journal may not be one of the leading journals of Japan, but it is read by many persons of the student class, and many of its recent critical contributors have been men whose profession it is to inspire young men with ideas. Is it, then, any wonder that such attacks upon Japan's ally arouse feelings the very reverse of those which make for closer harmony and friendship?

In its issue of February 17, 1916, the "Japan Chronicle" said editorially (my italics):

Most interesting development of all, however, is the announcement made, baldly and unequivocally, by one of the premier newspapers of the country that Count Okuma's assurances are of no value, and that Japan *is* tired of the alliance and displeased with Britain's attitude towards her. . . . The "Osaka Mainichi" thinks it not unnatural that Count Okuma, as prime minister of Japan, should give public expression to assurances to the contrary, but the fact remains that the dissatisfaction of the Japanese at the British attitude toward them is real and genuine, "and the desire for a revision of the Anglo-Japanese alliance is generally expressed among the Japanese." ... The following are the principal grounds stated by the Osaka paper on which this widespread Japanese dissatisfaction at the British attitude is alleged to be based: Firstly, the discriminatory treatment of Japanese in Canada, Australia, and other British territories. Secondly—and here we come on familiar ground once more—"in China all the British, officials and others, unite in obstructing the development of Japanese interests." Thirdly, in spite of the fact that Japan is vitally interested in the China question, *the Anglo-Japanese alliance refuses to recognize Japan's supremacy in China, and Great Britain would not assist Japan in the event of war breaking out between her and the United States over the China question."* Then we are told that Japan continues to bear the one-sided obligation with regard to India, while the British are trying to prevent the free influx into India of Japanese people and Japanese goods. ... The idea that the recent outbursts in the Japanese press are the result of German machinations is rather far fetched. There are certain papers in Tokio and Osaka that for a 100 yen note would print anything about anybody, but it is absurd to think that a paper of the standing of the "Osaka Mainichi" could be thus influenced, nor is it to be supposed that the university professors, military men, Diet members, and government officials who have been and are still so diligently writing "Messages to England" have been bribed with German money to pursue the course they have. As we have already pointed out, it is the restraining effect of the Anglo-Japanese alliance on the ambitions in China of a certain section of Japanese which is the real explanation of the attacks now being made on Great Britain and the Anglo-Japanese alliance, and the "Osaka Mainichi" makes no attempt to conceal the fact.

The "Far East" (Tokio) of February 19, 1916, said:

A section of the Japanese press having devoted a great amount of space to the effort to prove the Anglo-Japanese alliance a one-sided compact, by which Britain only benefits, one of the leading magazines in a recent issue takes the British ambassador to task for not courting popularity among the people of this country! This is the sum and substance of an article in "Nippon and Nipponjin," Dr. Miyake's journal, which devotes a long article to what must now be a congenial task with many Japanese publicists, the general abuse of England and all things British. We do not propose to reproduce this article, which might well be ignored if the fact also could be ignored that it is written by a man prominent in Tokio journalism and read by thousands of the better classes of the people. . . . Turning to a wider field Dr. Miyake puts a new construction on the alliance. *The further Britain goes in India the further Japan can go in China, is his view of that piratical compact between England and Japan!*

Japan's aggressions in China are not the only cause of friction between Japan's policy and that of Great Britain. The amended alliance included India in its scope, which served to attract Japanese interest to that country, an interest which has been manifested, at times, in ways that are annoying to Great Britain. The last time I visited India, in 1906, the Government had found it necessary to limit the activities of Japanese propagandists there, who were playing upon the anti-British sentiment of the native population. Since the alliance has required Japan to act in aiding to defend India in certain circumstances, Japanese gradually have assumed a protective attitude toward the Indian peoples, and there has been a subtle and continuous propaganda to extend Japanese influence in India, usually on the basis of alleged racial and religious community. The Japanese press seldom misses an opportunity to dilate on this subject, and an occasion occurred in the autumn of 1915, when the arrest in Japan of two Indians charged with seditious activity against Great Britain, and who had sought refuge in Japan, caused discussion. On the eve of being deported from Japan under circumstances which insured their falling into the hands of British authorities, these Indians were aided to escape by Japanese sympathizers. The sympathy of the Japanese press with the Indian revolutionists was outspoken. In December, 1915, the "Yorozu" said editorially:

While there are various rumors as to the unrest in India and revolutionary tendencies there, the British people are strenuously endeavoring to deny these rumors. At the same time they are taking every precaution to keep the revolutionary elements under control. But the unrest in India to-day is something unavoidable. The question which we must study is whether Japan will be called upon to mobilize in India in case of a rebellion in that country. The British people are using the idea of Japanese mobilization as a weapon to subjugate the Indians, because while the Indians are not afraid of the British soldiers so much, they would never think of opposing the Japanese army. But this is something which will have a far-reaching effect upon the peace of the Orient. We Japanese ought to consider this matter very carefully. In spite of the British declaration that Japan would mobilize, there is no provision in the Anglo-Japanese treaty which calls for a Japanese mobilization in case of civil war in India. If a third power should attack India, Japan must help. But in the case of a civil war, Japan has no duty to help England to oppress the Indians. If Englishmen think that they can use Japan in that way it is a great mistake; it is too selfish of them to think so. By the way, has not England abused Japan too much in the past? We never considered it as an honor to be told that Japan's foreign office is in Downing Street, London. The criticism that the Foreign Minister of Japan is an agent of Sir Edward Grey does not give a pleasing impression to the Japanese people. Japan is an independent nation of the world. She does not need to work for England like a dog or a horse. Now the Indians are only wishing to secure self-government, not independence. Their recent awakening gives them the right to ask for self-government. The Russian people asked and secured the Duma at the time of the war with Japan, Poland secured her self-government in the present great war, and now India has sent 200,000 men to help England in the European War, and it is proper for the King of England to give the Indians self-government in appreciation of the services rendered by the Indians in the war. If Englishmen should grudge it, it may not be a proper thing. Perhaps there are many Englishmen who favor giving self-government to the Indians. As we are at war with Germany, we had advocated sending an expedition to Europe. But we had never thought of making ourselves slaves of England, and oppress the Indians against whom we have no grudge. We had an intimate friendship with India from ancient times. We consider the three hundred million Indians as if they were our own brethren. Our trade with India has increased year by year. If we should ever send an expedition to India when we are not pledged to do so by any of the treaties, thereby hurting the feelings of the Indians, it will be a great loss of our own prestige and a great mistake of policy. The English say that the Germans are smuggling arms to India. But we cannot believe it. The German hand seems to have reached Persia. But the German army has not even reached Asia Minor. German arms may have been smuggled in there. But the desire of the Indians for self-government did not develop on account of the German instigation. We Japanese should study this situation of India very carefully indeed.

This comment of the Japanese newspaper contains inaccuracies, but its animus and point of view are extremely significant. At about the same time, another influential Japanese paper said:

Recently, stories were in the air that Japan may send an expedition to India to suppress the rebellion there. But all these things are not in the treaty of alliance, which only provides that in case a third power should attack one party to the alliance, in the far East and India, the other party should come to the assistance. It does not say that Japan should assist England in putting down an internal rebellion in India. At any rate, the Okuma ministry goes astray very often from the limitations of the treaty of alliance. It is natural that the nation entertains doubts as to the reason why Japan joined the London declaration.

The closing sentence refers to Japan's acceptance of the joint declaration of the belligerent allies that none would conclude peace or make terms of peace separately, which was strongly criticized in Japan as placing limitations on Japan's freedom to get all she could out of the war. A volume could be filled with recent publications by Japanese showing that they expect a revolt in India against British rule, that they sympathize with such an aspiration of the Indians, that Japan is the proper successor to Great Britain as India's overlord and protector, and the leader of an Oriental revolt against all Western assumptions of superiority.

Additional points of friction between Japanese and British policies in China soon followed upon Japan's temporary suspension of pressure, after securing the agreement signed in May, 1915. Japan's meddling in China's internal affairs continued. When it was proposed to change the form of government from a republic to a monarchy, Japan assumed leadership in the warning to the Chinese Government which was made also by Great Britain, France, Russia, and Italy. Very curiously, this participation by the other Entente Allies was taken by many Japanese publicists as a reflection on Japan. One Japanese newspaper, the "Yomiuri," remarked that "the joining of Italy in giving warning to China shows that Italy must have thought it profitable to join in order to share the benefits accruing therefrom. In other words, she has joined the three other European powers in limiting the activity of Japan in the Orient. The European powers do not like to see Japan extending her power in China. Hence they would join Japan in whatever she does in order to be a restraining factor."

This feeling among Japanese that policy of the Entente Powers in China was designed to check Japan there found further expression when the proposal to have China join the belligerent Entente was published. The "Yomiuri" said:

The news circulated by the Associated Press is to the effect that the Powers which joined Japan in sending the warning to China regarding the monarchy plan have decided to drag China in to join the Entente Powers in order to restrain the activity of a certain Power in China. This means that England, France, Russia, and Italy are trying to "rescue" China from Japan. And Japan has not been consulted about this plan as yet. We warned our government authorities at the time Italy joined in sending the warning to China, that such might be an outcome of the joint warning to China. The four other Powers joined Japan at the time, because they wanted to restrain Japan in whatever she may do there. If we thought that they joined us in order to assist us, it was a great mistake. Our prediction has come true. The four Powers have made it impossible for Japan to take any independent action in the Orient. This is a great diplomatic failure. Japan had not committed many very serious diplomatic mistakes, until the Okuma ministry came into power. The Okuma ministry has besmirched the stainless diplomatic history of Japan. Under the present circumstances, unless we are ready to fight against the four Powers there will be nothing for us to do but to agree to join the four Powers in the attempt to induce China to join the Entente Powers. The government authorities may deny this Washington news as being an attempt of the German spies or of the pro-Yuan propagandists. But our countrymen have long been deceived by the foreign office people and they would not believe the denial if it is made. The British foreign minister has declared that England would leave everything to Japan in leading the China policy of the Powers. But now the four Powers have taken action to restrain Japan's activity in China, thereby disillusionizing the Japanese foreign office authorities.

Again, it is not the accuracy or inaccuracy of the statements, but deductions made by the Japanese editor that are interesting. The Japanese press freely accused Sir John Jordan, British minister to China, of having instigated the proposal that China join the Entente belligerent combination during the Great War, implying treachery to Japan; and these imputations were also made guardedly by the semi-official press. Such comment indicates how, in many Japanese minds, the Anglo-Japanese alliance is now regarded as a hindrance rather than an advantage to Japan, because of its restrictions upon Japan's policy in China, due to its fundamental clash with British interests there. The wave of anti-British criticism in Japan was resented by Great Britain, and the Japanese Government took steps to repress it. Count Okuma and other ministers gave out statements protesting Japan's adherence to the alliance, and the Japanese semi-official press changed its tone. But that Japan's world policy is inimical to British interests wherever they touch in Asia, is demonstrated repeatedly by the logic of events.

CHAPTER XIV

JAPAN AND THE UNITED STATES

Issues between these nations—Japan's real attitude toward America—Sources of friction—Initiated by Japan—Japan's population problem—Failure of Japanese emigration to Asia—Effects on Japan-American relations—A new problem—The two viewpoints—The American position—As the Japanese see it—Japan's growth of population—Asiatic multiplication—East vs. West—The line of least resistance—The doctrine of "irrepressible expansion"—Its meaning to America—The dead-lock—Significance of the Gulick plan.

ISSUES between Japan and the United States, contacts which create these issues, and relations dependent on them cannot be entirely separated from interests and policies of other nations in any comprehensive survey; but when restricted to the Pacific basin, where its major elements must be worked out, this problem comprises two principal factors—direct contacts of the two Governments and peoples, and conditions involved with the fate of China. Both factors are surcharged with forces making for international friction, and war.

History proves the fallacy of assuming that generous motives and good intentions of one people will always be understood and accepted by another people or nation as they are meant. It is probable that most Americans are puzzled to understand why Japan-American relations, which for so long a time presented only amicable aspects, in their later stages have developed frictions that show ominous portents. As a people and nation, Americans long have felt only friendly sentiments toward Orientals, including, or rather especially Japanese; and there never has been in either the general attitude of Americans, or the policy of the United States Government as

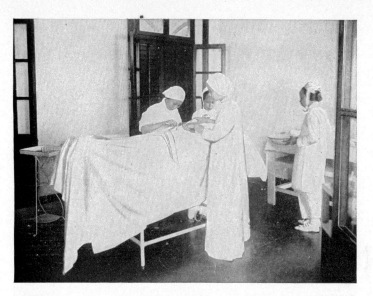

Chinese women are educated in medical work by the mission hospitals

St. Luke's Hospital, Shanghai, an American institution

Americans conceive its objects, any hostile intent or invidious designs against Japan. What Americans in general have not comprehended is that, in recent times, this attitude of theirs has meant little to Japanese, who doubt its sincerity, and do not reciprocate. To most Americans, talk of war between Japan and the United States has seemed foolish, because they have not perceived anything to fight about; and if the purposes of Japan as a nation, and the ideals of the Japanese as a people, *vis-à-vis* America, complemented the sentiments of Americans, then to expect war between these nations would be foolish. It is evident, then, that whatever elements of doubt exist about this matter lie chiefly, with Americans, in ignorance or misunderstanding of the real motives, ambitions, and purposes of Japan. I will present my conclusions about some of these questions in summary, as follows:

(a) Japan is making deliberate preparations in anticipation, if not actually in expectation, of a collision with the United States.

(b) Japanese popular thought and sentiment have been deliberately prepared for this eventuality by the Government, and are hostile toward the United States.

(c) While the Japanese Government and press have formulated and stimulated this sentiment in Japan, a Japanese propaganda in America has almost succeeded in lulling that nation into a false security, and has exerted an influence to prevent and retard measures to prepare the United States against an armed clash.

(d) The fate of China, the stability of the Monroe Doctrine (now embracing the new ideal of Pan-Americanism), the balance of power in the Pacific Ocean, and whether a yellow peril ever will become a reality, are questions included in the outcome of the relations of Japan and the United States.

(e) The great European War destroyed the international balance of power in the far East, creating a condition which enabled Japan to disturb that region, and by reaction also to menace the peace of America.

(f) Constructive action by the United States is required to help recreate that balance of power.

In modern times, issues which may lead to war between great nations do not spring up suddenly, out of an unforeseen condition or an impulsive quarrel; but are a gradual growth, usually derived from a fundamental need or aspiration of one or more nations. The serious issues that exist between Japan and America are of that nature, and their causes, and political development, lie chiefly with Japan. This is why Americans are comparatively unfamiliar with them. There is almost nothing in the course of American political evolution, within the last century, and since relations with Japan began, which has altered the national attitude toward questions on which these issues turn. America's general attitude and policy toward China has not changed, in principle, although it has been occasionally modified by circumstances. America stands, as always, for fair treatment of China, respect of her nationality, preservation of her integrity, and as among foreign nations and interests an equal position and opportunity for all. Japan until very recently has professed the same principles and objects. America's attitude toward Asiatic immigration has not changed materially for half a century, since the question first came up; yet for a long time no friction with Japan arose on this question. Therefore, in respect to both major elements of the problem, it is a shift of attitude by Japan that has led to irritation. In trying to grasp the new situation caused by Japan's changed attitude, Americans are blinded and confused by the fact that Japan, in so far as is possible, has concealed her shifts of policy, and pretends to stand where she formerly did. It requires a close scrutiny of conditions which have caused Japan to change her attitude toward America to reveal the truth.

It is clear that the immigration question between Japan and the United States does not spring from any activities of Americans in Japan, or in the far East. It springs from activities of Japanese in the Americas. Its initiative comes from Japan, and the attitude of America is entirely defensive. Americans did not raise the issue, although by force of circumstances they may seem to have started or given occasion for the argument about it, thereby creating an international question. The true origin of this issue, therefore, is to be found in the causes for Japanese emigration to the Western Hemisphere. This points back to the Russo-Japanese War and its aftermath. Among the professed motives which Japan gave for making war against Russia was the alleged necessity to secure additional territory where surplus Japanese population could go. So persistently and with such plausibility was this idea propagated throughout the world that it is given place in discussion of this problem by Westerners after Japan has dropped it. The idea of Korea and Manchuria, providing a satisfactory field for Japan's excess population is no longer widely entertained in Japan, and no longer, if it ever did, has a place in Japan's genuine, as distinguished from her pretended, foreign policy. Some wrong assumptions about this question are widely accepted. It is incorrect to say that Japan is overpopulated in a territorial sense, for a large area of the territory of Japan proper is sparsely populated, and over one third of the arable land in Japan is uncultivated. Therefore it is not lack of land that impels Japanese to emigrate; it is a desire for economic betterment. There is a good deal of room, expressed in land, in Korea and Manchuria. Manchuria has long been a part of China, and large sections of China are as densely populated as any sections of Japan. Yet Chinese have not gone to Manchuria in large numbers for various reasons, among which are climate and lack of communications and security. Those conditions are improving, and China now would like to use Manchuria for her own surplus population; but she has been blocked by Japan. This being so, one cannot accept an assumption of a right of Japan to annex Korea and Manchuria on those grounds. If it is a question of rights and justice, then China's right should supersede Japan's, for China's need of her own undeveloped territory is as great. If the legality and ethics of the question are considered, China has a prior and better title. I call attention to both the legal and moral aspects of this proposition, and their bearing upon Japanese emigration to America.

But a curious, though logical, outcome of Japan's efforts to colonize in Korea and Manchuria and in other parts of China is that, notwithstanding the unjust preferential conditions maintained for them by their Government in comparison with Koreans and Chinese, Japanese immigration to the continent of Asia is comparatively a failure. The reason is simple. In going to Korea and China, Japanese find that they have moved into an even lower standard of living than obtains in Japan; that is, to a more cramped economic field, not a wider one. Japanese cannot, even with preferential facilities, compete in large numbers with their neighbor Orientals. Chinese and Koreans are able to, and do, undercut Japanese in business economies and standards of living. Preferential exactions in their behalf by the Japanese Government enables some Japanese to improve their state by pursuing commercial and other occupations in China, but to the millions of Japan's peasantry China offers no lure and little opportunity for betterment. The application of this situation to Japan's contacts with America is easily deduced. It is not toward the East, with its lower economic level, that Japan's millions yearn; but toward the West, with its higher economic standards, under which Japanese of all classes can cut and still find room for an immense improvement of their condition. In this situation is found the cause for the effort of Japan to sustain the position of Japanese in the United States, and Japan's approaches in Mexico and other American countries. It provides the key to one phase of Japan's modern attitude toward the United States. In the last few years (1910–16) two points have taken clear shape in Japanese thought—Korea and China do not provide a satisfactory outlet for them, and the most desirable field for their emigration (North and South America) is practically barred to them by the United States. This question has gradually come to embrace all of the American nations, for a Japanese colonization of any countries on the Western Hemisphere, in its eventual political and economic reactions, would affect the United States scarcely less than a Japanese colonization of United States territory. To Americans this issue probably will seem more important than the fate of China and conditions there, though it is not really so. It is nearer, and therefore looms larger.

There are two distinct points of view on the emigration (or immigration) question—Japan's and America's. Americans understand their own viewpoint pretty well. It is briefly: Orientals have lower economic standards, and therefore their presence among Westerners disturbs our earning and living conditions; they have different political and religious ideas, which cannot easily be adjusted to those of the West, if at all; they have different racial and social characteristics, and therefore cannot be fully assimilated into our social body. So the people of the United States cannot endure their presence among them in large numbers.

Japan's point of view is merely that her people want to go to Western countries and to have the same rights and opportunities there that other nationalities have. That point of view, with all it comprehends, is well set out by Japanese themselves. No other topic of national interest has been more discussed in modern Japan than this one; her statesmen, journalists, educators, and scientists have covered the subject in all its aspects and phases in the course of its development from an academic to an active and imminent political issue, and the trend of their thought and opinion is deeply significant. Summarized, Japan's viewpoint is: The Japanese are the superior race of the world; by this virtue they are destined to dominate civilization and culture throughout the world; to accomplish this national destiny requires the utmost concentration and exertion of the national strength; the contemptuous attitude of the West toward Orientals requires the Orient to demonstrate its superior military power; to this end, Japan must unite Oriental peoples under her leadership and control; for Japanese to lose their nationality and racial characteristics by contamination of Westerners must be prevented, and therefore they should not as emigrants merge with other nations; nevertheless, it is necessary for Japanese to have the right to live in Western countries and have equal privileges there; these things must be accomplished by arms if necessary; no sacrifices are too great for Japanese to make to secure these objects.

It is pertinent to show that Japanese thinkers no longer regard Asia as a desirable field for Japanese colonization. I use the word colonization, instead of emigration, for that is a distinction which lies at the root of Japan's foreign policy. In an address made in 1914 Professor Kichisaburo Endo of the Imperial University, Tokio, said: "It is impossible for our peeople, who from elementary schooldays have been bred with teachings of loyalty and patriotism, to lose their characters and adopt those of the country to which they emigrated. The suggestion that they can, completely ignores the history of the country. There are some Japanese who tried to refute the common contention of the American people that the Japanese are utterly unassimilable. It is undisputed, when weighed very carefully, that we may prove to be most refractory for assimilation by another race. As a Japanese of manly spirit will never be swallowed up by the national characteristics of other peoples, the refutal is impossible." The "Kokumin," one of the most influential newspapers in Japan, said in 1914: "It is deprecatory for Japanese subjects to emigrate to foreign countries and change their nationality by naturalization. Japan is one of the rising nations of the world, and it is the height of absurdity that Japan should send out many able youths as emigrants to foreign lands. After all, the average Japanese transcends every other people of decadent nations, in ability and talent." In 1913 the "Osaka Mainichi" said: "At present there are seven Japanese in the State of California who have been naturalized, and the Japanese residing in

America call them traitors to their nation and will not deign to speak with them. The Japanese cannot expand in America without becoming naturalized and when we come to this we are confronted with the problems of our family system, and our system of education becomes a barrier.'' An English journalist, staff correspondent of the ''Morning Post'' (London), wrote in 1915: ''The general opinion amongst foreigners is that Japan does not favor her nationals abandoning their citizenship, and that therefore she cannot ask any foreign nation to allow them that privilege. To request an alien power to concede a Japanese subject the right to abandon his allegiance to the Emperor of Japan might seem to many Japanese as an act of blasphemy. To all true Japanese the Emperor is divine; allegiance to the sovereign is the most sacred and inalienable of all relations. Renunciation of citizenship would mean to a Japanese an act of treason, and it is a question whether his fellow-countrymen would not regard it as such and treat him accordingly.'' These comments, culled out of many similar ones, suffice to show that Japan's attitude toward her emigrants is peculiar in that she demands a place for them in other countries, but wants to retain their political allegiance. That the Japanese Government recognizes the technical impossibility of maintaining this position was shown by its action, in 1916, in removing official restraint upon Japanese born abroad who want to become citizens of other nations. A foreign-born Japanese hereafter can renounce his allegiance to the Mikado technically, and his new status will be recognized by the Japanese Government. The practical effect of this new provision will be negligible. If an American wants to reside in England and have equal position there with Englishmen, he becomes a British subject, and *vice versa*. Most foreigners who become permanent residents of the United States also become citizens of that nation. With such emigrants there are no basic characteristics opposed to their assimilation in other Western countries. If it should occur that immigrants of any single nationality would settle in the United States in large numbers, and decline to become American citizens, there is little doubt that the condition so created would be regarded with apprehension by the American Government, and as a possible menace to its institutions and existence, and some kind of regulation would be attempted. The residence of foreigners in any nation in excess of the national population would be a cause of uneasiness —that is, if German, or British, or Russian residents in the United States, or all aliens combined, should outnumber the native and naturalized population.

The following comments show how Japanese now regard Asiatic countries as a field for emigration, or colonization. In 1914 the "Japan Financial and Economic Monthly" said: "It is a fact that the authorities show discriminatory treatment of the natives. . . . Twenty years have elapsed since Formosa was ceded to Japan, but no intermarriage between Japanese and Formosans is legally allowed. Only that education which is necessary to gain a livelihood is given to the natives; the higher education necessary for civilized people is denied them. No franchise is given the Formosans. The total Japanese population of Formosa is only 120,000, whereas the natives number 3,000,000. It will require at least a million Japanese in Formosa to thoroughly Japanese the natives with as little loss of time as possible. The Formosan authorities have started the encouragement of Japanese immigration as an official enterprise. But since the revenue from the sugar excise has been transferred to the charge of the mother country, it is doubtful whether the scheme can be carried out with success."

Immediately after the Russo-Japanese War the Japanese Government made great efforts to stimulate Japanese emigration to Korea and Manchuria, with some success at first, but after a few years the flow stopped, and then began to recede. This caused criticism of the Government, and it was charged that government enterprises in Manchuria, like railways and mines, were depriving Japanese of opportunity by employing Chinese and Koreans. An official of the South Manchurian

Athletics are becoming popular, and are in the curriculum of both boys' and girls' schools. China scored the most points in the last Far Eastern Olympic Games

The new China.

Railway Company stated in the "Japan Mail" of August 1, 1914, that "the Japanese could not compete with the Chinese laborers, who work for 20 to 30 sen a day and subsist on 4 to 5 sen a day." (A sen is ½ cent United States currency.) Commenting on this fact, the "Yamato" said: "Japanese laborers are superior to the Chinese in mode of living, but they cannot challenge the Chinese coolies in the field of hard labor. Japanese laborers are not welcomed in Manchuria and are excluded in North America. How will the emigration question be solved? This is a serious question that calls for an immediate solution." When Japan, in 1914, occupied Shantung Province in China, there was an inrush of Japanese immigrants, but this time the Government, having the examples of Formosa, Korea, and Manchuria in mind, published a report of Mr. Shirani, Civil Governor of the Kwangtung leased territory (Port Arthur and Dairen), who said, referring to Shantung: "The question I now will expound is, will it become an equally promising colony for our people as Formosa or Manchuria? To be frank, whatever data I have collected and studied disheartens me, as I am overwhelmingly led to conclude in the negative." Regarding Korea, the Japan "Monthly Bulletin of Economic and Social Intelligence" said in 1913: "Land is cultivated only partially or imperfectly. The population is sparse. Colonization is limited almost exclusively to reclamation work without any special attempt to create small or medium-sized farms. The Government is encouraging emigration. Mr. Ishizaki of the 'Osaka Shosen Kaisha' says that wide tracts of land excellent for pastoral use lie neglected in Korea." About Hokkaido, the northern island of Japan proper, the same publication said: "This part is very thinly populated and the land is either not cultivated or cultivated in a very primitive manner. During 1912 the immigration into Hokkaido was 61,156 as against 13,963 emigrants—a net increase of 47,193. It will be seen that the number of people who leave Hokkaido each year to return to Japan proper is still very considerable. This is due to many

causes, not the least important of which is the comparative
severity of the climate to which the Japanese from the southern
provinces cannot always adapt themselves.'' The report of
the Japan Sociological Society for 1915 said: ''The present
tendency is to drive Japan's surplus population into Korea
and China, where density of population is almost as congested
as in Japan; a movement which, if it continues, is likely to lead
to a clash and war between Oriental races. . . . From a hu-
mane point of view it would undoubtedly be better for Oriental
emigration to distribute itself in Canada, the United States,
South America, and Oceanica, *as is its present desire and
natural tendency.* The attempt to turn Japanese emigration
into Asia is purely artificial and arbitrary, and, as has been
suggested, is liable to produce trouble in China and the Indies.''

It is germane, at this point, to demonstrate briefly some
matters which bear on sociological and economic effects and
probabilities, of the modern attitude of Japanese toward their
emigration, the political problems growing out of this attitude,
and how these problems touch the United States. It is not
necessary to review here certain general effects of Oriental
immigration to Western countries. Volumes have been written on the subject, which is not a new topic. Every Western
State that has felt the pressure of Asiatic immigration has
legislated to exclude it, among them the British States of
Canada and Australasia. Antipathy to some results of Asiatic
immigration is not confined to the United States, but is general among Westerners wherever the condition occurs. It
may be mentioned that Japanese resentment is as keen against
British States that exclude them as it is against America. The
following comment of the ''Kokumin'' in August, 1914, is interesting: ''Australia is a British country, but its geographical
position and the temper of its people hold the country in
closer touch with the United States than with the fatherland,
and a federation of ideas between Australia and the United
States seems to have been effected. Whatever is proposed in
America is copied by Australia. . . . So the people of Aus-

tralia passed a law barring Asiatic labor from its shores, after the United States had affected it. Our diplomats deal with any problem that occurs in Australia through the Foreign Office in England. This is proper, indeed, but they should not forget the fact that all questions affecting Japanese in Australia and Canada can be traced to the United States, and unless a fundamental solution is made with America, no satisfactory result may be expected by negotiations with Australia through the British foreign office.'' And the ''Japan Magazine'' of August, 1914, said: ''We quite concur in the conviction of the Japanese press that as the question with the United States affects similar questions with the British colonies, it ought to be settled once and for all on the strictest basis of justice and fair play, so as to preclude any further issue.'' The breadth of the issue as it affects Japan is thus recognized, coupled with a conviction that it must be settled with America first. At times the view has been advanced in the United States that any menace involved in the Japanese, and behind that the whole Asiatic immigration question, does not threaten America especially, but will fall equally on all Western countries. This is true as to principle, but it is not necessarily true as to practice. If a flood is loosed, its natural course will be to spread over territory according to gravity: but if it is obstructed at some places by dykes, its greater volume will be diverted to places not protected by dykes. Asiatic emigration, if unrestricted, might move toward the vast undeveloped possessions of Russia in Asia, or to British possessions in Canada, Australasia, and South Africa, with as much incentive as it would have toward the United States and South America. But if it is excluded from those regions, its incentive toward the United States and South America will be augmented and accelerated.

What this pressure may become is intimated by the report of the Japan Sociological Society for 1915, as published in the ''Japan Magazine'': ''The Japan Sociological Society estimates that the earth is capable of sustaining comfortably about 2,300,000,000 people according to the *American standard of living;* and if they adopt the German standard as many as 5,600,000,000 can live well on the earth; but if they live according to the Japanese standard, 22,400,000,000 could easily find sustenance on mother earth. The present population of the earth is estimated at about 1,750,000,000, and, at the present rate of increase, in the next 150 years it will have reached about 10,000,000,000.'' This Japanese scientific society has reached a conclusion that, at present comparative standards of living, ten Japanese can live where one American can—thus fixing the economic and sociological ratio between these nationalities at 10 to 1. Other Asiatic standards are lower than Japanese. Another factor in this computation is the ratio of increase of population. Approximately, the population of the world has doubled in the last eighty years, with the rate of increase compounding not only in arithmetical progression, but also by reason of the application of scientific discoveries to human existence. If the same ratio of increase is maintained for the next 150 years, the earth's population would be about 6,000,000,000. But the Japan Sociological Society puts the earth's population at 10,000,000,000 in 150 years from now, indicating that the former ratio of progression will be stimulated by some races multiplying more rapidly. Analysis shows that that estimate is based on a calculation that Asiatics will hereafter multiply much more rapidly than Western races, especially if they can by emigration spread into countries where their conditions of life will be bettered. The present population of the earth is nearly equally divided between the two predominating civilizations. At the present ratio of increase, the white races double in number in eighty to ninety years, while Asiatics under favorable conditions double in thirty years. On this basis, the world may have to provide room for 300,000,-000 more Orientals in the next twenty-five or thirty years. Japanese official statistics show that the native population in Korea has increased in four years (1910–14) 17 per cent., which will double it in about twenty-four years. The population in Japan is increasing almost as rapidly. In China and India various conditions have checked the natural growth of population, but the rate of increase is swelling in both those countries with the introduction of better sanitation and raising of economic standards. In this connection the differences of sex ethics, as derived from religion, law, and customs, between the East and the West, have an important bearing on the comparative ratios of multiplication.

Japanese statesmen and scientists apparently are now convinced that Asia and the islands of the far East do not offer a satisfactory field for Japanese population expansion, in comparison with the Western Hemisphere, for both political and economic reasons. The economic reason is that the greater the difference between standards, the greater is the opportunity for the lower standard to improve. Such clashes of economic standards usually cause a double shift toward readjustment— the competition of the lower standard pulls the higher standard down until they meet at a medium point, and thereafter move along together, or the descending higher standard succumbs entirely to the control of the ascending lower one. This assumes that population and other elements, in the clash, are approximately equal, or have free play to operate naturally. The normal tendency of all standards is, of course, upward. The report of the Japan Sociological Society gives two standards of Western existence—German and American. By them, four Japanese can exist where one person does under the German standard, but ten Japanese can exist where one person now does under the American standard. As between these two standards, Japanese would prefer to transplant to the American, for obvious reasons. Moreover, land is required, and undeveloped or underdeveloped land in large quantity is not to be found in Europe, but may be found in other continents. There is such land in Canada, in the United States, in Siberia, in Australasia, in South Africa, in Mexico, in South America. Why, then, do Japanese particularly select the United States and South America as their destined field for emigration and colonization?—and why is Japan's world policy shaped to that end?

One reason I have indicated—the economic preference. The other reason lies in the rule of least resistance. Japan realizes that she cannot expand in Siberia now, and perhaps never. Russia bars the way there, and the Russo-Japanese War showed Japan the limit of her offensive power in that direction. That war did much to wake Russia to these aspects of her own problem in Asia, and ever since the war Russia has made great efforts to raise a human and military barrier in her Eastern possessions. Russia expects to have to provide for another 150,000,000 of her own people within a century, and intends to hold Siberia for them. In the last ten years Russia has been rushing the colonization of eastern Siberia and the Altais slopes, has double-tracked the Siberian Railway, and built the Amur Railway. Russia is a military power. Japan cannot break through there in the present century. It seems equally difficult for Japan to force her emigrants upon British possessions in America, Africa, and the Antipodes, for those are protected by the British navy and their own military strength. What is left, of the desirable fields? Territory of the United States, and those regions presumably encompassed by the Monroe Doctrine. These not only are the more desirable to Japanese, but they also are poorly defended. Against any Japanese propulsion toward Europe, or possessions of European nations, will be arrayed military and naval power which, in such an issue, would be able to create formidable combinations to oppose an Asiatic menace. Across the Pacific, more delectable, more accessible, undefended by its own strength and unprotected by any strong international combination, lies the American hemisphere. This condition contains, also, a clue to Russia's apparent willingness to come to an understanding with Japan in eastern Asia at this time. Russia looks ahead. She sees this Asiatic pressure coming and knows that the flood, when it breaks, will surge mightily for an outlet somewhere. Russia does not want its force to break upon her possessions in Asia. She has established colonies as buffers; and has built military dykes, and will strengthen them; but there may be no need that Russia's dykes should withstand the pressure. If the flood is diverted elsewhere, its pressure on Russia will be relieved. Consequently, Russia may be willing to see Japanese emigration take an opposite course. The same reasoning applies to other Powers. "Welt-Politik" as it is now adjusted, and is shaping, inevitably will throw almost the full force of Asia's expansive energy upon America.

Running through arguments which Japan advances in justification or in trying to justify, to Americans, her policy in China and on the emigration question, is the doctrine of "irrepressible expansion." This doctrine is much used in modern times as an excuse, or a reason, for territorial and commercial aggressions. When a nation, within its own territorial boundaries, becomes congested, or thinks it is congested, or proves that it is congested by some comparison of its existing internal conditions with what it wants or claims for itself, it is customary for it to base such claims on alleged "necessity" to expand. In recent years Germany has used this argument. Japan is now using it, and her use of the doctrine of "irrepressible expansion" has found many supporters in America. Japan's apologists in the United States accept, and even advocate Japan's claim of a "right" to room to expand in Asia, at the expense of China. Other Americans, who perceive the moral and legal obliquity of such a claim by Japan, are willing to tolerate it because of a presumption that Japanese emigration to Asia would relieve its pressure on America, and thus tend to solve a grave issue between Japan and the United States. That Japanese emigration to Asia will not satisfy Japan's irrepressible expansion, as Japanese conceive it, has been demonstrated, so by conceding China as a "legitimate" field for it, whether China consents or not, Americans admit a dangerous principle, which already has reacted on their own nation, to its confusion. Sifted down, Japan's apologists try to justify her predatory expansion by citing the alleged overpopulation of that country, and the alleged necessity to acquire more territory. This amounts to asserting a doctrine that the claimed needs of one people are a true warrant for them to satisfy these needs by taking from others. Suppose this argument was advanced: "Americans have a very high standard of living, and cannot live comfortably and develop their civilization in a cramped condition. They require plenty of room. The country is becoming overcrowded. It is true that there is a great deal of uncultivated land in the United States, but it is not as rich as Americans like to have; and much of it only can be brought under cultivation by spending large sums on irrigation and reclamation work. It is more convenient to take lands in Canada and Mexico. The Canadians now do not use nearly all of the land in their country, and the same is true of the Mexicans. We therefore are justified in taking possession of it; and since our civilization requires that wherever we go we shall extend our own Government and ideals, we must annex those regions. Of course this policy will be of great benefit to the Canadians and Mexicans, for we will improve their countries and will give them a much better government." Suppose, further, that in order to annex Canada and Mexico it was necessary to conquer or to overawe them, and that required a very large army and navy. Suppose the United States, in order to carry out such a policy, would tax Americans 60 per cent. of their per capita income; and would spend 50 per cent. of the revenue thus raised on the army and navy that would be needed to conquer or overawe Mexico and Canada. Suppose also that a part of the money so spent on armaments would suffice to irrigate and reclaim enough uncultivated and improfitable lands in the United States to provide room for the natural expansion of population for an indefinite time. Suppose, instead of spending hundreds of millions on irrigation and reclamation projects in the Western States of America, it was seriously proposed that that money, with great additions, would be used to create an army and navy to acquire land in Canada and Mexico. This hypothetical case is almost an exact paral-

Photograph, Underwood & Underwood, N. Y.

Famine refugees in China.   Famine relief work has been done chiefly by Americans

lel of Japan's present policy in Asia. It has been argued in the Japanese Diet, and measures to that end have been advocated, that by modern irrigation and reclamation methods a large area in Korea can be made productive; and parts of Japan proper can be made desirable for agriculture that are now unused. Even Japanese have objected to spending so much of the revenues for armaments to support a policy of territorial expansion as long as large areas in Japan's present territories are uncultivated, and can be made productive by spending money for improvements. This principle applies to the whole economic and sociological question in Japan. Japan's world policy is stretching the doctrines of "imperative necessity" and "irrepressible expansion" to the limit.

When one analyzes Japan's imbued conception of her "irrepressible expansion" doctrine, in its applications to America, a condition is uncovered that cannot be ameliorated by arguments, or satisfied by concessions to "honor." In support of her point of view, Japan advances certain arguments, some of which seem plausible at first blush, but all of which are inconsistent in some degree, and almost wholly irreconcilable with what the United States can possibly concede. Japan insists that her subjects shall have the same position and rights in the United States as, let us say, English, or Germans, or Dutch, or French. That seems fair on the surface; but consider. With whom does it rest to say who shall and who shall not join in American nationality, and share its political and social life? With the American nation, of course. To submit that decision in any part to a foreign nation would qualify American sovereignty. This is not meant as an argument to exclude Japanese. I only contend that Americans have the exclusive right to decide the conditions of citizenship and residence in their own territories. A good deal can be said in favor of Japanese as residents of any nation. That is not the question between the two nations. Americans reserve to themselves the right to exclude or admit whom they will, according to standards of citizenship which they make for themselves. From this position, I am sure, Americans cannot be budged except by superior force of arms. The small group of intelligent statesmen that controls Japan understand this perfectly, yet they keep the question alive. It is inconsistent for any nation to try to force its subjects or citizens upon other nations by process of expatriation. Japan does not desire her subjects to become naturalized in the United States, for thereby they would be lost to Japan, if their change was genuine; but only insists that Japanese in America must be treated like other foreigners. Here, again, America's answer necessarily is that she herself must reserve and exercise the right to discriminate among foreigners, according to circumstances. The American general immigration laws are a long list of discriminations; furthermore, Japan imposes, in that country, similar disabilities on foreign residents there to which she objects in the United States, and excludes Chinese laborers.[1] Behind Japan's outward position there is a deeper motive. It is clear that no concessions that are possible for the United States to make, without qualifying its internal sovereign powers, can meet what Japanese really want to obtain. Here is a deadlock, which can be loosened only by one side receding completely, or by a fight.

In these circumstances, I regard with some uneasiness efforts that have been made to convince Americans that this issue can be compromised in a way satisfactory to Japanese. Following the suspension of official negotiations in 1914,[2] a plan to substitute for the "gentlemen's agreement" an arrangement which would save Japan's susceptibilities was advanced, originating in Japan. Dr. Sydney L. Gulick, an American employed at a university in Japan, was selected to propagate this plan in America. The so-called Gulick plan is for the United States to avoid discriminating between Japanese and other immigrants and foreign residents by amending its general immigration law in some particulars. This amendment would limit all classes of immigrants, as to nationality, to a

[1] Appendix P and Y.   [2] Appendix X.

stated per cent. of previous immigrants and residents of that
nationality. Under Dr. Gulick's proposed formula, the number of Japanese who could legally enter would be few, while
it would but slightly affect the normal influx of immigrants
of other nationalities. By this device, Japanese would be on
the same legal status as other foreigners entering America,
while being practically excluded. Analysis shows that this
device does not touch the fundamental question at issue. Even
as a "face-saving" scheme it is no improvement on the "gentlemen's agreement," whereby Japan herself retards Japanese
emigration to the United States by refusing passports to her
nationals. The "gentlemen's agreement" is based on the fiction that Japan herself voluntarily prevents the expatriation
of her subjects, and their residence abroad in large numbers.
The Gulick scheme is based on a similar fiction that, by a
technical trick, a law which seems to place Japanese on the
same basis with other foreign immigrants to the United States,
while actually excluding them, gets around the difficulty.
There is no real difference. Japanese would be excluded just
the same; while the United States would qualify its power to
deal with other classes of immigration irrespective of their
nationality. Lurking in the Gulick device is a tentative recognition, by the United States, that Japanese colonization of
other American republics does not infringe the Monroe Doctrine. That perhaps is why the Japanese Government favors
it above the "gentlemen's agreement." But the real significance of this Gulick plan lies deeper. Japanese statesmen
must know that it offers no solution that will satisfy Japan,
and that will open a clear way for Japanese emigration and colonization in the Western Hemisphere. So its proposal at this
juncture is, logically, in the nature of a device to distract attention, to delude Americans into believing that the cloud has
passed; while Japan continues to prepare to challenge by
arms for a fundamental adjustment in accord with her own
viewpoint and desires.

CHAPTER XV

What constitutes defense?—Defense of territory and sovereignty—Defense of a policy—What is involved—Japan's treaty obligations—The "open door" covenants—Influence of Japan's policy on other Powers—Reversion to "sphere" policy—The Asama incident—Implied intimidation of the United States—Baron Shibusawa's mission to America—The "coöperation" idea—Meaning of this proposal—Efforts to gild the pill—A Jap-ized Monroe Doctrine—How it would work—Will America betray China?

O N one point public opinion in America is correct in its conception of modern contacts of Japan and the United States. In almost all discussion of this problem by Americans the defensive idea is uppermost. There is no disposition by Americans to political aggression in any part of the Orient, or to obtain any unfair commercial advantage there. But most Americans are confused about what is to be defended by their nation in the Orient, and how it should be defended. I have shown, as between Japan and the United States, that American rights and interests that are menaced by Japan's policy shape into two questions—the situation of China, and Asiatic immigration. In respect to the immigration issue, it is clear to Americans that with them it takes a purely defensive form. About questions involved with the situation and fate of China, American opinion is not clear, as to their defensive or aggressive character. As Americans understand the "open door" policy, it only means fair play among commercial competitors coupled with respect of China's independence, and contains no essence of aggression on China or any nation. Yet, why the United States should defend its position under the "open door" in China is by no means as clear to American public opinion as why the Government should defend their country against objectionable immigration which seeks to enter America by force. The mandatory nature of the obligation of a Government to defend its own territories and its sovereign rights within those territories is plain enough, but the obligation of a Government to defend interests and rights outside its territories is not so clear to the average citizen. The reason for this vagueness of popular thought is because the thing to be defended is, in one case, tangible and linked with the law of self-preservation, and in the other case the thing to be defended is a *policy*. Yet every war the United States has had, including the Revolution, was about policy, or principle (which is usually the same thing); the great European War was caused by conflict of policies; nearly every war of the last two centuries was about policy; and it is practically certain that most future wars will be about policy. Belgium went to war, in 1914, because her territory was invaded; but her territory was invaded because policies of greater nations that did not concern Belgium, had collided. In modern times, and probably in the future, nations not only will be brought into war by their own policies, but they also will be dragged in by policies of other nations. From this modern condition of civilization we may draw the conclusion that to sustain a policy often is as obligatory and necessary to a nation as to defend its own territory and sovereignty. The two points where the policies of Japan and the United States are antagonistic are closely related, in any plan by the United States to defend its rights. America's preparations to defend its stand on the immigration issue, based on Japan's present position and territory and population, obviously would not be adequate if Japan gets control over the immense population and resources of China. As Japan expands in the Orient and thereby increases her actual and potential power, America's defensive requirements will increase accordingly. If the United States will not defend its policy in China and the Pacific Ocean while it still can be defended there, it may later have to take even greater military measures for defense of its own territory and sovereignty and standards of living against a consolidated Orient, under Japan's control, than would suffice to protect its China policy now. Even with a purely defensive policy, there is a question of where the first line of defense should be established. Some Americans think their national defensive front against a Japanese menace should be on the western shores of the United States; others think it should be in China and some islands of the Pacific, and everywhere the interests of the two nations touch.

The policy of the United States in the far East has two phases—moral and material. These are distinct, yet they often are so closely interlocked as to be almost indistinguishable. Moral aspects of the policy embrace certain obligations to China and to other Powers from historic relations and under the terms of treaties; certain obligations to uphold Christianity, human liberties, justice, education, scientific progress; certain especial obligations in respect to the Philippines. The moral principles of any policy will have expression in material matters, or have no practical expression at all. Moral responsibility remains nothing but a phrase unless it is translated into practical effort.

The tendency of far Eastern affairs that led to the existing situation began something more than twenty years ago, just prior to the China-Japan War, and it then found expression in efforts of several Powers to establish and protect their special interests and positions in China. Realizing that the tendency known as the "sphere of influence" policy would lead to international strife, and probably to the dismemberment of China, the United States moved officially to check it by international agreement. Initiative was taken by John Hay, then American secretary of state, and what is known as the Hay Doctrine was formulated, in 1899.[1] The *status quo* thereby created was disturbed by the Russo-Japanese War, and the subsequent actions of Japan. In the Portsmouth treaty,[2] Japan and Rus-

[1] Appendix K.   [2] Appendix C.

sia explicitly agreed to respect the "open door" in Manchuria. Following that war, a number of treaties and agreements concerning China were made between the Powers, and these provide the legal basis for international relations in the far East. There are four treaties relating to China, as follows: (a) The Franco-Japanese agreement signed in June, 1907; [3] (b) the Japan-United States (Root-Takahira) agreement signed in November, 1908; [4] (c) The Russo-Japanese convention signed in July, 1907; [5] (d) The renewed Anglo-Japanese alliance signed in July, 1911. [6] Each of these instruments has a particular clause about the "open door" and integrity of China. That clause of the Franco-Japanese agreement reads: *"The Governments of Japan and France, being agreed to respect the independence and integrity of China, as well as the principle of equal treatment in that country for the commerce and subjects or citizens of all nations . . . engage to support each other for assuring the peace and security in these regions, with a view to maintain the respective situation and the territorial rights of the two high contracting parties in the continent of Asia."* A clause of the Russo-Japanese convention reads: *"The two high contracting parties agree to recognize the independence and the territorial integrity of the Chinese Empire, and the principle of equal opportunity for the commerce and industry of all nations in the said Empire, and they engage to uphold and defend the maintenance of the status quo and the respect of that principle by all the peaceful means possible to them."* The Root-Takahira agreement says: *"They [America and Japan] are also determined to preserve the common interests of the Powers in China by supporting by all pacific means at their disposal the independence and integrity of China, and the principle of equal opportunity for the commerce and industry of all nations in that empire."* The Anglo-Japanese alliance gives as one of its objects: *"The preservation of the common interests of all Powers in China by ensuring the independence and integrity of the Chinese*

[3] Appendix M.   [4] Appendix Q.   [5] Appendix D.   [6] Appendix L.

Empire and the principle of equal opportunity for the commerce and industry of all nations in China.'' It will be noted that Japan is on record in five separate treaties to respect the independence of China, and to act there in accordance with the ''open door'' commercial policy. Thus four Powers directly interested in China took pains to pin Japan down in written agreements. The other Power directly interested in China, Germany, is on record as supporting these doctrines by Count von Bülow's response to Mr. Hay's note. Serious infringements of the Hay Doctrine since its promulgation have been due chiefly to Japan's course and policy. Some other Powers have at times committed or assented to evasions of the principle, but analysis shows that those acts usually were shaped to meet some situation caused by Japan. Any agreement of several parties can be undermined by one of them. A departure from the ''open door'' policy by one Power unsettles the whole doctrine. It is as if a number of railways agree on common rates, and thereafter one of the railways secretly or surreptitiously alters them. As soon as the duplicity is discovered, the other railways will try to protect themselves. Japan's course in Manchuria, Korea, and China has driven other Powers to reassert ''spheres of influence'' formerly claimed by them, as a means of self-protection in case the Hay Doctrine cannot be sustained. Japan's intrigues and persistent disregard of treaties are a chief cause of China's troubles, and of international friction in the far East.

The Hay Doctrine was not a makeshift. When it was accepted by the Powers, in 1899, it was taken as a workable diplomatic formula that opened a way out of the disturbing ''sphere'' muddle in China. The Powers then saw that the ''sphere'' policy was founded on a theory of international collisions of interests, instead of harmony of interests, and that it would be a cause of war if permitted to go on. Joseph H. Choate, then American ambassador to Great Britain, in his note presenting the Hay agreement to Lord Salisbury, said: ''It is the desire of my Government that the interests of its citizens may not be prejudiced through exclusive treatment by any of the controlling Powers within their respective 'spheres of interest' in China, and it hopes . . . to remove dangerous sources of international irritation, and thereby hasten united action of the Powers at Peking to promote the administrative reforms so greatly needed for strengthening the Imperial Government and maintaining the integrity of China.'' It is an interesting reflection, that no other nation has its independence and integrity assured by so many treaties, founded on sound principles of law and equity, and subscribed to by so many Powers, as China has. Yet no nation is in a more precarious and insecure position, in respect to its independence and territorial integrity, than China is to-day. Written treaties alone assure nothing in international affairs.

Japan's procedure when she saw, or thought she saw, in the Great War an opportunity to overthrow the Hay Doctrine, and to put in its place her own exclusive domination of China, has phases of peculiar interest to the United States. Japan's demands in twenty-one articles were presented to China, at Peking, on January 18, 1915. It is now known, as disclosed by the Japanese Government, that the demands were handed to Mr. Hioki, the Japanese minister to China, on December 3, 1914; six weeks before they were presented. Japan's military operations against Germany in China were completed on November 16, by the capitulation of Tsingtau. Immediately afterward, Mr. Hioki was summoned to Tokio from Peking, to consult with his Government. When he returned to Peking he had the demands in his possession, with instructions. This indicates that Japan's extraordinary demands were not a hasty afterthought, but were part of a general plan formulated before Tsingtau fell, and when some nations, and many people in Western countries, were still beguiled by Japan's promise to restore Kiaochou to China. Yet Mr. Hioki waited six weeks after he returned to Peking before he presented the demands. Japan was waiting for a propitious moment. The Japanese Government knew that its demands were revolutionary in character, that they overturned every principle on which the existing international comity in China was founded, that they aimed at the destruction of China's independence; and that for these reasons they inevitably would arouse antagonism and opposition. As Japan then surveyed the situation, she did not fear effective opposition from any of the European Powers. She knew they would be irritated—especially Great Britain—but her allies had their hands full with their own affairs nearer home. The United States remained. That was the most uncertain of important outstanding factors. Japan had no fear of America's military power, but a demonstration, or a strong protest by the United States, might influence other Powers and China, and have a serious effect on Japan's plans. These circumstances lend interest to some contemporaneous events.

Soon after Japan entered the war against Germany, a strong Japanese fleet was sent to cruise in the Pacific, although Japan had stated that her naval operations would be confined to Chinese waters. The German naval victory off the coast of Chili provided a reason, or excuse, for a Japanese fleet to cruise in American waters, presumably to assist in locating and defeating the German squadron. It was subsequently demonstrated that this Japanese fleet had other objects. In December, 1914, the Japanese battleship *Asama* went aground in Turtle Bay, on the coast of Lower California, in Mexican territory. In this connection, Japan's tentative efforts to obtain a coaling station on that coast are remembered. It was nearly three months after the *Asama* went aground before the United States Government learned definitely of her presence there. By that time, other Japanese warships had gone to the *Asama's* assistance, either having advance instructions, or being summoned by wireless. The *Asama* remained in Turtle Bay, being refloated and having temporary repairs, until June, 1915. During that time she was attended by from seven to ten other Japanese warships, and by several Japanese auxiliary naval vessels. One or two British warships that were cruising in that locality looking for German sea raiders also dropped anchor from time to time.   Now consider the location of Turtle Bay, strategically, in relation to the Panama Canal.   The American battle fleet was in the Atlantic Ocean.   For several months, until after Japan had forced China to sign the "agreement" in May, 1915, a Japanese fleet lay at Turtle Bay, or during the whole course of the negotiations at Peking.   Independent investigations indicated that the position of the *Asama* where she grounded was never serious, and that she sustained no damage; in fact, it was plainly intimated that she was purposely slipped on a soft mud-bank, to provide an excuse to assemble a Japanese fleet at Turtle Bay at that juncture.   At any rate, it was not until a Japanese fleet was assembled at Turtle Bay that Mr. Hioki presented the demands of his Government at Peking, and the Japanese fleet did not leave Turtle Bay until the "agreement" had been extorted from China. By then, slides had blocked the canal, and such a strategical disposition was not required.   The relation of these circumstances to Japan's course in China, and to action of the United States pertaining thereto, is of course conjectural, but much significance was attached to them in the far East, where it was regarded as a move to discourage an American protest.   It is a fact that during a period of the negotiations when the attitude of the United States was doubtful, Japan had a fleet in American waters, and convenient to strike at the Canal, that was superior to the American naval force in the Pacific. Japanese diplomacy is seldom separated from force, although the connection between the two often is covered up.

In a previous chapter, I have narrated the course of those negotiations, and the part known to have been taken by the United States.   At the eleventh hour the United States Government placed its position on record, in its note of May 16, 1915.   There is no doubt, however, that the American Government acted with reluctance, and that since Japan suspended negotiations on the immigration question and served notice of her intention to obtain satisfaction by other means, Washington has kept the soft-pedal on Japan-American issues. Even the note of May 16, which one would presume that the United States would desire the widest publicity for, was not given to the press by the State Department. It became public by the alertness of the Peking correspondent (Putnam-Weale) of the "Daily Telegraph" (London), who cabled it to that newspaper. There are many intimations that American diplomacy, in its far Eastern relations, in recent years, has labored under a degree of intimidation, due to the nation's military and naval unpreparedness. On several important occasions it has yielded principles to expediency, and has failed to sustain vigorously and openly its own treaty rights, and international justice.

Having forced China to make an agreement, by which Japan strengthened her position in that country, Japan for a time dropped the mailed fist and reverted to diplomacy to secure that position. Baron E. Shibusawa, Japan's leading financier, was sent on a visit to America in the autumn of 1915. His mission was to present arguments, and to state the position of Japan in some matters. Although Baron Shibusawa spoke as an individual, it was well understood that his utterances were intended to reflect the policy of his Government. He made a number of addresses in America, in the same vein. In those addresses Baron Shibusawa, in euphemistic language, told American business men, and also the Government, that Japan had scrapped the "open door" treaties, and now asserts a superior and exclusive position in China. Japan had obtained by threat of force an agreement with China, and Baron Shibusawa was delegated to inform Americans of Japan's construction of this agreement. He made it quite clear. He said that American capital should unite with Japanese energy and talent to develop China's resources, and dressed the proposition in a lot of pleasant euphemisms. He meant that if Americans want hereafter to participate in commerce and finance in China, they only can do so through Japan, and with Japan's consent. China does not count. America's treaties with China do not count. The Root-Takahira agreement does not count. Japan is the dictator. In a speech delivered in New York, Baron Shibusawa warned Americans that their "activities in China might lead to hostile competition [with Japan], mutual distrust, and bitter animosity, which may be disastrous." His words plainly contain an implied menace. The Japanese Government could not use such language without seeming to be provocative, so it sent an unofficial spokesman to say it. Thus, with a few words, are a score of treaties and conventions wiped out, and the Hay Doctrine is thrown on the scrap-heap, in so far as Japan alone can put it there.

An attempt was made to gild the pill which Baron Shibusawa set before Americans. For some months before his arrival in America, the Japanese press and Japanese press services in the United States had been conducting an inspired propaganda for that purpose. These arguments were dressed in various disguises, of more or less superficial plausibility. The chief ones are: Japan intends to insure the independence of China and the "open door" there by formulating a Japanese Monroe Doctrine for the far East; Japan desires to coöperate with America in protecting and developing China. It is worth while to examine these propositions.

A trick of Japanese diplomacy which one finds constantly repeated in its preparatory propaganda is to take some popularly accepted policy of another nation and draw a real or pretended analogy between it and some policy of Japan. In deceiving American public opinion, Japan has seized upon the fact that a certain long-standing policy of the United States is embodied in the Monroe Doctrine, to advance the idea that Japan is herself morally entitled to announce a similar doctrine as applying to the Orient—and that such a doctrine is applicable to Japan's present policy toward China. In order to see whether the Monroe Doctrine, as advanced and practised by the United States, is adjustable to what Japan is trying to accomplish in the far East, we must first discover what the Monroe Doctrine is. Japanese statesmen and publicists who advance this argument begin by predicating their hypothesis on an assumption which is an insult to America—that, in effect, the Monroe Doctrine is a diplomatic fiction behind which the intention of the United States to absorb or dominate the other American republics is veiled. The Monroe Doctrine is not that, on its face. As enunciated, the doctrine professes exactly opposite objects. It pretends to safeguard the weaker American republics against possible aggressions of stronger nations, and especially from having the monarchial institutions of Europe imposed upon them contrary to their wishes—for at the time when President Monroe enunciated his doctrine, Europe was essentially monarchial in form of government, and the Holy Alliance designed to extend and perpetuate those institutions. That was the essence of the doctrine when it was formulated—and that, to Americans, is its essence yet. Applications of the doctrine have changed with the changes of conditions. Americans no longer fear the reactions upon their own republican institutions from an extension of the monarchial idea to the American Hemisphere. But they are alive to possibilities involved in the domination of South and Central Americas by powerful military nations of Europe and Asia. So the doctrine has survived long after its original incentive became innocuous. It is upheld by almost unanimous popular sentiment in the United States, and is ostensibly accepted by a majority of European Powers.

But, as Japanese statesmen and press insinuate, it is possible for a policy enunciated by Governments to mean something different than what it says. As to that, I concede that Japan can speak with a certain degree of expertness about two-faced aspects of international attitudes, and professions. The Monroe Doctrine might say one thing and mean another. Its real test is how the United States has applied it, during the century of its existence. A hundred years is a long time in political evolution, can ring a good many changes, and can justify, or plausibly seem to justify, radical reversions. How has the Monroe Doctrine worked in practice? It will be admitted—for the present status of the Americas speaks for itself—that in so far as it has had any influence, the doctrine has operated to protect the weaker American republics from encroachments of European Powers, and from having the monarchial system imposed on them. I need not cite instances, which are numerous, of how the doctrine has been invoked, and applied. Japan insinuates that this is all very well—but that the United States has merely been preventing the European Powers from swallowing South and Central Americas, because it intends in good time to swallow them itself. Let us examine that thought, in the light of facts. Take Mexico. For years a condition has existed in Mexico that is ideal if the United States wanted a pretext to seize that country. If other instances are required, take Cuba, take Panama, take the Philippines. And take other aspects of the attitude of the United States relating to South and Central American countries. Has the Monroe Doctrine been invoked to prevent the extension of European financial influence and commerce in those countries, and to secure for the trade of the United States a paramount and preferential position there? The world's commercial and financial statistics answer these questions conclusively. That the trade and financial influence of the United States in Central and South Americas is inferior, in comparison with several European nations, is well known—and it is equally well known that the United States never has made the least effort, or shown the least desire, to establish for itself a paramount and preferential and exclusive position there.

Thus we see that the Monroe Doctrine was intended to accomplish two principal things—(a) *To preserve the territorial integrity and political autonomy of the weak American republics;* (b) *To secure and preserve in those countries the commercial principle of the "open door" for all nations.* And when we look back at the record of history, from the enunciation of the doctrine to the present day, we see clearly that it has worked out that way.

Suppose that the United States had used, or would hereafter use, the Monroe Doctrine to apply in South America a commercial and financial policy like Japan has practised in Korea and Manchuria, and which is embodied in her demands on China in 1915. Suppose that the Monroe Doctrine would be construed to mean that no railway could be built in South America except under conditions dictated by the United States; that no mines or other natural resources could be exploited there without the United States being first consulted; that no foreign loan could be made to any South American nation without the consent of the United States being first obtained, and except with American participation (whether Americans had the money to lend or not); that the United States must be consulted in all important industrial enterprises requiring foreign capital; that Americans must be employed as political, financial, and military "advisers" to South American Governments; that South American Governments must consult the United States when they want to purchase armaments, and must purchase a majority of such supplies from the United States; that when foreign capital is used to build railways in those countries, American managers must be employed, and the traffic rates be fixed so as to give American commodities an advantage over other foreign goods; that supplies used in railways and other utilities in those countries must be purchased in the United States, or be purchased through American firms; that American goods entering those countries will be given preferential customs rates; that Americans shall have a right to own lands and reside in all parts of South America, and not be subject to the laws of those countries; that Americans must be heads of police in important South American cities; that South American Governments could not lease any of their own territories without first consulting the United States; that no contracts to build naval bases or harbor works in those countries would be permitted without first obtaining the consent of the United States; that the United States would have to be consulted when South American countries desired to change their fiscal systems.

Every condition I have enumerated, Japan already has put into effect in Manchuria, and wherever she has succeeded in establishing a "sphere of influence." If the United States placed such a construction on the Monroe Doctrine, for how long would other Powers accept the doctrine without protest?

Is that how a Jap-ized Monroe Doctrine for China, and the Orient, will work out? Is what Japan is trying to do in China to-day rightly comparable to President Monroe's purposes when he formulated his famous doctrine? The Monroe Doctrine was designed to protect the political autonomy of the countries it covers, and to preserve the "open door" there, and has done it. *In short, the Monroe Doctrine, in its theory, and also in its practical application, is almost exactly what the "territorial integrity" and "open door" doctrines in respect to China are, as they were originally advocated by Great Britain, and afterwards formulated by the United States.* So there is already one Monroe Doctrine that applies to China—a doctrine which all the Powers interested in the fate of China have subscribed to, and which presumably is still binding upon them, since none of them has openly repudiated it. Now Japan wants to create another doctrine that is applicable to China. By so proposing, Japan suggests that the present international doctrine regarding China is not satisfactory, and needs to be changed. Yet to America Japan pretends that what she is trying to do in China in no way violates, or is contrary to, the "open door" and "territorial integrity" policies as formulated by John Hay. In conjecturing about what kind of a doctrine Japan wants to substitute for these policies—what her idea of a Monroe Doctrine for the far East under her hegemony is—it is reasonable, and logical, to assume that it would resemble the Japanese conception of respect for the territorial integrity and political autonomy of these countries which Japan has shown in Korea and

Manchuria, and her idea of the "open door" that she has *demonstrated* in those regions. And if that is Japan's conception of a Monroe Doctrine for China, it is plain that a Jap-ized doctrine will be the antithesis of the real Monroe Doctrine.

The twin brother of Japan's Monroe-Doctrine-for-China idea is Baron Shibusawa's "coöperation" proposal. It has a superficial plausibility. One way, it seems like: "Let us not engage in irritating competition in China. Let us join hands, and work together. We need each other." That has a good sound. But what does it actually mean? Taking advantage of extraordinary circumstances, Japan wrung an agreement from China whereby Japan, unless prevented by outside influence, can compel China to do whatever Japan wishes, under menace of force. China needs foreign capital and foreign knowledge to aid in developing her wonderful resources, and she wants this assistance, too; but China wants it to enter under conditions that will not qualify or limit China's sovereignty, or injuriously exploit China, or drag China into trouble with other foreign Powers. In that China is right. Entering China in certain forms, foreign capital is a danger to her national existence. Now Japan, having an "agreement" exacted by compulsion, virtually makes a proposition founded on these circumstances: China will not, except under compulsion, grant facilities in her territory to foreign investments or give guarantees such as some foreign investors want. Great Britain and the United States, the nations to which China logically looks for foreign advice and capital, and that are also able and competent to provide them, are inhibited by their ideals from putting such compulsion on China. Japan is in a convenient position to overawe China and exact any terms from her, and Japan is willing to use her power that way. But Japan herself cannot finance large enterprises in China. Therefore, a good combination would be for Japan to exercise police power over China, to regulate her; and the United States and Great Britain provide the capital, to be spent under Japanese direction. In short, Japan offers to coerce China, while England and America furnish money for Japanese to exploit her. One can see how this scheme would provide an attractive temporary opportunity for a small group of British and American financiers, which in a decade or so might make a good commission at a minimum of risk, provided their own Governments would countenance the deal. But it also would mean a permanent injury to other and larger British and American financial and commercial interests. It would mean the betrayal of China. It would, for the sake of quick and easy profit for some financiers, help establish Japan in a position to dominate China politically and economically, to the handicap of trade and enterprises of other nations. It would divert American capital to finance Japan's competing commercial campaign in China instead of financing American trade there. What has happened in Manchuria, in Korea, and in Shantung since Japan occupied that province, would happen in the whole of China. In view of those facts, Baron Shibusawa's proposition is amazing. In the Chinchow-Aigun Railway scheme, in the Bethelem Steel Corporation construction contracts in Fukien, and in other projected enterprises, Japan used political intrigue backed by menace to debar American finance and industry from China; and obstructed other American plans favored by Chinese. Japan's working hypothesis is plain. She first tries to create a condition so that American finance and commerce cannot enter China without Japan's consent. It is not enough for Japan to obtain political domination of China, and exclusive commercial position there; for while Japan could then prevent other nations from entering China, she could not develop China rapidly without capital, and Japan has no spare capital of her own. Japan wants foreign capital for use in China, in order to exploit China and to make that people an auxiliary to Japan's power; but she wants foreign capital in China to be under Japanese control, and its use limited as Japan wishes and as Japan's Imperial interests require. A certain amount of foreign business can be done in those circumstances, but Japan will take the cream, and when developments reach a sustaining stage the foreign support can be eliminated if that is desirable, without the foreigners or China being consulted. This plan would put foreign capital and trade in China on the same basis as it now is in Japan. Having obtained that control, Japan will be in a position to say to American finance: "China offers a fine field for investment, but you cannot operate there independently, for Japan forbids it. But if you will fall in with Japan, your investments will be protected, and you will be allowed a fair profit until Japan can dispense with your aid."

A fundamental presumption of the Shibusawa plan for "coöperation" of American capital with Japan in China rests on the assumption that Japan can provide capable persons to direct and manage such enterprises, and that they will do better under Japanese direction and management than they would under American or Chinese management. Americans do not admit that Japanese are superior to them as engineers, builders, financiers, and business men. Take the item of railways, which probably offers the largest immediate opportunity for development in China. Baron Shibusawa's idea is that Americans would finance railways in China, and that Japanese would build, operate and control them. This proposal assumes several things—that Japanese are competent railway builders and managers, and that Chinese either are not competent, or are not to be considered. Railways in Japan are managed by the Government. How have they been managed? In 1915 "Jiji Shimpo," a leading Japanese newspaper, said: "The government management of railways has improved neither the service nor the revenue therefrom; and the Government is continually compelled to borrow money to promote efficiency. The fact that railways in Japan are not made to pay their way as in other countries shows that they are not properly managed. Railways managed as the Government manages them would, as private enterprises, be compelled to

Efforts are being made by American missionaries and the American Red Cross Society to employ Chinese famine and flood refugees in reclamation work, and to prevent recurrence of these disasters. Scenes showing this work

go into bankruptcy; but the Government makes the nation supply the deficiency.'' Japan has in past years imposed many Japanese engineers on China, and few of them have been satisfactory. China to-day abounds with incompetent Japanese engineers and mechanics, just as China abounds with inferior Japanese imitations of Western machinery and appliances. While Chinese are not very advanced in modern mechanics and science, there are many young Chinese who have received technical education in Western schools, and some of them already have made brilliant records. Many Chinese are taking technical courses in American colleges, the means being provided by rebate of America's share of the ''Boxer'' indemnity. They expect to return to China and help in the industrial and political reconstruction of their nation. The sentiments of Chinese, if they are superseded or displaced by Japanese in this work, with America's approval, can be understood.

To develop China's resources requires, beside tranquillity, these things: capital, constructive skill, scientific management, labor. No country in the world is better supplied with good labor than China is. China herself can supply some technical experts now, and will supply more as time passes. China still needs a certain degree of foreign aid in management. Much of the capital must come from abroad, although Chinese can supply some. What necessary element must Japan furnish, that requires Americans to coöperate with Japanese in such enterprises in China? If Japanese want to build a railway in China, and can provide the capital, and China is willing, then the United States would not object, or interfere. If Americans want to build a railway in China, and can provide the capital, and China is willing, and there is nothing in the project to conflict with existing treaties or agreements, then why should Japan object? and say: ''Let me in, and let me boss the job, or you can't do it.'' This is the Shibusawa ''coöperation'' proposal, in a nutshell. Baron Shibusawa was entertained in America, and listened to politely; but his coöperation idea made little impression among American financiers, who probably did not see why they should ask Japan's permission to do obliquely what may be done honorably and independently, or by coöperation with other foreign interests that can supply a quota of the necessary capital. Yet when he returned to Japan, statements were published which created the impression that his mission had been successful, and that Americans would coöperate with Japan in China. This news was widely published in the far East, and in China it caused almost consternation, for it was construed as meaning that the United States had been induced to accept Japan's claims in China. How damaging this idea is to American popularity and prestige in China is apparent; and the matter was of such importance that official inquiries were cabled to America, whereupon leading American bankers emphatically denied the imputation, and stated that they would not participate in any projects in China except under conditions that harmonize with the integrity of China, with the "open door" there, and with the announced policy of the United States Government.

As near as Japan's official attitude can be discovered now, it assumes that the "agreement" signed at Peking in May, 1915, is binding on China and other Powers, and that Japan's interpretation of the agreement is to be accepted. It may turn out that way, but it is pertinent to point out that Japan's interpretation has not as yet been accepted, publicly, by any Power. Even China took care, in her official statement of the negotiations,[7] to intimate plainly that she signed the agreement under compulsion, and with a reservation, which was communicated to all of the Powers, that China disclaims all intention to rescind or qualify existing agreements with other nations. China, therefore, served notice that she morally rejects the agreement. The United States Government, in

[7] Appendix R.

its note of May 16, also formally rejects the agreement in so far as it infringes American rights in China under existing treaties. The other Powers, engaged in war, did not commit themselves. Thus the question remained open, for settlement in the future.

CHAPTER XVI

JAPAN AND THE UNITED STATES—*Concluded*

America's attitude defensive—Japan not threatened with attack—Armaments to support foreign policies—Aggressive character of Japan's policies—Japan's challenge to the Monroe Doctrine—Japan and Mexico—Trend of Japanese thought—The strategy of Japan's diplomacy—Its applications to Europe—Its application to weakness and pacifism—American policies threatened—Shall they be defended?—Where to begin the defense—Japan's advantageous position—Analogy of Hay and Monroe doctrines—Can Japan be defeated?—Strategical propositions involved—America's inability to strike—Solution of the difficulty—A Philippine-American alliance.

I HAVE shown that the attitude of the United States toward the Oriental problem is defensive: first, defensive of the right of Americans to decide upon the character of immigration to their own country; second, defensive of rights and principles set out and guaranteed by existing treaties among all the Powers, and of the particular rights and interests of Americans—that is, defense of a policy.

What is Japan's attitude? In respect to Japan's territory, and internal organisms, are they threatened? Does any Power plan an invasion of Japan, or an encroachment upon Japan's administrative prerogatives? If so, there is nothing in world conditions which give premonitions of such designs and purposes. Japanese themselves entertain no such anxiety. In the vast amount of discussion, in the press and the Diet, that attends the recurring army and navy budgets, with their constantly mounting expenditures, the idea of Japan's territory being attacked never enters. Not only does no Power have any sufficient reason so to attack Japan, but no Power has the strength to make such an attack successful, except at disproportionate cost, so long as Japan maintains a fairly large and efficient army and reserve. Japan, within herself, is safe; and the Japanese know it. Yet the nation spends approximately half of its total revenue for armaments, when to do this it is necessary to take half of the total meager earnings of the people in taxation. Why did the Premier, Count Okuma, who also is President of the Japan Peace Society, say in the Diet on December 7, 1915: "Not a single day can be lost in carrying out the naval increase program"? Either Japanese statesmen are mad, or there exists in this chain of circumstances a definite purpose. About the general objects of Japan's purpose in increasing her armaments there is no secrecy—they are admittedly required to protect a policy which operates outside of Japan's own territory. Moreover, unless it is shown that policies to which Japan is committed by treaties are impeached or menaced (when her attitude would be *defensive*), her purpose must be to promote some policy that differs from, or is in addition to, policies to which international sanction has been obtained. This is Japan's true position now. She already has discarded, in so far as her separate action can, the existing international policy in the far East; furthermore, she is developing new phases of policy which require armed power to promote them.

As between Japan and the United States, therefore, America's position is that of defending her own sovereign rights and policies which are a part of existing international law. Japan's position is that of seeking to qualify America's sovereignty, and to overthrow those policies, and to replace the policies by others which are more satisfactory to Japan. In principle, on these issues, America's position is passive, Japan's is aggressive; America's is defensive, Japan's is offensive. These nations clash on questions of *policy*. Some Americans now think (ignoring their country's history) that no nation ought to go to war about a foreign policy, and especially that the United States ought not to defend, or assert, any policy by arms; yet many pacifists who advocate a retreat for the United States on these questions at the same time profess to see nothing wrong in Japan using force, or threat of force, to impose her will and rule over other nations and peoples, even to impose her will and rule over American rights and interests abroad.

Defined as policies, the principal questions where Japan and the United States are opposed are the Hay Doctrine and the Monroe Doctrine. Many Americans, who hazily perceive that there is a difficulty between Japan and the United States about the "open door" in China, do not comprehend how it is that Japan also is challenging the Monroe Doctrine. Japanese diplomacy usually approaches a proposition obliquely; then when a certain position is attained, a more direct method is adopted. Thus Japan began her campaign to destroy the Hay Doctrine by openly professing adherence to that doctrine, and by signing eight separate agreements to sustain it; in that way diverting suspicion of her motives until a change in the situation could be effected and she could come out against it— as she now has done. Japan began her war to annex Korea by declaring that her purpose was to protect Korea's independence, and guaranteeing that independence. Following the same method, Japanese diplomacy commenced its campaign to destroy the Monroe Doctrine by professing to Americans admiration for the principles and operation of the doctrine, and by pretending to model Japan's policy toward China after it. Many Americans even now cannot see that Japan is threatening the Monroe Doctrine.

I previously have analyzed the conditions which tend to impel Japan's emigration toward the Western Hemisphere. It is fully recognized in Japan that such a tendency touches the Monroe Doctrine; only Americans are still blind to the fact. Take an example. Japanese emigration to Mexico has in recent years received considerable stimulus from the Japanese Government. So far, with Mexico in disorder, and with the number of Japanese there comparatively few, no serious question caused by their presence has arisen between Mexico and Japan. Political and economic and sociological problems due to immigration do not come up quickly. For one thing, it requires the presence of immigrants in considerable numbers and for some time to develop the conditions which cause friction with the native or established population. The process is gradual, and usually takes years. Japanese immigration to Mexico, in small numbers, is not likely to disturb conditions to an extent to make them undesirable; they mix with the natives easily, and could assimilate with them were it not for the Japanese sense of racial and political superiority over the lower and middle classes of Mexicans, and the mandate which every Japanese emigrant carries from their own race and nation to preserve wherever they go their racial characteristics uncontaminated, and to retain allegiance to the mother country. If Japanese immigration to Mexico is unrestrained, the Japanese population there might increase to several millions in a decade. Several millions of Japanese in Mexico, by natural increase, would become ten millions in half a century, would submerge the natives, and dominate the country. That ten millions of Japanese in Mexico would create grave complications for the United States, is obvious. But long before Japanese population in Mexico attained that figure, it is reasonably sure that their presence and activities there, from what is known of their conduct in other countries where they regard the natives as inferiors (Korea, Manchuria, and Formosa), would create friction. In that situation, this condition might arise: Mexico might want to place a limit on Japanese immigration, and attempt to legislate to that end. Taking Japan's course toward the United States as a premise, Japan would take offense at such action by Mexico. If Mexico persisted in excluding Japanese, and Japan continued to object, then a serious issue would be raised between Mexico and Japan. If Japan attempted to coerce Mexico, Mexico might invoke the Monroe Doctrine and appeal to the United States. That would be just such a condition as the Monroe Doctrine was designed to meet—to prevent a weak American State from having its autonomy forcibly subverted by a foreign Power. In those circumstances, if Japan by force compelled Mexico to admit Japanese, and to give them full rights and privileges, then in effect the sovereignty of Mexico would pass to Japan, against the will of the Mexicans. Japan's course in Korea and China demonstrates both the principle and the method that might be employed. I take it that none will dispute that such a sequence of events would come within the scope of the Monroe Doctrine as it was conceived by its originator, and as it has been interpreted in the past. If the point should be conceded, and Japan would be permitted to absorb or dominate Mexico, the outcome would be that the military power of Japan, now separated from the United States by the Pacific Ocean, would be transferred to a contiguous land border. The political principles applicable to such a case of Mexico are similarly applicable to any other country on the American Hemisphere.

Is this example far-fetched? On that point, some prominent Japanese may be heard. In the issue of "Shin Nijon" for July, 1914, Count Okuma, in outlining the policy of his Government, wrote: "The United States early in the nineteenth century declared the Monroe Doctrine, thereby preventing the European Powers from invading America *and at the same time undertaking not to meddle in affairs outside of the American continent*. But she could not continue in that policy long. Her economic development necessitated that she should seek outlets for her products abroad, and a field for the investment of her surplus capital. *To-day the Monroe Doctrine is in fact an impossibility*." Count Okuma is, of course, wrong in saying that the Monroe Doctrine engaged not to meddle in affairs outside of the American continent. It did no such thing, although the advisability of attaching this corollary to it often has been discussed, and there have been numerous attempts to read that interpretation into it. Count Okuma had an object in so stating the doctrine to the Japanese. This object is revealed in much Japanese discussion of the subject, and it is put as follows by K. K.

Kawakami, a Japanese author on problems of emigration: "If, however, the United States must object to Japanese enterprise *in Mexico,* she may do it and still remain at peace with Japan. But in that case America must also be ready and willing to accept a similar exclusion policy which Japan may reasonably adopt with regard to American enterprise in *China,* Manchuria, and Korea. America cannot impose upon any foreign nation a condition which she is not herself ready to accept." Note the implied claim of Japan's protectorate or suzerainty over China.

Many Japanese writers are at pains to try to show that the Monroe Doctrine does not cover the question of immigration, while at the same time arguing that, if it does, and could be construed to exclude Japanese from the Americas, then it logically follows that the United States should concede Japan a free hand in China. Mr. Kawakami further wrote: "The United States shall not object to bona-fide commercial enterprise, *including immigration* of the Japanese in such countries of Central and South America, as there is no hostile feeling toward the Japanese. If, however, the United States must object to such enterprises, then she must also be ready to acquiesce in Japanese objection to *American enterprises* in Korea, Manchuria, and *China.*" In an address delivered in the United States in 1915, Dr. Toyokichi Iyenaga said: "Some say Japan pays scant respect to the Monroe Doctrine and might even dare to assail it. I believe not. Japan has no political interest or ambition in South America. *She only wants her people to go there for trade and the pursuit of other industries. And the Monroe Doctrine has nothing to do with the question of immigration, which is, of course, the domestic matter of each sovereign State of South America.*" The contention that the doctrine does not apply to immigration is again emphasized. In discussing the intention of the United States to fortify the Panama Canal, to which he objected, K. Nakashoji, ex-minister of communications, wrote in the "Dai Nijon" for March, 1915: "When the war is over

America will discard the Monroe Doctrine, for pan-Americanism as a new principle of twentieth-century politics. *That the racial competition will be prevalent in the future is too plain to need elucidation.* In the face of this state of affairs, the Japanese people have been providentially dispensed to harmonize the civilizations of the East and West and benefit 1,000,000,000 people of Asia thereby. It must not be forgotten that it is important for them to join hands with the Russians, Britons, and Chinese and obtain a predominant position for solving the Pacific question. But luck will never smile on the idle; therefore the people of Japan must take due measures for accomplishing the object."

Those quotations illustrate a general trend of Japanese thought on these questions. Dr. Iyenaga is correct in saying that the question of immigration is the exclusive concern of each sovereign State. The Monroe Doctrine logically cannot be applied to such a condition, or to any condition, *except at the invitation of an American State.* If it should happen that Japanese immigration to some American countries would be satisfactory to the people and Governments of those countries, the Monroe Doctrine as it was originally conceived would not seem to apply. But it is practically certain, as things are, that extensive Japanese immigration into American countries will in time cause frictions, and then from those frictions a delicate international situation may develop, which will come within the scope of the Monroe Doctrine. Mr. Nakashoji's comments are interesting as introducing a strategical suggestion. He argues that Japan should join with Russia, Great Britain, and China to obtain a predominant position for solving the Pacific Ocean question. In conjunction with a discussion of the Monroe Doctrine, that is significant. Japanese statesmen know that the doctrine is none too popular with European Powers, that some of them would be glad to see it abandoned or broken down, and that others would not object if it was disputed or come to its defense. Japan's diplomatic strategy, therefore, takes that condition to work on. If by diverting Asiatic emigration to the Western Hemisphere, possessions of some European Powers are thereby relieved of its pressure, and at the same time the Monroe Doctrine is broken and South America opened to the colonization of certain Powers, it might help solve European problems by relieving tension at some points, and making openings in new directions. Indeed, it is possible for the influence and diplomacy of Japan, by its application to American and Asiatic problems, to divert the course of world politics, and give it a new turn. If that comes about it is evident that the effects on the position and security and prosperity of the United States will be tremendous, probably detrimental, and perhaps disastrous. That Mexico is included in Japan's survey is demonstrated both by wide discussion and events. In recent years many agents of Japan have been in Mexico, ingratiating themselves with all factions, and obscurely meddling in Mexican politics. Eminent Mexicans have been given enthusiastic receptions in Japan, and Japanese officials have visited Mexico. An alliance has been suggested. Many references are made in the Japanese press about the possibility of Japan intervening in Mexico to protect Japan's interests there, or to sustain Mexico in disputes with the United States. Japan has tried to obtain coaling stations and a naval base there. As in Korea, then in Manchuria, then in China, and now in Mexico, Japan plays the old trick of first establishing a presumption by discussion, then assuming that presumption to be a right, then asserting the right in some oblique diplomatic manner, then backing it by a display of power. It is the Oriental habit of moving by circumlocution. In dealing with weak nations, and nations of strongly pacific disposition, this method is very effective. Often a point can be scored, and a concession secured, because of the stupidity of those in a Government who have to deal with these affairs, and who grant something without comprehending what really is being done, and the significance of the act in its subsequent results. On other occasions, with weak and pacific nations, even when their responsible officials comprehend the consequences of yielding to such arguments and pressure, they often will yield a little rather than risk hostilities, or a serious complication. In that way nations can be and often are deprived of their rights by degrees. In problems now focusing in the Pacific Ocean and its surrounding continents, there is serious danger that, because of ignorance and indifference of the American people about these problems and their meanings, American statesmanship may make concessions out of timidity or reluctance to face an issue which a few years hence will dangerously react upon the United States, and seriously embarrass its policy.

If the policy of Japan threatens, or comes into adverse contact with the Monroe Doctrine, what then? Shall the United States sustain the doctrine, or abandon it rather than fight, or risk a fight, if it should come to that? Such a clash would be chiefly about abstract issues—about policy. Those who oppose wars about policy probably would, in such an event, prefer to abandon the Monroe Doctrine rather than defend it with force. On the other hand, the chances are that a majority of Americans, foreseeing that to permit Japan to dominate Mexico and populate that country with millions of Japanese giving allegiance to their mother land will in time transfer the point of contact in disputes between Japan and the United States from a vague region somewhere across an ocean to the Rio Grande, may decide that it is better, if necessary, to fight to sustain the doctrine in its original scope and meanings. And having accepted that responsibility as an unavoidable burden, those Americans may extend their vision farther, and consider, since to defend or not to defend a policy can lead to such a situation, if it may not be better to begin the defense of the policy at some point more distant from their own national territory, if that is possible; they may reason that if a policy ultimately must be defended, prudence requires that the best way to defend it, and the best place to defend it, and the best means to defend it, should be discovered and provided for without delay. And since a policy

rests legally and ethically upon its essential principles, then
the point to begin to defend a policy would seem to be at
the place, and on the occasion, when its vital principles are
first attacked. In this connection, the close analogy, in principle, of the Monroe Doctrine with the Hay Doctrine is
obvious.

Where, when, and how to defend the policies of the United
States in a collision with Japan are interesting questions. In
defending a policy it is not possible to draw a geographical
line and say to the enemy: "If you cross that line we will
fire." In defending the territory of a country it is easy to draw
a line, although nations threatened with invasion prefer, if that
is possible, to meet the enemy outside their territorial boundaries, and to keep him out. But when a policy is to be defended, it often happens that an enemy can gain every important point, and practically overthrow a policy, without once
attacking the territory of its opponent. This could happen in a
war between Japan and the United States about the Hay and
(or) Monroe doctrines. It is possible for Japan or any Power
to destroy both these doctrines without landing a single soldier
in the United States, or firing a shot at the coast defenses of
America. In the following discussion of strategical phases of
this proposition, I will assume that the United States wants to
sustain and defend these policies. If the contrary is assumed
there is no problem; or the problem will be postponed for one
or two generations, to come up then in different form and
at closer contact. The United States can, for the time, avoid
trouble about the Hay Doctrine by abandoning it, and accepting the consequences; if its possessions in the Pacific Ocean
are coveted by another Power, the United States can avoid
trouble, for the time, by abandoning them; if the Monroe
Doctrine is objected to by another Power, it can be abandoned;
if other Powers, without asking the consent of the United
States, decide to tear up treaties which protect American interests and rights in the far East, the United States can
meekly abandon them. On the other hand, if Americans want

to sustain the Monroe and Hay doctrines, and their treaty rights in the far East, and to have an influence in the political and commercial development of that region, they should face the fact that they cannot be sustained by any war conducted, from the American side, on the borders of the United States.

In any war about conflict of policies, the belligerent that controls the major strategical factors will win. Both the Hay and Monroe doctrines apply to conditions outside of the United States and its territories, therefore any nation or nations that can control the regions where the policies apply practically can say aye or nay to the policies. If the United States and Japan would go to war about these policies, the only way the United States can gain its point, and compel Japan to yield her will to the will of America, is to inflict such injury and detriment on Japan that she will submit. It is evident that Japan can do to American rights what she wishes in China, in the Pacific Ocean, and in South America without attacking the main territories of the United States. To prevent Japan from having her way in the regions where the Monroe and Hay doctrines apply, Japan must be injured and impeded to an extent that she will feel it, and be restricted so that she cannot make her power felt in those regions. Can the United States do that? If not, then it follows that the two major foreign policies of our nation are at the mercy of Japan, to accept or reject as she chooses, in so far as the United States can defend them.

How can Japan be injured, impeded, and restricted by force or influence applied by the United States? There are two methods—diplomatic and military. Consideration is given to the diplomatic method elsewhere, so I will here discuss only the military method. A military invasion of Japan proper would be so difficult and costly, in comparison with other means, that it can be dismissed as impractical; therefore compulsion on Japan is confined to injuries and impediments that can be applied to her externally. There are two means of doing that—blockade, and occupation of Japan's continental and detached possessions. This discussion will be here confined to a war in which the United States and Japan are the only belligerents, for any other presumption brings in diplomatic considerations. It can be said that a complete blockade of Japan by the United States alone is not possible under existing conditions. Japan's geographical position is very advantageous strategically. She has a large merchant marine, a good navy, and she lies close to the mainland of Asia. By the Siberian railways she has a route to Europe which requires only a short intra-marine haul, across the Sea of Japan to Vladivostok, or across the Korea strait from Shimonoseki to Fusan, from where there are rail connections with Siberia and China. The marine routes to China all are comparatively protected and short, across the Yellow Sea to Shanghai, to Tsingtau, or to ports in the Gulf of Pechili. Her marine route to Europe passes by way of Hongkong, Singapore, Ceylon, and the Suez Canal. Unless the United States can seriously interfere with these marine routes of Japan, there is no way of impeding her commerce, and of making a war react injuriously upon her internal situation. It is obvious that the United States army, however large, has no offensive power to obstruct Japan's commerce; that is for the American navy to do. The American navy cannot do it unless it has a numerical superiority over the Japanese navy, and naval bases in the far East. With a view to obtaining expert opinion on these questions to supplement my own, I asked American and foreign army and navy officers the following questions:

1. What is the tonnage (Japanese merchant marine) available for transport and other military uses in a war with the United States, deducting that required to keep Japan's necessary commerce going?

2. What tonnage is required, in event of war between Japan and the United States, in the following instances: (a) A Japanese attack upon an adequately defended naval base in

the Philippines (for the purpose of this question, assume a combined native and American force of 100,000 concentrated in the vicinity of Manila; and that a Japanese force of 200,-000 is required to attack it successfully), (b) A Japanese attack upon Guam (assuming adequate defensive works and garrison), (c) A Japanese attack on Hawaii (same assumptions), (d) A Japanese invasion of the United States or Panama, (e) Japanese operations or strategical dispositions in Korea and Manchuria to safeguard against moves by China or Russia?

3. What time is required to organize and carry out any of the operations indicated in Question 2?

4. What is Japan's situation in respect to supplying herself with supplies and munitions of war, in case American naval operations would impede the importation of such articles or their ingredients?

5. To what extent can the United States, in the event of war threatening, or happening, impede the acquisition by Japan, and acquire for itself, neutral vessels suitable for transport and auxiliary purposes? Is this chiefly a financial competition, or do other factors apply?

6. What military force and defensive works are required to hold and protect a naval base in the Philippines against a Japanese attack, for one year, or indefinitely?

7. Is it feasible to organize a native Filipino force which, with a small American force and American staff direction, can defend a naval base in the Philippines against Japanese attack?—and if so, what size of such native force is required?

8. If such an adequate native military force existed in the Philippines, with adequate defensive works and naval base facilities, what would be the strategical values of such a position toward these conditions—(a) menace to Japan's trade routes with China and Europe, (b) deterring effects on Japanese naval operations in the Pacific Ocean, (c) effects upon a Japanese effort to invade America, or to attack the Panama canal, (d) advantages to American naval operations in

Grounds of the Woman's Academy at Seoul, Korea, an American mission

Students of Pyeng Yang Academy, Korea, an American school. Christian mission schools may be closed or restricted by Japan

Asiatic waters, (e) influence upon Japan by proximity to China, with the possibility of anti-Japanese moves there?

9. In the event of war between Japan and the United States, without the participation of any other Powers, does not the only chance for the United States to impose its contentions over Japan (or to win) depend on sea control?—and is it possible to apply naval force to the defeat of Japan without having advanced American naval bases and strategical positions contiguous to Asiatic waters?

10. Is an American naval and military position in the Pacific founded on a hypothesis of simply defending the Hawaiian Islands and continental territory of the United States compatible with the exercise of any real influence in the fate of China, and the protection and advancement of American interests in China?

11. What is the strategical value of Guam in respect to these propositions? What force and defensive works are required to hold Guam against a Japanese naval attack?—or against a combined naval and military attack? Is Guam so situated as to make such defense feasible?

12. What theoretical naval superiority over Japan is required to give reasonable assurance of the security of American interests and possessions in the Pacific?

13. What parts do China and Russia take, strategically, in a theoretical war between Japan and the United States (or a strong conflict of interests)?—would not any effort of the United States to utilize the land forces of China against Japan, need the Philippines as a means of maintaining communications with China, and possibly to supply China with arms and munitions?

14. To what extent are present defensive facilities and preparations in the Philippines, Guam, and Hawaii deficient and insufficient?

15. Is an American fleet permanently maintained in the Pacific Ocean necessary to protect American possessions and

interests there? and if so, what should be the size of this fleet?

Circumstances restrict publication of information and opinions of this character by army and navy officers, but I can say that the replies that were given coincided with my own views except, in some cases, about minor matters. The expert opinions were practically unanimous about all major strategical propositions. The technical details of working out problems like these probably would be tedious to laymen, and I will try to elucidate the propositions in an untechnical way. It is interesting, however, to insert the table on page 307, compiled by the General Staff Corps of the United States army, and published in September, 1915, in a War College bulletin.

These figures are based on conditions prior to the Great War. A report in 1916 of the Japanese ministry of marine shows over 1,500,000 tonnage of Japanese deep-sea vessels.

Since analysis shows that Japan, in enforcing her will over that of the United States regarding the Hay Doctrine and the Monroe Doctrine, does not need to attempt an invasion of the continental territory of the United States, such an operation can be dismissed from this discussion. The tabulation of the General Staff, as applied to Japan, estimates only a Japanese attempt to invade the United States; but the figures given can easily be adapted to apply to Japanese attacks on the Philippines, Guam, Hawaii, or the Panama Canal. A Japanese attack on the canal would have to make a longer marine haul than an attack on the Pacific coast States, while an attack on the Philippines and other places in the Pacific would require a shorter haul. If the United States would entirely abandon the Philippines, there would be no need to make calculations about their defense; but for the purpose of this argument the Philippines are being considered not in their own capacity, but as a base for operations by the American navy against Japan's marine routes to Asia and Europe. This takes us back to Questions 9 and 10, given previously: (9) "In the event

PREPAREDNESS OF THE GREAT POWERS FOR OVER-SEA EXPEDITIONS.

Nation.	Strength of army.	Tonnage available of ships with capacity over—			First expedition using 50 per cent of tonnage given.[3]		Second expedition using 75 per cent of tonnage given.		Time needed to—	
		3,000 tons.	2,000 tons.	1,000 tons.	Men.	Animals.	Men.	Animals.	Load and cross ocean with first expedition.	Return, load and re-cross with second expedition.
									Days.	*Days.*
Austria-Hungary	4,320,000	....	762,756	....	72,000	14,000	108,000	21,600	20.7	40.4
France	5,000,000	....	1,705,931	....	160,931	32,186	243,295	48,279	15.8	30.0
Germany	5,000,000	3,569,962	4,018,185	....	387,000	81,270	440,000	94,600	15.8	30.8
Great Britain	1,695,000	13,000,000	....	....	170,000	90,000	....	....	14.0	27.0
Italy	2,600,000	....	1,065,321	....	91,000	13,650	136,000	20,475	18.3	35.0
Japan	2,212,000	....	....	2 1,013,985	95,745	24,416	142,622	36,623	22.5	41.0
Russia	5,000,000	....	428,019	....	37,630	7,940	66,444	11,918	20.5	40.0

1 240,500 territorials.

2 Japanese field regulations indicate the intention to use steamers of 1,000 tons; for this reason and because of the large amount of steamers between 10 and 12 knots speed, all Japanese steamers over 10 knots speed and a thousand tons gross have been considered.

3 Fifty per cent. has been assumed as the figure representing the amount of shipping in or within call of home ports at outbreak of war.

NOTE.—The allowance prescribed in our Field Service Regulations of 3 tons per man and 8 tons per animal for ships over 5,000 tons and 4 tons per man and 10 tons per animal for vessels under 5,000 tons has been used in estimating the capacity of ships, except where the regulations of any country prescribe a different allowance. These allowances include rations, water, forage, etc., for the voyage and a margin for three months' reserve supplies. The tonnage allowance covers men, animals, and all accessories and is sufficient to provide for vehicles (including guns).

Fighting power is the result of organization, training, and equipment backed by the resources of the country. Available shipping is a matter of commercial statistics.

of a war between Japan and the United States, without the participation of other Powers, does not the only chance for the United States to impose its contentions over Japan (or to win) depend on sea control?—and is it possible to apply naval force to the defeat of Japan without having advanced American naval bases and strategical positions contiguous to Asiatic waters?'' and (10) ''Is an American naval and military position in the Pacific founded on a hypothesis of simply defending the Hawaiian Islands and continental territory of the United States, compatible with the exercise of any real influence in the fate of China, and the protection and advancement of American interests in China?'' Every expert, American and foreign, to whom the questions were submitted, and who replied at all, answered that without a foothold contiguous to Asia, and naval bases and facilities there, the American navy cannot, with conditions as they are and are likely to be, put pressure on Japan by seriously impeding her marine communications. And unless the American navy can do that, it is not feasible for the United States alone to defeat Japan on an issue arising from the Hay Doctrine.

The problem of defending the Monroe Doctrine against Japan is somewhat different. The Monroe Doctrine can be defended by preventing Japan from exercising her power in South America; and bases at Guam and Hawaii, and a base in the South Pacific, could serve those objects. If, however, Guam and Hawaii are left inadequately defended and unequipped for naval bases, the problem of defending the Monroe Doctrine will be difficult; while with those places in Japan's possession an invasion of the United States is much easier. The problem of defense in the Pacific is largely one of disposition and distribution. Of naval experts I have consulted, none placed the American naval force required to protect American interests in the Pacific at less than a 50 per cent. superiority over the Japanese navy, and a majority placed the margin of effectiveness at 100 per cent.; that is, the American navy should be twice as large as the Japanese

Typical modern school in the Philippine provinces. The great educational work of the United States is the outstanding, feature of American administration of the islands. Every locality now has good schools

navy. Let us assume, then, that the American navy is maintained at not less than 50 per cent. superiority over the Japanese navy, and that the United States standing army is maintained at 200,000 men, with adequate reserves. How should these forces be disposed in respect to possible trouble with Japan? In making a disposition of forces, the effects in deterring Japan from provoking war are almost as important as their use after war starts. The General Staff Corps of the United States army estimates (War College Bulletin, 1915) that 82,000 troops are needed to garrison the Philippines, Hawaii, Panama, Alaska, and Porto Rico. This estimate allows about 28,000 men for the Philippines, and makes no allowance for Guam. Present army and navy plans are predicated on an assumption that if Guam is used as a base, the Philippine base will be abandoned. At recent Congressional inquiries, some army and navy officers expressed opinions favoring the abandonment of the Philippines for Guam as the advanced base in the Pacific, but only in case it should be decided not to retain any political connection with the Philippines, and not to improve the existing force and defensive facilities there. Army and navy experts, as a rule, are not in favor of abandoning the Philippines (of course, this argument applies exclusively to naval and military strategical considerations); but think it would be better to abandon them unless they are provided with adequate defenses, and to retire to Guam or Hawaii. Properly defended bases at Guam and the Philippines have great strategical values, and would handicap and complicate any Japanese attack upon Hawaii, Panama, or United States continental territory; indeed, if supported by sufficient mobile American naval force they would make such attacks impracticable. An American line of defense in the Pacific with an advanced outpost at Guam, or Hawaii, has little offensive power against Japan; that is, while it might suffice to prevent Japan from overthrowing the Monroe Doctrine, or invading continental America, it would be unable to *inflict any damage on Japan,* and consequently would be powerless to impose terms on her; and it could not defend the Hay Doctrine. The best the United States could get out of a war fought under those conditions would be a draw; the enemy might be repulsed, but he could not be punished, or penalized, nor could any restraints as to his future action be imposed. The General Staff allotments I have quoted are based on a disposition of the whole United States army requiring a total strength of a little over 200,000—not an excessive number. This total required strength would not be reduced by taking the 28,000 men allotted to the Philippines and stationing them at Guam, or scattering them among other posts. An elucidation of this question requires examination of elements connected with the Philippines.

In doing this, I will touch but lightly on political and moral aspects of the Philippine question, in its relations to the United States. From the standpoint of the broader policy of the United States in the Pacific, and the problem of defending this policy, the local issue of administration of the islands is not essential, although they are connected. I believe that all interests will be better served by the United States retaining supervision over the islands; but as so many Americans want to give them up, for various and contradictory reasons, I will show that the existence of a strong American outpost there is not incompatible with Philippine independence, but probably is necessary to secure it. Many American politicians, in speaking of "independence" for the Philippines, have in mind only an excuse for American sovereignty to quit the islands gracefully. That has a good sound; a different sound, for instance, than proposing to sell the islands, or to trade them, with or without their consent, treating its inhabitants as political chattels. To turn the millions of Christian Filipinos over to be ruled and exploited by a non-Christian Power also has an ugly sound, and this phase of the question is kept in the background by the advocates of abandonment. To quit the islands under those conditions only can be advocated and defended on the ground of *expediency,* on the theory that somehow, by so doing, the United States will be relieved of expense, and of danger. This theory disregards the issue of moral responsibility; it disregards the question whether such a course will entail expense and danger to the Philippines, and eventual subjugation of the Filipinos. It does not take into account how, if it is not possible for a great nation like the United States to protect the Philippines, the Philippines could defend themselves. But in thinking about independence Filipinos must consider these matters, must consider how they can maintain their independence, how to preserve order internally, and to repel external aggressions. I presume that most Americans would regard a condition whereby the Philippines might be substantially independent to manage their own affairs, be free peacefully and without outside interference to pursue their destiny and to progress, be secure in their liberties, and be able financially to sustain that status, as an ideal one, and a proper outcome of the uplift work the United States has done there. For the Philippines to have a few years of "independence," then to fall under the dominion of an Asiatic Power, and take a place similar to Korea and Formosa, to be inferior in all respects to their overlords, to be restricted as to education, in the practice of Christianity, in participation in commercial and industrial development of their own country, hardly would satisfy the aspirations of Filipinos, or the conscience of America. Is there a way by which desires of both Filipinos and Americans can be accomplished? If there is such a way, ought it not to be taken?

The General Staff allots 28,000 American troops to defend a base in the Philippines under existing international conditions. Let us consider this problem in another way. If the Philippines become independent, they will require an army to police the country and as a means for defense. If the support of the United States is withdrawn entirely, then the Philippine army will have to be increased accordingly. Experience with the native Philippine scouts and constabulary has demonstrated that they make good troops. A fairly efficient Filipino army, therefore, is a matter of funds and organization; and such an army can be maintained for about one-fifth what an American force of the same size costs there.   Suppose that the Philippine Government would organize and maintain a standing army of 100,000, with a larger reserve which could quickly double or treble the army in war.   Suppose that the United States would retain a naval base in the islands, with a comparatively small garrison.   Suppose that the Philippine Republic and the United States would make a treaty, whereby in the event of either becoming involved in war with an Asiatic Power they would support each other; that this treaty would require the United States to provide a number of military officers to help train the Filipino army, that the United States would supply the Philippine Republic with arms and equipment, and that in war the United States Staff would direct the joint operations. Such an arrangement would seem to assure most of the objects, in so far as foresight and moderate preparation can assure these things, of both Filipinos and Americans.   It would relieve the Philippines of all expense for naval equipment and coast defenses; for the United States navy would provide that defense. It would enable the United States not only to grant independence to the Philippines, but to aid in securing it.   It would make it possible for the United States, in addition to accomplishing those objects, to be in a position to defend its policy in the far East without extra expense and without increasing its naval and military organizations above the size required merely to maintain a purely defensive security in the Western Hemisphere.   By such an arrangement, a garrison of 10,000 United States troops would be sufficient in the Philippines, and the 18,000 thus relieved would be available for Guam and other points.

What I am trying to demonstrate is this: It requires no larger army and navy, no greater expense, to do the things which the United States is morally obligated to do in the Philippines and which best serves the interest of the Philippines than not to do them, while to do those things will also put the United States in a position to sustain its policy in the far East and to retain influence in the tremendous questions focussed in that region. As to risk of war, to do those things tends to lessen it by discouraging aggressive Powers from forcing issues with America that cannot be sustained by equity and justice. I contend that a basis can be found to safeguard all of America's moral obligations and policies in the Pacific, and to give them reasonable protection, without incurring extraordinary danger, and without maintaining additional naval and military force exclusively for that purpose. It is quite feasible, in granting independence to the Philippines, to make it obligatory for the Philippines to maintain a specified military organization, in return for aid from America in maintaining that independence. The advantages to the Filipinos are obvious.

With a well-fortified naval base in the Philippines, which in war would be supported by a native Filipino army of 100,000 to 200,000 troops under American staff direction, no anxiety need be felt for their security against an attack by Japan, provided the American navy is offensively superior to the Japanese navy. So situated, a Japanese army of at least 250,000 would be required for an attack on the Philippines. That would be a major military operation, and if it was undertaken Japan could not at the same time undertake another major oversea military operation, for lack of sufficient marine transport and naval convoys. In that situation, in contemplating war against the United States on any question, and not possessing decisive naval superiority, Japan's operations would be subject to severe strategical limitations. Her facilities for oversea military operations would limit her to one major expedition at a time. If she attacked the Philippines, other American territories would be immune, except from excursions, until the Philippine operations were concluded; if she elected to attack Hawaii, or Panama, or the Pacific coast, the Philippines would be comparatively immune, and would exist as a base for commerce-destroying operations against Japan's lines of communication with Asia and Europe. With a base in the Philippines protected by such an alliance, or an arrangement similar in its results; with an adequately defended and garrisoned base at Guam, and another at Hawaii; with the canal adequately fortified and garrisoned, the American navy would have both defensive and offensive striking power in the Pacific Ocean and Asiatic waters, enabling it to support not only policies applying to continental America, but also policies applying to the far East.

CHAPTER XVII

CONDITIONS AFFECTING AMERICA'S SECURITY

How a war can begin—Qualifying influences—Incidental restrictions on Japan—A new phase of war—Japan's munition business—An unexpected windfall—Government monopoly—Opportunity for naval expansion—Bringing Japan's arsenals up to date—Is America financing an enemy?—Conditions of the Great War—Capital and patriotism—American credits to belligerents—The position of Russia—The principle involved—The relations of capital to nationality—Japan's naval program—Elements of time and cost—Japan's self-sufficiency in construction—Extent of Japan's dependence—Will Japan pass America?

ANY well-prepared nation, bent solely on its own aims, can start a war. It does not require provocation, or excuse, or justification. It can invent or incite provocation, take that as excuse, and depend on might for justification. Japan is the instigator of a trouble-making formula in the far East which seriously includes the United States in its effects, and probably also as a participant. But there are measures which pacific nations can take to qualify and deter a trouble-making formula. I do not refer to treaties; they at most usually record understandings that are predicated on ephemeral conditions, and are worthless unless supported by force. Modern nations touch each other so intimately, so variously, that it is always possible for any strong nation to exercise a great influence on all other nations; an influence that can be applied frequently by pacific means.

As I wish to attract attention to specific facts, I will illustrate by citing certain conditions existing in the far East, and try to show their relations to the United States. Take Japan's course in the Great War. I have indicated Japan's motives in participating, by seizing Tsingtau and some islands in the

315

Pacific Ocean, and by taking the opportunity to intimidate China. In this policy she was influenced at times by other nations, and by the United States. Although official published action of the American Government, in respect to Japan's demands on China, was limited to taking certain exceptions, America did exert, perhaps unwittingly, a considerable influence upon Japan's course. Japan's intimidation of China, which culminated in the so-called agreement signed in May, 1915, coincided in its latter stages with the great Teutonic drive against Russia, which brought out sharply Russia's deficiencies of munitions. Just about then, too, all the Entente belligerents were beginning to realize that munitions might decide the war. Russia in her need already had almost denuded Japan of surplus munitions, purchased at high prices. As a consequence, the crisis with China forced by Japan, when it encountered resistence by China, caught Japan unprepared in the sense of being short of munitions. This was the world situation, in respect to munitions supply, at that time: the Allies had, apart from the nations fighting in Europe, only two effective sources of supply—the United States and Japan. There was a strong agitation in America against the export of munitions in large quantities, and at that time none was able to foretell just what position the United States Government would eventually take on this question. It appeared that a number of considerations would apply. With Japan threatening a fundamental American policy in China, which might involve the United States, the American Government might see the advisability of keeping munitions at home; or America might be drawn into war for other reasons. Also, if Japan was to reap the profits of supplying Russia with munitions, she could not herself embark on a war against China, which would ruffle her own allies and America. At that juncture, beyond doubt, also came in another influence of Great Britain, France, and Russia. Their need for munitions was paramount—without them they faced defeat in Europe, or a prolongation of the war indefinitely. Those Powers exerted influence with Japan to induce

American defenses in the Pacific Ocean. El Fraile, a rock in the south channel of the entrance to Manila Bay, which is being fortified

Landing at Corregidor Island, the "Gibraltar of the far East," commanding the entrance to Manila Bay

her to take a course which would not stem the flow of munitions from America, and also would permit Japan to supply her own maximum production to Russia. What the allied Powers promised Japan, to be redeemed afterward, is not known; although the Japanese Diet and the Japanese press pointedly hinted at "compensations" for Japan relaxing her grip on China's throat, which the future would reveal.

A glance at some elements of Japan's internal situation will illuminate this. For years Japan has been straining her finances to provide for an extraordinary naval and military expansion, and some necessary factors were unavoidably delinquent, among which was facilities in Japan for the manufacture of war munitions. Japan, like other nations, had not fully grasped the proportionate relation of ammunition to modern warfare. She knew she was deficient, but how badly deficient she did not begin to comprehend until the Great War had been going on for some time. I am inclined to think that this discovery (which synchronized with a similar discovery of Japan's European allies) provided the crucial factor in the various matters that combined to make Japan partly suspend her pressure on China. Japan's military experts decided that, before anything more could be risked, it was necessary to improve and greatly augment Japan's means to manufacture war munitions. And there was the means to hand, aptly provided by the urgent needs of the Allies in Europe. The reason why Japan was behindhand in manufacturing equipment for war was her limited funds. Strain as she did, she still had not been able to find the money to do all that she wanted to do. Some parts of her military machine lagged a little, and her arsenal equipment, like that of all the allied Powers, was behind the other branches. Here was an unexpected and most welcome opportunity to remedy that defect. The need of her allies created a means to build up munition factories in Japan to supply them, and also provided a way for Japan to finance this important branch of her military preparedness, which she previously had been too poor to do.

From estimates derived from Japanese sources, munition orders exceeding $500,000,000 were placed in Japan in the years 1915–16. Taking prevailing conditions and practice as a criterion, it is fair to assume that a profit of 15 per cent. was made on those orders. It is estimated that before the Great War ends Japan will get a billion dollars' worth of munition orders. A 15 per cent. profit on what she received in 1915 would be about $75,000,000. A similar profit on what she will probably get would be $75,000,000—a total of $150,000,000. A Japanese economic writer, Mr. Tsumura, has analyzed the process whereby the principal industries of Japan have been brought under the control of the Government. He states that in 1901 the Government had 27 per cent. of the total capitalization of the industries of the country; 31 per cent. in 1902; 32 per cent. in 1903; 33 per cent. in 1904; 35 per cent. in 1905; 41 per cent. in 1906; 59 per cent. in 1907; 87 per cent. in 1908. I believe the proportion receded slightly in recent years. It is estimated that the Government owns nearly one half of the entire valuation of all properties in Japan. This is a chief cause for the poverty of the people, and has been brought about by two main causes—exploitation of the people by the commercial and financial oligarchy, and the convenience which this system provides for the Government to levy taxation by indirect methods. The Japanese annual budgets plainly show (although much is withheld) the effects of Japan's expansion policy upon her national finances. When Japan devoted herself to internal improvement her national debt remained low. Only $25,000,000 was added to it during the first sixteen years of the late emperor's reign, when the total debt (1883) was $140,000,000. In 1902 the debt was $265,000,000, but it rose to $1,050,000,000 in 1906 owing to the war against Russia. No money indemnity was obtained from Russia, and according to Mr. Tsumura Japan's national debt had swollen in 1911 to $1,277,709,000, of which $1,218,714,500 was owed abroad. Japan's annual interest charge on her debt is now over one third of the total expenditure of the Government. In 1912 the total ordinary budget was $205,500,000; of which only $61,000,000 was for administration, the remainder going for armaments and interest. Of late years Japan has had an extraordinary budget for naval expansion, which in the last year brought the total to over $300,000,000; while the tonnage of the Japanese navy has increased from 50,000 at the time of war with China (1895–05) to over 500,000 now. In the same period the Japanese standing army has been increased from seven divisions to nineteen divisions; two more divisions have just been authorized for "the protection of Korea," and the program calls for an increase to twenty-five divisions. Japan's military and naval expansion is entirely responsible for the burdensome taxation, and the recurring fiscal deficits. When the chance for Japan to increase her production of war munitions came, the Government saw its opportunity, and ordained that only the Government should undertake the manufacture of ammunition and other purely war materials. This created a government monopoly of these products, enabling the Government to decide exclusively the details of this expansion, and, what is equally important, to include the profits in the government revenues without publishing them. In this way the Japanese Government has found the way vastly to expand its means to produce war munitions, and also the money to facilitate its naval and military expansion. It could be argued (indeed, it has been argued in the Diet), that this windfall might better be devoted to other uses, to lightening the burden of taxation, and to internal improvements, rather than be spent on further increases of armaments. It could be used to reduce the national debt, and to meet maturing obligations, some of which are pressing. In an interview with Minister Taketomi of the Japanese Department of Finance, published in 1915, he estimated the *deficit* for the current fiscal year at yen 10,000,000 ($5,000,000), and further ascribed the deficit to a decrease of revenue from all taxes, and especially from government-controlled enterprises; and that the finance department contemplated meeting maturing obligations by new issues of bonds. This statement, taken in connection with the fact that the Japanese Government expected to get hundreds of millions of profits on munition orders, is significant. We have a finance minister announcing a fiscal deficit, coupled with a suggestion that maturing bonds cannot be met out of revenues, and therefore will be converted. There is no doubt that Japan, out of munition profits, had funds to balance her budget deficit, to meet maturing foreign-held bonds, and for other purposes too. Yet the Govment prefers to keep its munition profits as a special fund to be used—how?—while it borrows abroad the money to convert maturing bonds. The use Japan intends to make of her munition profits is indicated by the announcement of Admiral Kato, minister for naval affairs, that the naval increases must take precedence, and Count Okuma's statement in the Diet, that not a day can be lost in carrying out the plan of the Japan National Defense Council. This plan is called a *repletion* of the navy, and means a gradual replacement of old ships with new and more powerful ones. By this device, the number of units in Japan's active navy will not seem to grow, on paper; but in reality her building program will be accelerated. This repletion scheme apparently is in addition to the published program for eight super-dreadnoughts and eight battle-cruisers. It seems that the repletion plan was decided on in the autumn of 1914, but the censorship was used to suppress the information, and to mislead the world about it.

Let us look a little farther. If Japan conserves her munition profits for naval and military expansion, thus not having to arouse her own population by demands for new revenue, perhaps also being able to escape the notice of other nations, while she meets maturing foreign obligations by new loans, she will be able to get on a war basis without difficulty, and without attracting much attention. How is this war preparedness being financed? Japan is not financing it by herself. That is clear. Analysis shows that the United States has helped to finance Japan's preparedness, in this way. Japan is making war munitions, and selling them principally to Russia. Russia

herself had no money to pay for them; the financing of the transactions was handled by Great Britain and France. Great
Britain and France were themselves large purchasers of munitions derived principally from America. In the autumn of
1915 those Powers arranged a credit loan of $500,000,000 in
the United States, and more may be asked for. The establishment of these credits in the United States releases British and
French capital which can be lent to Russia, which nation in turn
pays it to Japan. Thus, indirectly, American credit has as-
sisted in financing Japan's war preparations.

So we arrive at a paradox. Against what nation, or nations,
are Japan's war preparations directed? Japan has got all she
can at the expense of Germany, and all she can get out of the
Great War, unless she is "compensated" for sending troops
to Europe at the expense of China and the United States. Is
Japan arming against China alone? Japan's ordinary armaments are more than sufficient to defeat or overawe China.
What theoretically formidable enemy remains? The logic of
this situation points to the United States as the nation Japan
is preparing against. If this is true, we have American financiers helping to finance a military and naval program directed against the United States.

Such a situation is not as peculiar as it seems at first thought;
indeed, it is a commonplace for capital of one nation, or nationality, to finance warlike and other activities of competing and
even hostile nations. "Capital knows no patriotism" is a saying which, if not quite exact, at least approximates modern conditions. For many years (as brought out in reports of the
British Board of Trade) British capital (or London financiers)
has been largely financing Germany's world trade campaign,
thus freeing German capital to finance Germany's military
and naval preparations. Great Britain was among the latest
of the European Powers to grasp the modern significance of that
system, and her Government is devising means to put checks on
British capital in its international ramification hereafter. Germany, France, Russia (although Russia is not much of a lender

or investor outside her own domains), and Japan some time
ago took steps to prevent their own capital from being employed in ways that may contravene the national policy and
interests. In those nations few large financial operations extending abroad can be carried through except with the Government's approval. In France, Germany, and Japan, securities cannot be listed on the bourses without the approval of the
Government; which means that investors of those nations will
hesitate to purchase securities not so listed, and consequently
places a limitation on the underwriters. That system confines
the foreign financing of bankers and capitalists of those nations
to comparatively small operations, unless they come under some
degree of government supervision. Under that system it is not
feasible for an issue of foreign bonds to be floated in a country
except with government approval, unless bankers are prepared
to take up the loan with their reserve funds. The system
imposes certain, and at times irksome, restrictions on capital;
but it has the merit of preventing a Government's broad political policy from unwittingly getting at cross purposes with big
financial interests of its own nationals, or *vice versa;* and also
tends to prevent a nation's capital from being used, unbeknown
to its Government and people, for their own undoing. If American financiers would coöperate with Japan in China under the
terms proposed by Baron Shibusawa, it would be a case of
capital knowing no patriotism. In such instances, if capital
of and by itself has no patriotism, some means should be found
by moral suasion to instil patriotism; or if that is not possible,
to restrain it within patriotic bounds by legal restrictions.
When the American credit to the Allies of $500,000,000 was be-
ing negotiated, it was called to the attention of the financiers and
the Government at Washington, that the credit did not include
Russia, and that it ought to include Russia. By the terms
and conditions of the loan (or credit), the apparent exclusion
of Russia was a subterfuge; for while the credit was to Great
Britain and France, it would aid those nations to make advances
to Russia and their other allies. How funds so obtained by

Russia financed Russia's munition transactions with Japan I have shown; and the exclusion of Russia from that American loan was a fiction. To America it had the disadvantage, in respect to Russia, of freeing Russia from obligation to America, while at the same time benefiting by America's financing. Russia, technically, is obligated to Japan for furnishing the munitions, and to her European allies for being financed; while the nation which makes the trade possible takes neither material or political gain, so far as Russia is concerned, from the transaction. Those who urged that Russia should be directly included in these credits did not do so in a spirit of opposition to credits to the Allies. The principle of such credits is sound; but they should be so framed as to reap all possible advantages for, and to contain no serious disadvantages to, the United States. If America aids in financing Russia, let America obtain from Russia the moral and political credit such action calls for, which would partly offset the obvious political and material benefits Japan reaps from that situation. Since America can confer such assistance, the converse is true—she can work a corresponding disadvantage by withholding it. This is a leverage of great political power, which it is legitimate to exert; which should be exerted to secure recognition for American viewpoint and American interests in places where these are affected by a war, and by its settlement. On that basis, the need of the Allies to draw on American resources in prosecuting military operations could be applied to conditions in the far East, and conduced to preserve a *status quo* in the Pacific that will coincide with America's interests and policy.

Having these conditions in mind, I submitted to naval experts the following questions:

1. Assuming that Japan has in hand $150,000,000 obtained in addition to ordinary revenues, which she devotes to expansion of her navy, what program would be possible?

2. What is the state of Japan's marine building facilities, and what would be their maximum production under pressure?

3. To what extent can Japan produce armor plate, and big naval guns?

4. Is it now feasible for Japan to produce within herself all the ingredients of a modern battleship, and other modern naval craft?

5. To what extent can Japan, during the Great War, derive such supplies from other countries?

6. To what extent does Japan obtain armor plate from the United States?

7. Assuming that Japan spends $150,000,000 on naval expansion, in addition to her regular building program, how rapidly can she increase her naval strength?

8. Assuming such acceleration of Japan's naval program, how will it affect the comparative naval power of Japan and the United States, taking the present rate of American construction?

9. In money cost per unit (including operation), what result, in comparison with America, can Japan procure in naval construction with a given amount: that is, what naval power can Japan obtain by spending $150,000,000 compared with what the United States will get for the same sum under present conditions?

10. What measure of acceleration is required (assuming this advance in Japan's strength), for the United States to maintain naval predominance over Japan?

11. Taking present conditions in the United States navy, and proposed legislation recommended by the department, and an increase of the Japanese navy as above indicated, what would be the comparative naval strengths of the two nations in three and five years?

Taking my own information and that supplied by naval experts on these matters, if Japan has the funds available she can pass the United States in naval strength within a few years unless the usual American building program and process are increased and accelerated. Japan now can lay down five capital ships simultaneously, and in a year can provide ways

Philippine native troops. A company of Moros

Philippine native troops. A company of constabulary

to lay at least three more. She has ample ways to build smaller ships. Heretofore Japan has built warships slowly, about as slowly as they are built in America; but lack of funds has retarded Japan. She also has been delayed by her desire, for economy and national security, to produce in Japan all the ingredients of all types of warships. She is now able to do this. Japan makes at the Muroran and Kure government plants armor-plate up to 12-inch, and naval guns of the largest calibers now used. What maximum output of armor-plate and big guns the Japanese plants have is a military secret; but it is doubtful if within the next few years they can supply plate and guns for as many capital ships as the yards can lay down. While the Great War continues, and perhaps for some time afterward, Japan cannot obtain armor-plate and big guns from abroad, unless they come from America. A deficiency in any important ingredient checks construction, so the measure of Japan's naval construction capacity may be her ability to supply any single ingredient. Japan cannot build capital ships any faster than she can provide guns and armor for them, or engines, or steel plates. Japan's munition business has provided means to supply and reinforce some former deficiencies and insufficiencies in her arsenals and navy yards. However, there are physical limitations on naval construction by Japan exclusively. Just what they are is accurately known only to the Japanese naval staff. It is possible that Japan is drawing materials and naval supplies from America, as well as financial help. Japan has an advantage over America of about 20 per cent. in cost of warship construction, and over 100 per cent. in cost of naval maintenance; that is, Japan can build warships 20 per cent. cheaper than they are built in the United States, and it costs about twice as much to maintain an American warship as it does to maintain a Japanese ship because of different standards and conditions of service. So for a given amount, Japan can get more warships than the United States can. For $150,-000,000 Japan can build about twelve capital ships—super-dreadnoughts and battle-cruisers. It has been taking Japan three to three and one-half years to build a capital ship, but she can shorten that time a great deal. It has been taking three to four years to build a capital ship in America, and experts estimate that it can be done in twenty months. On this basis of figuring, Japan can by spending an additional $250,000,000 build twenty new capital ships in four years. At the rate of increase provided by Congress, that would carry Japan ahead of the United States in naval strength. Japan, however, can only pass the United States by sufferance. There are facilities to build sixteen capital ships simultaneously in the United States, and guns, armor, and other furnishing probably also can be supplied without much delay. Japan cannot pass America in naval strength unless Americans are willing. The American General Naval Board advocates a program which will provide twenty-eight modern capital ships by 1922, which is considered necessary to keep ahead of Japan. At present the United States is well ahead of Japan in battleships, but has no battle and scout cruisers. Japan has four battle-cruisers in commission, and several of the newest type of scout cruisers are under construction.

CHAPTER XVIII

THE MEASURE OF SUFFICIENCY IN NATIONAL PREPAREDNESS

Elements of this proposition—The two standards—Powers and dependent nations—Examples of China and Belgium—Belgium's strategical position—Her measure of sufficiency—China's position—Her measure of sufficiency—The pacifist and armed theories of preparedness—Relation of preparedness and unpreparedness to international security—Modern origins of war—The clash of commerce and industry—The balance of power—Its effects on America—The naval balance—The international balance of interest—Old bases of security destroyed—America's weakness revealed.

IN efforts to readjust their national life and organization to new forces in the world, whose existence they hardly had suspected, Americans seem to agree on one point—all are for "adequate preparedness" for defense. But there is wide divergence of opinion about what constitutes "adequate preparedness." Extreme pacifists think that treaties with other nations are all the security needed; the other extreme requires a superior military and naval power over any nation or combination of nations. Between these extremes, popular thought is confused, and so are many administrators. What constitutes the measure of sufficiency for the security of a nation? Can this be determined? And if so, what is the measure of sufficiency in military and naval forces for the United States?

This is a proposition which can be worked out by approximation. It depends on a balancing of elements and probabilities. It rests on a sliding scale according to fluctuations of national ambitions and interests and armaments. These ambitions, interests, and armaments, fluent as they are, nevertheless are as tangible as any elements of modern civilization with which political science has to deal; they come within the scope of practi-

cal human affairs. In theory, justice requires that the measure
of sufficiency for the security of nations in their existence and
rights is the same for all. In practice, there evidently are at
least two standards. In this respect, nations can be divided
into two classes: (a) Those able, with qualifications, to protect
and enforce their own rights in the world; and (b) those whose
strength is not sufficient to sustain their own rights, which
therefore depend on a balance of power among other nations.

When the Great War began, the United States assumed for
itself a position among the nations (usually called Powers),
which are able to protect and enforce their rights in the world,
and therefore to direct their own destiny. Events have shaken
this assumption. Most Americans now realize that their nation
has slight physical power to enforce its rights abroad; but the
United States still ranks among the Powers because of its vast
potentialities, and by reason of circumstances which make it
feasible for them to be converted into actual power. It is the
availability for use of resources, not merely their existence, that
hereafter will determine the position and influence of nations in
the modern world. The natural resources of China are exceeded
by no nation; yet she is in grave danger of falling into vassal-
age. It is doubtful if China still has control over her own
national destiny. By a wrong philosophy and long disuse of
her resources she has lost control over them, and to-day cannot even use them internally except under qualifications imposed by foreign Powers. China will not now be permitted
to arm to protect herself, if some Powers can prevent it, and it
is probable that they can. China is an example of a State
which, with all elements of becoming a Power herself, has taken
a course that has placed her in the class of nations whose
sovereignty and rights depend on external forces. Belgium is
an example of nations in that class because of circumstances
that, in modern times, are mostly beyond her control. Belgium has not the resources to become a Power—her national
rights and existence hang in the balance among the Powers.
China and Belgium are in the same class for different reasons

and causes, and their fates in the Great War provide a practical illustration of some phases of the problem of sufficiency in preparedness for defense.

It may be well to take up, in order, the two chief theorems of national, or international, peace and security, as demonstrated by the cases of Belgium and China—the extreme pacifist as distinguished from the armed defense theorem: for the problem of a scientific measure of sufficiency is purely academic if the pacifist theorem is correct. Both Belgium and China, being comparatively weak in armaments, depended on a balance of power, as expressed in treaties, for security. In both cases principal Powers had subscribed to treaties giving satisfactory assurances; but what both Belgium and China really depended on was a balance of interests among the Powers that would offset predatory policies and armed aggressions of any of them. Both China and Belgium have suffered the detriments of a state of war within their territories. They are losers by the war without hope of gain from its outcome, and with little prospect of compensation for their losses. But there are fundamental differences about the ways that Belgium and China became involved. Belgium geographically lies almost directly between Berlin and Paris, and offers the shortest and easiest way to move armies between those capitals. That was her misfortune. In European military circles it was well understood that in a war between France and Germany singly, both nations probably would respect the neutraliy of Belgium. It was equally well understood that if Germany had to fight France and Russia at the same time, Germany almost certainly would march troops across Belgium and Luxembourg. At war with both France and Russia, or a greater combination of nations, Germany's chance for success would be to defeat France quickly, before the whole power of Russia could be applied on her other frontier. In those circumstances, it was a foregone conclusion with military experts (and also, we may be sure, with Governments), that Belgium's neutrality would be infringed upon to a greater or less extent. In that connection it is pertinent to point out that while it would be advantageous to Germany to march troops quickly across Belgium, it would not be equally advantageous for Russia and France to do that. Therefore, France and Russia would not be likely to initiate violation of Belgium's neutrality, for it would not be to their interest to do so. The interest of France and Russia would be served by keeping Belgium neutral, or if they could not keep her neutral to have her on their side. In considering Germany's action, and criticisms passed on it, one cannot help reflecting about what action the Allies would have taken toward Belgium if the strategical conditions in the first stage of the war had turned the other way. Perhaps an answer to that thought can be found in the treatment of China. By the interference of Japan, Kiaochou, a leasehold of Germany in China, was attacked. The position of Kiaochou was not connected in any important way with the main operations of the war, nor could it affect the outcome. To neutralize it by agreement would have required but a few weeks for diplomacy to arrange had there been a real desire of the belligerents to respect China's neutrality. For Kiaochou to parallel Belgium it would have to lie somewhere in the convenient path of an Allied invasion of Germany. It does not so lie. Whether Kiaochou was for the time occupied by Germans or Japanese or Chinese could not importantly affect the decision of the war.

With exception that the position of Belgium is of great strategical importance in relation to the main war operations, and might decide their eventual outcome, while the position of Kiaochou was of negligible strategical importance and could not affect the outcome of the war, the legal and moral aspects of the plights of Belgium and China are analogous. There was a military excuse—not a right, not a justification, but an excuse —for Germany's violation of Belgium's neutrality. There was not a reasonable military excuse for violation of China's neutrality in the attack on Tsingtau. In the case of Belgium, strategical military motives as applied among the belligerents inspired the action; in China, the motive was provided by politi-

cal designs of a single Power casually and unnecessarily included in the war.   Both Belgium and China therefore were
vicariously involved in war; Belgium because of anxiety of
belligerents to strike each other, and China because of designs
upon her territory and sovereignty.   Thus we have two methods by which weak nations can be dragged into war, without
their consent, practically demonstrated as to motives and circumstances.   There is nothing in the cases of China and Belgium that could not have been foreseen and either wholly or
partly insured against by themselves.   Belgium was constantly
threatened by a collision of great Powers whose armaments she
could not equal, so it was not possible for her to be absolutely secure.   Her measure of armed sufficiency must therefore
be fixed at her maximum of preparedness.   Assume that when
war began Belgium was at her maximum of armed preparedness.
Would that have made any difference?   It might.   The strategical advantage to Germany in August, 1914, of striking
at France through Belgium turned on two factors—time and
cost in men.   Some military critics contend that, as it was, the
resistence offered by Belgium defeated Germany's strategical
object.   If Belgium's armed strength at the beginning of war
had been three or four times what it was, it is reasonable to
assume that she would have been immune from invasion in case
she desired to remain neutral.   In those circumstances the cost
and delay to either side, in violating Belgium's territory,
would have more than offset any advantage that could be
gained; *ergo,* it would be poor strategy, and still poorer politics.
If Belgium could have mobilized a million men simultaneously
with the other grand mobilizations, the probability of her
neutrality being forcibly violated would have been small.
She could have remained, like Switzerland, Holland, and Den-
mark, free of war and able to keep her industry and commerce
going with restrictions.   Or if she had wanted to enter the war,
on either side, she could have made conditions.   In short, she
might in some degree have been master of her own fate, instead of a pawn in the game of greater nations.

China's situation was different in many particulars. China has certain advantages denied to Belgium. One of these is geographical separation (called isolation before it was learned that there is no such thing in international affairs). China thought she did not lie in the way of any vital conflict of the Powers. Even if they got to fighting about China, the principal points of contact would be in Europe, or away from China. China overlooked one thing, however. She did not foresee that a general European war would, by temporarily detaching those factors in the balance of power upon which China's security depended, leave China exposed to the full force of a near-by Power. That is what happened. Japan seized the opportunity to advance her designs in China. Suddenly deprived of the protection of a "balance," China had no means to protect herself. Yet China's measure of sufficiency is not hard to determine, and she formerly has been able to supply it herself. China required an armed force sufficient to stand off a sudden attack from Japan, in the event of other checks upon Japan being removed. An efficient army of half a million, with some fortifications, would have sufficed.

The relation of preparedness and unpreparedness of nations to the peace and the security of other nations and of the world is pointedly brought out by China's case. If China had been fairly strong and prepared, the whole situation in the far East during the war would have been different. China herself would have been able, with or without general consent, to neutralize Kiaochou. Japan would not have been called on, nor have had an excuse to interfere; and could not have seized the opportunity to aggress on China; and the disturbing reactions from that situation upon China's internal affairs, upon America, and the whole world, would not have occurred. In the modern world a helpless nation, which is at the same time rich, is perhaps the greatest cause for international friction and war that can be; its failure to provide protection for itself invites aggressions that spring from cupidity and ambition, and compels other nations to bear proportionately excessive armaments

America's defenses in the Pacific Ocean.   Landing a big gun at Honolulu

U. S. naval base at Pearl Harbor, near Honolulu (uncompleted)

to sustain a balance of power. Moreover, the armed nations usually find a means of charging the cost of their extra-armaments on the weaker nations.

As origins of modern wars are more studied, the feeling is growing among men who regard politics scientifically, that their fundamental cause, or one of their fundamental causes, is a clash of commercial ambitions and interests among nations. This view has been expressed by learned commentators who advance the argument that the "open door" of equal opportunity is the only equitable basis for international commerce. But that is not the theorem which has animated some European statesmanship, and which helped to drag the world into war. The commercial and industrial elements of some nations exult in the opportunity provided by war to cripple commerce and industry of other nations and to seize their markets, thereby placing them at a disadvantage for many years, or permanently disabling them. Taking this and other circumstances as a hint that statesmanship, as now conceived, will use military and naval force—in short, will make war from such motives, it appears that a great expansion of American foreign commerce will hereafter bring the national interests within the scope of such policies. If Americans succeed in their wish and purpose to procure a goodly share of world commerce, they will attract to their nation the same jealousies and antagonisms which have involved other Powers in war with each other. Even by making a strong and promising effort that way, they will excite apprehension and opposition among nations whose policies of statecraft are strongly to sustain their nationals against competitors, and to obstruct by diplomacy all powerful competitive effort. The course of development of the United States has caused it almost to escape, so far, this especial form of international hostility. But a strong international competition is plainly marked out ahead of America which, unless there is a reversal of certain tendencies of statecraft, will lay the United States open to foreign military and naval pressure politically applied to commercial opportunity. If that is true, then it is evident that America has a deep interest in the world's balance of power. If it were not for the pressure of American industrial development outward into foreign commerce, the nation might go on indefinitely without being vitally affected, and without having its security touched by the semi-hostile competition for trade among other Powers. But every sign given by reactions of the Great War upon America tends directly toward the commencement of a strong outward economic pressure. That war completely and finally broke down the so-called isolation of the United States. Its economic isolation was undermined long before, and the Great War forever ended its political isolation.

The United States hereafter will not be able to feel unconcerned about alliances among the major Powers. America has had no thought of a war against Great Britain, but in recent years American statesmanship has been compelled to face the possibility of eventual friction with Japan that might depend on force, or a show of force. If the possibility of Great Britain, under the Anglo-Japanese alliance, siding with Japan against the United States was thought of (and military men always are thinking of such possibilities), the situation in Europe was believed to preclude Great Britain from taking part. It was felt that the German navy would hold the British navy in European waters, and to a certain extent offset its application against America. In that way, the line-up of the Powers in Europe deterred any one of them, or any existing combination of them, from aggression upon America, and from interfering in a broil between America and an Asiatic nation. From this it can be deduced how the position and security of the United States may be affected by variations in the balance of power in Europe. It is possible for the Great War to disturb or destroy the old balance of power in Europe. Suppose that Germany is defeated, her territory diminished, her navy destroyed or transferred to her enemies, and her army disbanded, or decreased to a limit inferior to the military establishments of other Powers. That would at once treble the armed strength of Great Britain *vis-à-vis* the United States. Some say that a war between Great Britain and the United States is impossible; but people said that about the war which began in 1914. As conditions have been, as between Great Britain and America, the probability of an issue between them that would lead to war was slight. Those conditions are passing, and will never be restored. The rise of Japan and her alliance with Great Britain creates complications. If Germany is crushed, and put out of business for a while as a competitor for world trade, a powerful competitor will take her place— the United States. Under those circumstances, would the fears and animosities inspired by Germany's expansive commercial efforts be inherited by America? If world statesmanship was predicated on the same theorem of commercial expansion that has guided the United States, there would be no threatening portent in this prospect. But analysis of modern conditions reveals that the "open door" theorem of commercial expansion and opportunity is not the theorem which dominates the statecraft of all the Powers. Unless the European theorem is changed, the propulsion of American economic energy into world commerce is premonitory of a clash. A primary requisite of a true "open door" policy is freedom of the seas, and no freedom of the seas is secure that is policed by, and therefore subject to the domination of any single Power which is at the same time a leading competitor of other nations. If there is an overturn of the balance of power that has existed in Europe for forty years, the effects upon America will be greater than effects upon many States in Europe.

Analysis of certain conditions of world politics within the last half century shows that a fundamental factor in estimating the measure of armed sufficiency for the United States was a collision of interest and policy which kept European Powers arrayed against each other, and which lately has resolved into two major groups headed, respectively, by Great Britain and Germany. If that condition is altered, or seriously modified, the hypothesis, in its relations to America, will be upset. Assuming that Germany might have ambitions and designs that would bring her into conflict with the United States, then if Great Britain was opposed to German expansion, the British navy might be considered as conducing to America's security. But that is a line of reasoning which, with conditions altered, can be taken the opposite way. If Great Britain should get into a position whereby her major, or immediately predominating interest, brought her into opposition with the United States, then it might be the German navy which, by partly or wholly neutralizing the British navy, would affect the balance of power in America's favor. Therefore, the measure of armed sufficiency for the United States now and hereafter cannot be stated in fixed terms, as of Germany, or of Great Britain, or of Japan, or of any nation or nations—but will turn on *the balance of power* among the principal nations. There is nothing fixed and stable about an international balance of power. It depends on a number of elements, of which military and naval strength are only two. Its real criterion always is in the *balance of interest*, and that shifts frequently. However, this is certain—*a considerable armed strength is indispensable to a place in the balance of power.* President Wilson in 1916 mentioned that internationally the United States faces two ways— the Atlantic and Pacific oceans—and confronts serious problems on both facets. America's foreign policy (which in the past pursued a stiffer and more definite course than in recent times) has been predicated on the existence of a division of interests and power among European nations and also among Asiatic nations. Just as a division of Europe into two groups of about equal armed power, and equally threatening each other, conduced to the security of the United States, so does a similar division of interest and power among Asiatic nations tend to protect America against attack from that direction. For instance, with China a comparatively strong nation, and with Russia also powerful in the far East, Japan only can successfully attack America by composing her differences with those nations, and with their passive assent, or help. Since, as con ditions are, Japan's divergences of interest and causes of friction with China and Russia equal her probable frictions with America, they constitute a check upon her. If Japan obtains the hegemony of China, the situation in the Pacific as it effects America will change.

This outline of principles and world conditions provides the basis for calculating the measure of armed sufficiency needed for the security and protection of American national territory and interests. The details can be left to naval and military experts. It is obvious, however, that naval power constitutes America's first line of defense, and her primary factor of influence in an international balance of power. Taking conditions as they are, and as they seem to be shaping, the United States needs a naval force second only to that of Great Britain, and a time may come when it will have to be equal to the British navy. That is for Great Britain to say, as much as for America. Great Britain can take a course that will enable the United States safely to remain in second naval rank, or she can compel that nation to build against her. If a balance of power exists, East and West, that militates against Great Britain assuming a domineering attitude on the high seas, and toward American foreign trade, then the United States need not be made uneasy by the part a superior British navy can take in a dispute between these two nations exclusively, because of the exposed position of Canada. This assumes, of course, that an efficient military organization is maintained as a complement of the American navy. In the past the security of the United States was favorably affected by the then existing opinion about military affairs and national strength. It was widely believed that an efficient army and military organization could be provided quickly by a nation that possessed the money and natural resources, and that oceans interposed serious obstacles. The ideas of Americans which gave them a sense of security were to a considerable extent held abroad, in estimating the difficulties and risks involved in war against the United States. The world also thought that the American nation was united and that, at bottom, the American spirit was martial, and would instantly respond to repel any menace, or an attempt to intimidate the nation. Events have modified all those opinions. In considering their national security hereafter, Americans must regard the question in the light of what the world now thinks of America, as well as how Americans regard the world.

CHAPTER XIX

AMERICA AND CHINA

Decline of American prestige in China—Moral and material factors—Basis of American moral influence—American missions—Missionary work and influence threatened—The danger—The example of Korea—The ethical dilemma—Moves in China—Propagation of Buddhism—Japan's inconsistency—Clash of Christianity with Japan's policy—Viewpoint of American missionaries—Material phases—American financial participation—Withdrawal of American Banking Group—Effects upon China—The Hwei River scheme—Conditions affecting foreign investments—Other examples—The Fukien incident—Decline of American trade—Reasons therefor—American foreign investments—Principles involved.

A S far as it is possible in international contacts, the relations between China and the United States always have been friendly. This attitude is mutual, only obscured and ruffled occasionally and temporarily by some workings of the American exclusion laws. Ever since diplomatic relations were established, the broad policies of the two nations have been harmonious. When China began to fall into international difficulties the United States took an intelligent and lively interest in her situation, and initiated many actions calculated to relieve pressure on her, to preserve her integrity and autonomy. In lesser affairs, as between themselves, America has acted liberally toward China. All Chinese who know anything of such matters know this, and the knowledge has in time percolated into all strata of popular opinion with cumulative effect. There never has been and there is not now any issue between China and America tending toward a serious schism. In so far as their national policy and popular predisposition can affect these matters, the United States ranks first among foreign nations in the estimation of Chinese.

Yet American prestige in China is declining. That conclusion is the net result of striking an equation between matters conducing to American popularity with Chinese, and matters tending to undermine American influence with them. The decline is both moral and material. A decline of material interests is comparatively easy to measure; it can be expressed in trade statistics and investments. A decline of moral influence is hard to measure, for it is intangible. It cannot be expressed by statistics, and eludes figures of speech. "Prestige" comes near to expressing moral influence, but prestige can mean so many things. It sounds paradoxical, yet it is true that while American moral repute has been steadily mounting in China for decades to its present high point, other elements in recent years just as steadily have been breaking down American prestige. Perhaps I can make this clear by putting it that American moral prestige in China is now sentimental. It has almost no practical force in China because Chinese have discovered that it has little practical application. They have discovered that international morality that has no practical application is only a platitude. A sentiment may be a very pretty thing, but it takes action to apply it to affairs. And even the morality of a so-called moral sentiment can be questioned when it dissolves in phrases, and by its default allows wrong and injustice to dominate.

American moral influence with Chinese rests chiefly on its manifestations in China, or effects in China which can be traced to American action, inaction, or policy. The great humanitarian work done by Americans in China—religious, educational, medical—forms the bed-rock of American moral influence there. Frequently this work is credited with containing the whole of American moral influence; but that is a short-sighted view. The moral influence of missions is their outstanding quality and is undimmed by other features. It stands nakedly altruistic, labor without profit, benefits given freely. The missions—especially schools and hospitals—have come to be appreciated by Chinese of all classes, who make extensive use of the advantages they offer. The benefits, frequently conferred without charge, are obvious. Missions therefore are distinct from other foreign activities. Justice and the reign of law are as important to civilization as education. A foreign law-court in China is as much a moral influence as a church or a school. But there are many features about the administration of justice that are disagreeable, and arouse terror and resentment. Industries which give employment under improved conditions, railways and ship lines that extend communications, electric lighting and telephone systems, devices for the improvement of agriculture, the activities of commerce, all contain powerful moral influences. But the *quid pro quo* appears distinctly in all of them, which contrasts with the ideal nature of humanitarian work. About the religious results of foreign missions in China I am uncertain, as I am uncertain about spiritual forces in America. Statistics of conversions to Christianity manifestly cannot tell the story of foreign religious influence in China any more than church attendance can give the measure of morality in America. It is easier to estimate the work of mission schools and hospitals. The practical results can be seen everywhere. There may be uncertainty about the spiritual effect of Christianity with Chinese, but it is evident that modern education helps Chinese boys and girls to become better citizens, and that to relieve physical suffering and improve the public health and living conditions works out in China much the same as elsewhere. These schools and hospitals send out thousands of young Chinese into the modern professions, or with some degree of Western education, to spread their knowledge among the people. The civilizing force of foreign missions in China is incalculable, and in this work America has taken a leading part. Tremendous human effort, and hundreds of millions of dollars, have been expended in mission work, in providing it with facilities and in preparing for its extension. Missions in China have almost driven their original enemies—superstition and the ignorance of strangeness—from the field, with great results accomplished, and greater results ahead. Now Christian missions are threatened with restraint upon their labors and upon the moral influence so slowly and painfully built up.

This threat does not come from China, but from Japan. In the demands which Japan presented to China in 1915 were provisions that Japanese shall have the right to own land anywhere in China for the building of Japanese hospitals, churches, and schools. On its face, this provision seems similar to rights accorded Christian missions; and it is taken as an intimation of Japan's purpose to propagate Buddhism in China. It also must be taken in connection with the demands as a whole, which obviously aimed to establish Japan's suzerainty over China, a purpose which Japan has not relinquished. It is the possible association of Japanese suzerainty in China with a Japanese Buddhist propagation there that alarms Christian missionaries, who have Korea as an object lesson. Japan's annexation of Korea is recent history. First the country was occupied by Japanese troops during the war with Russia, under a guarantee of protecting Korea's independence. After the war, Japan gradually absorbed Korea's administration, forcing the Korean Emperor against his will to sign an agreement submitting to Japan's authority. Annexation followed. Soon after the Japanese occupation it became evident that the change boded no good to Christian missions in Korea. Koreans bitterly resented the subjugation of their country, and for years carried on a quasi-rebellion and feeble political obstruction to Japanese rule, and to the subordination of Koreans to Japanese interests and exploitation. Notwithstanding that a large majority of missionaries in Korea have at all times made a sincere effort to be neutral between the native population and the Japanese, and to work in harmony with the Japanese administration, their presence was the cause of some political complications. Prince Ito recognized this when he became Resident-General at Seoul, and he said that he feared Korean Christians would form a political solidarity antagonistic to Japan as a result of ideas and doctrines inculcated by American missionaries. The foundation for this presumption easily may be perceived.

Christianity has made greater comparative progress in Korea than elsewhere in the Orient. There are over half a million professed believers, and over 1800 mission schools and churches. A large majority of them are conducted under American auspices, which means that American ideas of personal rights and political liberty insidiously are injected into the minds of the people. This is the political danger which Ito foresaw, for such notions are inimical to Japan's policy in her dependencies. They also are repugnant to political institutions in Japan; but there the proletariat is homogeneous with the oligarchy and imbued with patriotic devotion to the Emperor, while in Korea the people are unsympathetic to Japanese rule and are easily incited to oppose it. Ito also foresaw that Japan probably would lose the sympathy of foreign missionaries in Korea, who naturally would incline toward the people among whom they have worked for so long, and whom they regard as being equal to Japanese in all fundamental elements of character. That proved to be the case. Japanese administration did not progress far before missionaries began to see that Koreans are the under dogs, and to resent Japan's treatment of them. This led to some friction between missionaries and the Residency, although except in a few instances no rupture occurred. When Prince Ito was assassinated by a Korean, the Japanese press plainly intimated that American missionary influence was connected with the crime because by criticizing Japanese administration in Korea missionaries incited Koreans to resist it. That incident served to emphasize the predicament of American missionaries in Korea after Japan's occupation of that country. They were caught between the horns of an ethical dilemma. In Western countries, if churchmen and religious teachers believe that injustice is being done to a large part of the population, or even to a small number, they consider it a duty to remonstrate with those who are responsible for the condition, and if other means fail to redress it, to agitate to secure betterment. Protests of the clergy in Belgium and of American missionaries in Armenia during the Great War are examples of that attitude, of which history provides many instances. Having knowledge of conditions in Korea oppressive to the native population, should the missionaries be silent? This is their dilemma; and they solved it in three ways according to their lights and consciences. The greater number abstained from actions which rightly can be construed as interference between Japanese authorities and Koreans, and which might be considered pernicious political activity; indeed, they were cautioned by Japan. Some have chosen to speak out on behalf of the Koreans; and a few have been vociferous in approbation of Japan's policy. Those who have remained quiet have been troubled in spirit, and have yielded only to pressure of circumstances. This pressure is applied from Japan and from America. Representations were made to the mission boards that it was advisable to check anti-Japanese propensities of missionaries in Korea, whose attitude threatened to make their position there untenable. In facing that problem the missionaries encounter a number of difficulties. To accomplish the real object of their work requires them to secure and retain the confidence of Koreans, and they are puzzled how to do this if they take or are tacitly forced into a pro-Japanese attitude. At times the Japanese press has accused American missionaries in Korea of inciting anti-Japanese sentiment. This they easily might do; they have a good political machine in the mission schools and churches which directly reach the more intelligent and progressive Koreans. But the missionaries generally have maintained a neutral attitude. One aspect of this question is interesting: The Tokio Government strongly objects to any criticism of Japan's Korean policy by missionaries, but it gives the widest possible publicity to any favorable expressions by them, and shows its appreciation by conferring decorations. Thus one side of the picture is suppressed, and only favorable aspects of Japan's rule are presented. A significant phase of this question is whatever light it throws on the psychological effects of Japan's rise and military power upon the old militant spirit of the Christian world.

Prior to the annexation of Korea, when Japan desired to keep a soft-pedal on affairs in that country, the Japanese Government handled the Christian missions issue as delicately as it could. But when annexation was accomplished, a stronger policy was adopted. In an official report by the Japanese Governor-General published in 1914, summarizing the results of the first three years following annexation, this language is used: "If the separation of education and religion be enforced all at once these mission schools will be obliged to close their doors, and there being a dearth in the government and public schools able to take their place, their closure will leave a great gap in the educational work in Chosen. For this reason, for the time being the authorities concerned pay attention only to the prevention of evil that may occur on account of the presence of these schools, intending later to enforce the principle of education standing aloof from religion." This cannot be intelligently read otherwise than as an announcement of Japan's intention to close foreign mission schools in Korea (Chosen), although when it is to be done remains doubtful. So far, the mission schools, although under a vague official ban, have not lost ground, because the Koreans prefer them to the government schools, and more students apply than can be accommodated. Soon after Japan seized Korea the Japanese Government made a regulation refusing passports to Koreans who want to finish their education in America. Thus avenues for American thought to penetrate Korea are being closed. Separate schools are maintained for Japanese and Korean children in Korea, sustaining the caste idea. On the other hand, Japan is working to stimulate Buddhism in Korea. The Japanese official report on Chosen, quoted above, also says: "Provisions were also included in the ordinance for reviving Buddhism and its propagation. Thanks to this ordinance, more than 20,000 priests and nuns living in about 1400 temples and monasteries were enabled to engage in their work." Shintoism (a form of Buddhism), and the cult of Emperor divinity, which are opposed to the teachings of Christianity, are inculcated in the schools of Japan, and also in the government schools in Korea. Apparently it is desired to exclude only one religion (Christianity) from the schools. Administrative educational restriction in Korea is aimed at foreign missionary work.

When, therefore, Japan coupled a move to obtain administrative control over China with provisions to propagate Buddhism through a school system there, American missionaries in China were alarmed, and privately protested to their Government. Yet, in expressing their objections to Japan's course, missionaries in China are subject to restraints similar to those imposed on such criticism in Korea. When Japan violated China's neutrality in 1914, and marched her troops into the interior of Shantung Province, the Chinese population were subjected to many indignities and deprivations by the Japanese soldiers, which inspired some missionaries to write to the newspapers giving their observations, and protesting.[1] Efforts were at once made to suppress this criticism on the ground that it is unwise to antagonize Japan, and some missionaries who had spoken out were cautioned by their superiors. While generally refraining from outspoken agitation, some strong representations nevertheless were made privately to Washington. I will quote from a letter written by a leading American missionary in 1915 to President Woodrow Wilson: "In the very nature of the case, every American missionary, Catholic and Protestant, sympathizes with China in her desire to preserve her independence and integrity. Indeed, while our missionaries are not preaching politics, our usefulness with the Chinese would be immediately at an end if they felt that we were out of sympathy with their aspirations to preserve their national freedom and independence. The Japanese Government understands that all missionaries, and especially Americans, whether they express it or not, feel in their hearts hostility to any effort on Japan's part to secure the control of China by threats of

[1] Appendix T.

force. Christianity inspires individuals to be loyal to God rather than to man, and to contend for freedom to worship Him according to the dictates of their consciences. Such convictions necessarily are in conflict with any attempt at military dictation to a nation by an alien Government and race. The Japanese Government as instinctively feels the antagonism of Christianity to her progress in Korea and in China as the Roman Government felt the antagonism of early Christianity to her imperial despotism. Hence, Japan's attempts through threats of force and through her efforts to impose secrecy upon China, to secure the control of this nation, in the very nature of the case will lead her also to hinder, cripple, and if possible to destroy the work of Christian missionaries in China. . . . In case our appeal to you fails, which seems incredible, it can fail only through your conviction that our people are unwilling to see our Government put forth any effort to guard American interests and the interests of humanity in the far East. In that case, greatly as we dread appearing in print upon any subject which may appear controversial, we are willing to assist in all possible ways in letting the American people know of the events which are transpiring in the far East. Our people have a right to this knowledge, and we shall be unwilling longer to stand idly by and see consummated plans which will bring to naught that for which we have given our lives and that which we count dearer than life itself. We cannot remain dumb oracles and witness this national outrage of Japan upon China.''

The view of the Chinese Government on this question is expressed in its official account of the China-Japan negotiations of 1915, as follows:

The two articles relating to the acquisition of land for schools, hospitals, and temples as well as to the right of missionary propaganda, would, in the opinion of the Chinese Government, have presented grave obstacles to the consolidation of the friendly feeling subsisting between the two people. The religions of the two countries are identical and, therefore, the need for a missionary propaganda to be carried on in China by Japanese does not exist. The natural rivalry between Chinese and Japanese followers of the same faith would tend to create incessant disputes and friction. Whereas Western missionaries live apart from the Chinese communities among which they labor, Japanese monks would live with the Chinese; and the similarity of their physical characteristics, their religious garb, and their habits of life would render it impossible to distinguish them for purposes of affording the protection which the Japanese Government would require should be extended to them under the system of extra-territoriality now obtaining in China. Moreover, a general apprehension exists among the Chinese people that these peculiar conditions favoring conspiracies for political purposes might be taken advantage of by some unscrupulous Chinese.

I take it that few who are acquainted with conditions in the far East, and who are not inhibited from candor, will dispute that there is a fundamental clash between Japan's imperial policy in Asia and the principles and teachings of Christian missions. From this it follows logically that unless Japan's policy in China is opposed by Christian missionary influence, Christian tenets will have to be suppressed and sacrificed, and missionary moral influence with the Chinese will become negligible; and if Japan's policy succeeds, it will in time undermine mission work and missionary influence and replace it with Buddhist influence. That is an apparent object of Japan's policy in China. One notices that the Japanese Government, which in Korea aims to use the conjunction of Christianity with the mission schools in that country as a reason for suppressing those schools, apparently intends to use Japanese schools in China as a means to promote Japan's political influence by propagation of the Buddhist religion, and to check the spread of Christian influence. What is held to be wrong for Christian missions to do in Korea is by Japan considered right for Japanese Buddhist missions to do in China, under circumstances where the moral justification is infinitely less. It need not be presumed that the Japanese Government really cares about the propagation of Buddhism. That religion is neglected in Japan. It happens that Buddhism is a strong religion in China, and therefore provides good ground for Japanese political work among Chinese.

The process of undermining American moral influence, or

prestige, in China has recently been proceeding more, in its obvious manifestations, from the applications of the policy of the American Government to American material enterprises and interests there. Here again the policy of the American Government is correct in ideals, and is superficially energetic. But for several years, and especially during the administration of Woodrow Wilson, the American policy in China has almost invariably yielded or temporized or withdrawn when it encountered serious opposition, and when action or progress entailed risk of serious opposition. Up to a point, following its formulation into an international understanding by the Hay Doctrine, American policy in China proceeded evenly. Few serious obstacles or questions developed until after the Russo-Japanese War, when Mr. Knox brought forward his plan to neutralize Manchuria. The failure of that well-intentioned and practical plan proved definitely that with several Powers their acceptance and support of the Hay Doctrine was perfunctory, while some of them privately opposed it. Mr. Knox extricated his proposal as best he could, without yielding any of the principles he contended for. But thereafter it was well understood that any large American projects in China might expect to encounter the diplomatic hostility of certain Powers. Nevertheless, the effort to save the "open door" for American enterprise was not abandoned during the Taft administration. The American banking group continued to participate in the Hukiang loans, and became a member of the 4-Power and later the 6-Power groups, only to feel its position so insecure that, failing a positive assurance of its Government's support, it withdrew. Since then there has not been a fair chance for large American participation in China's development. Events had proven conclusively that such participation would encounter foreign diplomatic opposition, and it could not succeed without strong official support to offset that. President Wilson's utterances about the withdrawal of the American banking group from the reorganization loan had immense momentary popularity in China, as also did the contemporary announcement that independent American bankers would float a Chinese loan. Chinese soon discovered that the practical results of President Wilson's policy were not what they had expected. The 5-Power banking group was not seriously affected by the withdrawal of the American bankers, and by the action of the American Government; indeed, the group's attitude was something like "good riddance." Within the 6-Power group, the Americans had at times rather blocked progress by always insisting on being liberal to China, and by sticking for a strict adherence to the "open door" and "integrity of China" principles. Instead of the American withdrawal breaking up the group, and forcing it to modify its terms and conditions, the terms and conditions were merely tightened a little. China soon discovered that there was no genuine prospect to obtain an independent American loan. She therefore was compelled to accept the terms of the 5-Power group. The immediate effect in China of President Wilson's policy was a tightening of the hold of the 5-Power group, and the removal of the friendly and liberal influence of America in China's financial affairs. The immediate result of President Wilson's policy in America, by destroying the confidence of American financiers in the policy of the administration, was to create a situation whereby the flotation of any considerable Chinese loans in America was impossible. In theory and utterance, the policy of the Wilson administration promised well for China; in practice it worked detriment to China, in so far as it had any influence.

Even after the withdrawal of the American banking group from the reorganization loan, efforts to promote American enterprises in China continued. Some Americans failed to perceive the true significance of that event, and still thought it was feasible to operate in China. The American Government, perhaps a little astonished by the results of its attitude to the banking group, let it be known that it would like to promote American participation in the development of China, and would support any legitimate projects to that end which did not tend to trespass on China's autonomy. In explaining its attitude toward the banking group, the Washington administration (*vide* Mr. Bryan) had intimated its objection to "dollar diplomacy," an explanation which, with its applications to American internal politics, was not unpopular in America. The administration was willing to aid American projects in China that did not try to do so-and-so, and to expect so-and-so from their Government. It soon became evident that unless so-and-so was done, no important American project in China could be promoted—so-and-so meaning certain conditions that are necessary to assure the legal security and profitable operation of enterprises in China.

A practical demonstration of this soon occurred. For a long time American missionaries in China and the American Red Cross Society had coöperated in famine relief work in China, caused usually by the flooding of some rivers there. The recurrence of these disasters, and the growing tendency of Chinese officials and people to depend on American charity for relief, while doing nothing themselves to prevent the floods, in time caused American missionaries to refuse to support further appeals to the charity of Americans unless the Chinese would coöperate with Americans in a plan to prevent the floods and to reclaim the devastated areas. In this idea the so-called Hwei River reclamation project was born. This is a plan to control the flow of the Hwei River by engineering works, and to reclaim and irrigate large sections of fertile lands. The scheme was similar to reclamation and irrigation projects in western America. The American Red Cross Society employed C. D. Jamison, an American engineer, to make preliminary surveys and estimates, and on his recommendation a board of distinguished American engineers visited China in 1914 and surveyed the region. They reported that the scheme was feasible from an engineering standpoint. The next step was to finance it. The scheme contemplated that the reclaimed lands would be opened for settlement, and would yield returns that would pay interest and principal on the cost of reclamation work. If the plan succeeded, a terrible annual affliction would be prevented, and a large population provided with means to exist by their own labor instead of upon foreign charity. This project has an obvious sentimental appeal; it was charity linked with practical development and permanent improvement. The State Department, which under Mr. Bryan's administration deplored "dollar diplomacy," heartily approved the Hwei River scheme, coming before it draped in the mantle of charity and associated with missionary work. The scheme was entirely worthy of support. But it required to be financed, just as if it was an ordinary business enterprise seeking the support of "dollar diplomacy"; and the financiers wanted security for the investment. That brought the scheme square up against the same conditions that affect every large foreign enterprise in China. The scheme was feasible. Experts estimated that it would require a certain amount of money to complete it. The operating charges would be so much; the interest on the investment would be so much; the probable revenue would be so much. The revenue would come from the people who would farm the lands, in taxation and rents. If disorder broke out in that region, and outlaws overran the country, the people could not produce and it might not be possible to collect taxes and rents. So a very necessary factor of security was police power, and protection to the property. If internal disorder was widespread and the Chinese Government (as frequently happens) could not restore order and could not provide protection, then either a foreign police power must protect the property or it would not be protected. If the property was not protected, and the taxes and rents were not collected, the repairs might fall behind, and the investment would decline in value and might vanish. If the Chinese Government (as in that case) assured the interest and principal of the investment, and from rebellion or revolution or any cause it could not or would not protect the property, then either a foreign police power must assume that duty or leave the tangible assets of the investment unprotected. And, as conditions are in China now, it is not possible to protect such investments

Photo, International Film Service, Inc.

Japanese battle-cruiser "Kongo." Speed 28 knots: displacement 27,500 tons; armament eight 14-inch guns and sixteen 6-inch guns. Japan has four of this type of ship in commission. The United States has none

without in some degree infringing or qualifying China's administrative autonomy. That is the dilemma. Latter-day American policy has said that it will not lend support to American projects or investments in China when to do so carries the possibility of interfering in China's affairs, or using diplomatic pressure. That is equivalent to debarring American enterprises and investments from China. When it reached the stage where it was to be financed, the humanitarian Hwei River reclamation scheme was in the same position as a railway or loan deal; it had to satisfy investors. As this cannot be done without the backing of the American Government, the scheme is suspended.

Any kind of a project in China that requires foreign capital must meet this condition. It is fruitless to argue now about how this came about, or about the abstract justice or injustice to China. The fact remains that China cannot procure capital abroad without satisfying foreign investors as to their security, and as investors depend on their bankers, China must satisfy the leading foreign bankers; which, reduced to practice, means that the entities who must be satisfied are those which composed the financial syndicate that negotiated the Chinese reorganization loan. When the American Government acts on a method that discourages leading American bankers from supporting foreign enterprises, it creates a condition preventing American participation in such enterprises. In the case of China, no matter how much Chinese may want to deal with Americans, they are debarred, and China is driven willy-nilly to deal with other nations. If that situation forces worse terms and perils upon her, is it not possible that Chinese may think that American support and friendship have no practical value, and that any reliance on them has disagreeable consequences? Continue this process long enough, and there will be very little of American prestige in China left. For the Chinese are a practical people.

An incident that was very damaging to American prestige in China is the so-called Bethlehem Steel loan. During the

visit of Prince Tsai-tsun (then Minister of Marine) to the
United States in 1909 he signed an agreement with Charles M.
Schwab, by which China was to borrow tls. 30,000,000 for naval
purposes.   The deal contemplated the purchase of naval materials from the Bethlehem Company, which undertook to finance
the transaction.   It is probable that the company agreed to accept Chinese government bonds in payment for materials and
construction; it to hold or dispose of the bonds.   After the
revolution the new Government of China wanted to repudiate
this agreement, but it could not do so justly, and it accepted the
contract.   The matter was held in abeyance for some time,
waiting upon a decision by China how to apply it.   After much
discussion, it was suggested that a part of the proposed loan
would be applied to the construction of a naval base on the coast
of China.   A board was appointed to decide where this base
should be built, and a port in Fukien Province was selected.   A
project for a principal naval base in China had been mooted
for years, and its construction and the supply of materials was
a desirable piece of business for which there was considerable
competition.   British and Japanese firms were among the competitors.   When news about the Fukien base was published in
1914, there was much discussion about it, especially in the
Japanese press, which took the attitude that the project in
some way intruded on the rights of Japan, and was a blow
aimed at Japan.   The Japanese press represented the matter
as an insidious scheme to establish an American naval base
opposite Formosa, and in Japan's claimed "sphere" in that
part of China.   Taking these false reports as a basis for action,
the Japanese Government made representations to the State
Department.   I believe that Viscount Chinda told Mr. Bryan
that Japan would regard it as an "unfriendly act" if American money was used in financing enterprises in Fukien.   At
any rate, the bluff worked.   Viscount Chinda so impressed
Mr. Bryan that a telegram was sent to the American legation
at Peking, giving instructions to inform China that the United
States would not support the American interest.   I was in-

formed that this telegram was couched in terms so humiliating to America that it was modified on the request of the American minister; but even then the action amounted to a partial concession by the United States of Japan's preferential position in Fukien. Having attended to America, Japan next asked China's intentions in the matter. Left in the lurch by the United States, China saved her face as best she could, by suavely stating that she never had had any intention of using American money in Fukien. Japan later clinched her point by certain stipulations of the agreement she wrung from China in 1915. Thus was the "open door" closed to American enterprise in another part of China, and contrary to the wishes of China. In this incident, China was again given an object lesson, proving that the United States will not back its nationals in sustaining their rights under the "open door" in China, and the same notice was again given to Americans.

The broad effects of this policy are apparent. Americans and Chinese may proceed with business negotiations to a point of agreement. In the course of this process the American interest competes on an equal basis with all other foreign interests. If that competition fails, diplomacy can invoke the pressure of its Government, and take the business away from the Americans. After several applications of the process it is conclusively demonstrated to Chinese that it is useless to waste time considering important propositions from Americans, and to Americans that it is useless wasting time and money trying for the business. In the Bethlehem case, China was willing to do business with Americans, but Japan would not allow her to. That humiliates China, but she is too weak to resist. Americans wanted to do business with China, but Japan would not allow them to. Japan had absolutely no right to interfere, and is bound by several treaties to respect the "open door" policy. Her refusal to allow Americans to do business in Fukien is very humiliating to the United States as a nation, but the American Government allows the affront and injustice to pass unchallenged. In Chinese eyes, therefore, China and the United States are getting to be in the same class as nations in comparison with the real Powers; and China only gets into trouble by trying to trade with Americans, or by listening to American propositions and advice.

The instances I have cited have the character of finance and investment rather than of commerce, although the principle of "business follows the loan" runs through them. In respect to straight commerce, American interests in China have suffered as much as in other lines of business. American exports to China fell in ten years (1905–1915) from about 28 per cent. of China's total imports to less than 8 per cent. Various causes contributed to this decline, the principle cause being conditions due to international policies. The annual report of the American Association of China, made at Shanghai on December 29, 1914, said:

Turning now from trade in general to some particular considerations—what is the outlook? American cotton formerly held a premier position in Manchuria. Under Russian occupation, every nation stood on an equal footing in Manchuria. The same duties and charges were assessed against all and facilities for distributing goods and doing business in general were satisfactory. Now it is all changed. Under Japanese administration, no chance to advance its own trade is overlooked and to competitors the means taken appear to be a departure from fair trading. In fact, they constitute a most serious violation of the open door principle on which the diplomacy of the United States in China is based. Japanese competition takes the form of a system of rebates not only in freight and steamer rates, but in remission of duties and charges which are assessed against all other nations. In addition to this many forms of petty annoyances have been worked out for the non-Japanese trader, and the imitation of established trade-marks is common.

Now that the Japanese are in Shantung, not the mere foothold that the Germans held at Tsingtau, but with an apparent determination to dominate the Province, the same tactics may be expected, since it would be exactly in line with the course employed in Korea and Manchuria. With Dalny on the northern promontory and Tsingtau on the southern Japan has secured a potential control of the trade of North China from the Russian frontier to the Yangtze upon whose valley her traders have long cast covetous eyes. In this connection it will become apparent that not only ourselves, but other nationalities face a loss of trade.

In iron and steel products conditions are on a different basis but scarcely less disadvantageous to the American. Here also the open door is largely a myth, for even with open bidding on railway materials, rails and rolling stock, bridges and the like, the specifications are such as to give European competitors an immense advantage. Unfortunately there is no international standard.

The policy of the United States Government is discouraging the investment of American capital in Chinese railways and in loans to the Republic has been detrimental to our merchants, but as the administration gains a clearer view of the situation in China and begins to recognize the things that must be done if the United States is to share in this vast trade area, there are possibilities of some modifications of this policy which is believed to have been put forth without sufficient investigation and, at that, on sentimental grounds. This Association should use every means in its power to awaken the Government in Washington, through whatever means it can find, to the necessity for a more vigorous policy in China to secure for us and to hold open when secured as liberal advantages for the extension of our trade as are now enjoyed by other nationalities.

A potent element in securing the sales of their product in foreign countries that is often overlooked by the manufacturer at home is the placing of his agencies wherever possible in the hands of Americans. As it is now, some products that might be enjoying a wide field are now being restricted by being in the hands of those who— other considerations being equal—naturally prefer to promote the sale of their own nationals. Efforts to bring this home to the United States manufacturer should be made, as he stands a chance of having his product blanketed by the agency being in the hands of one who holds it merely to prevent competition with goods made by one of his own nationality.

The expectations about effects on other foreign commerce of Japan's occupation of Shantung and Tsingtau voiced in that report have been fulfilled. Japan's methods in Shantung differ in no essential particular from her methods in Manchuria and Korea, and the principle of her obstruction to American investments in Fukien.

American policy in China can be taken as affecting directly both China and the United States. If America abandons the Hay Doctrine and withdraws completely from active participation in affairs in the far East, how will China be affected? China will be affected to the extent that a force favorable to her, and aiding her to resist aggressions, will be removed from the international consortium. None of China's problems will be solved, and her ability to deal with them will be further limited, and she will be drawn further into the grip of Powers intending to subjugate her. One factor that promised relief from pressures and exactions will be eliminated; one influence that worked favorably for China will be removed. That is not a good thing for China, and China will understand perfectly. China also will understand that America's course is actuated by indifference and timidity. China's position vis-à-vis America will be that of seeing a professed friend leave her to be submerged by her difficulties, or to be rescued by other Powers. I distinguish between popularity and prestige. Even in this course, America might retain a certain popularity with Chinese, by continuing to bestow missionary benefits upon them, and by a repetition of friendly expressions. But in the serious work of life and national existence China's important dealings and contacts would be with other nations; and practical aid would come from them, if it came at all. The influence of America on these matters would be negligible; and consequently the prestige of America with Chinese would be negligible.

Effects on America of a retreat from China and the far East are considered elsewhere in their broader strategical aspects; but in respect to economic matters there are some interesting points. Prior to the Great War, the part of American finance in China was circumscribed by the limitations of the market for foreign securities in America, and by the subordination of the American money market to British and European influence. It was practically impossible for the most powerful financial combination in America to float a large foreign loan without joining with British and French financiers, for there was behind the American bankers no considerable investing public to absorb the securities. London and Paris ruled the international money market, with Berlin as a growing factor. Even British bankers were chary of assuming great foreign loans without consulting Paris, for the Paris bourse has long controlled the European investor. Paris and London fixed exchange rates, and dictated the conditions of international credits. A principal factor in enabling French and British bankers to do this was that their Governments consistently pursued policies designed to sustain investments abroad. If a French or British investor bought a Chinese bond, of an issue supported by their Governments and underwritten by leading bankers, they knew that the police power of the French and (or) British Governments backed the investment and sustained its security against illegal impairments. It was this combination of assurances that made such bonds a safe investment, subject only to customary business risks. Prior to the Great War there was not much money in America available for foreign investments, and in participating in Chinese loans American bankers had to safeguard themselves by leaving a way open to turn any unsold bonds over to their British and French associates. There is a prospect that after the war and in the future America will have money to lend abroad, and that Americans will desire to make their surplus capital a means to extend the nation's foreign commerce through such investments. The money and the desire are not sufficient, however. Other elements are necessary. A basis for sound security must be provided: that is, some reliable authority must assume the obligation to protect these investments in their legal rights. Only Governments can do that; only Governments should do it. For a Government to protect foreign investments of its nationals requires the means and the will to do so. The great wealth and population and potential power of the United States gives it the means to protect the rights and property of its nationals abroad, and the will of the Government about this question is for the American people to determine.

That American capital, as such, will not venture abroad without being assured of legal protection is a foregone conclusion.

That American capital, in large amount, will not enter China as such, under a policy like the American Government has recently followed, is certain. But capital is the most mobile of economic elements. It can change its flag without much difficulty. As long as there are Governments in the world that can and will protect foreign investments, capital need not be shut off from such investments. If it should come to pass that only one Government in the world is able to protect its foreign investments, and will protect them, then it would follow inevitably that all the capital in the world seeking foreign investments will become concentrated under the legal protection of that Government. Foreign investments and commerce require certain facilities. Legal protection in the countries where investments are made is one; freedom of transport is another. If "trade follows the loan," then the trade financed by foreign loans must be protected in transit over the world. This means it must be protected on the high seas as well as on land. Governments, then, which provide these facilities will be the desirable ones for such capital and such trade to be allied with. If but one Government in the world is able to provide these facilities, and does provide them, then that one Government will in time draw to it a majority of the international capital and commerce in the world. If hereafter there is free American capital available for international financing and commerce and economic development, it will first try to gain the support and protection of its own Government in such undertakings. But if the American Government should continue to refuse to provide and assure these necessary facilities, American capital need not thereby be inhibited from international exploitation. It can move. It can change its nationality. For instance, if American money is needed (as it probably will be) to float Chinese loans, it can be procured provided American investors want to lend the money. It only is necessary for British and French and German bankers to underwrite the loans, separately or in combination, with the support of those Governments. The bonds can then be sold in America, through American bankers.

They will be a safe investment, for they will be under the protection of the French or (and) British or (and) German Governments, and an American can put his money into them without fear, and subject only to the recognized business risks. By that system, it is feasible for American capital in any amount to participate in foreign enterprises, but it must operate under other flags, and depend on other Governments for protection. That will not matter so much to the bondholder—his interest will come just the same, and his principal is reasonably secure. But it will make a great difference to American industry and commerce, and in general application to American prestige in the world. If it becomes necessary for American finance and trade in foreign countries to adopt a quasi-foreign nationality to secure facilities and protection, the inevitable tendency will be for them to combine their citizenship with the nationality that aids and protects them. Already this tendency is noticeable. In China many major American interests operate as foreign corporations, not that they wish to do that, but for practical business reasons. It is certain, however, that the dreamed-of predominance of America as the world's financial and commercial center, never can happen under such a policy as has been pursued by America in China lately. A good deal of American foreign business can be done, but the direction and control over it will not really rest with Americans. And the power that does control the international economic processes of America eventually will strongly influence, if it does not actually dominate, America's internal economic and political development.

Against such a combination of circumstances that has developed recently, the efforts of individual Americans to build up American interests and trade in China have been almost fruitless. They have constantly struggled with difficulties caused by international politics without an equalizing support of their own Government, and lack facilities which their Government should provide, and which are provided by other Governments. American diplomatic and consular officers in China nearly without exception are anxious to aid their national interests, and work hard to do it; but they are powerless when not sustained by their Government at Washington. To talk of promoting American interests and of developing trade in any country and at the same time having a Government that refuses or fails to protect those interests and that trade, is an absurdity. Such a policy defeats American corporate and individual energy abroad. In respect to these foreign contacts, the acts of the American Government frequently show a lack of coöperation and coördination among its various departments. The Department of Commerce in some of its branches may be working energetically and intelligently to build up American trade with China, while another branch of the Government sweeps the results away. The annual report of the American Association of China, adopted at Shanghai on December 30, 1915, contained this comment: "The absence of American ships has, during this year, been a source of such inconvenience and loss to American merchants that we can only hope it will press home the fact of the heavy handicap to American trade caused by our being without ships that fly our flag. Our merchants in many cases have not been able to carry out their engagements by reason of not having been able to secure tonnage, as the shipping companies of other nationalities have discriminated in favor of their own people. It has not been a matter of first come first served, but first and last the space has gone to merchants whose nationality was that of the ships. This is a matter which this Association has repeatedly brought to the attention of our authorities and it is to be hoped that the conditions which the war in Europe has so emphatically brought to the attention of our people at home—conditions which directly affect our trade, even to the extent of taking it out of our hands and presenting it to our competitors—will hasten the day when we shall again see our ships in these ports, and our merchants saved the humiliations of 1915."

The reference is to the complete withdrawal of the Pacific Mail Steamship Company from business, as a result of the

Seaman's Act passed by Congress, that went into effect in 1915. There must be a fundamental reversion of practice at Washington if the disintegration of American interests and prestige in China is to be checked, and they are set to moving forward again.

CHAPTER XX

Relation of the West to China—The existing international formula—
The Hay Doctrine—Its principles still sound—International moral
responsibility—Its application to China—Can the Hay Doctrine be enforced?—Its weakness—False position of America—Dangers of aloofness
—A new consortium necessary—Its composition—Opposing ideals and
interests—Where does England stand?—Russia, France and Germany—
Elements of America's strength—What the United States may have to
do—Costs and compensations to America—Some possible consequences—
Practical basis for coöperation in China needed.

THE future of China, and the course of vital world-
forces closely involved with her fate, must be seriously affected and perhaps will be decided by the
policies of foreign Powers; and the application of these policies
to China will depend on relations among the Powers themselves.
An international policy for China cannot be based exclusively
on the interests of the Powers as they touch in China. With
one exception, the Powers have interests elsewhere that are now
considered more important, or more pressing, than China's fate.
Japan is the exception. The China question is to Japan the
most important issue in the world. By the fate of China, the
fate of Japan as a world Power will be decided. Turning one
way, China by her bulk and greater resources in time may supersede Japan as leader in the Orient. Turning another way,
China may be made to transfuse her latent strength and wealth
into the veins of Japan, and make Japan the most powerful
empire in the world.

In considering the relation of the West to China, and what
Western Powers can and ought to do in her behalf and in their
own interest, some formula is necessary. One assumes that it

is desirable for this formula to have a sound moral basis.   It also must have expression; that is, be put into words.   Then it must be given ordinance and authority.   *Then it must be enforced.*

What would constitute a sound moral basis for an international formula in China?   Equity and justice would seem to be necessary ingredients—equity and justice as among foreign Powers supporting and enforcing the formula, and equity and justice to China.   Justice to China would seem to require respect for her national rights as they have existed and have been recognized for centuries; equity to China would seem to require fair treatment of her in all her international contacts.   Justice and equity as between foreign interests in China would seem to require fair and equal treatment and opportunity there, and mutual respect for interests in existence and rights guaranteed by existing obligations.   When we inspect the situation of China, we find that such a formula already exists.   The Hay Doctrine embodies, as well as skilled international lawyers could devise, the principles and conditions I have outlined as being theoretically desirable.   The Hay Doctrine also has the force of ordinance and authority, for it was formally ratified by six Governments, constituting a majority of the so-called Powers. What, then, is lacking?   The Hay Doctrine needs to be *enforced.*

The Hay Doctrine was formulated by the United States Government; which only means that one nation took the initiative and prepared a memorandum of principles, and then presented this memorandum separately to several other chiefly interested Governments with a request that they would approve it. One presumes that there was some discussion, confidentially, among the chancelleries before the memorandum took acceptable form; anyhow, it was brought into acceptable form and duly accepted.   Could a better formula than the Hay Doctrine be devised now?   I do not think so.   The Hay Doctrine is simple.   It includes the essential principles.   It covers the essential points at issue.   It does not make the mistake of trying to incorporate details. Mind, the Hay Doctrine is not merely a single note or treaty. It is a series of notes and treaties, all professing the same ends, and in their progressive expressions reiterating the essential principles. It is like a constitution, stating the fundamental law. Subsequent acts and policies were to be modeled and construed in harmony with it. The Hay Doctrine could be revised, reformulated, restated; but if its principles were retained nothing would be changed fundamentally. It would do no good to revise and restate a fair-play doctrine for China unless it was *enforced*. Can such a doctrine be enforced?

Occurrences of the Great War caused much discussion about the foundations and enforcement of international law. The case of Belgium especially was commented on. Many eminent men and jurists argued that the United States was morally and legally obligated to resist, with force if necessary, open and inexcusable disregard of international covenants. In an issue of November, 1914, the "Outlook" (New York), in commenting on some utterances of Theodore Roosevelt about this question, said:

In the face of the greatest crisis that has come upon the world in modern times, shall the United States repudiate its past, attempt to follow theories which it has never observed, and evade the responsibility of doing its share in maintaining the public law of nations? If so, it must take the consequences of its inaction: it must withdraw from the family of nations, must make up its mind to engage in no agreements with other nations that entail mutual obligations, must abandon its hope of substituting arbitration and international court action for war; for all these things rest upon the maintenance of a public law of nations that corresponds to the common law that governs individuals. We do not believe that Americans would regard such a withdrawal from the world as desirable even if it were possible. If it is both impossible and undersirable, then there remains only one honorable alternative—to accept with courage and firmness every opportunity to affirm our interest in maintaining this public law. To say that the United States can be neutral on this subject is equivalent to saying that the United States acquiesces in the doctrine that, after all, there is not, and should not be, any such thing as the public law of civilized nations.

The principles and ideas thus enunciated I believe to be sound—sound in morals, and sound as to practical politics; for moral ideals about political affairs which cannot be fitted to methods of practical politics are ineffective; and morals that are inoperative are not morals at all—they are merely phrases. Because the Great War concentrated attention upon affairs and conditions in Europe, most contemporary commentators predicated their analyses entirely on those affairs and conditions. But the principles and ideals are general. They can apply, and should be made to apply, to all parts of the world, to all conditions which imperil international relations, and which tend to embroil nations. Mr. Roosevelt, Robert Bacon, the "Outlook," and many other experienced American critics of affairs have taken the position that the United States, when apprised of the trend of events that preceded the Great War, should have taken vigorous measures to secure respect for the neutralities of weak nations that wished to keep out of the conflict, and for the Hague conventions; that the United States should not have been satisfied to do nothing, and be sorry about such infractions, but should have intervened actively to sustain peace and justice.

Now consider the situation of China, and events which involved that country in the war, and which threaten her independence. Germany is blamed for violating the neutrality of Belgium. Germany's reply is the doctrine of "imperative necessity." I need not argue the bases of that doctrine, as opposed to the doctrine of inviolability of treaties and conventions. In that instance, the doctrine of "imperative necessity" did apply to the situation, as to fact, although the morality of the doctrine can be disputed. In violating China's neutrality, Japan cannot with reason apply the doctrine of "imperative necessity"; indeed, it was not pleaded. Not only was China's neutrality violated in military operations against Tsingtau, but the greater part of a Chinese province was occupied by Japan, where at once were set in motion the familiar processes by which Japan closed the "open door" in Manchuria and usurped the sovereignty of that part of China. Vested interests in Shantung were seized on specious pretexts. As a bald, ruthless, unscrupulous aggression on a helpless and friendly neighbor, Japan's course in China in 1914 and to 1916 stands apart. If Germany indirectly violated treaties with the United States by invading Belgium, then Japan has directly and doubly violated treaties with America by her course in China. If what happened in Europe is thought to concern the United States so deeply on moral grounds, and also on grounds of intelligent self-interest, then what is happening in China concerns America in a greater degree on the same grounds. Issues and principles touched by the case of Belgium are identical with those involved with the case of China, as to abstract morality; while the case of China is of more importance, in its practical aspects and its bearings on the interests and security of America. What is happening in China presages further dissension between Japan and America, and also contains the germ of a possible breach between Great Britain and America. America's interest in the case of Belgium is mostly academic, and the responsibility is purely a moral one. The American Government's interest in the fate of China is intensely practical, and the responsibility is that of supporting its own definite treaty obligations, rights, and interests.

From an American standpoint—indeed, from the broad international standpoint—the far Eastern question is this: Can the Hay Doctrine be enforced? It has been suggested that these issues be submitted to a Pacific Ocean conference for discussion and formulation by general agreement. But the issues have been fully discussed, and an agreement based on sound principles has been reached. Moreover, that understanding is embodied in treaties signed by the principal Powers. What reason is there to presume that another similar agreement would fare any better, or work out a better solution than the Hay Doctrine? Unless certain nations will abandon their present policies and courses, no new agreement can be reached.

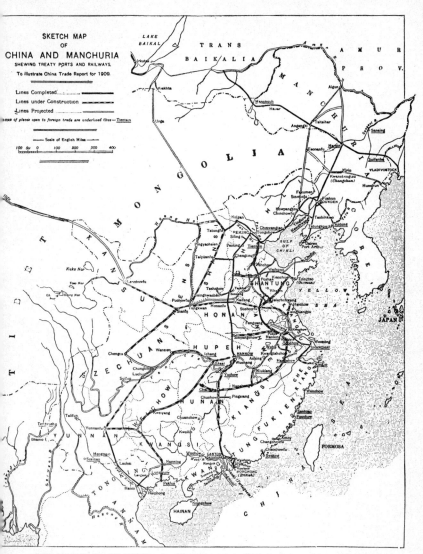

RAILWAY MAP OF CHINA, showing relation of the Shantung lines to the general system.
From the Far Eastern Review

Unless the nations would *observe* and sustain a new agreement, there is no use making one. What are the prospects to improve the Hay Doctrine, or to replace it with a new agreement that would strike a measure of international equity and satisfaction? It is evident that either an agreement must be formulated that will satisfy *all* the Powers, and China, or the agreement must be supported by enough Powers to enforce it in opposition to the dissenters. There is another alternative. All agreements can be dissolved, and each of the Powers can follow its own course regardless of the others. That would lead inevitably to war.

The Hay Doctrine is as sound and as just and as equitable now as when it was first advanced. It was so meritorious that it was accepted by all the Powers. Why, then, has it failed in application? The Hay agreement lost vitality because it included some nations that were not sincere in accepting it, and did not want it to succeed. That is, the agreement violated a principle of contract which rejects elements that are antagonistic to the main purposes and interests of the contractors. The Hay Doctrine is satisfactory as a formulation of principles. It broke down when it included in the agreement nations whose real policies are opposed to those principles. Certain fallacious presumptions then entertained in diplomacy and statecraft led to that mistake. There was uncertainty about the real attitudes of some Powers. But it was thought that, by including them in the agreement, they could be bound to respect and support the doctrine; in short, the weakening of the Hay agreement was due to a blind and rather ridiculous faith in written treaties. Apparently it was assumed by some Governments that if the agreement was once signed by the principal Powers, it would enforce itself automatically. The signing of a treaty will no more enforce it than putting a law in a statute book will enforce the law. The United States Government got the Powers to agree to the Hay Doctrine, and then seemed to think that it had done its part. The doctrine was left for other Powers to enforce, or to enforce itself.

So it appears that the need is not to make a new international rule for China, but to enforce the rule already enacted. First, consider what part the United States can take. Is it still desirable, as an American policy, to apply the Hay Doctrine? The recent attitude of the American Government seems to be that it is very desirable to maintain the Hay Doctrine, but the United States is under no responsibility or obligation to enforce it. Put another way, the idea at Washington seems to be that although the doctrine is essential to the protection and advancement of American position and interests in China, and to the independence of China, the issues are not important enough to risk friction with any Powers by effort to sustain them; that is, America wants the Hay Doctrine to stand, but it will do nothing positive to enforce it. If by dint of moral eloquence and diplomatic persuasion the United States can talk other Powers into respecting the doctrine, and induce them even to maintain it against opposing Powers by the threat of force or the use of force, then America will get whatever benefits that come, without taking any of the responsibility or risks. It is plain that hereafter the "open door" and "integrity of China" policies cannot be maintained by moral protestations. At least one Power—Japan—has practically come out against them, and has given unmistakable intimations that only compulsion in some form will make her respect and observe them. A repudiation of the Hay Doctrine by Japan, and perhaps by Russia too, can be expected. The doctrine need not fall on that account. If Japan repudiates it formally, as she already has done in practice, the real situation will not be changed. Japan will be on the outside openly opposing the doctrine instead of on the inside secretly knifing it. I think it will be better that way. A profession of new principles, or a re-profession of old principles, and an international realignment in the far East, must come anyhow. A new consortium— perhaps two—will be formed. Will America be in a consortium, or will she hold aloof? This is one of the most important questions the United States Government has to decide.

If America holds aloof in the coming reorganization in the far East, her international influence in that part of the world will drop to practically nothing.   Whatever replaces the Hay Doctrine, and even if some of its principles are retained in its successor, the position and interests of the United States in that case would have only casual consideration.   The course of events would be directed by other Powers without particular regard to America's interests and wishes, and without consulting the Washington Government.   America will continue to be deeply affected by whatever happens—more deeply affected in all probability than any other Western nation—but by aloofness she will lose direct influence over the forces that beat upon her.   America will be a spectator, wondering what will happen, fearing what will happen, and without power to shape or turn events by the influence of her diplomacy. America will have resigned her seat at the far Eastern council of nations.   And America will not placate Japan, nor divert the ultimate purposes of Japan's policy in its relation to America, by abandoning the Hay Doctrine.   Japanese are apt to construe such action as a confession of weakness, prompted by timidity and cowardice.

However, America will have the option of taking part in solving the Eastern question.   I think she will be even urged to take part; for the power and influence of America can be a tremendous force.   But I am sure of one thing: America will not be invited to join a consortium, America will not be permitted to join a consortium, unless she will assume her full measure of responsibility and pay her share of the costs.   She will not be allowed to pose as an international altruist benignly uttering moral platitudes and fixing moral standards for other nations to set their conduct by, claiming an equal position and say, taking a goodly share of any benefits that come, and evading the risks.   She must come in, with all that means; or stay out, with all that means.   She cannot be a dilettante meddler.   This is the rôle the United States has performed in China during the last five years.   It has accomplished nothing of permanent value, least of all any lasting good to China. In some of its aspects, American policy in China has in recent times been almost as disturbing to international comity as the weakness of China. America has stood a monitor, warning the other nations of infringements or infractions of the Hay Doctrine, when, as they gradually have come to learn, the United States Government has had no intention of strongly backing the doctrine, or of helping to enforce it, or of doing more than mildly chide the violators. If America does help maintain international equity and equilibrium in the far East hereafter, her part is clearly defined. She must become a member of an alliance, or *entente*. She will have to agree to do certain things in the event of certain contingencies, and will have to provide the means to do them. This requires the maintenance of specified military and naval strength and certain strategical dispositions of that force.

What would be the composition of a consortium or entente or alliance organized to enforce the "open door" and "integrity of China" policies? To work out successfully, it should include Powers whose interests harmonize with these principles, and exclude Powers whose interests (or policies) conflict with these principles. Interests and policies of a nation are not always coöperative, although they always are supposed to be and are designed to be. For instance, the genuine interests of a nation in China might be in harmony with the Hay Doctrine, but the policy of that nation might be antagonistic to the doctrine because of error of statesmen who decide the policy. I believe, and American statesmen apparently have always believed, that the "open door" and "integrity of China" policies are to the genuine and permanent interest of Japan, and of all nations. This assumes that the principles of fair play, of equal opportunity, and respect for the rights of weaker nations and backward peoples, if faithfully observed, will work out beneficially for all nations and for the world. But fair play and equal opportunity are not principles that underlie all national policies when applied externally. Selfish advantage, national

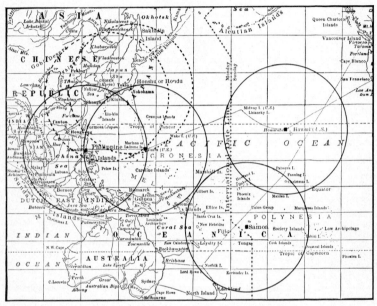

Map illustrating the strategical position of the United States in the Pacific Ocean, and the Far East, with bases at Hawaii, Guam, the Philippines and Samoa. The circles have a diameter of 3,000 miles, within which distance naval operations from a central base can be conducted efficiently. The dotted circles show the scope from the chief naval bases in Japan. With bases at these points, adequately supplied and fortified, it is possible for the United States to protect its position and policies in the Far East. Without these bases, these policies cannot be protected effectively.

aggrandizement, territorial acquisition, unfair competition, predatory ambitions, are motives that dictate some national policies; and diplomacy is never without a plausible dogma to predicate such policies on. American statesmen apparently were so convinced that Japan's true interest lies in supporting the Hay Doctrine that they at one time gave full credit to Japan's acceptance of it. It may be that when Japan first accepted the doctrine, her statesmen did think it was to Japan's advantage; and it is certain that they thought it to Japan's advantage to pretend to think that way. Nearly everybody seemed to be fooled, including Great Britain. There was one exception—Russia. An eminent Russian diplomatist, especially skilled in far Eastern politics, told me more than ten years ago that Japan was humbugging about the Hay Doctrine, and was humbugging America in all ways. Russia and Japan were at outs then, and the Russian statesman could speak privately without restraint; that is, his own nation's policy did not restrain him from expressing those views, as it might now. I agreed with him at that time, although few Americans thought that way then. It took a decade for events to demonstrate obviously that present-day Japanese statesmen regard American policy in China, as expressed by the Hay Doctrine, as being absolutely opposed to the interests of Japan. This is no longer a secret. The Tokio "Nichi-Nichi" of January 29, 1916, remarked editorially, apropos America's opposition to Japan in China: "The situation between Japan and America is like two trains running toward each other on the same track." Prominent Japanese have said almost as forcible phrases in the Diet. Japanese opinion is practically unanimous on this question. Therefore it seems worse than useless to include Japan in any consortium to maintain the Hay Doctrine. She will be with the opposition. The question arises, naturally, if it is possible to win Japan over to support the "open door" and "integrity of China" principles. Japan may be compelled to observe these principles, but she cannot now be persuaded sincerely to support them. Her statesmanship, her preparations, her plans, and her dispositions are committed to the other course, which accords with her present national ambitions and ideals. These will not be suddenly reversed; they will not be reversed at all except from necessity, although they may be retarded or suspended by considerations of expediency.

What nations would join with the United States in sustaining and enforcing the Hay Doctrine? This proposition requires examination, for such an entente should not be a makeshift or haphazard arrangement. I have previously indicated the bearings of European politics on this situation; and an approximately accurate answer to the question depends on the outcome of the Great War, and the balance of power thereafter among the belligerents. This much can be foreseen: Russia, Great Britain, and France have what can be called primary interests in China. Germany has a strong tentative interest there. Other European nations can be classed as negative, falling in according to their alignments in European politics. We therefore have only six Powers to reckon with—Great Britain, Russia, Germany, France, Japan, and the United States— those which composed the 6-Power financial group. What combinations are possible, that could provide the needed strength? A combination of France, Great Britain, and the United States might do. If Germany was added, the consortium would be all-powerful. But first let us try to discover how the attitudes of these Powers would incline logically. We have two of them already placed—Japan and the United States—on opposite sides of the question. Great Britain's preference, other things being approximately equal, probably is to maintain the "open door" and independence of China policies. Great Britain was first to advocate these principles, and while at times she has lapsed in observing them, it is likely, having in mind the world-situation after the war, that she will recognize that an enforcement of the Hay Doctrine is the only real promise of a permanent peace in the Orient that is consistent with British interests and prestige and honor. If Great Britain takes this view, then France also will be strongly inclined to accept it, for France has not enough to gain by a different course to make her pull that way.

Russia's position is doubtful. I take it that Russia has no enthusiasm for the Hay Doctrine; but neither has she any strong reasons for opposing it now. Her situation after the war will be such that considerations applying to her position in Europe may decide how she will align in the far East. Taken solely by Russia's Oriental interests, she can play the game either way on about equal chances; that is, by lining up with Japan, or by lining up with America. But analysis shows that after the war Japan can really give Russia nothing that Russia requires at this stage of her development—money and support in Europe. Neither has Russia anything to fear from Japan in the far East if Japan is opposed there by a strong entente of Powers which also is friendly to Russia. It is tolerably clear that Russia cannot for several decades dispense with close associations with France and Great Britain. Financial considerations strongly influence this. Furthermore, it seems likely that for several decades close financial associations with America will be almost, if not quite, a necessity for France and England; and Russia also is not indifferent to this consideration. It is evident that after the war the comparative financial strength and influence of America among the Powers will be greatly enhanced, provided the American Government pursues a favorable policy to promote and permit it. In many ways her coöperation will be needed, even if it is not desired. Europe hardly will expect to work freely and amicably with American finance and industry while excluding it from China, or conniving with its exclusion; unless Europe expects to be able completely to overawe America, and to dictate the conditions under which America shall exist and develop.

What of Germany? Germany's alliances in Europe, aside from the Powers now combined against her, are not applicable to strengthen her hand in the far East except as they support her influence in Europe. Taking Germany's interest in China, I believe her disposition is to sustain the "open door" and the integrity of China, because I believe that such a policy is to the advantage of Germany on broad lines. Since the German Government subscribed to the Hay Doctrine, it has, by and large, rather "played the game." Germany's Shantung agreement (which called forth the action of Mr. Hay) was distinctly based on the "sphere of influence" thesis; but Germany has since then fairly well observed her promise, made by Count von Bülow to Mr. Hay, not to construe the Shantung agreement in contradiction to the "open door" principle; and Germany has been guilty of no serious infringements of the doctrine in other parts of China. It is only doing justice to Germany to state this; and that since the disagreeable incident of her taking leasehold of Kiaochou, German activities in China, as applied to China, have been comparatively free from disturbing features. Presuming that after the war Germany will naturally incline to continue this policy toward China, it must be some diversion of German interest, or some new application of far Eastern conditions to Germany's position in Europe that would array her with Japan, and against the Hay Doctrine. If peace finds Germany so circumscribed and menaced in Europe that she wants to strengthen her position, then it might be possible that she would make an alliance with Japan for purely strategical reasons. There is no genuine sympathy between those nations, and no real community of their interests in Asia.

I have not given China a rating in a consortium to enforce the Hay Doctrine, for China is both the reason and object of the doctrine. China is herself too weak to sustain it, and consequently her contribution to its enforcement for a long time will be sentimental and coöperative. Only those nations which purpose to impose on China by force are indifferent to her good will. China's good will is very important to all nations that intend and expect to develop interests there by friendly intercourse. And China asks nothing but justice. However, China's course within herself, her ability or ineptness in government, her adaptability or obstruction to progress, her willingness or backwardness to do what she can for herself and to facilitate external stimulants and aids, her receptiveness to good advice, her appreciation of friendly intentions, and the development of a national patriotism and spirit that carry promise of national cohesiveness and reconstruction, all must exert a strong influence on the course of events.   China may so misconduct her affairs, may display such incompetence, or internal dissension, that her case will be considered hopeless, and compel some foreign supervision of the country.   China has to some extent lost control over her own fate, but it is possible for her to recover it.

Many take it as a foregone conclusion, with affairs shaping as they are in the far East and the world, that England must or will support America in sustaining the Hay Doctrine.   That is the logic of the situation in its major bearings.   I believe that England's inclination will be that way in a comparison of alternatives.   The Anglo-Japanese alliance never has been wholly satisfactory to Great Britain; it never has been at all satisfactory to British colonies bordering the Pacific Ocean.   It contains deep-lying embarrassments and insidious dangers.   It is a makeshift for both England and Japan.   The existing political terms and conditions of the alliance no longer serve Japan's aims; they cannot be adjusted to Japan's policy unless they are radically changed, or secretly enervated.   To do that would require Great Britain to make sacrifices and concessions which she does not want to make.   But is there a way out for Great Britain?   It is clear that Great Britain cannot hereafter play it both ways with Japan and America; she will not find it possible to hold the sympathy of both of these nations.   This argument already has been put with force and clearness by the Japanese press and by Japanese officials.   It undoubtedly will be put with equal force and clearness by American diplomats sooner or later.   What will England do?   I imagine the British Government stating its case, confidentially, something like this: ''You Americans want to keep the door open in China, so that your commerce and your finance can enter on equal

terms. You also want to maintain the integrity and autonomy
of China. You have moral grounds for this—justice and humanity and the integrity of treaties, and all that—and we will
give you credit for a reasonable amount of genuine altruism;
your national record entitles you to that. But deeper than
that, you begin to see that there may in time be an Oriental
peril for you. You have seen within a few years a small
Oriental nation rise to be a formidable Power by learning and
applying Western military science; from that you reason that
if this method and disposition are communicated to the whole
of eastern Asia, and that region becomes consolidated under
one arrogant and aggressive and predatory Government, then
you had better look out lest the weight of that impact will be
thrown against your country, and your institutions, and your
standards of life. We admit that Great Britain had much to do
with building up Japan's power; but we did not fully calculate
her rate of progress, and did not guess accurately the consequent shifting of her disposition and policy. We see it now,
and don't like it much better than Americans do. But Great
Britain's imperial interests require certain checks and balances,
which to have any effect must be represented by military and
naval strength, and a readiness to use this strength. The alliance with Japan has, for a time, supplied a quota of this balance.
If we drop it, what will take its place? We are none too secure
as it is; our world interests and position are exposed to so
many reactions that we cannot sustain a strong policy in the
Pacific if we become opposed to Japan, unless her defection is
made up elsewhere. With Great Britain, in these matters, it
is give and take. If we take something from Japan, we must
be willing to give something. It has seemed to us that America, in the far East, has been wanting to take without giving.
You want the door kept open, but you don't want to have to
provide any of the police required to keep it open, and to keep
depredators out, or to commit yourselves to a responsibility
calling for force. We are not deluded. We know that the
door cannot be kept open in China without force that will be

used, and that other nations know will be used, if occasion requires. We have been supplying our part of this moral and physical force; but at times we have been compelled to yield a little to what our allies want, in order to maintain a general balance. Suppose England drops the alliance with Japan. That will throw Japan to the other side; or even if she has to play a lone hand, we are not strong enough, or cannot take the risk, or do not think it is worth while, to fight her in the far East. Will America supply to our grand balance what we will lose by dropping Japan? Will America agree to maintain its navy and army at a certain standard, to prepare certain necessary defenses and facilities, to make certain strategical dispositions of its navy and army in conjunction with our own, and those of other nations perhaps, and to use those forces in a common, stipulated cause if occasion arises? If America will do that, we can talk business. If you won't, then we are compelled to drop a hint about 'four-flushing,' and whatever dispositions are made in respect to these international questions will have to count America out. If other Powers have to spend the money to provide international police power, and the men to do the work, and have to suffer the losses and take the odium and the risks, then they will run the game without consulting America.''

That is what it amounts to. Americans must understand that their nation has operated on credit as a first-class Power in international politics as long as it can. In the future it will be necessary for it to deliver the goods, or drop back into a second-rate position and a second-rate influence. It is folly to think that by abstaining from active participation in these affairs America will avoid their influence and consequences. It also is folly to think that by refusing to supply its quota of international responsibility and police power the United States can avoid paying its share of the cost of them. I suppose, even in the backwoods where resides the mythical American farmer whose viewpoint is now supposed to decide the attitude of the American Government toward problems of foreign relations and world politics, that it is understood that foreign trade is desirable, is necessary to a well-balanced American industrial development, and is inevitable anyhow, for there is no way America can avoid such commerce. It will be forced on the nation, as it was forced on Japan, and as it is being forced on China; unless Americans surround their country with forts and drive off all ships that approach their shores. This international trade must be policed, just as trade inside the United States is protected. On the high seas, going and coming, in foreign countries as well as in America, this commerce must have legal status and police protection in its legal rights. If the United States will not take part in establishing this legal status, and in enforcing the law, then American foreign trade will operate under laws and regulations made by other nations, and enforced by other nations. Americans will not enjoy these privileges and benefits without cost. They will have to pay their share. They cannot escape payment. It will not be necessary for the Powers that make the laws and do the policing to enter the United States to collect America's share of the cost. That can be collected at some external point of transit —in freights, in tariffs, in indirect charges. Let us, for example, assume that the business of enforcing international law and protecting American foreign trade is entrusted to Great Britain. A good many Americans seem to be in favor of that, on the theory that it would save Americans a lot of trouble and responsibility. Police would be needed to protect the trade and to enforce the laws, and in international affairs this police work is done by armies and navies. Unless all the other Powers would abide by Great Britain's administration, and concede her supreme authority, it would be necessary for Great Britain to have a great navy and a large army. That would cost a great deal. If America refused to pay her quota of cost, Great Britain could and no doubt would exact the money by levying on the commerce. Americans could not question the rulings of Great Britain; they could not avoid paying what Great Britain decided should be paid. If retaliations were threatened or at-

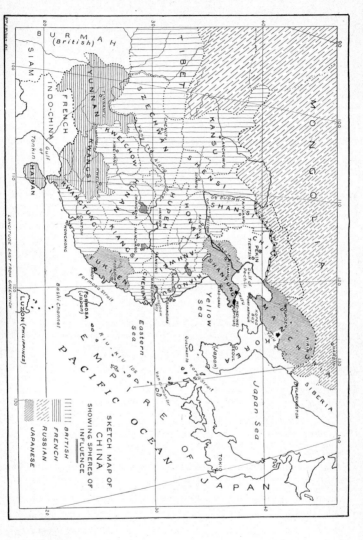

Map showing the division of China into "spheres of influence," with Japan in occupation of the sphere formerly held by Germany. The United States has no "sphere"

tempted, America would be powerless to enforce them. The only way Americans could, under that system, have any direct say in their foreign relations would be to become a part of the British Empire, and participate in the British Government. If other questions arose, between America and other Powers, it would be their fiat and Great Britain's that would decide the issues. In time America by that process would lose control over her internal affairs to some extent. This is exactly the situation of China to-day. That is why a Hay Doctrine, or something like it, is necessary to prevent China's political nationality from vanishing from the earth. It is possible for a few armed Powers to charge the cost of their armaments on the pacifist nations, while holding the power themselves. This has happened among classes and sections within Governments; why cannot it happen among nations?

Taking Japan and America as the logical extreme opposites of the Eastern question, with the other Powers ranging between them, what have Japan and America each to offer to attract to themselves a preponderating consortium to support their policies? America has, besides a promise of fair play and equal opportunity, every element that is needed in such a combination—money, resources, intelligence, science; and a sufficient surplus of all to be able to spare some for foreign development. Japan has only military and naval strength, and her limitations are defined by the extent of her foreign credit. There is no doubt which is the better partner, the more able physically to fulfil its undertakings. There ought, after Japan's recent course in China, to be no doubt which is the more reliable ally. If America will provide an equal naval and military force to Japan's, or a force which in combination with those of other Powers will counterbalance Japan's, she can almost select her own partners in the far East. Under the present conditions, Japan is an international nuisance, and she may easily grow into an international peril. It seems incredible that Japan's policy in China can prevail over the enlightened and equitable Hay Doctrine; it seems incredible that the lower morality and the lesser material interests (Japan's trade and investments in China are not one tenth of those of Western nations) shall supersede the greater ones; it seems incredible that the Western Powers will permit Japan's aggravating world policy to progress unimpeded. Yet Japan's policy may gain the upper hand by default of effective opposition, and by a general demoralization and confusion of Western statesmanship which will prevent the organization of a consortium to check her.

There are several methods for trying to maintain a nation's internal and international rights. One is frankly dependent —by becoming a political vassal, or henchman, of a real Power. Another way is by diplomatic intrigue, by playing upon opposing policies and interests of stronger nations, and arraying them against each other to create an equilibrium. This has been China's way. We see how it has worked out. Another way is for a nation, having the population and resources that permit it, to provide an armed strength sufficient to sustain its own prestige and rights, and to give its wishes and dictum weight in international affairs. There are no other practical methods, and none is likely to be developed by civilization soon. Of course it happens that weak nations do at times enjoy the privileges of security and autonomy, but only by the sufferance and toleration of real Powers. There is a point where even a nation having population and resources sufficient to become a real Power can lose ability to choose between these methods. At one time, not many years ago, China could have made her own choice without much difficulty, but she allowed it to pass, and did not apply a part of her resources to create national strength. Now she is not free to choose. She cannot prepare for defense if she wants to, except by permission of the Powers, and if some Powers have their way this permission will not be given. Thus national irresolution and supineness lead logically to national enervation and subjugation.

America probably still is free to choose among these methods, but none can say how long this option will run. The whirligig of "Welt-politik" spins faster than it used to, is animated by new and subtle forces which agitate civilization through innumerable contacts, whose effects no corner of the earth can escape. There is a tendency to measure these issues by costs in dollars, especially in America. Some argue that preparedness for defense may be a good thing, but it costs too much. Preparedness for defense is frequently likened to fire insurance, and the comparison is accurate in many ways. Many persons do not insure because they can comprehend distinctly the money needed for payments, while the return is less tangible. One thing is present, and actual, the other is future and problematical. In some countries state insurance is forcing the laggards and improvidents to bear their part of this and other forms of economic equalization. National defense is a form of state insurance. In respect to American policy in the far East and the cost of insuring it by increasing armaments, the economies of the proposition can be figured in general terms. A method of treating this question that is advocated in America is by avoidance; that is, give up the Hay Doctrine and the Philippines, and any other outlying possessions and outposts that may, by coming within the scope of aggressive policies of other Powers, involve the United States. Apart from the fact that no real problem ever is solved by avoidance, it may be that it will cost less, in dollars, to prepare to defend American policy and possessions abroad than to abdicate them. It is roughly estimated that China's administrative, commercial, and economic development in the next twenty years will need $2,000,000,000 of foreign capital. Under a genuine application of the Hay Doctrine, America would have approximately one fourth of this financing, assuming that within this period Great Britain, France, Germany, and the United States are the principal financial nations. The returns from this investment would be partly interest and partly trade. Five per cent. interest on $500,000,000 is $25,-000,000 income annually. The capital will go into industrial undertakings mostly—railways and such facilities. In such construction about one third of the capital is applied to materials—an item of about $135,000,000 of business for

America's share. Such industrial enterprises require about
12 per cent. annual renewals—about $15,000,000 annual ex-
port trade. Interest and profits coming to America would be
about $30,000,000 yearly, besides the original profits and com-
missions. This is business arising entirely from *investments,*
and which, as conditions are in China, will go to the nation
providing the capital. That kind of business is distinct from
straight commerce, which is done on the selling qualities of the
goods. There is a vast future trade in China for America under the "open door," which abandonment of the Hay Doctrine
will cut off. To that can be added trade in the Philippines
under the present or a similar association of those islands with
the United States. These figures are roughly sketched in to
show that the money returns from sustaining an American
policy in China and the Pacific may more than pay the cost of
maintaining armaments to sustain the policy, leaving other
considerations (the graver ones) out of the estimate.

In this connection, some other matters are full of suggestion.
In recent times a fatally wrong hypothesis about some foreign
contacts of the United States has been propagated in America,
which, if it is not shaken off, inevitably will dam the current
of national progress by reversing processes that have built up
the nation. The development of America has been due to two
main elements—natural resources and people. The natural resources were useless without people to set them to working.
People came to America and were induced to remain and merge
with the nation because by the American political system they
were offered greater advantages and opportunities than they
had in other countries. These comparative conditions are not
permanent or perpetual. The world is going through an evolution which causes a constant shifting of elements that apply
to these conditions. If conditions arise whereby other nations,
in comparison with America, give people better advantages
and opportunities under the changing circumstances of civilization and economic evolution, and better facilities to work, and
better protection for their lives and property, then the tide

will turn, and gradually people will drift away from America in their political allegiance, toward those better advantages and facilities and protection.   It is not from accident or preference that many Americans now do business in China, and in other countries, as British and other foreign corporations.   If the proposal to abandon the Philippines without making any provision for their stability and security is carried out, there will be some interesting manifestations of this principle.   I never have met a superior type of business man or investor in the Philippines who has any faith in the ability of the Filipinos to conduct a stable government now, and to preserve their nationality without foreign aid.   If United States authority and protection is withdrawn from the islands, the principal American interests and property there will be driven to seek protection, and the greater part of them probably will get under the British flag as soon as they can; and many Filipino-owned interests will do the same thing.   That is what I would do if I had worked to build up a property and interests in the Philippines, and the United States should withdraw entirely.   No announcement that, after withdrawal, the United States will protect American property and investments in the islands will satisfy Americans or others with a practical foreign experience, in view of recent events.   The American Government that would withdraw from the Philippines in these circumstances probably would thereafter desert American interests there like they recently have been abandoned in Mexico and China, and on the high seas.   A few more years of this kind of foreign policy will begin to alienate the political allegiance of Americans living and doing business abroad, for they will begin to yield to practical influences tending to bring their business and their political nationality under the same flag.   This tendency contains grave consequences for the American nation.   It can cause internal reactions.   Experience has shown the unreliability of purely sentimental fealty as a basis for American popular loyalty to the State, for in the progressive evolution of the American citizen from European ancestry there is much uncertainty about the exact stage of that progress where the different elements of the population will fix their sentimental allegiance, unless their citizenship is joined with obvious material benefits derived from it and dependent on it.   Allegiance attaches ultimately to home and property, is the dogma on which democracy rests and on which the American nation is founded. Modern political intelligence sees a little farther, and is coming to attach allegiance to the Government that gives security to home and property wherever it is, rather than to a Government in whose territory residence is conditionally held.

One cannot fail to notice in the far East the cumulative effects of current acts and policy of the American Government in its foreign relations.   The Chinese long have regarded the United States as a great Power.   A few years ago there was a ruthless massacre of Chinese in Mexico which deeply touched the growing patriotic sentiment and pride of Chinese at home, who felt that their national weakness was responsible for such incidents. Then followed a period in Mexico when many Americans lost their lives and property, yet the United States obtained no more satisfaction than China got, and was even less urgent than China in demanding satisfaction.   Orientals interpret such a policy to mean that the United States is too weak or too timid to protect its citizens and their property abroad.   It is not possible for an American to explain the American policy in Mexico to Orientals so they will comprehend it.   I have tried.   A series of events in recent years has devitalized American diplomacy in the far East to an extent that will hamper its influence there for a long time.   I have the best information that when the Wai Chiao-pu (Chinese foreign office) was asking delay in the negotiations with Japan in 1915, Mr. Hioki, the Japanese minister at Peking, stated that his Government was averse to postponement because of the possibility of international complications.   He said frankly that Japan was concerned about the attitude of America, and wanted to adjust the Chinese questions "while the present American Government is in power."

No new entente or alliance to enforce the "open door" and uphold the integrity of China can work out successfully unless a practical basis for coöperation is found. Experience has proven this. Mr. Knox recognized it, and his plan for the neutralization of railways in Manchuria was a move to that end. I heard that Mr. Knox, after Japan and Russia rejected his proposal, and Great Britain and France had sided with their allies, said: "Very well; but they will have to come to that in the end." The American banking group recognized it when, after futile independent efforts, it entered into coöperation with an international group. Something must be done to stop the international scramble for advantages and strategical position in China, which will continue with growing aggravation as long as the "sphere" theory is applied. After the association of Sun Yat Sen with the rebellion of 1913 had caused the revocation of the charter of the Chinese National Railway Corporation, George Bronson Rea devised a plan for international coöperation in railway development in China, with the approval of the Chinese Government, providing for an equitable coöperation of British, French, German, and American interests. Mr. Rea visited Europe and the United States to present this plan. At a meeting held in Paris in April, 1914, the financial and constructing groups of the four Powers approved a plan for an international corporation with headquarters in Switzerland. The American, French, and German Governments also approved it. The British Goverment approved it "in principle," but inclined to preserve a British "sphere" by insisting that only British interests should operate in certain parts of China. The Great War stopped these negotiations, and the matter rests. Mr. Rea's plan in principle is the same as Mr. Knox's Manchuria scheme, applied to the whole of China. Unless the Powers will agree to some practical method of coöperation in finance and major development, the "open door" will continue to be evaded.

Another international arrangement in China which the Great War disturbed is the 5-Power banking group and its

undertakings. Germany is a member of the 5-Power group,
and German banks are participators in the financing of the
Reorganization Loan. The war disrupted German financial
and commercial connections throughout the whole world with
Great Britain, France, Russia and Japan, the other Powers
composing this group. There is naturally speculation about
the future of the 5-Power group, and a reorganization will be
necessary for many reasons, to meet the changed conditions
that will follow the war. The group may not be able to, or
may not want after the war to carry out its undertakings as
they were originally conceived. It probably will be difficult
to float Chinese bonds in Europe and England for some time
after the war, for all the belligerent nations will be heavy bor-
rowers for their own reorganization and reconstruction. The
need to sustain their foreign trade will induce those Powers,
however, to make provision for financing those interests; and
China cannot be overlooked or abandoned. Interests that have
taken half a century to construct will not be allowed to disintegrate if that can be prevented. As I write, discussion of
these matters is influenced by the rancors, hostilities and
alarms bred by the war; and a disposition is shown by French,
British and Russians to exclude Germany from any future participation in international financing in China. That is a
wrong and dangerous disposition, in which America should
not join. The "open door" in China will not be really open
if it is shut to Germany—there can be no assurance of harmony and peace in a financial consortium that, because of hostility, refuses to work with nations that are able and are entitled to participate. If a new group is organized, it should
include Germany, if Germany wants to join, and if she can
do her share of the financing. A reorganized group should
include America too, for practical as well as international reasons, for American money will actually be needed to an extent
that has not occurred heretofore. Opportunity once more
unexpectedly beckons to America. But American finance will
not be able safely to participate, as such, however it may wish

to, unless it is strongly and definitely supported by the diplomacy and power of the American Government.   Failing to get that support, American money that is supplied to help finance China, or important undertakings in that country, will be driven to operate under other flags, by the process of first being lent to European, British or Japanese bankers, who in turn, with the backing of their Governments, will use it in China.

These far Eastern questions demand solution.   It is possible to adjust them to a pacific formula, and to restrain them within that formula.   If allowed to go on nagging and ruffling international susceptibilities at every turn, they will bring war.   However they are adjusted, however they turn, America cannot escape the effects of these forces.

APPENDICES

APPENDIX A

CORRESPONDENCE AND UTTERANCES OF THE UNITED
STATES, JAPANESE AND RUSSIAN GOVERNMENTS
RELATING TO THE PROPOSAL TO NEUTRALIZE
RAILWAYS IN MANCHURIA

No. 1—Mr. Knox's Statement to the Press.
No. 2—Reply of the Russian Government.
No. 3—Reply of the Japanese Government.
No. 4—Response of the United States Government to the Russian Counter-proposal.

1.

Statement Given to the Press
Department of State, Washington,
January 6, 1916.

In reply to an inquiry as to the truth of the St. Petersburg report relating to the neutralization of railways in Manchuria, the Secretary of State to-day said:

The proposition of the United States to the interested Powers looking to the neutralization of the Manchurian railroads discloses the end toward which American policy in the far East has been recently directed.

Late in May last this Government learned that an understanding had been reached between important British, French, and German financial groups, supported by their Governments, by which they were to furnish funds for the construction of two great railways in China. This Government, believing that sympathetic coöperation between the Governments most vitally interested would best subserve the policies of the maintenance of Chinese political integrity and equality of commercial opportunity, suggested that American coöperation with the powerful international financial group already formed would be useful to further the policies to which all were alike pledged.

This Government pointed out that the greatest danger at present in China to the open door and the development of foreign trade arose from disagreements among the great Western nations, and expressed the opinion that nothing would afford so impressive an object lesson to China and the world as the sight of the four great capitalist nations—Great Britain, Germany, France, and the United States—standing together for equality of commercial opportunity.

Owing to the strong opposition that had developed in certain official quarters in China and elsewhere, the President, in July last, felt warranted in resorting to the somewhat unusual method of communicating directly with His Imperial Highness Prince Chun, Regent of the Chinese Empire, informing the latter that he was greatly discouraged at the reports of certain prejudiced opposition to the Chinese Government's arranging for equal participation by American capital in the Hukuang loan. The President pointed out that the wishes of the United States were based upon broad national and impersonal principles of equity and good policy, in which a due regard for the best interests of China had a common part. He reasserted his intense personal interest in making use of American capital in the development of China an instrument in the promotion of China's welfare and an increase in her material prosperity without entanglements or embarrassments that might affect the growth of her independent political power and the preservation of her territorial integrity.

As a result of this communication, an agreement was soon reached with the Chinese Government that American bankers should take one fourth of the total loan and that Americans and American materials should have all the same rights, privileges, preferences, and discretions for all present and prospective lines that were reserved to the British, German, and French nationals and materials under the terms of their original agreement except only the right to appoint chief engineers for the two sections about to be placed under contract. As to the latter point, China gave assurance that American engineers would be employed upon the engineering corps of both roads and that the present waiving of America's right to chief engineers would in no way prejudice its rights in that regard when future extensions should be constructed. After several months of continuous negotiations, the right to such American all-around equal participation has been acknowledged and a final settlement on this basis has been all but completed.

The grounds for this energetic action on the part of the United States Government have not been generally understood. Railroad loans floated by China have in the past generally been given an Imperial guaranty and secured by first mortgages on the lines constructed or by pledging provincial revenues as security. The proposed hypothecation of China's internal revenues for a loan was therefore regarded as involving important political considerations. The fact that the loan was to carry an Imperial guaranty and be secured on the internal revenues made it of the greatest importance that the United States should participate therein in order that this Government might be in a position as an interested party to exercise an influence equal to that of any of the other three Powers in any question arising through the pledging of China's national resources, and to enable the United States, moreover, at the proper time again to support China in urgent and desirable fiscal administrative reforms, such as the abolition of *likin,* the revision of the customs tariff, and general fiscal and monetary rehabilitation.

There were, however, stronger reasons and broader grounds. In fact, the action of the Government in respect to the pending loan was but the first step in a new phase of the traditional policy of the United States in China and with special reference to Manchuria. As is well known, the essential principles of the Hay policy of the open door are the preservation of the territorial and jurisdictional integrity of the Chinese Empire and equal commercial opportunity in China for all nations. This Government believes that one of the most effective, if not the most effective, way to secure for China the undisturbed enjoyment of all political rights in Manchuria and to promote the normal development of the eastern provinces under the policy of the open door practically applied, would be to take the railroads of Manchuria out of Eastern politics and place them under an economic and impartial administration by vesting in China the ownership of its railroads; the funds for that purpose to be furnished by the nationals of such interested Powers as might be willing to participate and who are pledged to the policy of the open door and equal opportunity, the Powers participating to operate the railway system during the period of the loan and enjoy the usual preferences in supplying materials.

Such a policy would naturally require for its execution the cooperation not only of China, but also of Japan and Russia, who already have extensive railway rights in Manchuria. The advantages of such a plan are obvious. It would insure unimpaired Chinese sovereignty, the commercial and industrial development of the Manchurian provinces, and furnish a substantial reason for the early solution of the problems of fiscal and monetary reform which are now receiving such earnest attention by the Chinese Government. It would afford an opportunity for both Russia and Japan to shift their onerous duties, responsibilities, and expenses in connection with these railways to the shoulders of the combined Powers, including themselves. Such a policy, moreover, would effect a complete commerical neutralization of Manchuria, and in so doing make a large contribution to the peace of the world by converting the provinces of Manchuria into an immense commercial neutral zone.

The recent signature of an ad referendum agreement between a representative of the Chinese Government and the financial representatives of the United States and Great Britain to finance and construct a railway line from Chinchow to Aigun gave the United States an opportunity to lay this proposal before the Government of Great Britain for its consideration, and it is gratifying to be able to state that the project has already received the approval in principle of that Government. There are reasons to believe that such a plan might also meet with like favorable consideration on the part of Russia. Germany and China cordially approve the American suggestion, and certain press reports from Japan indicate that the project may likewise be received with favor by that country. For instance, a recent article on the subject in the "Japan Mail" ends with these significant words:

"One cannot conceal from oneself the fact that if all the railways forming part of the system which connects the West with the far East were converted into a neutral estate, a great contribution will be made to the peace of the world."

2.

Ambassador Rockhill to the Secretary of State
(Extract)

No. 12

American Embassy,
St. Petersburg, January 22, 1910.

Sir:

I have the honor to enclose herewith the *aide-memoire* from the ministry for foreign affairs in reply to the memorandum submitted to it by this embassy, embodying the proposals contained in your cabled instructions of November 6, last, for the neutralization of the railway lines in Manchuria.

This aide-memoire was received by the embassy yesterday afternoon. This morning's newspapers contained the official communiqué giving the substance of the aide-memoire. The comments of the press are distinctly divided along purely political lines; the Government and Conservative organs being opposed to the general proposal, the liberal press in favor of it; while both are disposed to favor a fuller consideration of the question of Russian participation in the Chinchow-Aigun Railway.

I have, etc.,

W. W. ROCKHILL.

(Enclosure)

THE AIDE-MEMOIRE

The Imperial Government did not fail to submit to the most serious examination the alternative proposed by the Government of the United States of America, tending on the one hand to establish an international administration and control of the railroads in Manchuria and on the other hand to engage Russian capital in the enterprise of the Chinchow-Tsitsihar-Aigun Railway. The Federal Government sees in this proposition the best means of maintaining in their entirety the political rights of China in Manchuria and of contributing to the development of this province by applying to it the principle of the open door.

It is with a feeling of deep satisfaction that the Imperial Government notes the testimony borne by the United States Government to the sincere desire with which Russia is animated to support in Manchuria the policy of the open door and of equal opportunity, as well as to guarantee to China her full sovereignty there.

However, nothing appears at the present time to threaten either this sovereignty or the open door policy in Manchuria. Consequently the Imperial Government cannot discover in the present condition of Manchuria any reason necessitating the placing on the order of the day of the questions raised by the United States Government.

At the same time the Imperial Government believes that it must declare with absolute frankness that the establishment of an international administration and control of the Manchuria railroads as proposed by the Federal Government would seriously injure Russian interests, both public and private, to which the Imperial Government attaches a capital importance. This proposition cannot, therefore, meet with a favorable reception on its part.

In making this statement the Imperial Government is pleased to hope that, appreciating at their just value the immense material sacrifices and moral efforts at the expense of which these interests were created, the Federal Government will look at this question from the same standpoint as the Imperial Government, which standpoint is equitable in every respect. The Imperial Government, believing that the interests involved in the Chinese Eastern Railway are notorious, believes that it may confine itself to stating their substance succinctly.

It is important above all to remark that at the same time this immense enterprise was put into execution under extraordinary conditions, the Chinese Eastern Railway Company insured itself, for the whole duration of the concession—that is, for eighty years —both on the part of the Chinese and of the Russian Government, well-defined rights and privileges which it did not consent to relinquish unless China redeemed the whole enterprise, but in no event before the expiration of a period of thirty-six years. The company therefore adopted its plan of operation with the conviction of being able to realize this long period of time guaranteed to it by the very act of concession. Now thirty years still separate it from the expiration of the shortest of these periods.

It is evident that, under these conditions, to urge it to relinquish its rights and privileges would be to inflict on these interests an injury which nothing could warrant. For this the Imperial Government sees no sufficient reason.

On the other hand, the fact must not be lost sight of that, being obliged to operate in a country where European civilization does not exist, the company was compelled to make great expenditures not only for the construction of the railroad proper, but also in connection with numerous auxiliary works. It was also necessary to create and organize various kinds of administrations and services connected in one way or another with the railroad. Finally, thanks to the public confidence which was enjoyed by the company, numerous private enterprises, more or less connected with the railroad, arose along the Chinese eastern line, very considerable capital being invested in them. It is hardly possible to enumerate the numerous interests grouped about this line to-day, and this is a sufficient reason why the Imperial Government deems itself obliged to use the greatest circumspection in making any modification whatever of this state of affairs which is the source of so many interests.

There is still another final consideration which still more greatly obliges the Imperial Government to observe great prudence. The development of Manchuria and the exploitation of its natural resources are not the only purposes pursued by the Chinese Eastern Railway. The latter is of a public interest of the first order to Russia. It constitutes the principal line of communication between the Russian possessions in the far East and the rest of the empire; it is also the great artery by which these possessions are supplied with Russian merchandise. In this way the line is but an integral part of the great Trans-Siberian Railway, which is used by almost all of western Europe in its relations with the far East. It is this consideration that decided the Russian Government to guarantee, at a very considerable expense, the capital invested in the construction of the Chinese Eastern Railway, and to cover the deficit resulting from its operation. It cannot, therefore, be a matter of indifference to the Imperial Government whether it is an international organ that administers a line of such importance, or, on the contrary, a

Russian stock company which is obliged not to fix the rates and conditions of transportation of merchandise by the Chinese Eastern Railroad without the consent of the Russian Government, and which, by the very nature of the concession obtained, is closely connected with the interests of the nation.

These are the considerations which, from the Russian standpoint, determine in a conclusive manner the attitude of the Imperial Government toward the proposition of the United States Government regarding the international administration and control of the Manchurian railroads. There are others, however, of a general character which likewise do not plead in favor of this proposition.

The Imperial Government is of the opinion that the proposition of the United States does not sufficiently guarantee that the new order of things will have a satisfactory result from a financial standpoint. At all events the organization proposed for Manchuria is of a tentative character, which has not only never been tried in China but is unusual in itself. To decide in favor of it on so vast a scale as proposed by the Federal Government, relinquishing for this purpose a system that has been tested, would only be possible with a certainty of obtaining favorable results. The Imperial Government regrets that it does not have this certainty.

Taking up, now, the second alternative of the American proposition, the Imperial Government considers itself obliged to declare that it regards the project of construction of the Chinchow-Tsitsihar-Aigun Railroad as being of capital importance to Russia. Its accomplishment will open up a new route, giving access from the south not only to the Chinese Eastern Railway, but directly to Russian possessions at Aigun. This shows adequently the strategic and political importance of the enterprise. Moreover, the construction of this line will essentially modify the conditions under which eastern Mongolia and the north of Manchuria are served by the Chinese Eastern Railway. Now, the Imperial Government cannot realize the consequences of this proposition and decide on the attitude which it ought to assume in regard thereto unless it is informed of the basis on which it reposes. For these reasons the Imperial Government, which being willing in principle to take this question under consideration, hopes that it will be enabled to know the basis of the proposition in due time in order that it may, after a thorough examination, reach a final attitude with regard to the proposition itself as well as to its participation therein.

It is the same with any future project concerning a financial participation in the construction of railroads in Manchuria. The Imperial Government considers that it must reserve the privilege of examining every project of this kind from a double standpoint of its political and strategical interests and of the interests of the Chinese Eastern Railway. Then only could it take a position in regard to each of the lines which might be projected.

3.

Ambassador O'Brien to the Secretary of State
(Extract)

(No. 978)
American Embassy,
Tokyo, January 24, 1910.

Sir:

I have the honor to inclose herewith a copy of the note from Count Komura, to me, dated the 22d instant, in relation to the proposal to neutralize certain railways in Manchuria, etc.

I have, etc.,

T. J. O'BRIEN.

(Enclosure)

The Minister for Foreign Affairs to Ambassador O'Brien

Department of Foreign Affairs,
Tokyo, January 21, 1910.

Monsieur L'Ambassador:

The note which your Excellency did me the honor of addressing to me under the date of the 18th ultimo, in reference to the internationalization and administration of the railways of Manchuria, was duly received and has had, it is scarcely necessary to add, the most serious attention of the Government of His Majesty the Emperor.

The Imperial Government are well aware that the proposal of the United States is entirely disinterested, and that it has for its single inspiration a desire to promote what your Excellency's Government conceives to be the best interests of China, and I beg you to accept my assurances that the Imperial Government, upholding in all sincerity as they do the integrity of the Chinese Empire and the principle of equal opportunity in all parts of China, would unhesitatingly lend their undivided support to the project if they would bring themselves to the conclusion that its realization would accomplish the result desired.

The relations of friendship and good understanding which so long existed between our two countries, and the common desire of both that nothing may be permitted to weaken the sentiment of mutual good will and confidence, afford, I am happy to believe, ample assurance that a frank exposition of the reasons which prevent my

Government from giving their support to the scheme will not be misunderstood or misconstrued.

The most serious objection to the proposal in question lies in the fact that it contemplates a very important departure from the terms of the treaty of Portsmouth. That treaty was designed to establish in Manchuria a permanent order of things, and the Imperial Government firmly believed that in a strict and loyal adhesion to its provisions are to be found the highest guaranties of enduring peace and repose in this part of the world and of the orderly advancement of Manchuria. Not the least difficult of the many difficult and important problems that were definitely solved at Portsmouth was the question of railways. That adjustment subsequently received the deliberate confirmation of the Chinese Government in the treaty of Peking, and the railway operations now carried on in southern Manchuria are consistent with the original concessions which were with equal deliberation granted by the same power.

Nor can the Imperial Government see in the present condition of things in Manchuria anything so exceptional as to make it necessary or desirable to set up there an exceptional system not required in other parts of China. There is nothing in the actual situation in that region, so far as the Imperial Government are aware, which exceptionally interferes with the undisturbed enjoyment by China of her political rights. So far as the question of the open door is concerned, the principle of equal opportunity possesses in its application to Manchuria a more comprehensive signification than it has elsewhere in China, since in the virtue of Article VII of the treaty of Portsmouth the Japanese and Russian railways in those provinces are dedicated exclusively to commercial and industrial uses. Finally in the matter of railway administration, it is impossible for the Imperial Government to believe that the substitution of an international in place of a national régime would prove advantageous or beneficial. On the contrary, it seems to them that in the presence of such a system, economy and efficiency would, in the nature of things, be obliged to yield to political exigencies, and that the divided responsibility of the system would inevitably mean an absence of due responsibility, to the serious disadvantage of the public and the detriment of the service.

These are the principal reasons why the project under examination does not commend itself to the favorable consideration of the Imperial Government. But there are other cogent reasons which cannot be ignored.

In the regions affected by the Japanese railways in Manchuria there have been numerous Japanese industrial and commercial undertakings which owed their inception, as they owe their continual existence, to the fact that the Imperial Government, possessing the railways in question, are able to extend to those enterprises and to the persons engaged in them due protection and defense against attack and pillage by lawless bands that still infest the country. In the development of these enterprises, which are contributing in such a marked degree to the prosperity and progress of Manchuria, a large number of Japanese subjects and large sums of Japanese money are enlisted, and the Imperial Government could not in good faith or with a due sense of their responsibility consent to surrender the means by which such protection and defense are made possible.

The observations which I have now the honor to present to your Excellency, and which I venture to hope may prove as convincing to your Excellency's Government as they are convincing to my own have reference to the plan in its widest sense, but they are, I should add, no less applicable to the scheme in its more restricted form, since the two plans are in principle the same and differ only in degree.

In conclusion, I wish to express to your Excellency the sincere appreciation of my Government for the courteous intimation of the United States concerning the projected Chinchow-Aigun line, and to say that in principle the Imperial Government will be prepared to participate in the enterprise with the other Powers interested in the question. But as that question is clearly distinguishable from the main subject of your Excellency's note, I will, with your permission, reserve this minor point for separate and independent attention when the necessary details regarding the matter are known. I avail myself, etc.,

COUNT KOMURA.

4.

Memorandum to the Russian Embassy

Department of State,
Washington, April 18, 1910.

The Government of the United States has given most careful consideration to the Memorandum of the Imperial Russian Government, presented through the Embassy at Washington on February 24, 1910.

The American Government learns with regret that thus far the Imperial Russian Government still inclines to the view that the projected railway from Chinchow to Aigun, to be built by China by means of a foreign loan, would be injurious to the national and economic interests of Russia, as seemed, at the time, to be apprehended also of the more comprehensive proposals of the United States.

The rights of American citizens in the projected Chinchow-Tsitsihar-Aigun line, like those of the British company concerned, are based upon a contract ratified by the Imperial Chinese Government. In lending its support to this enterprise on the part of its nationals the American Government has felt that it was acting not only in harmony with its traditional policy relating to China but also in full accord with its broad rights under existing treaties. In view of this policy which has repeatedly been recognized and accepted by the Powers, the Government of the United States could scarcely be supposed in any way to commit itself to a recognition of exclusive rights of any Power within any portion of the Chinese Empire, under agreements such as that of 1899 between Russia and China, referred to in the Memorandum of the Imperial Russian Government, even if it did not seem incontrovertible that these had been spontaneously superseded precisely by the terms of other subsequent treaty provisions on the part of Russia.

This principle indeed has long been generally accepted by the Powers, including the Imperial Russian Government, notably in the exchange of notes of 1899 and 1902, relating to the policy of equal opportunity throughout the Chinese Empire, and it has more recently been reaffirmed in numerous international agreements until it has became an integral part of the law governing and controlling the relations and intercourse of the interested nations.

Moreover, having in view the rights enjoyed by the Government of the United States under prior treaties, it should be observed that the Government of China obviously could not by means of preferential agreements with any single Power dispose of rights which it had already granted by treaty generally to other nations, and the United States would therefore be forced to contend that to invoke, in derogation of general treaty rights, such an agreement as the Russo-Chinese understanding of 1899 might nullify stipulations of treaties between China and foreign Powers, and thus seriously curtail the rights of the nationals of other countries.

While the Government of the United States is led to make this candid statement of what it would hold to be the indisputable rights of its own nationals under its treaties with China, it is confident that the relations of friendship that have so long obtained between the two countries must absolutely preclude the idea that the American Government is in any respect unmindful of the important interests of Russia in eastern Asia.

The Government of the United States has from the first freely given repeated assurances of its sincere desire for coöperation with Russia in the matter of the construction of railways in China, and it rests confident in the belief that the Imperial Russian Government is not unappreciative of the assurances so given.

From this point of view it naturally follows that the American Government welcomes the principle of the proposal of the Imperial Russian Government (as to a possible line from Kalgan to Kiakhta) for the especial reason that it is happy to see therein the clearest expression of a reciprocal disposition on the part of Russia to co-operate with the United States in jointly aiding China's railway and commercial development. It is peculiarly gratifying to the United States to find this new reason to hope that the same principle as that embodied in the American proposals of last December may yet find useful fruition through its appeal to the wise policy of the Imperial Russian Government.

Without further examination of a possible Kalgan-Kiakhta project as an independent one, and without proceeding to a consideration of such fundamental questions as that of China's disposition in the matter, the conditions of possible participation, etc., the Government of the United States ventures to revert, then, to the Chinchow-Aigun project.

While the Government of the United States, for the reasons already given, could not be expected to admit the right of any third Power to obstruct the lawful enterprise of American citizens in any part of the Empire of China, and has, moreover, no reason to believe that Russia would wish to assert any such right, it is at the same time prepared to use its influence with its own nationals and with the Chinese Government to secure the full and friendly consideration of such modification of the Chinchow-Tsitsihar-Aigun project as the Imperial Government of Russia might wish to propose. The American Government has indeed taken the greatest pleasure in instructing its representative at Peking in this sense.

Looking to the eventuality of avail by Russia of the opportunity thus created, the American Government would suggest, as a practical step, that so soon as an agreement is reached in principle between the interested Governments, the details of the Chinchow-Tsitsihar-Aigun line and of the possible modifications of the project should be referred to the representatives of the respective financial groups and of the Chinese Government, who are primarily concerned in any phase of these projects, whether the more comprehensive or a single line.

Pending further discussion of broader plans of coöperation, the American group's representative at Peking and his British associate are desirous of making precise the practical provisions for at least the first stages of the Chinchow-Tsitsihar-Aigun line to which it is believed there can be no possible objection, and the American Government hopes that, in view of the present fair prospects of more important coöperation and of harmony of policy, the Imperial Russian Government will now find it consistent with its broader policy to authorize its representative at Peking to reassure the Government of China of the withdrawal of Russia's remonstrance, a deference for which, due to Russia's universally recognized interests, has alone delayed the efforts of those concerned.

APPENDIX B

I. CHINESE REORGANIZATION LOAN AGREEMENT

This Agreement, made at Peking on the twenty-sixth day of April, 1913, between The Government of the Republic of China (hereinafter called "The Chinese Government"), acting through its Premier, its Minister of Foreign Affairs, and its Minister of Finance, of the one part, and The Hongkong and Shanghai Banking Corporation, The Deutsch-Asiatische Bank, The Banque de l'Indo-Chine, The Russo-Asiatic Bank, and The Yokohama Specie Bank, Limited (hereinafter collectively called "The Banks"), of the other part,

WITNESSETH:

Whereas the Chinese Government desires to borrow the sum of Twenty-five Million Pounds Sterling (£25,000,000) equal to 511,250,-000 marks, 631,250,000 francs, 236,750,000 roubles, 244,900,000 yen, for general reorganization and administrative purposes (hereinafter to be specified) and proposes to evidence the above loan by the issue of its gold bonds for the principal amount above named, and *Whereas* the Banks are prepared to issue to the public on behalf of the Chinese Government the bonds of the above-named loan: *Therefore it is agreed as follows:*

ARTICLE I.—The Chinese Government hereby authorizes the Banks to issue either in one amount or in series, at their option, five per cent. (5 per cent.) gold bonds, to an aggregate amount of £25,000,000 equal to 511,250,000 marks, 631,250,000 francs, 236,750,000 roubles, 244,900,000 yen.

The Banks have the option to pay the whole or any portion of the proceeds of the loan to the Chinese Government in pounds sterling or the equivalent at the above parities in the currencies of the various countries in which the subscriptions have been made. The coupons attached to the preliminary certificates and to the definitive bonds shall be payable in the various countries at the above parities. The definitive bonds shall be subject to the same conditions when drawn, redeemed, or paid.

The loan shall be of the date of the first issue of bonds and shall be entitled "THE CHINESE GOVERNMENT FIVE PER CENT. REORGANIZATION GOLD LOAN OF 1913."

ART. II.—Subject to the provision in Article XIII hereinafter for

406

the payment of the first coupon, the net proceeds of the loan shall be used solely for the following purposes:

(a) Payment of liabilities due by the Chinese Government as detailed in Annex A to this Agreement.

(b) Redemption in full of outstanding provincial loans as detailed in Annex B to this Agreement.

(c) Provision for payment at due date of liabilities of the Chinese Government shortly maturing as shown in Annex C to this Agreement, including provision for foreign claims for damage and losses arising out of the Revolution.

(d) Disbandment of troops as detailed in Annex D to this Agreement.

(e) Current expenses of administration as estimated in Annex E to this Agreement.

(f) Reorganization of the Salt Administration as set forth in Annex F to this Agreement.

(g) Such other administrative purposes as may be mutually agreed upon between the Chinese Government and the Banks.

The aforesaid Annexes form part of this present Agreement.

ART. III.—This entire loan, and all advances which may be made in connection therewith, are hereby constituted a direct liability and obligation of the Chinese Government, which hereby pledges its good faith and credit for the punctual payment of the principal and interest of the loan and/or advances and for the performance of all the undertakings on its part herein assumed.

ART. IV.—This entire loan, together with any advances which may be made in connection therewith, is hereby secured in respect to both principal and interest by a charge upon the entire revenues of the Salt Administration of China, subject to previous loans and obligations already charged on the security thereof and not yet redeemed, as detailed in the statement attached to this Agreement, and it shall have priority both as regards principal and interest over all future loans, charges and mortgages charged upon the above-mentioned revenues so long as this loan or any part thereof shall be unredeemed. No loan, charge, or mortgage shall be raised or created which shall take precedence of or be on an equality with this loan, or which shall in any manner lessen or impair its security over the said revenues of the Salt Administration of China, so far as required for the annual service of this loan, and any future loan, charge or mortgage charged on the said revenues of the Salt Administration shall be made subject to this loan, and it shall be so expressed in every agreement for any such future loan, charge or mortgage.

If at a future time the annual collection of the Maritime Customs revenues should exceed the amount necessary to provide for all existing obligations charged thereon or which may have become chargeable thereon under existing agreements by reason of the abolition of *likin* consequent upon tariff revision, it is understood and agreed that such surplus shall be applied in the first instance to the security and service of this loan, the surplus of the salt revenues being thereby *pro tanto* increased and made available for the general purpose of the Chinese Government.

ART. V.—The Chinese Government engages to take immediate steps for the reorganization with the assistance of foreigners of the system of collection of the salt revenues of China assigned as security for this loan, in the manner which has been determined upon by the Ministry of Finance and which is as follows:

The Chinese Government will establish a Central Salt Administration (Yen Wu Shu) at Peking, under the control of the Minister of Finance. This Central Salt Administration will comprise a Chief Inspectorate of Salt Revenues (Chi Ho Tsung So) under a Chinese Chief Inspector (Tsung Pan), and a foreign Associate Chief Inspector (Hui Pan), who will constitute the chief authority for the superintendence of the issue of licenses and the compilation of reports and returns of revenues. In each salt-producing district there will be a branch office of the Chief Inspectorate (Chi Ho Fen So), under one Chinese and one foreign District Inspector (So Chang) who shall be jointly responsible for the collection and deposit of the salt revenues. The engagement and dismissal of these Chinese and foreign District Inspectors, and of the necessary Chinese and foreign staff at the Chief and Branch Inspectorates, will be decided jointly by the Chinese and foreign Chief Inspectors, with the approval of the Minister of Finance. It will be the duty of the District Inspectors jointly to superintend the issue of licenses and to collect all fees and salt dues; and to report all receipts and disbursements in full detail to the local Salt Commissioner (Yen Yun Ssu) and to the Chief Inspectorate in Peking, which will publish periodical reports of the same after submission to the Minister of Finance.

Release of salt against payment of dues in any District will be made only under joint signature of the Chinese and foreign District Inspectors, the revenues so collected to be lodged by them in a "Chinese Government Salt Revenue Account" with the Banks or with depositories approved by the Banks, and reported to the Chief Inspectorate for comparison with their returns. This Salt Revenue Account shall be drawn upon only under the joint signatures of the Chief Inspectors, whose duty it will be to protect the priority of the several obligations secured upon the salt revenues.

So long as the interest and principal of this loan are regularly paid there shall be no interference with the Salt Administration as herein provided, but if interest and/or principal be in default at due date, then after a reasonable period of grace the said organization shall forthwith be incorporated with the Maritime Customs and the revenues above pledged shall be administered for the account and in the interest of the bondholders.

ART. VI.—Pending the reorganization of the Salt Administration and commencing with the first month from the date of this loan, the Provinces of Chihli, Shantung, Honan and Kiangsu shall pay monthly into the Banks the funds necessary to meet the service of this loan in accordance with the amounts stated in the Schedule to be attached to this Agreement and fourteen days before the due date of each such amount. The payment of these amounts by the Provinces named is hereby secured by a first charge upon Central Government taxes of the respective provinces to be assigned and the Chinese Government engages to supply the banks with evidence that the obligations under this Agreement of the Provinces named are officially recognized by the proper authorities of the said Provinces.

So soon as the revenue collection of the Salt Administration over a period of one year shall be sufficient to cover the service of all loans and obligations now secured thereon, including that of this present loan, together with a margin sufficient to cover a further half yearly interest coupon of the latter, the said monthly contributions from the provinces shall be suspended, and the service of this loan shall then be paid from the revenues of the Salt Administration. So soon as the revenues of the Salt Administration shall have been maintained for three successive years at the figure above determined the aforesaid provincial liability shall be finally released.

ART. VII.—The Banks are hereby authorized to issue to subscribers to the loan gold bonds for the total amount of the loan in such denominations and for such amounts as shall be determined by the Banks. The form and language of the bonds shall be settled by the Banks in consultation with the Ministry of Finance or with the Chinese Ministers in London, Berlin, Paris, St. Petersburg and Tokio.

The Bonds shall be printed and/or engraved by the Banks at the expense of the Chinese Government and shall bear the facsimile of the signature of the Minister of Finance, in order to dispense with the necessity of his signing them all in person, and of the seal of the Chinese Government. The Chinese Minister in London and/or Berlin and/or Paris and/or St. Petersburg and/or Tokio at the option of the Banks shall previous to the issue of the bonds authenticate them with a facsimile of his signature and of his seal as a proof that the issue and sale of the bonds are duly authorized by and binding upon the Chinese Government. Representatives of the Banks in London, Berlin, Paris, St. Petersburg or Yokohama, as the case may be may countersign the bonds as agents for the issue of the loan.

ART. VIII.—The rate of interest for the loan shall be five per cent. (5%) per annum on the nominal principal and shall be paid by the Chinese Government to the bondholders half-yearly through the or their designated agents, upon presentation of the proper coupons. Coupons shall be payable in Pounds Sterling or the equivalent in Marks, Francs, Roubles and Yen as provided in Article I. The said interest shall be calculated from the date on which the loan is issued to the public.

ART. IX.—The term of the loan should be forty-seven (47) years. Repayments of principal shall commence with the 11th year, and shall be made by yearly sinking fund of 98,397,945,% equal to £245,-994:17:3 equivalent to 5,030,594.94 Marks, 6,211,370.28 Francs, 2,329,571.35 Roubles, 2,409,765.67 Yen, which shall be paid by the Chinese Government to the Banks in monthly instalments in accordance with the amounts stated in the Schedule to be attached to this Agreement, and fourteen days before the due date of each such amount.

If at any time after the lapse of seventeen years from the date of the loan the Chinese Government should desire to redeem the whole outstanding amount of the loan or any part of it not yet due for repayment in accordance with the Schedule to be attached hereto it may do so up to the end of the thirty-second year by a payment of a premium of two and one-half per cent. (2½%) on the face value of the bonds, that is to say by the payment of £102:10/— for each £100 Bond, and after the end of the thirty-second year it may make such extra redemption without premium, but in each and every case of such extra redemption the Chinese Government shall give six months' previous notice in writing to the Banks and such extra redemption shall be effected by additional drawings of bonds to take place on the date of an ordinary drawing as provided for in the prospectus of the loan.

When the loan has been fully repaid this Agreement will immediately become null and void.

ART. X.—Payments by the Chinese Government for interest and amortization shall be made monthly in accordance with the amounts stated in the Schedule to be attached to this Agreement, and fourteen days before the due date of each such amount in equal shares to the Banks by the Ministry of Finance, which shall hand to the Banks in Shanghai funds in Shanghai sycee and/or coin of the national currency, so soon as the said currency shall have been effectively established, sufficient to meet each such payment in gold in Europe and/or in Japan exchange for which shall be settled with the Banks on the same day. These payments may however be made in gold in Europe, and/or in Japan, fourteen days before their due date, if the Chinese Government should happen to have gold funds bona-fide at its disposal in Europe and/or Japan, not remitted from China for the purpose, and should desire so to use them. Interest upon the said monthly instalments until they are required for the service of the loan to the bondholders shall be allowed by the Banks to the Chinese Government at the rate of 2% per annum.

In reimbursement of expenses connected with the payment of interest and with the repayment of principal of the loan the Banks are hereby granted by the Chinese Government a commission of one-fourth per cent. ($\frac{1}{4}$%) on the annual loan service, the said commission to be paid half-yearly to the banks as provided in the Schedule to be attached to this Agreement.

ART. XI.—All details necessary for the prospectus of the loan and in connection with the payment of interest and the repayment of principal of the loan and with the withdrawing of bonds for redemption, not herein explicitly provided for, shall be left for arrangement by the Banks in consultation with the Chinese Minister in London, Berlin, Paris, St. Petersburg and/or Tokio.

The Banks are hereby authorized to issue the prospectus of the loan as soon as possible after the signing of this Agreement, and the Chinese Government will instruct the Chinese Ministers in the various capitals named above to coöperate with the Banks in any matters requiring conjoint action and to sign when requested the prospectus of the loan.

ART. XII.—All bonds, coupons and payments made and received in connection with the service of this loan shall be exempt from all Chinese taxes and imposts during the currency of this loan.

ART. XIII.—The price of the present loan or of any series thereof to the Chinese Government shall be the price of its issue to the public on the London market less a deduction by the Banks of six per cent. (6%) of the nominal value of the bonds, the issue price in London to be not less than Ninety per cent. (90%), securing to China a net price of not less than Eighty-four per cent. (84%) for the entire loan. The Banks shall be responsible for all expenses connected with the issue of the loan except the printing and/or engraving of the bonds.

It shall be left to the Banks to determine the most favorable moment for issue, and the Minister of Finance shall be notified in advance in order that the necessary instructions may be given to the Chinese Ministers abroad.

The Banks shall retain on deposit in Europe and/or Japan from the first proceeds of the loan a sufficient amount to meet the first half-year's interest and the Bank's commission of $\frac{1}{4}\%$ thereon, and the Chinese Government hereby authorizes the Banks to pay the said first half-year's interest and commission from the funds so retained. At the same time the funds to be paid by the Provinces into the Banks in China for service of the loan as provided in Article VI of this Agreement shall accumulate during the six months covered by the first half-year's interest so retained, and shall be held as a reserve fund to provide against any possible interruption of such payments by the Provinces, until the suspension of the latter takes place under the provision of the said Article.

After deductions from the proceeds of the loan of an amount sufficient for the payment of the first coupon and for the repayment with accrued interest of any advances made by the Banks on account of this loan, and after provision has been made for items a, b, and c in terms of Article II of this Agreement, the balance of the net proceeds of the loan shall be placed to the credit of a "Chinese Government Reorganization Loan Account" with the Hongkong and Shanghai Banking Corporation, the Deutsch-Asiatische Bank, the Banque de l'Indo-Chine, the Russo-Asiatic Bank and the Yokohama Specie Bank, Limited, in London, Berlin, Paris, St. Petersburg or Yokohama, in instalments and on dates conforming to the conditions allowed by the prospectus to the subscribers to the loan.

Transfers of loan funds to China from the Banks in Europe and Japan shall be made through the Banks in China as nearly as possible in equal amounts from each of the Banks, the rates of exchange for each transfer from Europe or Japan, being settled simultaneously with the transferring Banks on the same day. In the event of equal transfers being found to be impracticable a mutually satisfactory procedure for making the transfers above referred to shall be arranged between the Minister of Finance and/or the Banks.

Interest at the rate of three (3) per cent. per annum shall be granted on the balance of loan funds held in London, Berlin, Paris, St. Petersburg or Yokohama: interest on the credit portion of the loan funds kept in China by the transferring Banks will be allowed at the Banks' rate for current accounts to be arranged.

Withdrawals of that portion of the loan proceeds held in the aforesaid Chinese Government Reorganization Loan Account in Europe or Japan shall be at the order of the Ministry of Finance subject to the provisions of Article XIV hereinafter. Transfers of loan funds to China shall be made in amounts to be arranged from time to time with the Banks but shall not exceed £500,000 in any one week, and funds so transferred shall be held by the transferring Banks in China until required for the purposes for which the loan is made, and withdrawn as hereinafter provided in Article XIV.

ART. XIV.—The Chinese Government engages at once to put into effective operation an Account and Audit Department, under the Provisional Regulations Promulgated by a Presidential Order dated the 15th of November, 1912, and published in the Official Gazette of November 16th, 1912, copy and translation of which are hereto attached in Annex H of this Agreement, subject to the understanding that any modifications which may be found necessary shall not impair their effect in regard to this loan.

The Chinese and foreign Directors of the Bureau of National Loans shall witness their approval of all requisitions for loan funds by their joint signatures thereon. Withdraws of loan funds from the Banks shall be for amounts corresponding to the actual requirements of disbursements.

Cheques and/or orders upon the Banks for the withdrawal of loan funds shall be signed by a duly authorized representative of the Minister of Finance and shall be sent, together with the supporting requisitions duly signed as above, and the relative "orders to pay" (Fa k'uan ming-ling), to a representative of the Banks to be designated. The said representative of the Banks, after satisfying himself that the expenditure is in accordance with Article II of this Agreement and the Annexes therein referred to, shall forthwith countersign the cheque and return it to the Ministry of Finance for presentation to and payment by the Banks.

Should the said representative of the Banks be in doubt in respect to disbursements of loan funds which have been made, he shall be entitled to make inquiries of the foreign Director of the Bureau of National Loans and to call upon him for the production of receipts and vouchers for inspection.

ART. XV.—In the event of any bond or bonds issued from this loan being lost, stolen or destroyed, the Bank or Banks concerned may notify the Ministry of Finance and the Chinese Ministers in London, Berlin, Paris, St. Petersburg or Tokio, as the case may be, who shall authorize the Bank or Banks concerned to insert an advertisement in the public newspapers stating that payment of such bond or bonds has been stopped; and to take such other steps as many appear advisable or necessary according to the laws or customs of the country concerned. Should any bond or bonds be destroyed, or should such lost or stolen bond or bonds not be recovered after a lapse of time to be fixed by the Banks, the Chinese Ministers in London, Berlin, Paris, St. Petersburg or Tokio, as the case may be, shall execute a duplicate bond or duplicate bonds for a like amount and deliver the same to the Bank or Banks representing the owner or owners of such lost, stolen or destroyed bond or bonds, which Bank or Banks shall pay all expenses in connection with such delivery and execution of such duplicate bond or bonds for the account of the owner or owners of such bond or bonds.

ART. XVI.—If before the publication of the prospectus for the issue of this loan any political or financial crisis should occur affecting the money markets or the prices of Chinese Government securities in such manner or to such degree as in the opinion of the Banks will render impossible the successful flotation and issue of this loan on the terms herein named, the Banks shall be granted a period of six months from the date on which this Agreement shall be signed within which to issue the loan to the public. If on the expiration of this period the markets are still unfavorable, then the Banks shall be entitled to ask the Chinese Government for extension of time. If the Chinese Government should refuse to grant the extension of time requested, this contract shall become null and void, subject always to the repayment to the Banks with accrued interest of any advances which may have been made by them on account of this loan. If this loan shall be issued in series under Article I hereof, the provisions of this clause shall, *mutatis mutandis*, apply to the issue of each series of the loan.

ART. XVII.—In the event of the Chinese Government desiring to issue further loans secured upon the revenue of the Salt Administration or to issue supplementary loans for purposes of the nature of those specified in Article II of this Agreement, the Chinese Government will give to the Banks the option of undertaking such loans on a commission basis of six per cent. (6%) of the nominal value of the bonds as provided in Article XII of this Agreement.

The Chinese Government further undertakes that for a period of six months after the complete issue of this present loan and payment of the last instalment therof in terms of the prospectus it will not proceed to the issue of any other Government loan or loans having a Government guarantee concluded later than April 10th, 1913, without the previous agreement of the Banks.

ART. XVIII.—The Hongkong and Shanghai Banking Corporation, the Deutsch-Asiatische Bank, the Banque de l'Indo-Chine, the Russo-Asiatic Bank and the Yokohama Specie Bank, Limited, shall take the loan in equal shares and without responsibility for each other.

ART. XIX.—The Hongkong and Shanghai Banking Corporation,

the Deutsch-Asiatische Bank, the Banque de l'Indo-Chine, the Russo-Asiatic Bank and the Yokohama Specie Bank, Limited, may, subject to all their obligations under this Agreement, transfer or delegate all or any of their rights, powers and discretions thereunder to any British, German, French, Russian or Japanese Company, Directors or Agents with power of further transfer and sub-delegation; such transfer, sub-transfer, delegation or sub-delegation to be subject, however, to the approval of the Chinese Government.

ART. XX.—This Agreement is signed on behalf of the Chinese Government by the Premier, the Minister of Foreign Affairs and the Minister of Finance under authority of a Presidential Order dated the twenty-second day of April, 1913, which has been officially communicated to the Ministers in Peking of Great Britain, Germany, France, Russia and Japan by the Waichiaopu.

ART. XXI.—Eight sets of this Agreement are executed in English and Chinese, three sets to be retained by the Chinese Government and five sets by the Banks. In the event of any doubt arising regarding the interpretation of this Agreement the English text shall rule.

Signed at Peking this twenty-sixth day of April, 1913.

Signed by: CHAO PING-CHUN, *Premier.*

LU CHENG HSIANG, *Minister of Foreign Affairs.*

CHOU HSUEH-HSI, *Minister of Finance.*

For the Hongkong and Shanghai Banking Corporation,
E. G. HILLIER, *Agent.*

For the Deutsch-Asiatische Bank,
H. CORDES.

For the Banque de l'Indo-Chine,
HENRY MAZOT.　　　　　　R. SAINT PIERRE.

For the Russo-Asiatic-Bank,
L. DE HOYER.

For the Yokohama Specie Bank,
M. ODAGIRI.

II. AGREEMENT FOR ADVANCES

This Agreement for advances on account of the "Chinese Government Five Per Cent. Reorganization Gold Loan" £25,000,000 is made between the Government of the Republic of China (hereinafter called "The Chinese Government"), acting through its Premier, its Minister of Foreign Affairs, and Minister of Finance, of the one part, and the Hongkong and Shanghai Banking Corporation, the Deutsch-Asiatische Bank, the Banque de l'Indo-Chine, the Russo-Asiatic Bank and the Yokohama Specie Bank, Limited (hereinafter collectively called "The Banks"), of the other part.

Whereas the above contracting parties have this day entered into an Agreement for a "Chinese Government Five Per Cent. Reorganization Gold Loan" of £25,000,000 and it has been agreed that the said loan shall be issued to the public as soon as possible at a price in London of not less than Ninety per cent. of the nominal value of the bonds, and *Whereas* the Chinese Government is in urgent need of funds pending the issue of the said loan to the public,

It is hereby agreed as follows:

ARTICLE I.—The Banks hereby agree to advance immediately upon the signature of this Agreement the equivalent of £2,000,000 Sterling as follows: £400,000, Marks 8,180,000, Francs 10,100,000, Roubles 3,788,000, Yen 3,918,400, to be held to the order of the Minister of Finance in London, Berlin, Paris, St. Petersburg and Yokohama respectively. The Chinese Government undertakes, if and when requested by the Banks, to evidence the said advances by the issue of Treasury Bills in the respective Currencies to be handed to the Banks.

ART. II.—Interest on the said advances of the aggregate equivalent of £2,000,000 shall be at the rate of Seven per cent. (7%) per annum, calculated from the date of this Agreement, and payable half-yearly and the principal with accrued interest shall be repaid from the first proceeds of the said "Chinese Government Five Per Cent. Reorganization Gold Loan" of £25,000,000 when issued, or in any case shall be repaid to the Banks by the Chinese Government within Twelve months from the date of this Agreement.

ART. III.—These present advances for the aggregate equivalent of £2,000,000, constitute a direct liability and obligation of the Chinese Government and are secured in respect to both principal and interest by the charge upon the entire revenues of the Salt Administration of China, in terms of Articles III and IV of the said Reorganization Loan Agreement.

ART. IV.—The said advances shall be used solely for the purposes specified in, and shall be treated as for account of, the Annexes D and E of the said Reorganization Loan Agreement; their disbursement shall be carried out in accordance with the provisions of Article XIV of that Agreement.

Arrangements will be made between the Minister of Finance and the Banks for the transfer of the said advances to China and the payment of the silver equivalent at the places where required.

ART. V.—The terms of this Agreement shall be officially communicated by the Waichiaopu to the Ministers of Great Britain, Germany, France, Russia and Japan in Peking.

ART. VI.—Eight sets of this Agreement are executed in English and Chinese, three sets to be retained by the Chinese Government and five sets by the Banks. In the event of any doubt regarding the interpretation of this Agreement the English text shall rule.

(Signed at Peking by the Contracting Parties this twenty-sixth day of April, 1913.) Signatures as above.

APPENDIX C

TREATY OF PEACE BETWEEN JAPAN AND RUSSIA

Signed at Portsmouth (New Hampshire), September 5 [Russian Calendar], 1905. Ratifications Exchanged at Washington, November 25, 1905.

His Majesty the Emperor of Japan on the one part, and His Majesty the Emperor of all the Russias on the other part, animated by the desire to restore the blessings of peace to Their countries and peoples, have resolved to conclude a Treaty of Peace, and have, for this purpose, named Their Plenipotentiaries, that is to say;

His Majesty the Emperor of Japan:

His Excellency Baron Komura Jutaro, Jusammi, Grand Cordon of the Imperial Order of the Rising Sun, His Minister for Foreign Affairs, and

His Excellency M. Takahira Kogoro, Jusammi, Grand Cordon of the Imperial Order of the Sacred Treasure, His Envoy Extraordinary and Minister Plenipotentiary to the United States of America; and

His Majesty the Emperor of all the Russias:

His Excellency M. Serge Witte, His Secretary of State and President of the Committee of Ministers of the Empire of Russia, and

His Excellency Baron Roman Rosen, Master of the Imperial Court of Russia and His Ambassador Extraordinary and Plenipotentiary to the United States of America:

Who, after having exchanged their full powers which were found to be in good and due form, have concluded the following Articles:

Article I. There shall henceforth be peace and amity between Their Majesties the Emperor of Japan and the Emperor of all the Russias and between Their respective States and subjects.

Art. II.—The Imperial Russian Government, acknowledging that Japan possesses in Korea paramount political, military and economical interests, engage neither to obstruct nor interfere with the measures of guidance, protection and control which the Imperial Government of Japan may find it necessary to take in Korea.

It is understood that Russian subjects in Korea shall be treated exactly in the same manner as the subjects or citizens of other foreign

Powers, that is to say, they shall be placed on the same footing as the subjects or citizens of the most favored nation.

It is also agreed that, in order to avoid all cause of misunderstanding, the two High Contracting Parties will abstain, on the Russo-Korean frontier, from taking any military measure which may menace the security of Russian or Korean territory.

ART. III.—Japan and Russia mutually engage:

1. To evacuate completely and simultaneously Manchuria except the territory affected by the lease of the Liao-tung Peninsula, in conformity with the provisions of additional Article I annexed to this Treaty; and

2. To restore entirely and completely to the exclusive administration of China all portions of Manchuria now in the occupation or under the control of the Japanese or Russian troops, with the exception of the territory above mentioned.

The Imperial Government of Russia declare that they have not in Manchuria any territorial advantages or preferential or exclusive concessions in impairment of Chinese sovereignty or inconsistent with the principle of equal opportunity.

ART. IV.—Japan and Russia reciprocally engage not to obstruct any general measures common to all countries, which China may take for the development of the commerce and industry of Manchuria.

ART. V.—The Imperial Russian Government transfer and assign to the Imperial Government of Japan, with the consent of the Government of China, the lease of Port Arthur, Talien and adjacent territory and territorial waters and all rights, privileges and concessions connected with or forming part of such lease, and they also transfer and assign to the Imperial Government of Japan all public works and properties in the territory affected by the above mentioned lease.

The two High Contracting Parties mutually engage to obtain the consent of the Chinese Government mentioned in the foregoing stipulation.

The Imperial Government of Japan on their part undertake that the proprietary rights of Russian subjects in the territory above referred to shall be perfectly respected.

ART. VI.—The Imperial Russian Government engage to transfer and assign to the Imperial Government of Japan, without compensation and with the consent of the Chinese Government, the railway between Chang-chun (Kuan-cheng-tze) and Port Arthur and all its branches, together with all rights, privileges and properties appertaining thereto in that region, as well as coal mines in the said region belonging to or worked for the benefit of the railway.

The two High Contracting Parties mutually engage to obtain the consent of the Government of China mentioned in the foregoing stipulation.

ART. VII.—Japan and Russia engage to exploit their respective railways in Manchuria exclusively for commercial and industrial purposes and in no wise for strategic purposes.

It is understood that that restriction does not apply to the railway in the territory affected by the lease of the Liao-tung Peninsula.

ART. VIII.—The Imperial Governments of Japan and Russia, with a view to promote and facilitate intercourse and traffic, will, as soon as possible, conclude a separate convention for the regulation of their connecting railway service in Manchuria.

ART. IX.—The Imperial Russian Government cede to the Imperial Government of Japan in perpetuity and full sovereignty, the southern portion of the Island of Saghalien and all islands adjacent thereto, and all public works and properties thereon. The fiftieth degree of north latitude is adopted as the northern boundary of the ceded territory. The exact alignment of such territory shall be determined in accordance with the provisions of additional Article II annexed to this Treaty.

Japan and Russia mutually agree not to construct in their respective possessions on the Island of Saghalien or the adjacent islands, any fortifications or other similar military works. They also respectively engage not to take any military measures which may impede the free navigation of the Straits of La Perouse and Tartary.

ART. X.—It is reserved to the Russian subjects inhabitants of the territory ceded to Japan, to sell their real property and retire to their country; but, if they prefer to remain in the ceded territory, they will be maintained and protected in the full exercise of their industries and rights of property, on condition of submitting to Japanese laws and jurisdiction. Japan shall have full liberty to withdraw the right of residence in, or to deport from, such territory, any inhabitants who labor under political or administrative disability. She engages, however, that the proprietary rights of such inhabitants shall be fully respected.

ART. XI.—Russia engages to arrange with Japan for granting to Japanese subjects rights of fishery along the coasts of the Russian possessions in the Japan, Okhotsk and Behring Seas.

It is agreed that the foregoing engagement shall not affect rights already belonging to Russian or foreign subjects in those regions.

ART. XII.—The Treaty of Commerce and Navigation between Japan and Russia having been annulled by the war, the Imperial Governments of Japan and Russia engage to adopt as the basis of their commercial relations, pending the conclusion of a new treaty of commerce and navigation on the basis of the Treaty which was in force previous to the present war, the system of reciprocal treatment on the footing of the most favored nation, in which are included import and export duties, customs formalities, transit and tonnage dues, and the admission and treatment of the agents, subjects and vessels of one country in the territories of the other.

ART. XIII.—As soon as possible after the present Treaty comes into force, all prisoners of war shall be reciprocally restored. The Imperial Governments of Japan and Russia shall each appoint a special Commissioner to take charge of prisoners. All prisoners in the hands of one Government shall be delivered to and received by the Commissioner of the other Government or by his duly authorized representative, in such convenient numbers and at such convenient ports of the delivering State as such delivering State shall notify in advance to the Commissioner of the receiving State.

The Governments of Japan and Russia shall present to each other, as soon as possible after the delivery of prisoners has been completed, a statement of the direct expenditures respectively incurred by them for the care and maintenance of prisoners from date of capture or surrender up to the time of death or delivery. Russia engages to repay to Japan, as soon as possible after the exchange of the statements as above provided, the difference between the actual amount so expended by Japan and the actual amount similarly disbursed by Russia.

ART. XIV.—The present Treaty shall be ratified by Their Majesties the Emperor of Japan and the Emperor of all the Russias. Such ratification shall, with as little delay as possible and in any case not later than fifty days from the date of signature of the Treaty, be announced to the Imperial Governments of Japan and Russia respectively through the French Minister in Tokyo and the Ambassador of the United States in Saint-Petersburg and from the date of the later of such announcements this Treaty shall in all its parts come into full force.

The formal exchange of the ratification shall take place at Washington as soon as possible.

ART. XV.—The present Treaty shall be signed in duplicate in both the English and French languages. The texts are in absolute conformity, but in case of discrepancy in interpretation, the French text shall prevail.

In witness whereof the respective Plenipotentiaries have signed and affixed their seals to the present Treaty of Peace.

Done at Portsmouth (New Hampshire) this fifth day of the ninth month of the thirty-eighth year of *Meiji,* corresponding to the twenty-third day of August (fifth September) one thousand nine hundred and five.

(Signed) SERGE WITTE. [L.S.]
(Signed) ROSEN. [L.S.]
(Signed) JUTARO KOMURA. [L.S.]
(Signed) K. TAKAHIRA. [L.S.]

In conformity with the provisions of Articles III and IX of the Treaty of Peace between Japan and Russia of this date, the undersigned Plenipotentiaries have concluded the following additional Article:

I. To ART. III.—The Imperial Governments of Japan and Russia mutually engage to commence the withdrawal of their military forces from the territory of Manchuria simultaneously and immediately after the Treaty of Peace comes into operation, and within a period of eighteen months from that date, the Armies of the two countries shall be completely withdrawn from Manchuria except from the leased territory of the Liao-tung Peninsula.

The forces of the two countries occupying the front positions shall be first withdrawn.

The High Contracting Parties reserve to themselves the right to maintain guards to protect their respective railway lines in Manchuria. The number of such guards shall not exceed fifteen per kilometer and within that maximum number, the Commanders of the Japanese and Russian Armies shall, by common accord, fix the number of such guards to be employed, as small as possible having in view the actual requirements.

The Commanders of the Japanese and Russian forces in Manchuria shall agree upon the details of the evacuation in conformity with the above principles, and shall take by common accord the measures necessary to carry out the evacuation as soon as possible and in any case not later than the period of eighteen months.

II. To ART. IX.—As soon as possible after the present Treaty comes into force, a Commission of Delimitation, composed of an equal number of members to be appointed respectively by the two High Contracting Parties, shall on the spot, mark in a permanent manner the exact boundary between the Japanese and Russian possessions on the Island of Saghalien. The Commission shall be bound, so far as topographical considerations permit, to follow the fiftieth parallel of north latitude as the boundary line, and in case any deflections from that line at any points are found to be necessary, compensation will be made by correlative deflections at other points. It shall also be the duty of the said Commission to prepare a list and description of the adjacent islands included in the cession and finally the Commission shall prepare and sign maps showing the boundaries of the ceded territory. The work of the Commission shall be subject to the approval of the High Contracting Parties.

The foregoing additional Articles are to be considered as ratified with the ratification of the Treaty of Peace to which they are annexed.

Portsmouth, the 5th day, 9th month, 38th year of *Meiji*, corresponding to the $\begin{cases} \text{23rd August,} \\ \text{5th September,} \end{cases}$ 1905.

(Signed) SERGE WITTE.   (Signed) J. KOMURA.
(Signed) ROSEN.   (Signed) K. TAKAHIRA.

APPENDIX D

CONVENTION BETWEEN JAPAN AND RUSSIA

SIGNED JULY 30, 1907

The Government of his Majesty the Emperor of Japan and the Government of his Majesty the Emperor of All the Russias, desiring to consolidate the relations of peace and good neighborhood which have happily been reëstablished between Japan and Russia, and wishing to remove for the future every cause of misunderstanding in the relations of the two Empires, have agreed to the following arrangements:—

ARTICLE I.—Each of the High Contracting Parties engages to respect the actual territorial integrity of the other, and all the rights accruing to one and the other Party from treaties, conventions and contracts in force between them and China, copies of which have been exchanged between the Contracting Parties (in so far as these rights are not incompatible with the principle of equal opportunity) of the Treaty signed at Portsmouth on the 5th day of September (23rd of August) 1905, as well as the special conventions concluded between Japan and Russia.

ART. II.—The two High Contracting Parties recognize the independence and the territorial integrity of the Empire of China and the principle of equal opportunity in whatever concerns the commerce and industry of all nations in that empire, and engage to sustain and defend the maintenance of the *status quo* and respect for this principle by all the pacific means within their reach.

In witness wherof, the undersigned, duly authorized by their respective Governments, have signed this Convention and have affixed their seals.

Done at St. Petersburg, the 30th day of the 7th month of the 40th year of *Meiji,* corresponding to the 30th (17th) of July, 1907.

(Signed) I. MOTONO.

(Signed) ISWOLSKY.

TREATY AND ADDITIONAL AGREEMENT BETWEEN JAPAN AND CHINA RELATING TO MANCHURIA

SIGNED AT PEKING, DECEMBER 22, 1905
RATIFICATIONS EXCHANGED AT PEKING, JANUARY 23, 1906

(Translation)

His Majesty the Emperor of Japan and His Majesty the Emperor of China, desiring to adjust certain matters of common concern growing out of the Treaty of Peace between Japan and Russia of September 5th, 1905, have resolved to conclude a Treaty with that object in view and have for that purpose named Their Plenipotentiaries, that is to say:

His Majesty the Emperor of Japan:

Baron Komura Jutaro, Jusammi, Grand Cordon of the Imperial Order of the Rising Sun, Minister for Foreign Affairs and Special Ambassador of His Majesty, and

Uchida Yasuya, Jushii, Second Class of the Imperial Order of the Rising Sun, His Majesty's Envoy Extraordinary and Minister Plenipotentiary; and

His Majesty the Emperor of China:

Prince Ching, Presiding Minister for Foreign Affairs, Councilor of State and Plenipotentiary of His Majesty,

Chu Hung-chi Minister for Foreign Affairs, Councilor of State and Plenipotentiary of His Majesty, and

Yuan Shih-Kai, Viceroy of the Province of Chihli, Junior Guardian of the Heir-Apparent, Minister Superintendent of Trade for the Northern Ports and Plenipotentiary of His Majesty;

Who, after having exchanged their full powers which were found to be in good and due form, have agreed upon and concluded the following Articles:

ARTICLE I.—The Imperial Chinese Government consent to all the transfers and assignments made by Russia to Japan by Articles V and VI of the Treaty of Peace above mentioned.

ART. II.—The Imperial Japanese Government engage that in regard to the leased territory as well as in the matter of railway construction and exploitation, they will, so far as circumstances permit, conform to the original agreements concluded between China and Russia. In case any question arises in the future on these subjects, the Japanese Government will decide it in consultation with the Chinese Government.

ART. III.—The present Treaty shall come into full force from the date of signature. It shall be ratified by Their Majesties the Emperor of Japan and the Emperor of China and the ratifications shall be exchanged at Peking as soon as possible, and not later than two months from the present date.

In witness whereof, the respective Plenipotentiaries have signed this Treaty in duplicate in the Japanese and Chinese languages and have thereto affixed their seals.

Done at Peking, this twenty-second day of the twelfth month of the thirty-eighth year of *Meiji,* corresponding to the twenty-sixth day of the eleventh moon of the thirty-first year of Kuang Hsü.

(Signed)   BARON KOMURA JUTARO, [L.S.]
> *Jusammi, Grand Cordon of the Imperial Order of the Rising Sun, Minister for Foreign Affairs and Special Ambassador of His Majesty the Emperor of Japan.*

(Signed)   UCHIDA YASUYA, [L.S.]
> *Jushii, Second Class of the Imperial Order of the Rising Sun, Envoy Extraordinary and Minister Plenipotentiary of His Majesty the Emperor of Japan.*

(Signed)   PRINCE CHING, [L.S.]
> *Presiding Minister for Foreign Affairs, Councilor of State and Plenipotentiary of His Majesty the Emperor of China.*

(Signed)   CHU HUNG-CHI, [L.S.]
> *Minister for Foreign Affairs, Councilor of State and Plenipotentiary of His Majesty the Emperor of China.*

(Signed)   YUAN SHIH-K'AI, [L.S.]
> *Viceroy of the Province of Chihli, Junior Guardian of the Heir-Apparent, Minister Superintendent of Trade for the Northern Ports and Plenipotentiary of His Majesty the Emperor of China.*

The Governments of Japan and China, with a view to regulate, for their guidance, certain questions in which they are both interested in Manchuria, in addition to those provided for in the Treaty signed this day, have agreed as follows:

ARTICLE I.—The Imperial Chinese Government agree that as soon as possible after the evacuation of Manchuria by the Japanese and Russian forces, the following cities and towns in Manchuria will be opened by China herself as places of international residence and trade:

In the Province of Shingking:
> Fengwangcheng; Liaoyang; Hsinmintum; Tieling; Tung-kiangtzu and Fakumen.

In the Province of Kirin:
> Changchun (Kuanchengtze); Kirin; Harbin; Ninguta; Hunchun and Sanhsing.

In the Province of Heilungkiang:
> Tsitsihar; Hailar, Aigun and Manchuli.

Art. II.—In view of the earnest desire expressed by the Imperial Chinese Government to have the Japanese and Russian troops and railway guards in Manchuria withdrawn as soon as possible, and in order to meet this desire, the Imperial Japanese Government, in the event of Russia agreeing to the withdrawal of her railway guards, or in case other proper measures are agreed to between China and Russia, consent to take similar steps accordingly. When tranquillity shall have been reëstablished in Manchuria and China shall have become herself capable of affording full protection to the lives and property of foreigners, Japan will withdraw her railway guards simultaneously with Russia.

Art. III.—The Imperial Japanese Government, immediately upon the withdrawal of their troops from any regions in Manchuria, shall notify the Imperial Chinese Government of the regions thus evacuated, and even within the period stipulated for the withdrawal of troops in the Additional Articles of the Treaty of Peace between Japan and Russia, the Chinese Government may send necessary troops to the evacuated regions of which they have been already notified as above mentioned, for the purpose of maintaining order and tranquillity in those regions. If, in the regions from which Japanese troops have not yet been withdrawn, any villages are disturbed or damaged by native bandits, the Chinese local authorities may also despatch a suitable military force for the purpose of capturing or dispersing those bandits. Such troops, however, shall not proceed within twenty Chinese li from the boundary of the territory where Japanese troops are stationed.

Art. IV.—The Imperial Government of Japan engage that Chinese public and private property in Manchuria, which they have occupied or expropriated on account of military necessity, shall be restored at the time the Japanese troops are withdrawn from Manchuria and that such property as is no longer required for military purposes shall be restored even before such withdrawal.

Art. V.—The Imperial Chinese Government engage to take all necessary measures to protect fully and completely the grounds in

Manchuria in which the tombs and monuments of the Japanese officers and soldiers who were killed in war are located.

ART. VI.—The Imperial Chinese Government agree that Japan has the right to maintain and work the military railway line constructed between Antung and Moukden and to improve the said line so as to make it fit for the conveyance of commercial and industrial goods of all nations. The term for which such right is conceded is fifteen years from the date of the completion of the improvements above provided for. The work of such improvements is to be completed within two years, exclusive of a period of twelve months during which it will have to be delayed owing to the necessity of using the existing line for the withdrawal of troops. The term of the concession above mention is therefore to expire in the 49th year of Kuang Hsü. At the expiration of that term, the said railway shall be sold to China at a price to be determined by appraisement of all its properties by a foreign expert who will be selected by both parties. The conveyance by the railway of the troops and munitions of war of the Chinese Government prior to such sale shall be dealt with in accordance with the regulations of the Eastern Chinese Railway. Regarding the manner in which the improvements of the railway are to be effected, it is agreed that the person undertaking the work on behalf of Japan shall consult with the Commissioner despatched for the purpose by China. The Chinese Government will also appoint a Commissioner to look after the business relating to the railway as is provided in the Agreement relating to the Eastern Chinese Railway. It is further agreed that detailed regulations shall be concluded regarding the tariffs for the carriage by the railway of the public and private goods of China.

ART. VII.—The Governments of Japan and China, with a view to promote and facilitate intercourse and traffic, will conclude, as soon as possible, a separate convention for the regulation of connecting services between the railway lines in South Manchuria and all the other railway lines in China.

ART. VIII.—The Imperial Chinese Government engage that all materials required for the railways in South Manchuria shall be exempt from all duties, taxes and likin.

ART. IX.—The methods of laying out the Japanese Settlement at Yingkou in the Province of Shingking, which has already been opened to trade, and at Antung and Moukden in the same Province, which are still unopen although stipulated to be opened, shall be separately arranged and determined by officials of Japan and China.

ART. X.—The Imperial Chinese Government agree that a joint-stock company of forestry composed of Japanese and Chinese capitalists shall be organized for the exploitation of the forests in the regions on the right bank of the River Yalu and that a detailed agreement shall be concluded in which the area and term of the concession as well as the organization of the company and all regulations concerning the joint work of exploitation shall be provided for. The Japanese and Chinese shareholders shall share equally in the profits of the undertaking.

ART. XI.—The Governments of Japan and China engage that in all that relates to frontier trade between Manchuria and Korea most favored nation treatment shall be reciprocally extended.

ART. XII.—The Governments of Japan and China engage that in all matters dealt with in the Treaty signed this day or in the present Agreement the most favorable treatment shall be reciprocally extended.

The present Agreement shall take effect from the date of signature. When the Treaty signed this day is ratified, this Agreement shall also be considered as approved.

In witness whereof, the Undersigned, duly authorized by their respective Governments, have signed the present Agreement in duplicate in the Japanese and Chinese languages and have thereto affixed their seals.

Done at Peking, this 22nd day of the 12th month of the 38th year of *Meiji,* corresponding to the 26th day of the 11th moon of the 31st year of Kuang Hsü.

(Signed)   BARON KOMURA JUTARO, [L.S.]
> *Jusammi, Grand Cordon of the Imperial Order of the Rising Sun, Minister for Foreign Affairs and Special Ambassador of His Majesty the Emperor of Japan.*

(Signed)   UCHIDA YASUYA, [L.S.]
> *Jushii, Second Class of the Imperial Order of the Rising Sun, Envoy Extraordinary and Minister Plenipotentiary of His Majesty the Emperor of Japan.*

(Signed)   PRINCE CHING, [L.S.]
> *Presiding Minister for Foreign Affairs, Councilor of State and Plenipotentiary of His Majesty the Emperor of China.*

(Signed)   CHU HUNG-CHI, [L.S.]
> *Minister of Foreign Affairs, Councilor of State and Plenipotentiary of His Majesty the Emperor of China.*

(Signed)   YUAN SHIH-K'AI, [L.S.]
> *Viceroy of the Province of Chihli, Junior Guardian of the Heir-Apparent, Minister Superintendent of Trade for the Northern Ports and Plenipotentiary of His Majesty the Emperor of China.*

APPENDIX F

SUMMARY OF SECRET PROTOCOLS TO PEKING TREATY OF DECEMBER 22D, 1905

The following was communicated by the Japanese Minister for Foreign Affairs to Mr. Wilson, Chargé d'Affaires of the United States at Tokyo, and by him transmitted to the Department of State under date February 16, 1906, as a summary of certain protocols to the Peking Agreement signed by the plenipotentiaries of Japan and China:

Whereas the protocols of the Conference recently held between the Plenipotentiaries of Japan and China with regard to Manchuria are to be kept strictly secret in deference to the desire of the Chinese Government, only such portions of those Protocols as possess the character of executory agreements are given in the following summary:

1. The railway between Changchun and Kirin will be constructed by China with capital to be raised by herself. She, however, agrees to borrow from Japan the insufficient amount of capital, which amount being about one-half of the total sum required. The contract concerning the loan shall, in due time, be concluded, following, *mutatis mutandis,* the loan contract entered into between the board of the Imperial Railways of North China and the Anglo-Chinese Syndicate. The term of the loan shall be twenty-five years, redeemable in yearly instalments.

2. The military railway constructed by Japan between Moukden and Hsinmintun shall be sold to China at a price to be fairly determined in consultation by Commissioners appointed for the purpose by the two Governments. China engages to reconstruct the line, making it her own railway, and to borrow from a Japanese corporation or corporations one-half of the capital required for the portion of the line east of Liao-ho for a term of eighteen years repayable in yearly instalments, and a contract shall be concluded, for the purpose following, *mutatis mutandis,* the loan contract entered into between the Board of the Imperial Railways of North China and the Anglo-Chinese Syndicate.

All other military railways in different localities shall be removed with the evacuation of the regions.

430

3. The Chinese Government engage, for the purpose of protecting the interests of the South Manchurian Railway, not to construct, prior to the recovery by them of the said railway, any main line in the neighborhood of and parallel to that railway, or any branch line which might be prejudicial to the interest of the above-mentioned railway.

4. China declares that she will adopt sufficient measures for securing Russia's faithful observance of the Russo-Chinese treaties with regard to the railways which Russia continues to possess in the northern part of Manchuria, and that it is her intention, in case Russia acts in contravention of such treaty stipulations, to approach her strongly with a view to have such action fully rectified.

5. When in the future, negotiations are to be opened between Japan and Russia for regulation of the connecting railway services (Article VIII of the Treaty of Peace between Japan and Russia), Japan shall give China previous notice. China shall communicate to Russia her desire to take part in the negotiations through commissioners to be despatched by her on the occasion, and Russia consenting shall participate in such negotiations.

6. With regard to the mines in the Province of Feng-tien, appertaining to the railway, whether already worked or not, fair and detailed arrangements shall be agreed upon for mutual observance.

7. The affairs relating to the connecting services as well as those of common concern in respect of the telegraph lines in the Province of Feng-tien and the cables between Port Arthur and Yen-tai shall be arranged from time to time as necessity may arise in consultation between the two countries.

8. The regulations respecting the places to be opened in Manchuria, shall be made by China herself, but the Japanese Minister at Peking must be previously consulted regarding the matter.

9. If no objection be offered on the part of Russia respecting to the navigation of the Sungari (by Japanese vessels), China shall consent to such navigation after negotiations.

10. The Chinese Plenipotentiaries declare that immediately after the withdrawal of the Japanese and Russia troops from Manchuria, China will proceed to take, in virtue of her sovereign right, full administrative measures to guarantee peace in that region and endeavor, by the same right, to promote good and remove evil as well as steadily to restore order, so that the residents of that region, natives and foreigners, may equally enjoy the security of life and occupation under the perfect protection of the Chinese Government. As to the means of restoring order, the Chinese Government are to take by themselves all adequate measures.

11. While relations of intimate friendship subsisted as at the present time between China and Japan, Japan and Russia had unfortunately engaged in war and fought in the territory of China. But peace has now been reëstablished and hostilities in Manchuria have ceased. And while it is undeniable that Japanese troops, before their withdrawal, have the power of exercising the rights accruing from military occupation, the Chinese Government declare that certain Japanese subjects in Manchuria have recently been observed to sometimes interfere with the local Chinese administration and to inflict damage to public and private property of China.

The Japanese Plenipotentiaries, considering that, should such interference and infliction of damage have been carried beyond military necessity, they are not proper acts, declare that they will communicate the purport of the above declaration of the Chinese Government to the Government of Japan, so that proper steps may be taken for controlling Japanese subjects in the Province of Feng-tien and promote the friendly relations between the two nations, and also for preventing them in future, from interfering with the Chinese administration or inflicting damage to public or private property without military necessity.

12. In regard to any public or private property of China which may have been purposely destroyed or used by Japanese subjects without any military necessity, the Governments of the two countries shall respectively make investigations and cause fair reparation to be made.

13. When the Chinese local authorities intend to despatch troops for the purpose of subduing native bandits in the regions not yet completely evacuated by Japanese troops, they shall not fail to previously consult with the Commander of the Japanese troops stationed in those regions so that all misunderstandings may be avoided.

14. The Japanese Plenipotentiaries declare that the Railway Guards stationed between Chang-chun and the boundary line of the leased territory of Port Arthur and Talien [Dalny], shall not be allowed, before their withdrawal, to unreasonably interfere with the local administration of China or to proceed without permission beyond the limits of the railway.

15. Chinese local authorities, who are to reside at Inkou, shall be allowed, even before the withdrawal of the Japanese troops, to proceed to that place and transact their official business. The date of their departure is to be determined, as soon as possible after the definite conclusion of this Treaty, by the Japanese Minister to China in consultation with the Waiwupu. As there is still in that place a considerable number of Japanese troops, quarantine regulations as

well as regulations for the prevention of contagious diseases shall be established by the authorities of the two countries in consultation with each other so that epidemics may be avoided.

16. The revenue of the Maritime Customs at Yin Kou [Newchwang] shall be deposited with the Yokohama Specie Bank and delivered to the Chinese local authorities at the time of evacuation. As to the revenue of the native Customs at that place and the taxes and imposts at all other places, which are to be appropriated for local expenditures, a statement of receipts and expenditures shall be delivered to the Chinese local authorities at the time of evacuation.

NOTE

In regard to the foregoing, see No. 1–B (?), Information Series, far East, being a memorandum of a conversation of January 28, 1908, in the course of which Tang Shao-yi, Governor of the Province of Fengtien, who signed the Peking Agreement, categorically denied the existence of any clause debarring China from paralleling the South Manchurian Railroad. Tang Shao-yi further gave distinct assurance that there was no secret agreement between Japan and China and that all the Legations had been apprised of this fact upon the conclusion of the Korean negotiations. Tang Shao-yi intimated that an agreement that China should not parallel the Japanese railroad had been sought and discussed, but not made, and implied that such discussion appeared in the signed minutes of the conference, the inference being that there was absolutely no agreement but simply evidence of a discussion of this subject.

APPENDIX G

CONVENTION BETWEEN THE GERMAN EMPIRE AND CHINA RESPECTING THE LEASE OF KIAO-CHOU

The incidents connected with the Mission in the Prefecture of Tsaochaufu, in Shantung, being now closed, the Imperial Chinese Government considers it advisable to give a special proof of their grateful appreciation of the friendship shown to them by Germany. The Imperial German and the Imperial Chinese Governments, therefore, inspired by the equal and mutual wish to strengthen the bonds of friendship which unite the two countries, and to develop the economic and commercial relations between the subjects of the two States, have concluded the following separate Convention:—

ARTICLE I.—His Majesty the Emperor of China, guided by the intention to strengthen the friendly relations between China and Germany, and at the same time to increase the military readiness of the Chinese Empire, engages, while reserving to himself all rights of sovereignty in a zone of 50 kilom. (100 Chinese li) surrounding the Bay of Kiao-chou at high-water, to permit the free passage of German troops within this zone at any time, as also to abstain from taking any measures, or issuing any Ordinances therein, without the previous consent of the German Government, and especially to place no obstacle in the way of any regulation of the water-courses which may prove to be necessary. His Majesty the Emperor of China, at the same time, reserves to himself the right to station troops within that zone, in agreement with the German Government, and to take other military measures.

ART. II.—With the intention of meeting the legitimate desire of His Majesty the German Emperor, that Germany, like other Powers, should hold a place on the Chinese Coast for the repair and equipment of her ships, for the storage of materials and provisions for the same, and for other arrangements connected therewith, His Majesty the Emperor of China cedes to Germany on lease, provisionally for ninety-nine years, both sides of the entrance to the Bay of Kiao-chou, Germany engages to construct, at a suitable moment, on the territory thus ceded, fortifications for the protection of the buildings to be constructed there and of the entrance to the harbor.

ART. III.—In order to avoid the possibility of conflicts, the Imperial Chinese Government will abstain from exercising rights of sovereignty in the ceded territory during the term of the lease and leaves the exercise of the same to Germany within the following limits:—

(1.) On the northern side of the entrance to the bay:

The peninsula bounded to the north-east by a line drawn from the north-eastern corner of Potato Island to Loshan Harbor

(2.) On the southern side of the entrance to the bay:

The peninsula bounded to the south-west of a line drawn from the south-westernmost point of the bay lying to the south-south-west of Chiposan Island in the direction of Tolosan Island.

(3.) The Island of Chiposan and Potato Island.

(4.) The whole water area of the bay up to the highest water-mark at present known.

(5.) All Islands lying seaward from Kiao-chou Bay, which may be of importance for its defense, such as Tolosan, Chalienchow, etc.

The High Contracting Parties reserve to themselves to delimitate more accurately, in accord with local traditions, the boundaries of the territory leased to Germany and of the 50-kilom. zone round the bay, by means of Commissioners to be appointed on both sides.

Chinese ships of war and merchant vessels shall enjoy the same privileges in the Bay of Kiao-chou as the ships of other nations on friendly terms with Germany; and the entrance, departure, and sojourn of Chinese ships in the bay shall not be subject to any restrictions other than those which the Imperial German Government, in virtue of the rights of sovereignty over the whole of the water area of the bay transferred to Germany, may at any time find it necessary to impose with regard to the ships of other nations.

ART. IV.—Germany engages to construct the necessary navigation signals on the islands and shallows at the entrance of the bay.

No dues shall be demanded from Chinese ships of war and merchant-vessels in the Bay of Kiao-chou, except those which may be levied upon other vessels for the purpose of maintaining the necessary harbor arrangements and quays.

ART. V.—Should Germany at some future time express the wish to return Kiao-chou Bay to China before the expiration of the lease, China engages to refund to Germany the expenditure she has incurred at Kiao-chou, and to cede to Germany a more suitable place.

Germany engages at no time to sublet the territory leased from China to another Power.

The Chinese population dwelling in the ceded territory shall at all times enjoy the protection of the German Government, provided that they behave in conformity with law and order; unless their land is required for other purposes they may remain there.

If land belonging to Chinese owners is required for any other purposes the owner will receive compensation therefor.

As regards the reëstablishment of Chinese Customs stations which formerly existed outside the ceded territory, but within the 50-kilom. zone, the Imperial German Government intends to come to an agreement with the Chinese Government for the definitive regulation of the Customs frontier, and the mode of collecting customs duties, in a manner which will safeguard all the interests of China, and proposes to enter into further negotiations on the subject.

SECTIONS II AND III

ARTICLE I.—The Chinese Government sanctions the construction by Germany of two lines of railway in Shantung. The first will run from Kiao-chou and Tsinanfu to the boundary of Shantung province via Weihsien, Tsinchow, Pashan, Tsechuen and Suiping. The second line will connect Kiao-chou with Chinchow, whence an extension will be constructed to Tsinan through Laiwuhsien. The construction of this extension shall not be begun until the first part of the line, the main line, is completed, in order to give the Chinese an opportunity of connecting this line in the most advantageous manner with their own railway system. What places the line from Tsinanfu to the provincial boundary shall take in en route are to be determined hereafter.

ART. II.—In order to carry out the above mentioned railway work a Chino-German Company shall be formed, with branches at whatever places may be necessary, and in this Company both German and Chinese subjects shall be at liberty to invest money as they so choose, and appoint directors for the management of the undertaking.

ART. III.—All arrangements in connection with the works specified shall be determined by a future conference of German and Chinese representatives. The Chinese Government should afford every facility and protection and extend every welcome to representatives of the German Railway Company operating in Chinese territory.

Profits derived from the working of these railways shall be justly divided pro rata between the shareholders without regard to nationality. The object of constructing these lines is solely the development of commerce. In inaugurating a railway system in Shantung Germany entertains no treacherous intentions towards China, and undertakes not to unlawfully seize any land in the province.

ART. IV.—The Chinese Government will allow German subjects to hold and develop mining property for a distance of 30 li from each side of these railways and along the whole extent of the lines. The following places where mining operations may be carried on are particularly specified along the northern railway from Kiao-chou to

Tsinan, Weihsien, Pashanhsien and various other points; and along the southern Kiao-chou-Tsinan Chinchow line, Chinchowfu, Laiwuhsien, etc.

Chinese capital may be invested in these operations and arrangements for carrying on the work shall hereafter be made by a joint conference of Chinese and German representatives.

All German subjects engaged in such work in Chinese territory shall be properly protected and welcomed by the Chinese authorities and all profits derived shall be fairly divided between Chinese and German shareholders according to the extent of the interest they hold in the undertakings.

In trying to develop mining property in China, Germany is actuated by no treacherous motives against this country, but seeks alone to increase commerce and improve the relations between the two countries.

The Chinese Government binds itself in all cases where foreign assistance, in persons, capital or material, may be needed for any purpose whatever within the Province of Shantung, to offer the said work or supplying materials, in the first instance to German manufacturers and merchants engaged in undertakings of the kind in question.

In case German manufacturers and merchants are not inclined to undertake the performance of such works or the furnishing of materials, China shall then be at liberty to act as she pleases.

The above Agreement shall be ratified by the Sovereigns of both the Contracting States, and the ratifications exchanged in such manner that, after the receipt in Berlin of the Treaty ratified by China, the copy ratified by Germany shall be handed to the Chinese Minister in Berlin.

The foregoing Treaty has been drawn up in four copies, two in German and two in Chinese, and was signed by the Representatives of the two Contracting States on the 6th March, 1898, corresponding to the 14th day of the second month in the twenty-fourth year of Kuang-hsu.

(Great Seal of the Tsung-li Yamen)
The Imperial German Minister,
(Signed) BARON VON HEYKING.
LI HUNG-CHANG (in Chinese)
Imperial Chinese Grand Secretary,
Minister of the Tsung-li Yamen, &c., &c.
WENG TUNG-HO (in Chinese)
Imperial Chinese Grand Secretary, Member of the
Council of State, Minister of the Tsung-li Yamen, &c., &c.

APPENDIX H

KIAO-CHOU-TSINANFU RAILWAY AGREEMENT

The Agreement for the construction of the Kiao-chou-Tsinanfu Railway was signed on March 21, 1900. The terms of the Agreement are as follows:

ARTICLE 1. According to the second clause in the Second Section of the German-Chinese Convention after the Tsaochou Mission Affair, the building of a railway line from Kiao-chou to Tsinanfu by a Chino-German Company is sanctioned, and in this Company, both German and Chinese subjects shall be at liberty to invest money.

At first, the management of this Company shall rest with the Germans, temporarily. A report of the shares taken up by the Chinese shall be made every six months to the Shantung Bureau of Foreign Affairs, and as soon as these shares shall exceed the amount of Tls. 100,000, the Governor of Shantung shall appoint a satisfactory official to become a member of the company and assist in clearly defining the regulations.

ART. 2. If said Company shall hereafter establish any branch office within the Province of Shantung, this Province will then appoint a satisfactory Chinese official for said branch office to assist in matters of consultation and operation.

ART. 3. The Governor of Shantung shall appoint a special official to assist in the locating of the railway; the high local officials or prominent gentry of various places will also be invited to assist. This will be done in order that the conditions of the various places may receive no injury. But as to scientific questions, these shall all be settled by the Engineer, and in all matters relating to the buying of land, the specially appointed official must be consulted. When the route has been investigated, the Company must prepare a map of the lines showing all the conditions, the scale to be 25,000 to 1, which map is to be handed in to the Governor of Shantung, after which the matter of buying the land will be considered, and as soon as the land is all purchased, the work on the construction can begin. But as to the buying of the land, this matter must be managed as heretofore, with uniform promptness and peacefulness, that the owners of land may have no excuse for putting obstacles in the way, which would result in delaying the work. The Company will be permitted to buy only so much land as is actually needed in the construction of the railway, including what will afterwards be needed for the operation of the line. For small car-housing stations, it will be permitted to buy a piece of land about 630 meters long (1 meter = 2 ft. 9.6 in. official measure, and 1 ft. official measure = 338 millimeters), and about 70 meters wide. For large car-housing stations it will be permitted to buy a piece of land about 730 meters long and about 100 meters wide. For railway stations of medium size a piece of land 850 meters long and 130 meters wide can be bought adjoining the walls (of the cities). For large railway stations the amount of land that can be bought will depend upon the special conditions of the case, except only that the necessary amount shall be the limit. When it is necessary, however, to buy earth to use in making fills or elevations, it will not be understood that this must all come from within the limits set down above.

Art. 4. In the construction of the line, whenever the Company finds a place upon its land where a space should be left for water to flow—whether a bridge should be built or a sluice opened—they must leave satisfactory space for the flow, in order that no harm or hindrance shall come to the populace or their fields.

Art. 5. The railroads must not injure or obstruct any city walls or public works within the Province, nor any important strategical positions that may be used for protection.

Art. 6. In constructing the railway, the Company must go around small villages and market towns, also ancestral halls, temples, graveyards, dwellings, and water-ways, orchards and vegetable gardens. These must not be made to suffer on account of the railway. And as for specially large and well arranged graveyards, these must receive special regard. In cases where it is impossible to avoid them, the matter should be thoroughly looked into and discussed by both parties and the high local officials must be requested to give two months' notice to the owner of the property, that he may construct a new graveyard at another place modeled after the original one. Any person in such a case, morevoer, must not be subjected to any financial loss.

Art. 7. In buying land the Company must use the Chinese units "kung" and "ch'ih" for measuring, one "kung" equaling five "ch'ih." (1 ch'ih = 338 millimeters, and in any locality one "mu"—360 "kung" or 9,000 square "ch'ih.") The Provincial Treasurer will furnish standard lengths for the "kung" and "ch'ih," that both parties may be guided by them. As to the Government tax, that matter will be dealt with in the same manner as is done in other parts of China where foreigners have bought land for the construction of railways.

ART. 8. In transporting materials and men for the measurement and survey of the land, the Company must keep off of the fields and vegetable gardens of the people, and in cases where real damage has been done by trampling on the fields, and action therefore is brought, the Company will be required by the local high officials to make good the loss, out of pity for the abused party.

ART. 9. Whenever the local officials are requested to appoint some one to assist the company, said company must provide such person with money for meals; and this money must be kept in an entirely different account from that in which the money is kept for the purchase of land from the owners. The latter should be handed over to the local officials, to be received by them and handed over in turn to the owners. At the same time the local officials must send the Company a certificate of purchase for the land.

ART. 10. If the Company desires to rent any buildings or rooms along the line of the railway, they must first notify the high local officials, whereupon the said officials will consult with the owners and draw up a contract for the rent on behalf of the Company.

ART. 11. All materials necessary for the construction of the railroad must be bought at the market price, and a fair price given therefor; or else the local officials may be requested to buy them for the Company.

ART. 12. All silver and other money used by the Company must be exchanged justly at the rate of the place at the time.

ART. 13. The Company will not be permitted to act upon its charter to operate off from the main line to connect with the mines, except for the purpose of bringing down rock, lime, etc., such, for example, as the branch line at Poashan Hsien connecting with the main line—such roads will not come under this prohibition. But whenever it is desired to build one of these short branch lines, permission must first be requested from the Governor of Shantung, that he may investigate the matter.

ART. 14. All section men appointed by the Company within the limits of Shantung Province must be provided with passports sealed by the officials of both countries. This is to assist the local officials in giving protection. Without such passport they can not assume the responsibility of protection.

ART. 15. All Chinese or Germans employed by the Company must be supplied with special certificates to that effect; sealed both by the local officials and the Company. This will facilitate the detection of impostors. When the road is being laid out, as well as when it is being constructed, it will be the duty of the Chinese officials to appoint men section by section, to accompany and assist (the railway employees) in looking after their things—such as wooden stakes, etc. Should any falsely assert himself to be in the employ of the Company, he shall be arrested and punished by the local officials.

ART. 16. Should it ever happen that it becomes necessary for soldiers to protect the railway outside of the 100 li zone (Kiao-chou concession) the Governor of Shantung shall detail such soldiers, and foreign soldiers can not be used. The Governor of Shantung having consented to use his utmost endeavors to protect the railway both in time of construction and operation, he must see to it that the railway receives no injury from bandits.

ART. 17. The object of constructing this line is solely the development of commerce, and it will not be permissible to transport foreign soldiers or munitions used by foreign soldiers to any place outside of the 100 li zone. If by any chance, the peaceful relations existing between China and any foreign Power become broken, the railway will still remain under the management of the Company, but the company must still observe the above rule. But if the offices are seized by an enemy, and the Company loses its control, then this Province will no longer assume the responsibility of protecting the line.

ART. 18. Should the Province be visited by famine or flood, so that it is necessary to send relief to the sufferers in the form of rice or clothes; or should there be any riot necessitating the use of soldiers, such soldiers (with their arms, provisions, and baggage) and such relief (as mentioned above) must be shipped at reduced rates according to such regulations as Germany has in her own country.

ART. 19. The Company must make satisfactory arrangements for the easy collection and receipt along its line, of such likin and Customs duties as are collectible in the Province on merchandise and domestic animals. As to the erection of Custom Houses, etc., the Customs officials of this Province will first discuss with the Company the amount to be expended, after which that matter will be taken up.

ART. 20. In the construction of the railway, the Company must employ among their men, people who live in the various villages along the line: and the Company shall also trade with them, that they may not be left out in the cold as it were.

ART. 21. All Chinese employed by the Company outside the German concession shall, if they break the law, be tried by the high local officials; and when a local official notifies the Company that according to Chinese law, a certain man should be tried as an offender, said offender shall not be given improper protection, or be in any way screened by the Company. If there be any offenders or law-breakers among the foreigners employed, and action be brought against them, they shall be tried by foreign law, and it will be the duty of the Company to make a thorough investigation of the case, and not show undue favor.

ART. 22. Competent men must be picked for work on the road, and natives of the place must be used as far as possible. Moreover, the price to be paid for labor must depend upon the various conditions of the place. If the laborers get into quarrels with the people, it will be the duty of the Chinese officials to arrest them and deal with them according to the law.

ART. 23. After the completion of the road, special men shall be detailed to watch and repair the line. Old residents in the various respective districts—men who have considerable means—shall be intrusted with the hiring of these men, in order to guarantee that the men who are hired will all be peaceful and reliable characters. Moreover, those who are intrusted with the hiring of the men must obtain from the local officials certificates for the men they hire. This is for convenience in investigation.

ART. 24. After all work in connection with the railway is completed and the road is being operated according to regulation, should there be any accident resulting in the injuring of any Chinese or damaging their property, the Company must repay them for their losses according to the conditions. At all times notices must be conspicuously placed. Damages must be paid also for all losses or injury to life or property caused by error or carelessness in the handling of the trains. Before the road is entirely completed, and when trains are running according to temporary schedule, this rule that damages must be paid for all losses or injury to life and property caused by error or carelessness in the handling of the trains, likewise holds good.

ART. 25. If there ever be any dangerous places in this province, such as flooded districts, fallen trestles, or damaged bridges, interfering with the operation of the railway, then these obstructions must be removed before the road can be operated again according to regulation.

ART. 26. If at any time, whether it be when the road is being located, constructed, or operated, the Company for some reason requests the Governor of Shantung to furnish soldiers for protection, it shall be his duty to investigate the matter immediately and grant the request, sending sufficient guards of soldiers to the place where they are needed. As to the amount of extra money which the Company shall pay such guards, this will be considered apart.

ART. 27. The title of and authority over all railroad lands outside the German concession, so far as they rested in the former owner originally, will revert from him to the Governor of Shantung. Title to, and authority over, the railroad lands within the German concession will revert to the German Governor.

ART. 28. The Chinese Government shall have the right to buy back this railroad in the future, but as to this matter, it will be considered separately later.

After the above articles have been adopted, signed, and sealed, they shall be sent to the Department and District officials, as well as to the various railway officials, that all may become familiar with them and act accordingly. Hereafter, if any alterations or additions are deemed necessary, they can be made only by consultation of the Governor of Shantung, or such competent and experienced officer as he may appoint, and the Company.

(Sgd.) YIN-CH'ANG,
Manager of Railway and Mining Affairs,
etc., etc., etc.,
YUAN (SHIH-K'AI),
Vice-President Board of War, Governor
of Shantung, etc., etc., etc.

Kuanghsu, XXVIth Year, Second Moon, 21st Day. March 21st, 1900. (Signed on the part of the Chino-German Co. by Schmidt and Michaelis.)

APPENDIX I.

BRITISH AND GERMAN AGREEMENT RE RAILWAY CONSTRUCTION IN CHINA

Minutes of Meeting held at New Court, St. Swithen's Lane, London, on the 1st and 2nd September, 1898.

Present:—Representing the German Syndicate—M.A. von Hansemann. Representing the British and Chinese Corporation, Ltd.—Mr. W. Keswick. Representing the Hongkong and Shanghai Banking Corporation—Mr. Ewen Cameron, Mr. Julius Brussel.

M. VON HANSEMANN proposed the following:—"It is desirable for the British and German Governments to agree about the sphere of interest of the two countries regarding the railway constructions in China, and to mutually support the interest of either country." This proposal was agreed to.

The following proposal of M. von Hansemann regarding the British and German spheres of interest for applications for Railway Concessions in China, viz.

"1.—British sphere of interest, viz.—The Yangtze Valley, subject to the connection of the Shantung lines to the Yangtze at Chinkiang: the provinces south of the Yangtze; the province of Shansi with connection to the Peking-Hankow line at a point south of Chengting and a connecting line to the Yangtze Valley, crossing the Hoangho Valley.

"2.—German sphere of interest, viz.—The Province of Shantung and the Hoangho Valley with connection to Tientsin and Chengting, or other point of the Peking-Hankow line, in the south with connection to the Yangtze at Chinkiang or Nanking. The Hoangho Valley is understood to be subject to the connecting lines in Shansi forming part of the British sphere of interest, and to the connecting line to the Yangtze Valley, also belonging to the said sphere of interest."

Was agreed to with the following alterations, viz.—"The line from Tientsin to Tsinan, or another point of the northern frontier of the Province of Shantung, and the line from the southern point of the Province of Shantung to Chinkiang to be constructed by the Anglo-German Syndicate (meaning the German Syndicate on the one part, and the Hongkong and Shanghai Banking Corporation and the

444

British and Chinese Corporation, Limited, on the other part) in the following manner, viz.—

"1—The capital for both lines to be raised jointly.

"2—The line from Tientsin or to Tsinan or another point on the northern frontier of the Province of Shantung to be built and equipped and worked by the German group.

"3—The line from the southern point of the province of Shantung to Chinkiang to be built and equipped and worked by the English Group.

"4—On completion the lines to be worked for joint account." So far the minutes of the proceedings of the meetings, and it is further agreed upon that neither the German Group nor the English Group will be bound to construct the lines assigned to their sphere unless the Shantung lines be constructed simultaneously.

Signed London, September 2, 1898.

Approved of and signed by A. VON HANSEMANN, W. KESWICK, EWEN CAMERON, JULIUS BRUSSEL.

APPENDIX J

AGREEMENT BETWEEN GREAT BRITAIN AND GERMANY DEFINING THEIR MUTUAL POLICY IN CHINA

SIGNED AT LONDON, 16TH OCTOBER, 1900

Her Britannic Majesty's Government and the Imperial German Government being desirous to maintain their interests in China and their rights under existing Treaties, have agreed to observe the following principles in regard to their mutual policy in China:

1.—It is a matter of joint and permanent international interest that the ports on the rivers and littoral of China should remain free and open to trade and to every legitimate form of economic activity for the nationals of all countries without distinction; and the two Governments agree on their part to uphold the same for all Chinese territory as far as they can exercise influence.

2.—Her Britannic Majesty's Government and the Imperial German Government will not, on their part, make use of the present complication to obtain for themselves any territorial advantages in Chinese dominions, and will direct their policy towards maintaining undiminished the territorial condition of the Chinese Empire.

3.—In case of another Power making use of the complications in China in order to obtain under any form whatever such territorial advantages, the two Contracting parties reserve to themselves to come to a preliminary understanding as to the eventual steps to be taken for the protection of their own interests in China.

4.—The two Governments will communicate this Agreement to the other Powers interested, and especially to Austria-Hungary, France, Italy, Japan, Russia, and the United States of America, and will invite them to accept the principles recorded in it.

SALISBURY.
HATZFELDT.

DECLARATION BY GREAT BRITAIN RESPECTING WEIHAIWEI

APRIL 19, 1898

England formally declares to Germany that in establishing herself at Weihaiwei, she has no intention of injuring or contesting the rights and interests of Germany in the Province of Shantung, or of creating difficulties for her in that province. It is especially understood that England will not construct any railroad communication from Weihaiwei and the district leased therewith into the interior of the Province of Shantung.

APPENDIX K

MR. HAY, AMERICAN SECRETARY OF STATE, TO MR. WHITE, AMERICAN AMBASSADOR TO GERMANY

Department of State,
Washington, September 6, 1899.

Sir:

At the time when the Government of the United States was informed by that of Germany that it had leased from His Majesty the Emperor of China the port of Kiaochou and the adjacent territory in the province of Shantung, assurances were given to the Ambassador of the United States at Berlin by the Imperial German Minister for Foreign affairs that the rights and privileges insured by treaties with China to citizens of the United States would not thereby suffer or be in anywise impaired within the area over which Germany had thus obtained control.

More recently, however, the British Government recognized by a formal agreement with Germany the exclusive right of the latter country to enjoy in said leased area and the contiguous "sphere of influence or interest" certain privileges, more especially those relating to railroads and mining enterprises; but, as the exact nature and extent of the rights thus recognized have not been clearly defined, it is possible that serious conflicts of interests may at any time arise, not only between British and German subjects within said area, but that the interests of our citizens may also be jeopardized thereby.

Earnestly desirous to remove any cause of irritation and to insure at the same time to the commerce of all nations in China the undoubted benefits which should accrue from a formal recognition by the various Powers claiming "spheres of interest" that they shall enjoy perfect equality of treatment for their commerce and navigation within such "spheres," the Government of the United States would be pleased to see His German Majesty's Government give formal assurances, and lend its coöperation in securing like assurances from the other interested Powers, that each within its respective sphere of whatever influence—

First. Will in no way interfere with any treaty port or any vested interest within any so-called "sphere of interest" or leased territory it may have in China.

Second. That the Chinese treaty tariff of the time being shall apply to all merchandise landed or shipped to all such ports as are within said "sphere of interest" (unless they be "free ports"), no matter to what nationality it may belong, and that duties so leviable shall be collected by the Chinese Government.

Third. That it will levy no higher harbor dues on vessels of another nationality frequenting any port in such "sphere" than shall be levied on vessels of its own nationality, and no higher railroad charges over lines built, controlled, or operated within its "sphere" on merchandise belonging to citizens or subjects of other nationalities transported through such "sphere" than shall be levied on similar merchandise belonging to its own nationals transported over equal distances.

The liberal policy pursued by His Imperial German Majesty in declaring Kiaochou a free port and in aiding the Chinese Government in the establishment there of a custom-house are so clearly in line with the proposition which this Government is anxious to see recognized that it entertains the strongest hope that Germany will give its acceptance and hearty support.

The recent Ukase of His Majesty the Emperor of Russia declaring the port of Ta-lien-wan open during the whole of the lease under which it is held from China to the merchant ships of all nations, coupled with the categorical assurances made to this Government by His Imperial Majesty's representative at this capital at the time, and since repeated to me by the present Russian Ambassador, seem to insure support of the Emperor to the proposed measure. Our Ambassador at the Court of St. Petersburg has in consequence been instructed to submit it to the Russian Government and to request their early consideration of it. A copy of my instruction on the subject to Mr. Tower is herewith enclosed for your confidential information.

The commercial interests of Great Britain and Japan will be so clearly served by the desired declaration of intentions, and the views of the Governments of these countries as to the desirability of the adoption of measures insuring the benefits of equality of treatment of all foreign trade throughout China are so similar to those entertained by the United States, that their acceptance of the proposition herein outlined and their coöperation in advocating their adoption by the other Powers can be confidently expected. I enclose herewith copy of the instruction which I have sent to Mr. Choate on the subject.

In view of the present favorable conditions, you are instructed to submit the above considerations to His Imperial German Majesty's Minister for Foreign Affairs, and to request his early consideration of the subject.

Copy of this instruction is sent to our Ambassadors at London and at St. Petersburg for their information.

I have, etc.

JOHN HAY.

COUNT VON BÜLOW, HIS IMPERIAL GERMAN MAJESTY'S MINISTER FOR FOREIGN AFFAIRS, TO MR. WHITE

(Translation.)

Foreign Office,
Berlin, February, 19, 1900.

Mr. Ambassador:

Your Excellency informed me, in a memorandum presented on the 24th of last month, that the Government of the United States of America had received satisfactory written replies from all the Powers to which an inquiry had been addressed similar to that contained in Your Excellency's note of September 26 last, in regard to the policy of the open door in China. While referring to this, Your Excellency thereupon expressed the wish that the Imperial Government would now also give its answer in writing.

Gladly complying with this wish, I have the honor to inform Your Excellency, repeating the statements already made verbally, as follows: As recognized by the Government of the United States of America, according to Your Excellency's note referred to above, the Imperial Government has, from the beginning, not only asserted, but also practically carried out to the fullest extent in its Chinese possessions absolute equality of treatment of all nations with regard to trade, navigation, and commerce. The Imperial Government entertains no thought of departing in the future from this principle, which at once excludes any prejudicial or disadvantageous commercial treatment of the citizens of the United States of America, so long as it is not forced to do so, on account of considerations of reciprocity, by a divergence from it by other governments. If, therefore, the other Powers interested in the industrial development of the Chinese Empire are willing to recognize the same principles, this can only be desired by the Imperial Government, which in this case upon being requested will gladly be ready to participate with the United States of America and the other Powers in an agreement made upon these lines, by which the same rights are reciprocally secured.

I avail myself, etc.

BÜLOW.

APPENDIX L

ANGLO-JAPANESE ALLIANCE

(1st) Agreement, Concluded January 30, 1902

ARTICLE I.—The High Contracting Parties, having mutually recognized the independence of China and Korea, declare themselves to be entirely uninfluenced by any aggressive tendencies in either country. Having in view, however, their special interests, of which those of Great Britain relate principally to China, while Japan, in addition to the interests which she possesses in China, is interested in a peculiar degree politically, as well as commercially and industrially, in Korea the High Contracting Parties recognize that it will be admissible for either of them to take such measures as may be indispensable in order to safeguard those interests if threatened either by the aggressive action of any other Power, or by disturbances arising in China or Korea, and necessitating the intervention of either of the High Contracting Parties for the protection of the lives and property of its subjects.

ART. II.—If either Great Britain or Japan, in the defense of their respective interests as above described, should become involved in war with another Power, the other High Contracting Party will maintain a strict neutrality, and use its efforts to prevent others from joining in hostilities against its Ally.

ART. III.—If, in the above event, any other Power or Powers should join in hostilities against that Ally, the other High Contracting Party will come to its assistance, and will conduct the war in common, and will make peace in mutual agreement with it.

ART. IV.—The High Contracting Parties agree that neither of them will, without consulting the other, enter into separate arrangements with another Power to the prejudice of the interests above described.

ART. V.—Whenever, in the opinion of either Great Britain or Japan, the above mentioned interests are in jeopardy the two Governments will communicate with each other fully and frankly.

ART. VI.—The present Agreement shall come into effect immediately after the date of its signature, and remain in force for five years from that date. In case neither of the High Contracting Parties should have notified twelve months before the expiration of the said five years the intention of terminating it, it shall remain binding until the expiration of one year from the day on which either of the High Contracting Parties shall have denounced it. But if, when the date fixed for its expiration arrives, either ally is actually engaged in war, the Alliance shall, ipse facto, continue until peace is concluded.

(2nd) Signed at London August 12, 1905.

THE MARQUESS OF LANDSDOWNE TO SIR C. HARDINGE

Foreign Office, September 6, 1905.

Sir,—I inclose, for your Excellency's information, a copy of a new Agreement concluded between His Majesty's Government and that of Japan in substitution for that of the 30th January, 1902. You will take an early opportunity of communicating the new Agreement to the Russian Government.

It was signed on the 12th August, and you will explain that it would have been immediately made public but for the fact that negotiations had at that time already commenced between Russia and Japan, and that the publication of such a document whilst those negotiations were still in progress would obviously have been improper and inopportune.

The Russian Government will, I trust, recognize that the new Agreement is an international instrument to which no exception can be taken by any of the Powers interested in the affairs of the far East. You should call special attention to the objects mentioned in the preamble as those by which the policy of the Contracting Parties is inspired. His Majesty's Government believe that they may count upon the good will and support of all the Powers in endeavoring to maintain peace in eastern Asia and in seeking to uphold the integrity and independence of the Chinese Empire and the principle of equal opportunities for the commerce and industry of all nations in that country.

On the other hand, the special interests of the Contracting Parties are of a kind upon which they are fully entitled to insist, and the announcement that those interests must be safeguarded is one which can create no surprise, and need give rise to no misgivings.

I call your special attention to the wording of Article II, which lays down distinctly that it is only in the case of an unprovoked attack made on one of the Contracting Parties by another Power or Powers, and when that Party is defending its territorial rights and special interests from aggressive action, that the other Party is bound to come to its assistance.

Article III, dealing with the question of Korea, is deserving of especial attention. It recognizes in the clearest terms the paramount position which Japan at this moment occupies and must henceforth occupy in Korea, and her right to take any measures which she may find necessary for the protection of her political, military, and economic interests in that country. It is, however, expressly provided that such measures must not be contrary to the principle of equal opportunities for the commerce and industry of other nations. The new Treaty no doubt differs at this point conspicuously from that of 1902. It has, however, become evident that Korea, owing to its close proximity to the Japanese Empire and its inability to stand alone, must fall under the control and tutelage of Japan.

His Majesty's Government observe with satisfaction that this point was readily conceded by Russia in the Treaty of Peace recently concluded with Japan, and they have every reason to believe that similar views are held by other Powers with regard to the relations which should subsist between Japan and Korea.

His Majesty's Government venture to anticipate that the alliance thus concluded, designed as it is with objects which are purely peaceful and for the protection of rights and interests the validity of which cannot be contested, will be regarded with approval by the Government to which you are accredited. They are justified in believing that its conclusion may not have been without effect in facilitating the settlement by which the war has been so happily brought to an end, and they earnestly trust that it may, for many years to come, be instrumental in securing the peace of the world in those regions which come within its scope.

I am, &c.,

(Signed)   LANSDOWNE.

(Inclosure.)

AGREEMENT BETWEEN THE UNITED KINGDOM AND JAPAN, SIGNED AT LONDON, AUGUST 12, 1905.

PREAMBLE

The Governments of Great Britain and Japan, being desirous of replacing the Agreement concluded between them on the 30th January, 1902, by fresh stipulations, have agreed upon the following Articles, which have for their object:—

(a) The consolidation and maintenance of the general peace in the regions of eastern Asia and of India;

(b) The preservation of the common interest of all Powers in

China by insuring the independence and integrity of the Chinese Empire and the principle of equal opportunities for the commerce and industry of all nations in China;

(c) The maintenance of the territorial rights of the High Contracting Parties in the regions of Eastern Asia and of India, and the defense of their special interests in the said regions:—

ARTICLE I.—It is agreed that whenever, in the opinion of either Great Britain or Japan, any of the rights and interests referred to in the preamble of this Agreement are in jeopardy, the two Governments will communicate with one another fully and frankly, and will consider in common the measures which should be taken to safeguard those menaced rights or interests.

ART. II.—If by reason of unprovoked attack or aggressive action, wherever arising, on the part of any other Power or Powers either Contracting Party should be involved in war in defense of its territorial rights or special interests mentioned in the preamble of this Agreement, the other Contracting Party will at once come to the assistance of its ally, and will conduct the war in common, and make peace in mutual agreement with it.

ART. III.—Japan possessing paramount political, military, and economic interests in Korea, Great Britain recognizes the right of Japan to take such measures of guidance, control, and protection in Korea as she may deem proper and necessary to safeguard and advance those interests, provided always that such measures are not contrary to the principle of equal opportunities for the commerce and industry of all nations.

ART. IV.—Great Britain having a special interest in all that concerns the security of the Indian frontier, Japan recognizes her right to take such measures in the proximity of that frontier as she may find necessary for safeguarding her Indian possessions.

ART. V.—The High Contracting Parties agree that neither of them will, without consulting the other, enter into separate arrangements with another Power to the prejudice of the objects described in the preamble of this Agreement.

ART. VI.—As regards the present war between Japan and Russia, Great Britain will continue to maintain strict neutrality unless some other Power or Powers should join in hostilities against Japan, in which case Great Britain will come to the assistance of Japan, and will conduct the war in common, and make peace in mutual agreement with Japan.

ART. VII.—The conditions under which armed assistance shall be afforded by either Power to the other in the circumstances mentioned in the present Agreement, and the means by which such assistance is to be made available, will be arranged by the Naval and Military authorities of the Contracting Parties, who will from time to time consult one another fully and freely upon all questions of mutual interest.

ART. VIII.—The present Agreement shall, subject to the provisions of Article VI, come into effect immediately after the date of its signature, and remain in force for ten years from that date.

In case neither of the High Contracting Parties should have notified twelve months before the expiration of the said ten years the intention of terminating it, it shall remain binding until the expiration of one year from the day on which either of the High Contracting Parties shall have denounced it. But if, when the date fixed for its expiration arrives, either ally is actually engaged in war, the alliance shall, *ipso facto*, continue until peace is concluded.

In faith whereof the Undersigned, duly authorized by their respective Governments, have signed this Agreement and have affixed thereto their Seals.

Done in duplicate at London, the 12th day of August, 1905.

(L.S.)   LANSDOWNE,
His Britannic Majesty's Principal Secretary
of State for Foreign Affairs.

(L.S)   TADASU HAYASHI,
Envoy Extraordinary and Minister Plenipotentiary of His
Majesty the Emperor of Japan at the Court of St. James.

(3rd) Alliance Treaty Signed July 13, 1911

PREAMBLE

The Government of Japan and the Government of Great Britain having in view the important changes which have taken place in the situation since the conclusion of the Anglo-Japanese Agreement of August 12, 1905, and believing that the revision of that Agreement responding to such changes would contribute to general stability and repose, have agreed upon the following stipulations to replace the Agreement above mentioned, such stipulations having the same object as the said Agreement, namely:—

A.—The consolidation and maintenance of the general peace in the regions of Eastern Asia and India.

B.—The preservation of the common interests of all the Powers in China by insuring the independence and integrity of the Chinese Empire and the principle of equal opportunities for the commerce and industry of all nations in China.

C.—The maintenance of the territorial rights of the High Contracting Parties in the regions of Eastern Asia and of India and the defense of their special interests on those regions:—

ARTICLE I.—It is agreed that whenever, in the opinion of either Japan or Great Britain, any of the rights and interests referred to in the preamble of this Agreement are in jeopardy, the two Governments will communicate with one another fully and frankly, and will consider in common the measures which should be taken to safeguard those menaced rights and interests.

ART. II.— If by reason of an unprovoked attack or aggressive action, wherever arising, on the part of any other Power or Powers, either of the High Contracting Parties should be involved in war in defense of its territorial rights or special interests mentioned in the preamble of this Agreement, the other High Contracting Party will at once come to the assistance of its Ally and will conduct the war in common and make peace in mutual agreement with it.

ART. III.—The High Contracting Parties agree that neither of them will, without consulting the other, enter into a separate agreement with another Power to the prejudice of the objects described in the preamble of this Agreement.

ART. IV.—Should either of the High Contracting Parties conclude a treaty of general arbitration with a third Power, it is agreed that nothing in this Agreement shall impose on such contracting party an obligation to go to war with the Power with whom such an arbitration treaty is in force.

ART. V.—The conditions under which armed assistance shall be afforded by either Power to the other in circumstances entered into the present Agreement, and the means by which such assistance is to be made available, will be arranged by the military and naval authorities of the High Contracting Parties, who will from time to time consult one another fully and frankly upon all questions of mutual interests.

ART. VI.—The present Agreement shall come into effect immediately after the date of its signature, and remain in force for ten years from that date (same proviso as first Agreement as to expiry).

In faith whereof the undersigned, duly authorized by their respective Governments, have signed this Agreement and have affixed their seals thereto. Done at London July 13, 1911.

> T. KATO, *the Ambassador of His Majesty the Emperor of Japan at the Court of St. James.*
>
> EDWARD GREY, *H.B.M.'s Secretary of State for Foreign Affairs.*

APPENDIX M

FRANCO-JAPANESE ARRANGEMENT

SIGNED AT PARIS, JUNE 10, 1907.

ARRANGEMENT

The Government of His Majesty the Emperor of Japan and the Government of the French Republic, animated by the desire to strengthen the relations of amity existing between them, and to remove from those relations all cause of misunderstanding for the future, have decided to conclude the following Arrangement:

"The Governments of Japan and France, being agreed to respect the independence and integrity of China, as well as the principle of equal treatment in that country for the commerce and subjects or citizens of all nations, and having a special interest to have the order and pacific state of things preserved especially in the regions of the Chinese Empire adjacent to the territories where they have the rights of sovereignty, protection or occupation, engage to support each other for assuring the peace and security in those regions, with a view to maintain the respective situation and the territorial rights of the two High Contracting Parties in the Continent of Asia."

In witness whereof, the Undersigned: His Excellency Monsieur Kurino, Ambassador Extraordinary and Plenipotentiary of His Majesty the Emperor of Japan to the President of the French Republic, and His Excellency Monsieur Stephen Pichon, Senator, Minister for Foreign Affairs, authorized by their respective Governments, have signed this Agreement and have affixed thereto their seals.

Done at Paris, the 10th of June, 1907.

(L. S.)   S. KURINO.
(L. S.)   S. PICHON.

DECLARATION

The two Governments of Japan and France, while reserving the negotiations for the conclusion of a Convention of Commerce in regard to the relations between Japan and French Indo-China, agree as follows:

The treatment of the most favored nation shall be accorded to the officers and subjects of Japan in French Indo-China in all that concerns their persons and the protection of their property, and the same treatment shall be applied to the subjects and protégés of French Indo-China in the Empire of Japan, until the expiration of the Treaty of Commerce and Navigation signed between Japan and France on the 4th of August, 1896.

Paris, the 10th of June, 1907.

(L. S.)   S. KURINO.
(L. S.)   S. PICHON.

APPENDIX N

CONVENTION BETWEEN THE UNITED KINGDOM AND RUSSIA RELATING TO PERSIA, AFGHANISTAN AND THIBET

SIGNED AT ST. PETERSBURG, AUGUST 31, 1907

RATIFICATIONS EXCHANGED AT ST. PETERSBURG, SEPTEMBER 23, 1907

CONVENTION

(Translation)

His Majesty the King of the United Kingdom of Great Britain and Ireland and of the British Dominions beyond the Seas, Emperor of India, and His Majesty the Emperor of All the Russias, animated by the sincere desire to settle by mutual agreement different questions concerning the interests of their States on the Continent of Asia, have determined to conclude Agreements destined to prevent all cause of misunderstanding between Great Britain and Russia in regard to the questions referred to, and have nominated for this purpose their respective Plenipotentiaries, to-wit:

His Majesty the King of the United Kingdom of Great Britain and Ireland and of the British Dominions beyond the Seas, Emperor of India, the Right Honorable Sir Arthur Nicolson, His Majesty's Ambassador Extraordinary and Plenipotentiary to His Majesty the Emperor of all the Russias;

His Majesty the Emperor of All the Russias, the Master of his Court Alexander Iswolsky, Minister for Foreign Affairs;

Who, having communicated to each other their full powers, found in good and due form, have agreed on the following:—

AGREEMENT CONCERNING PERSIA

The Governments of Great Britain and Russia having mutually engaged to respect the integrity and independence of Persia, and sincerely desiring the preservation of order throughout that country and its peaceful development, as well as the permanent establishment of equal advantages for the trade and industry of all other nations;

Considering that each of them has, for geographical and economic reasons, a special interest in the maintenance of peace and order in certain provinces of Persia adjoining, or in the neighborhood of, the Russian frontier on the one hand, and the frontiers of Afghanistan and Baluchistan on the other hand; and being desirous of avoiding all cause of conflict between their respective interests in the above-mentioned provinces of Persia;

Have agreed on the following terms:—

I.—Great Britain engages not to seek for herself, and not to support in favor of British subjects, or in favor of the subjects of third Powers, any Concessions of a political or commercial nature—such as Concessions for railways, banks, telegraphs, roads, transport, insurance, etc.—beyond a line starting from Kasr-i-Shirin, passing through Isfahan, Yezd, Kakhk, and ending at a point on the Persian frontier at the intersection of the Russian and Afghan frontiers, and not to oppose, directly or indirectly, demands for similar Concessions in this region which are supported by the Russian Government. It is understood that the above-mentioned places are included in the region in which Great Britain engages not to seek the Concessions referred to.

II.—Russia, on her part, engages not to seek for herself and not to support, in favor of Russian subjects, or in favor of the subjects of third Powers, any Concessions of a political or commercial nature—such as Concessions for railways, banks, telegraphs, roads, transport, insurance, etc.—beyond a line going from the Afghan frontier by way of Gazik, Birjand, Kerman, and ending at Bunder Abbas, and not to oppose, directly or indirectly, demands for similar Concessions in this region which are supported by the British Government. It is understood that the above-mentioned places are included in the region in which Russia engages not to seek the Concessions referred to.

III.—Russia, on her part, engages not to oppose, without previous arrangement with Great Britain, the grant of any concessions whatever to British subjects in the regions of Persia situated between the lines mentioned in Articles I and II.

Great Britain undertakes a similar engagement as regards the grant of Concessions to Russian subjects in the same regions of Persia.

All Concessions existing at present in the regions indicated in Articles I and II are maintained.

IV.—It is understood that the revenues of all the Persian customs, with the exception of those of Farsistan and of the Persian Gulf, revenues guaranteeing the amortization and the interest of the loans concluded by the Government of the Shah with the "Banque d'Escompte et des Prêts de Perse" up to the date of the signature of the present Agreement, shall be devoted to the same purpose as in the past.

It is equally understood that the revenues of the Persian customs of Farsistan and of the Persian Gulf, as well as those of the fisheries on the Persian shore of the Caspian Sea and those on the Posts and Telegraphs, shall be devoted, as in the past, to the service of the loans concluded by the Government of the Shah with the Imperial Bank of Persia up to the date of the signature of the present Agreement.

V.—In the event of irregularities occurring in the amortization or the payment of the interest of the Persian loans concluded with the "Banque d'Escompte et des Prêts de Perse" and with the Imperial Bank of Persia up to the date of the signature of the present Agreement, and in the event of the necessity arising for Russia to establish control over the sources of revenue guaranteeing the regular service of the loans concluded with the first-named bank, and situated in the region mentioned in Article II of the present Agreement, or for Great Britain to establish control over the sources of revenue guaranteeing the regular service of the loans concluded with the second-named bank, and situated in the region mentioned in Article I of the present Agreement, the British and Russian Governments undertake to enter beforehand into a friendly exchange of ideas with a view to determine, in agreement with each other, the measures of control in question and to avoid all interference which would not be in conformity with the principles governing the present Agreement.

CONVENTION CONCERNING AFGHANISTAN

The High Contracting Parties, in order to ensure perfect security on their respective frontiers in Central Asia and to maintain in these regions a solid and lasting peace, have concluded the following Convention:—

ARTICLE I.—His Britannic Majesty's Government declare that they have no intention of changing the political status of Afghanistan.

His Britannic Majesty's Government further engage to exercise their influence in Afghanistan only in a pacific sense, and they will not themselves take, nor encourage Afghanistan to take, any measures threatening Russia.

The Russian Government, on their part, declare that they recognize Afghanistan as outside the sphere of Russian influence, and they engage that all their political relations with Afghanistan shall be conducted through the intermediary of His Britannic Majesty's Government; they further engage not to send any Agents into Afghanistan.

ART. II.—The Government of His Britannic Majesty having declared in the Treaty signed at Kabul on the 21st March, 1905, that they recognize the Agreement and the engagements concluded with the late Ameer Abdur Rahman, and that they have no intention of interfering in the internal government of Afghan territory, Great Britain engages neither to annex nor to occupy in contravention of that Treaty any portion of Afghanistan or to interfere in the internal administration of the country, provided that the Ameer fulfils the engagements already contracted by him towards His Britannic Majesty's Government under the above-mentioned Treaty.

ART. III.—The Russian and Afghan authorities, specially designated for the purpose on the frontier or in the frontier provinces, may establish direct relations with each other for the settlement of local questions of a non-political character.

ART. IV.—His Britannic Majesty's Government and the Russian Government affirm their adherence to the principle of equality of commercial opportunity in Afghanistan, and they agree that any facilities which may have been, or shall be hereafter, obtained for British and British-Indian trade and traders, shall be equally enjoyed by Russian trade and traders. Should the progress of trade establish the necessity for Commercial Agents, the two Governments will agree as to what measures shall be taken, due regard, of course, being had to the Ameer's sovereign rights.

ART. V.—The present arrangements will only come into force when His Britannic Majesty's Government shall have notified to the Russian Government the consent of the Ameer to the terms stipulated above.

AGREEMENT CONCERNING THIBET

The Governments of Great Britain and Russia recognizing the suzerain rights of China in Thibet, and considering the fact that Great Britain, by reason of her geographical position, has a special interest in the maintenance of the *status quo* in the external relations of Thibet, have made the following Agreement:—

ARTICLE I.—The two High Contracting Parties engage to respect the territorial integrity of Thibet and to abstain from all interference in its internal administration.

ART. II.—In conformity with the admitted principle of the suzerainty of China over Thibet, Great Britain and Russia engage not to enter into negotiations with Thibet except through the intermediary of the Chinese Government. This engagement does not exclude the direct relations between British Commercial Agents and the Thibetan authorities provided for in Article V of the Convention between

Great Britain and Thibet of the 7th September, 1904, and confirmed by the Convention between Great Britain and China of the 27th April, 1906; nor does it modify the engagements entered into by Great Britain and China in Article I of the said Convention of 1906.

It is clearly understood that Buddhists, subjects of Great Britain or of Russia, may enter into direct relations on strictly religious matters with the Dalai Lama and the other representatives of Buddhism in Thibet; the Governments of Great Britain and Russia engage, so far as they are concerned, not to allow those relations to infringe the stipulations of the present Agreement.

ART. III.—The British and Russian Governments respectively engage not to send Representatives to Lhassa.

ART. IV.—The two High Contracting Parties engage neither to seek nor to obtain, whether for themselves or their subjects, any Concessions for railways, roads, telegraphs, and mines, or other rights in Thibet.

ART. V.—The two Governments agree that no part of the revenues of Thibet, whether in kind or in cash, shall be pledged or assigned to Great Britain or Russia or to any of their subjects.

ANNEX TO THE AGREEMENT BETWEEN GREAT BRITAIN AND RUSSIA CONCERNING THIBET

Great Britain reaffirms the Declaration, signed by his Excellency the Viceroy and Governor-General of India and appended to the ratification of the Convention of the 7th September, 1904, to the effect that the occupation of the Chumbi Valley by British forces shall cease after the payment of three annual instalments of the indemnity of 2,500,000 rupees, provided that the trade marts mentioned in Article II of that Convention have been effectively opened for three years, and that in the meantime the Thibetan authorities have faithfully complied in all respects with the terms of the said Convention of 1904. It is clearly understood that if the occupation of the Chumbi Valley by the British forces has, for any reason, not been terminated at the time anticipated in the above Declaration, the British and Russian Governments will enter upon a friendly exchange of views on this subject.

The present Convention shall be ratified, and the ratifications exchanged at St. Petersburg as soon as possible.

In witness whereof the respective Plenipotentiaries have signed the present Convention and affixed thereto their seals.

Done in duplicate at St. Petersburg, the 18th (31st) August, 1907.

(L. S.)   A. NICOLSON.

(L. S.)   ISWOLSKY.

AGREEMENT BETWEEN THE CHINESE GOVERNMENT AND THE RUSSO-CHINESE BANK FOR THE CONSTRUCTION AND MANAGEMENT OF THE CHINESE EASTERN RAILWAY

IMPERIAL SANCTION RECEIVED BY THE CHINESE ENVOY TO RUSSIA, HSU, DATED 29TH AUGUST, 1896. AGREEMENT SIGNED 8TH SEPTEMBER, 1896

(Translation from Chinese text)

1. China and Russia establish a Company, to be called the Chinese Eastern Railway Company, to construct and manage this railway. The seal to be used by the Company will be issued by the Chinese Government. The regulations of the Company will be in conformity with those of Russian railway companies. Shares may only be bought by Chinese and Russians. The Director of the Company will be appointed by China. His remuneration will be provided by the Company. He may live in Peking. His duty will be to supervise the task delegated to the Company by China, and to ascertain whether its obligations are faithfully performed. All business between the Company and the Chinese Government or any Chinese officials, either in Peking or the provinces, will also be managed by the Director. The Director will also investigate from time to time the accounts of the Company with the Chinese Government. An agent must be stationed at Peking for convenience of consultation.

2. For the purpose of surveying the course of the railway, the Chinese Director will depute an officer to act in conjunction with the Company's engineer and the local officials along the line of the route, who will arrange matters satisfactorily. Measures must be taken to pass round all houses, graves, villages and towns in the course of the railway.

3. Within twelve months of the issue of an Imperial Edict sanctioning this agreement the Company must have commenced work on the railway; and within six years from the date of the completion of the survey for the line and the handing over to the Company of the necessary land the whole line must be completed. The gage of the

line must be that of the Russian railway, i. e. 5 Russian feet, equivalent to 42 1-3 Chinese inches.

4. The Chinese Government will order all local officials concerned to do their utmost to assist the Company in regard to all material required for the construction of the railway, in engaging laborers and boats, carts, men, and horses for transport purposes, and in the purchase of grain and fodder. All these must be paid for by the Company at market rates. The Chinese Government will also afford facilities for transport.

5. The Chinese Government will take measures for the protection of the line and of the men employed thereon. The staff, Chinese and foreign, necessary for the line will be engaged as required by the Company. All crimes and lawsuits arising on the land of the company will be dealt with by the local officials in accordance with treaty.

6. As regards the land required by the Company for constructing, managing, and protecting the line and adjacent land, for procuring sand, earth, stones, and lime, if the land be Government land it will be given the Company without payment. If privately owned, the Company will provide funds for payment to the proprietors at market rates, either in one payment or as yearly rent. All the Company's land will be exempted from land tax. As soon as the land comes under the management of the Company they may erect thereon any buildings and carry on all kinds of work, and they may establish a telegraph line thereon worked by the Company for the Company's use. With the exception of mines, for which special arrangements must be made, all receipts of the Company for transport of passengers and freight, telegrams, etc., will be exempt from all taxation.

7. All materials required by the Company for the construction and repair of the line will be exempt from taxation.

8. All Russian troops, naval or military, and munitions of war, moved by the Russian Government by this railway, must be conveyed by the Company directly across the border. Apart from slight detentions en route, incidental to transfers, no other delays will be permitted for any cause.

9. Any foreign passengers by this line who may proceed into the interior away from the railway must be provided with Chinese passports authorizing them to proceed. Any person unprovided with such passports must be forbidden by the Company to proceed into the interior.

10. All goods and baggage coming from Russian territory, and again entering Russian territory by this line, will be exempt from taxation, but such goods and baggage, with the exception of personal luggage of passengers, must be carried by the Company in special

vans, and sealed by the customs officers on entering Chinese territory, and on leaving Chinese territory they must be examined by the customs officers to ascertain that the seals are intact, in which case they will be allowed to pass. If it be found that the seals have been opened en route the goods will be confiscated.

As to goods conveyed by this line from Russia to China or from China to Russia, they will pay duty according to the treaty tariff, i. e. an import or export duty, as the case may be, but subject to a reduction of 1-3 of the tariff rate. If such goods be conveyed to the interior they must pay transit duty in addition, i. e. half the amount of the duty already paid. Transit duty being paid, they are not to be taxed again on passing customs stations or likin barriers. But if transit duty be not paid they must pay duty at stations and likin barriers. China must establish customs stations at the two points where the line crosses the frontier.

11. Fares for passengers, freight for goods, and charges for loading and unloading will be fixed by the Company. Chinese Government despatches and letters must be carried by the Company free of cost. Chinese troops and munitions of war will be carried at half rates.

12. From the day of completion of the railway and the commencement of traffic, for a period of eighty years, all profit made by the line shall belong to the Company solely. Any loss must likewise be borne by it; the Chinese Government cannot be responsible. After eighty years the line and all its property are to revert to the Chinese Government without payment.

Thirty-six years after commencement of traffic China may take over the line on payment of the following and all capital and all moneys owed on account of the line and interest. As to profits made by the Company, should there be any not distributed to shareholders, these must be taken to be capital returned and be deducted from the price paid for the line. China must actually pay over the amount of purchase to Russia before receiving possession of the line.

On the day the line is completed and traffic commenced the Company will pay the Chinese Government five million treasury taels.

APPENDIX P

LAW CONCERNING MIXED RESIDENCE IN JAPAN

We, by the advice of our Privy Council, hereby give our sanction to matters relating to the residence and occupation, etc., of foreigners who either by virtue of Treaty or of custom have no freedom of residence and order the same to be promulgated.

(Imperial Seal and Sign-Manual.)

July 27th, 1899.

> Marquis Yamagata Aritomo,
> > *Minister President.*
> Marquis Saigo Yorimichi,
> > *Minister for Home Affairs.*
> Viscount Aoki Shuzo,
> > *Minister for Foreign Affairs.*
> Kiyoura Keigo,
> > *Minister for Justice.*

IMPERIAL ORDINANCE NO. 352

ARTICLE 1. Foreigners who either by virtue of Treaty or of custom have not freedom may hereafter reside, remove, carry on trade and do other acts outside the former Settlements and mixed residential districts. Provided that in the case of laborers they cannot reside or carry on their business outside the former Settlements or mixed residential districts unless under the special permission of the administrative authorities.

The classes of such laborers (referred to in the preceding clause) and details for the operation of this Ordinance shall be determined by the Minister for Home Affairs.

ART. 2. Persons infringing the proviso of clause 1 of the foregoing article shall be sentenced to a fine not exceeding Y. 100.

SUPPLEMENTARY RULES

ART. 3. This law shall be put into operation on and after August 4th, 1899.

ART. 4. Imperial Ordinance No. 137, of 1894, shall be rescinded after the date on which this Law comes into force.

467

Details relating to the operation of Imperial Ordinance No. 352, 1899, concerning the residence and occupation of foreigners who have no freedom of residence either by virtue of Treaty or of custom are decided as follows:—

July 28th, 1899.

MARQUIS SAIGO YORIMICHI,
Minister for Home Affairs.

ARTICLE 1.   The administrative authorities mentioned in Art. I of Imperial Ordinance No. 352, 1899, shall be the head of each prefecture and of Hokkaido.

ART. 2.   The laborers mentioned in Art. I of the same Law shall be men engaged in labor in agricultural, fishing, mining, civil engineering work, architectural, manufacturing, transporting, carting, stevedoring, and other miscellaneous work.   Provided that this rule is not applicable to those who are employed in household services such as cooking and waiting.

ART. 3.   Permission given to laborers (to reside in the interior) may be canceled by a local Governor when he deems it necessary to do so for the public welfare.

APPENDIX Q

NOTES EXCHANGED BETWEEN THE UNITED STATES AND JAPAN, NOVEMBER 30, 1908, DECLARING THEIR POLICY IN THE FAR EAST

Imperial Japanese Embassy, Washington,
November 30, 1908.

Sir:

The exchange of views between us, which has taken place at the several interviews which I have recently had the honor of holding with you, has shown that Japan and the United States holding important outlying insular possessions in the region of the Pacific Ocean, the Governments of the two countries are animated by a common aim, policy, and intention in that region.

Believing that a frank avowal of that aim, policy, and intention would not only tend to strengthen the relations of friendship and good neighborhood, which have immemorially existed between Japan and the United States, but would materially contribute to the preservation of the general peace, the Imperial Government have authorized me to present to you an outline of their understanding of that common aim, policy, and intention:

1. It is the wish of the two Governments to encourage the free and peaceful development of their commerce on the Pacific Ocean.

2. The policy of both Governments, uninfluenced by any aggressive tendencies, is directed to the maintenance of the existing *status quo* in the region above mentioned and to the defense of the principle of equal opportunity for commerce and industry in China.

3. They are accordingly firmly resolved reciprocally to respect the territorial possessions belonging to each other in said region.

4. They are also determined to preserve the common interest of all powers in China by supporting by all pacific means at their disposal the independence and integrity of China and the principle of equal opportunity for commerce and industry of all nations in that Empire.

5. Should any event occur threatening the *status quo* as above described or the principle of equal opportunity as above defined, it

remains for the two Governments to communicate with each other in order to arrive at an understanding as to what measures they may consider it useful to take.

If the foregoing outline accords with the view of the Government of the United States, I shall be gratified to receive your confirmation.

I take this opportunity to renew to Your Excellency the assurance of my highest consideration.

K. TAKAHIRA

HONORABLE ELIHU ROOT,
Secretary of State.

Department of State,
Washington, November 30, 1908.

Excellency:

I have the honor to acknowledge the receipt of your note of to-day setting forth the result of the exchange of views between us in our recent interviews defining the understanding of the two Governments in regard to their policy in the region of the Pacific Ocean.

It is a pleasure to inform you that this expression of mutual understanding is welcome to the Government of the United States as appropriate to the happy relations of the two countries and as the occasion for a concise mutual affirmation of that accordant policy respecting the far East which the two Governments have so frequently declared in the past.

I am happy to be able to confirm to Your Excellency, on behalf of the United States, the declaration of the two Governments embodied in the following words:

1. It is the wish of the two Governments to encourage the free and peaceful development of their commerce on the Pacific Ocean.

2. The policy of both Governments, uninfluenced by any aggressive tendencies, is directed to the maintenance of the existing *status quo* in the region above mentioned, and to the defense of the principle of equal opportunity for commerce and industry in China.

3. They are accordingly firmly resolved reciprocally to respect the territorial possessions belonging to each other in said region.

4. They are also determined to preserve the common interests of all powers in China by supporting by all pacific means at their disposal the independence and integrity of China and the principle of equal opportunity for commerce and industry of all nations in that Empire.

5. Should any event occur threatening the *status quo* as above described or the principle of equal opportunity as above defined, it remains for the two Governments to communicate with each other in

order to arrive at an understanding as to what measures they may consider it useful to take.

Accept, Excellency, the renewed assurance of my highest consideration.

ELIHU ROOT.

His Excellency
    BARON KOGORO TAKAHIRA,
        Japanese Ambassador.

APPENDIX R

OFFICIAL STATEMENT BY THE CHINESE GOVERNMENT RESPECTING THE SINO-JAPANESE NEGOTIATIONS NOW BROUGHT TO A CONCLUSION BY CHINA'S COMPLIANCE WITH THE TERMS OF JAPAN'S ULTIMATUM DELIVERED ON MAY 7, 1915

At three o'clock on the afternoon of May 7, 1915, His Excellency, the Japanese Minister in Peking delivered to the Chinese Government, in person an Ultimatum from the Imperial Japanese Government, with an accompanying Note of seven articles. The concluding sentences of the Ultimatum read thus:

"The Imperial Government hereby again offer their advice and hope that the Chinese Government, upon this advice, will give a satisfactory reply by six o'clock p. m. on the ninth day of May. It is hereby declared that if no satisfactory reply is received before or at the specified time the Imperial Government will take such steps as they may deem necessary."

The Chinese Government, having received and accepted the Ultimatum, feel constrained to make a frank and plain statement of the facts connected with the negotiations which were abruptly terminated by this drastic action on the part of Japan.

The Chinese Government have constantly aimed, as they still aim, at consolidating the friendship existing between China and Japan, and, in this period of travail in other parts of the world, have been particularly solicitous of preserving peace in the far East. Unexpectedly on January 18, 1915, His Excellency the Japanese Minister in Peking, in pursuance of instructions from his Government, adopted the unusual procedure of presenting to his Excellency the President of the Republic of China a list (hereto appended) of twenty-one momentous demands, arranged in five Groups. *The first four Groups were each introduced by a preamble, but there was no preamble or explanation to the fifth Group. In respect of the character of the demands in this Group, however, no difference was indicated in the document between them and those embodied in the preceding Groups.*

Although there was no cause for such a *démarche*, the Chinese Government, in deference to the wishes of the Imperial Japanese

472

Government, at once agreed to open negotiations on those articles which it was possible for China to consider, notwithstanding that it was palpable that the whole of the demands were intended to extend the rights and interests of Japan without securing a *quid pro quo* of any kind for China.

China approached the pending conferences in a spirit of utmost friendliness and with a determination to deal with all questions frankly and sincerely. Before negotiations were actually commenced, the Japanese Minister raised many questions with regard to the number of delegates proposed to represent China, the number of conferences to be held in each week, and the method of discussion. The Chinese Government, though their views differed from those of the Japanese Minister, yielded in all these respects to his contentions in the hope of avoiding any delay in the negotiations. The objections of the Japanese Minister to the customary recording and signing of the minutes of each conference, which the Chinese Government suggested as a necessary and advisable precaution, as well as one calculated to facilitate future reference, were also accepted. Nor did the Chinese Government retaliate in any way when in the course of the negotiations the Japanese Minister twice suspended the conferences, obviously with the object of compelling compliance with his views on certain points at the time under discussion. Even when delay was threatened owing to the unfortunate injury sustained by the Japanese Minister as a result of a fall from his horse, the Chinese delegates, in order to avert interruption, proposed that the conferences should be continued at the Japanese Legation, which proposal was accepted. Later, when, on March 22, the Japanese Government despatched large bodies of troops to South Manchuria and Shantung for the ostensible purpose of relieving the garrison—whose term of service had not then expired—the Japanese Minister stated at the conference, in reply to a direct question as to when the retiring troops would be withdrawn, that this would not be done until the negotiations could be brought to a satisfactory conclusion. Although this minatory step caused much excitement, indignation and alarm on the part of the Chinese people, and made it difficult for the Chinese Government to continue the conferences, they successfully exerted efforts to avert a rupture and thus enabled the negotiations smoothly to proceed. All this demonstrates that the Chinese Government were dominated by a sincere desire to expedite the progress of the conferences; and that the Japanese Government recognized this important fact was made clear on March 11 when the Japanese Minister conveyed to the Chinese Government an expression of his Government's appreciation of China's frankness and sincerity in the conduct of the negotiations.

One of the supplementary proposals was in these terms:

From February 2, when the negotiations were commenced, to April 17, twenty-four conferences were held in all. Throughout this whole period the Chinese Government steadfastly strove to arrive at an amicable settlement and made every concession possible.

Of the twenty-one demands originally submitted by Japan, China agreed to fifteen, some in principle and some textually, six being initialled by both parties.

IN THE MATTER OF THE DEMANDS TO WHICH CHINA AGREED

At the first conference, held on February 2, China agreed in principle to the first article of the Shantung group of demands which provides that China should give her assent to the transfer of Germany's rights in Shantung to Japan. The Chinese Government maintained at first that the subject of this demand related to the *post bellum* settlement, and, therefore, should be left over for discussion by all the parties interested at the Peace Conference. Failing to persuade the Japanese Minister to accept this view, the Chinese Government agreed to this demand in principle, and made certain supplementary proposals.

"The Japanese Government declares that when the Chinese Government give their assent to the disposition of interests above referred to, Japan will restore the Leased Territory of Kiao-chou to China, and further recognizes the right of the Chinese Government to participate in the negotiations referred to above between Japan and Germany."

The provision for a declaration to restore Kiao-chou was clearly not a demand on Japan but only a reiteration of Japan's voluntary statement in her Ultimatum to Germany on August 15, 1914 (a copy of which was officially transmitted to the Chinese Government for perusal on August 15), and repeated in public statements by the Japanese Premier. Appreciating the earnest desire of Japan to maintain the peace of the far East and to cement her friendship with China, as evidenced by this friendly offer, the Chinese Government left the entire question of the conditions of restoration to be determined by Japan, and refrained from making any reference thereto in the supplementary proposal. The suggestion relating to participation in the Conference between Japan and Germany was made in view of the fact that Shantung, the object of future negotiation between Japan and Germany, is a Chinese Province, and therefore China is the Power most concerned in the future of that territory.

Another supplementary proposal suggesting the assumption by Japan of responsibility for indemnification of the losses arising out of the military operations by Japan in and about the leased territory of Kiao-chou was necessitated by the fact that China was neutral *vis-à-vis* the war between Japan and Germany. Had China not inserted such a provision, her position in relation to this conflict might have been liable to misconstruction—the localities in which the operations took place being a portion of China's territory—and might also have exposed herself to a claim for indemnification of losses for which she was in no way responsible.

In a further supplementary proposal the Chinese Government suggested that, prior to the restoration of the Kiao-chou territory to China, the Maritime Customs, the telegraphs and post offices should be continued to be administered as heretofore; that the military railway, the telegraph lines, etc., which were installed by Japan to facilitate her military operations, should be removed forthwith; that the Japanese troops now stationed outside of the leased territory should be first withdrawn, and those within the territory should be recalled at the time when Kiao-chou is returned to China. Shantung being a Chinese Province, it was natural for China to be anxious concerning the restoration of the *status quo ante bellum*. Although the Chinese Government were confident that the Japanese Government would effect such restoration in pursuance of their official declaration, it was necessary for China, being neutral throughout the war, to place these matters on record.

At the third conference, held on February 22, China agreed to the second demand in the Shantung Group not to cede or lease to any Power any territory or island on the sea border of Shantung.

At the fifth conference, held on February 29, China agreed to give Japan the preference, provided Germany abandoned the privilege, to supply the capital for the construction of a railway from Chefoo or Lungkow to connect with the Kiao-chou-Tsinanfu Railway, in the event of China deciding to build that railway with foreign capital.

At the sixth conference, held on March 3, China, in the interests of foreign trade, agreed to open certain important cities in Shantung as trade marts under regulations approved by the Japanese Government, although this was a demand on the part of Japan for privileges additional to any that hitherto had been enjoyed by Germany and was not an outcome of the hostilities between Japan and Germany, nor, in the opinion of the Chinese Government, was its acceptance essential to the preservation of peace in the far East.

At the eighth conference, held on March 9, China agreed (1) to the extension of the term of the lease of Dairen and (2) Port Arthur, and (3) of the South Manchuria and (4) Antung-Mukden railways, all to 99 years.

Owing to the bitter experiences which China sustained in the past in connection with the leased portions of her territory, it has become her settled policy not to grant further leases nor to extend the term of those now in existence. Therefore, it was a significant indication of China's desire to meet Japan's wishes when she agreed to this exceptional departure from her settled policy.

At the same conference the Chinese Government also agreed to refrain from raising objections to the principle of coöperation in the Hanyehping Company, if the latter should arrive at an agreement in this respect with the Japanese capitalists concerned. With reference to this question it was pointed out to the Japanese Minister that, in the Provisional Constitution of the Republic of China, Chinese subjects are guaranteed the right of protection of their property and freedom to engage in any lawful occupation. The Government were precluded, therefore, from interfering with the private business of the people, and could not find any other solution than the one thus agreed to.

As regards the single article of the Fourth Group, and the preamble thereto, the Chinese Government held that they were inconsistent with Chinese sovereignty. However, China, at this conference, expressed her readiness to meet the wishes of Japan so far as it was possible without infringing her sovereignty, and agreed to make a voluntary pronouncement that she would not alienate any portion of her coast line.

In connection with the South Manchuria Railway it is worthy of note that the provision regarding the repurchase period in the agreement (36 years from 1902) was not mentioned in Japan's original proposal. Subsequently the Japanese Government, on the ground that the meaning of this provision was not clear, requested China to agree to its cancelation. To this request the Chinese Government acceded, though well aware that the proposed change could only benefit Japan. China thus relinquished the right to repurchase the railway at the expiration of another 23 years.

In connection with the Antung-Mukden Railway, the article, which was originally initialled at the conference, provided for the reversion of the railway to China at the end of 99 years without payment, but, at the subsequent meeting, the Japanese Minister requested that the reference to the reversion without payment be deleted from the initialled article. In acceding to the Japanese Minister's request, China again showed her sincere desire to expedite matters and to meet Japan's wishes even at the sacrifice of a point in her favor, to which Japan had already agreed.

At the eleventh conference, held on March 16, China agreed to give Japan preference in regard to loans for railway construction in South Manchuria.

At the thirteenth conference, held on March 23, China agreed (1) to the amendment of the Kirin-Changchun Railway loan agreement; (2) to give preference to Japan if the revenue of South Manchuria were offered as security for loans; (3) to give preference to Japanese in the event of the employment of advisers for South Manchuria; (4) to grant to Japanese the right of mining in nine specified areas in South Manchuria.

In its original form the demand with reference to mining in South Manchuria tended to create a monopoly for Japanese subjects, and, therefore, was entirely inconsistent with the principle of equal opportunity. The Chinese Government explained that they could not, in view of the treaty rights of other Powers, agree to this monopoly, but they readily gave their acceptance when Japan consented to the modification of the demand so as to mitigate its monopolistic character.

In connection with the Kirin-Changchun Railway, the amendment agreed to involve a fundamental revision of the original agreement on the basis of the existing railway loan contracts concluded by China with other foreign capitalists, as well as an engagement on the part of the Chinese Government to extend to this railway any better terms which may be hereafter accorded to other railway concessionaires in China. The capital of this railway was originally fifty per cent. Chinese and fifty per cent. Japanese. The effect of this undertaking is to transfer the capital originally held by the Chinese, as well as the full control and administration of the railway, to the Japanese.

At the twenty-first conference, held on April 10, China agreed, in regard to the demands concerning Fukien Province, to give Japan an assurance in accordance with Japan's wishes at a future time.

As regards demands 2 and 3 in the Manchuria Group, relating to the ownership of land for trade, manufacture, and agricultural enterprises, as well as for the right of settlement in the interior of South Manchuria, the Chinese Government, after discussion at several conferences, agreed to them in principle, but desired to introduce certain amendments concerning the control and protection of the Japanese subjects who might avail themselves of these rights. The course of the negotiations in connection with these amendments will be referred to subsequently.

Of the twenty-one original demands there were six, as previously mentioned, to which China could not agree on the ground that they were not proper subjects for international negotiation, conflicting as they did with the sovereign rights of China, the treaty rights of other Powers, and the principle of equal opportunity.

Thus, for example, the second article of the Hanyehping question in the original Third Group in particular seriously affected the principle of equal commercial opportunity.

The proposal that there should be joint administration by China and Japan of the police in China was clearly an interference with the Republic's domestic affairs, and consequently an infringement of her sovereignty. For that reason the Chinese Government could not take the demand into consideration. But when it was explained by the Japanese Minister that this referred only to South Manchuria, and he suggested that his Government would be satisfied if China agreed to engage Japanese as police advisers for that territory, the Chinese Government accepted the suggestion.

The two articles relating to the acquisition of land for schools, hospitals, and temples, as well as to the right of missionary propaganda, would, in the opinion of the Chinese Government, have presented grave obstacles to the consolidation of the friendly feeling subsisting between the two people. The religions of the two countries are identical and, therefore, the need for a missionary propaganda to be carried on in China by Japanese does not exist. The natural rivalry between Chinese and Japanese followers of the same faith would tend to create incessant disputes and friction. Whereas Western missionaries live apart from the Chinese communities among which they labor, Japanese monks would live with the Chinese; and the similarity of their physical characteristics, their religious garb, and their habits of life would render it impossible to distinguish them for purposes of affording the protection which the Japanese Government would require should be extended to them under the system of extra-territoriality now obtaining in China. Moreover a general apprehension exists among the Chinese people that these peculiar conditions favoring conspiracies for political purposes might be taken advantage of by some unscrupulous Chinese.

The demand for railway concessions in the Yangtze Valley conflicted with the Shanghai-Hangchow-Ningpo Railway Agreement of March 6, 1908, the Nanking-Changsha Railway Agreement of March 31, 1914, and the engagement of August 24, 1914, giving preference to British firms for the projected line from Nanchang to Chaochowfu. For this reason the Chinese Government found themselves unable to consider the demand, though the Japanese Minister, while informed of China's engagements with Great Britain, repeatedly pressed for its acceptance.

In respect to the demand for the appointment of influential Japanese to be advisers and instructors in political, financial and military affairs, the policy of the Chinese Government in regard to the appointment of advisers has been similar to that which has presumably guided the Japanese Government in like selection of the best qualified men irrespective of their nationality. As an indication of their desire to avail themselves of the services of eminent Japanese, one of the earliest appointments made to an advisership was that of Dr. Ariga, while later on Dr. Hirai and Mr. Nakayami were appointed to the Ministry of Communications.

It was considered that the demand that Japanese should be appointed in the three most important administrative departments, as well as the demand for the joint control of China's police, and the demand for an engagement to purchase a fixed amount of arms and ammunition from Japan or to establish joint arsenals in China, so clearly involved the sovereignty of the Republic that the Chinese Government were unable even to consider them.

For these reasons the Chinese Government, at the very outset of the negotiations, declared that they were unable to negotiate on the demands; but, in deference to the wishes of the Japanese Minister, the Chinese delegates consented to give the reasons for declining to enter into a discussion of them.

IN THE MATTER OF THE QUESTIONS OF DISPUTE INVOLVED IN SOME OF THE FOREGOING DEMANDS

The demand by Japan for the right of her subjects in South Manchuria to lease or own land, and to reside and travel, and to engage in business or manufacture of any kind whatever, was deemed by the Chinese Government to obtain for Japanese subjects in this region a privileged status beyond the terms of the treaties existing between the two nations, and to give them a freedom of action which would be a restriction of China's sovereignty and a serious infringement of her administrative rights. Should Japanese subjects be granted the right of owning land, it would mean that all the landed property in the region might fall into their hands, thereby endangering China's territorial integrity. Moreover, residence in the interior was incompatible with the existence of extra-territoriality, the relinquishment of which is necessary to the actual enjoyment of the privilege of inland residence, as evidenced in the practice of other nations.

Japan's unconditional demand for the privilege of inland residence accompanied with a desire to extend extra-territoriality into the interior of China and to enable Japanese subjects to monopolize all the interests in South Manchuria, was also palpably irreconcilable with the principle of equal opportunity. For this reason the Chinese Government were, in the first instance, unable to accept this demand as a basis of negotiation. Their profound regard for the friendly relations of the two countries, however, persuaded them to exert their utmost efforts, in spite of all the inherent difficulties, to seek a solution of a question which was practically impossible to solve. Knowing that the proposal made by Japan was incompatible with treaties, they nevertheless sought to meet her wishes within the limits of treaties. Accordingly they submitted a counter-proposal to open more places in South Manchuria to international trade and to establish Sino-Japanese joint reclamation companies.

This suggestion was made in the belief that the places to which Japanese subjects would desire to resort for purposes of trade, could not be other than important localities; if all these localities were opened to commerce, then they could reside, trade, and lease land there for joint reclamation. Thus Japanese subjects might enjoy the essence of the privilege of inland residence and would still be able to reconcile their position with China's treaties and the principle of equal opportunity.

After the Japanese Government declined to accept this suggestion, China withdrew it and replaced it with an amendment to the original articles. It was proposed in this amendment to grant to Japanese subjects the extra-treaty privilege of inland residence with the provisos that Japanese subjects in places outside of trade marts should observe Chinese police regulations and pay taxes in the same manner as Chinese; and that civil and criminal cases involving such Japanese subjects should be adjudicated by Chinese Authorities, the Japanese Consul attending merely to watch the proceedings. This suggestion was not an innovation; it was based upon the *modus operandi* now in force as regards the Korean settlers in inland districts in Chientao. But the Japanese Government again declined to accept it.

The Chinese Government thereupon made a third proposal along the line of what constitutes the present practice in Turkey, making a distinction, however, in favor of Japanese subjects, in the exercise of jurisdiction over civil and criminal cases. This was once more objected to by the Japanese Government.

Then the Chinese Government proposed to concede still another step—the fourth endeavor to meet Japan's wishes. They proposed to agree to the full text of Articles 2 and 3 relative to the question of inland residence, except that "the right of owning land" was changed into "the right of leasing land" and to the phrase "cultivating land" was added this clause: "the regulations for which shall be determined separately;" and, further, to add a supplementary article which embodied a *modus operandi* which the Chinese Government had constrained themselves to make, out of a desire to come to a settlement over this question. The view advanced in this supplementary article was based upon the Japanese Minister's declaration made on March 6, 1915, that a separate article embodying some compromise might be added to the original articles 2 and 3 for the purpose of avoiding any conflict with China's sovereignty or the system established by treaties. These suggestions made by the Chinese Government were not accepted by Japan.

As regards Eastern Inner Mongolia, not only have no treaties been entered into with Japan concerning this region, but also the people are so unaccustomed to foreign trade, that the Chinese Government invariably feel much anxiety about the safety of foreigners who elect to travel there. The Chinese Government, therefore, considered that it would not be in the interest of foreigners to open the whole territory to them for residence and commerce, and on these grounds based their original refusal to place Eastern Inner Mongolia on the same footing as South Manchuria. Still, their desire to meet the wishes of the Japanese Government eventually prompted them to offer to open a number of places in the region to foreign trade.

IN THE MATTER OF JAPAN'S REVISED DEMANDS

The foregoing is an outline of the negotiations up to April 17. It was hoped by the Chinese Government that the Japanese Government, in view of the great concessions made by China at the conferences held up to this time, would see a way of effecting an amicable settlement by modifying their position on certain points. In regard to these it had, by this time, become manifest that China would encounter almost insuperable difficulties in making further concessions.

The Japanese Government, however, suspended the negotiations until April 26 when they surprised the Chinese Government by presenting a new list of twenty-four demands (which is hereto appended), and requested the Chinese Government to accord their acceptance without delay, adding that this was their final proposal. At the same time the Japanese Minister stated that the Japanese Government would restore the leased territory of Kiaochow to China at an opportune time in the future and under proper conditions, if the

Chinese Government would agree to the new list of twenty-four demands without modification.

In this new list, although the term "special position" in the preamble of the Manchurian Group was changed to "economic relations," and although the character of the articles in the original Fifth Group was altered from Demands to a recital of alleged statements by the Chinese Foreign Minister, four new demands were introduced concerning Eastern Inner Mongolia. In deference to the wishes of the Japanese Government, the Chinese Government gave the revised list the most careful consideration; and being sincerely desirous of an early settlement offered new concessions in their reply presented to the Japanese Minister on May 1. (Annexed.)

In this reply the Chinese Government reinserted the proposal in reference to the retrocession of Kiaochow, which they advanced at the first conference on February 2, and which was postponed at the request of the Japanese Minister. This, therefore, was in no sense a new proposal.

The Chinese Government also proposed to agree to three of the four articles relating to Eastern Inner Mongolia. There was some difficulty in determining a definition of the boundaries of Eastern Inner Mongolia—this being a new expression in Chinese geographical terminology—but the Chinese Government, acting upon a statement made at a previous conference by the Japanese Minister that the Japanese Government meant the region under Chinese administrative jurisdiction, and taking note, in the list presented by the Japanese Minister, of the names of places in Eastern Inner Mongolia to be opened to trade, inferred that the so-called Eastern Inner Mongolia is that part of Inner Mongolia which is under the jurisdiction of South Manchuria and the Jehol Intendency; and refrained from placing any limitations upon the definition of this term.

The Chinese Government also withdrew their supplementary proposal reserving the right of making regulations for agricultural enterprises to be undertaken by Japanese settlers in South Manchuria.

In respect of the trial of cases involving land disputes between Japanese only, or between Japanese and Chinese, the Chinese Government accorded to the Japanese Consul the right of deputing an officer to watch the proceedings.

The Chinese Government also agreed to accept the suggestion of the Japanese Government to modify the term "police law and ordinances" into "police rules and regulations," thereby limiting the extent of control which the Chinese would have over Japanese subjects.

As regards the Hanyehping demand, the Chinese Government accepted the draft made by the Japanese Government, embodying an engagement by the Chinese Government not to convert the Company into a State-owned concern, nor to confiscate it, nor to force it to borrow foreign capital other than Japanese.

In respect of the Fukien question the Chinese Government also agreed to give an assurance in the amplified form suggested by the Japanese Government that the Chinese Government had not given their consent to any foreign nations to construct a dockyard, or a coaling station, or a naval base, or any other military establishment along the coast of Fukien Province; nor did they contemplate borrowing foreign capital for the foregoing purposes.

Having made these concessions which practically brought the views of China into line with those of Japan, and having explained in a note accompanying the reply the difficulty for China to make further concessions, the Chinese Government hoped that the Japanese Government would accept their reply of May 1, and thus bring the negotiations to an amicable conclusion.

The Japanese Government, however, expressed themselves as being dissatisfied with China's reply, and withdrew the conditional offer to restore Kiaochow to China made on April 26. It was further intimated that if the Chinese Government did not give their full compliance with the list of twenty-four demands, Japan would have recourse to drastic measures.

Upon receiving this intimation the Chinese Government, inspired by the conciliatory spirit which had been predominant from the very beginning of the negotiations and desirous of avoiding any possible rupture in the relations of the two countries, made a supreme effort to meet the situation, and represented to the Japanese Government that they would reconsider their position and make another attempt to find a solution that would be more satisfactory to Japan, in respect to those articles which China had declared could not be taken up for consideration, but to which Japan attached great importance. Even in the evening of May 6, after the Japanese Minister had notified the Chinese Government that the Ultimatum had arrived in Peking, the Chinese Government in the interests of peace still exerted efforts to save the situation by offering to meet Japan's wishes.

These overtures were again rejected, and thus exhausted the means at the disposal of the Chinese Government to prevent an *impasse*.

It is plain that the Chinese Government proceeded to the fullest extent of possible concession in view of the strong national sentiment manifested by the people throughout the whole period of negotiations. All that the Chinese Government strove to maintain was China's plenary sovereignty, the treaty rights of foreign Powers in China and the principle of equal opportunity.

To the profound regret of the Chinese Government, however, the tremendous sacrifices which they had shown themselves ready to make, proved unavailing, and an Ultimatum (the text of which is appended) was duly delivered to them by the Japanese Minister at three o'clock on the afternoon of May 7.

As to the allegations made in the Ultimatum against China, the Chinese Government hope that the foregoing outline of the history of the negotiations constitutes a clear, dispassionate, and complete reply.

In considering the nature of the course they should take with reference to the Ultimatum the Chinese Government was influenced by a desire to preserve the Chinese people, as well as the large number of foreign residents in China, from unnecessary suffering, and also to prevent the interests of friendly Powers from being imperiled. For these reasons the Chinese Government were constrained to comply in full with the terms of the Ultimatum (the reply being hereto appended), but in complying the Chinese disclaim any desire to associate themselves with any revision, which may thus be effected, of the various conventions and agreements concluded between other Powers in respect of the maintenance of China's territorial independence and integrity, the preservation of the *status quo,* and the principle of equal opportunity for the commerce and industry of all nations in China.

Memorandum Read by the Minister of Foreign Affairs to Mr. Hioki, the Japanese Minister, at a Conference Held at Waichiaopu, May 1, 1915.

The list of demands which the Japanese Government first presented to the Chinese Government consists of five Groups, the first relating to Shangtung, the second relating to South Manchuria and Eastern Inner Mongolia, the third relating to the Hanyehping Company, the fourth asking for non-alienation of the coast of the country, and the fifth relating to the questions of national advisers, national police, national arms, missionary propaganda, Yangtze Valley railways, and Fukien Province. Out of profound regard for the intentions entertained by Japan, the Chinese Government took these momentous demands into grave and careful consideration and decided to negotiate with the Japanese Government frankly and sincerely what were possible to negotiate. This is a manifestation to Japan of the most profound regard which the Chinese Government entertains for the relations between the two nations.

Ever since the opening of the negotiations China has been doing her best to hasten their progress, holding as many as three conferences a week. As regards the articles in the second group, the Chinese Government, being disposed to allow the Japanese Government to develop the economic relations of the two countries in South Manchuria, realizing that the Japanese Government attaches importance to its interests in that region, and wishing to meet the hopes of Japan, made a painful effort, without hesitation, to agree to the extension of the 25-year lease of Port Arthur and Dalny, the 36-year period of the South Manchuria railway and the 15-year period of the Antung-Mukden railway, all to 99 years; and to abandon its own cherished hopes to regain control of these places and properties at the expiration of their respective original terms of lease. It cannot but be admitted that this is a most genuine proof of China's friendship for Japan. As to the rights of opening mines in South Manchuria, the Chinese Government has already agreed to permit Japanese to work mines within the mining areas designated by Japan. China has further agreed to give Japan a right of preference in the event of borrowing foreign capital for building railways or of making a loan on the security of the local taxes in South Manchuria. The question of revising the arrangement for the Kirin-Changchun railway has been settled in accordance with the proposal made by Japan. The Chinese Government has further agreed to employ Japanese first in the event of employing foreign advisers on political, military, financial and police matters.

Furthermore, the provision about the repurchase period in the South Manchurian railway was not mentioned in Japan's original proposal. Subsequently, the Japanese Government alleging that its meaning was not clear, asked China to cancel the provision altogether. Again, Japan at first demanded the right of Japanese to carry on farming in South Manchuria, but subsequently she considered the word "farming" was not broad enough and asked to replace it with the phrase "agricultural enterprises." To these requests the Chinese Government, though well aware that the proposed changes could only benefit Japan, still acceded without delay. This, too, is a proof of China's frankness and sincerity toward Japan.

As regards matters relating to Shangtung, the Chinese Government has agreed to a majority of the demands.

The question of inland residence in South Manchuria is, in the opinion of the Chinese Government, incompatible with the treaties China has entered into with Japan and other Powers, still the Chinese Government did its best to consider how it was possible to avoid that incompatibility. At first, China suggested that the Chinese

Authorities should have full rights of jurisdiction over Japanese settlers. Japan declined to agree to it. Thereupon China reconsidered the question and revised her counter-proposal five or six times, each time making some definite concession, and went so far as to agree that all civil and criminal cases between Chinese and Japanese should be arranged according to existing treaties. Only cases relating to land or lease contracts were reserved to be adjudicated by Chinese Courts, as a mark of China's sovereignty over the region. This is another proof of China's readiness to concede as much as possible.

Eastern Inner Mongolia is not an enlightened region as yet and the conditions existing there are entirely different from those prevailing in South Manchuria. The two places, therefore, cannot be considered in the same light. Accordingly, China agreed to open commercial marts first, in the interests of foreign trade.

The Hanyehping Company mentioned in the third group is entirely a private company, and the Chinese Government is precluded from interfering with it and negotiating with another government to make any disposal of the same as the Government likes, but having regard for the interests of the Japanese capitalists, the Chinese Government agreed that whenever, in future, the said company and the Japanese capitalists should arrive at a satisfactory arrangement for coöperation, China will give her assent thereto. Thus the interests of the Japanese capitalists are amply safeguarded.

Although the demand in the fourth group asking for a declaration not to alienate China's coast is an infringement of her sovereign rights, yet the Chinese Government offered to make a voluntary pronouncement so far as it comports with China's sovereign rights. Thus, it is seen that the Chinese Government, in deference to the wishes of Japan, gave a most serious consideration even to those demands which gravely affect the sovereignty and territorial rights of China as well as the principle of equal opportunity and the treaties with foreign Powers. All this was a painful effort on the part of the Chinese Government to meet the situation—a fact of which the Japanese Government must be aware.

As regards the demands in the fifth group, they all infringe China's sovereignty, the treaty rights of other Powers or the principle of equal opportunity. Although Japan did not indicate any difference between this group and the preceding four in the list which she presented to China in respect of their character, the Chinese Government, in view of their palpably objectionable features, persuaded itself that these could not have been intended by Japan as anything other than Japan's mere advice to China. Accordingly China has declared from the very beginning that while she entertains the most profound regard for Japan's wishes, she was unable to admit that any of these matters could be made the subject of an understanding with Japan. Much as she desired to pay regard to Japan's wishes, China cannot but respect her own sovereign rights and the existing treaties with other Powers. In order to be rid of the seed for future misunderstanding and to strengthen the basis of friendship, China was constrained to iterate the reasons for refusing to negotiate on any of the articles in the fifth group, yet in view of Japan's wishes China has expressed her readiness to state that no foreign money was borrowed to construct harbor works in Fukien Province. Thus it is clear that China went so far as to seek a solution for Japan of a question that really did not admit of negotiation. Was there, then, evasion on the part of China?

Now, since the Japanese Government has presented a revised list of demands and declared at the same time that it will restore the leased territory of Kaiochow, the Chinese Government reconsiders the whole question and herewith submits a new reply to the friendly Japanese Government.

In this reply the unsettled articles in the first group are stated again for discussion. As regards the second group, those articles which have already been initialled are omitted. In connection with the question of inland residence the police regulation clause has been revised in a more restrictive sense. As for the trial of cases relating to land and lease contracts the Chinese Government now permits the Japanese Consul to send an officer to attend the proceedings. Of the four demands in connection with that part of Eastern Inner Mongolia which is within the jurisdiction of South Manchuria and the Jehol Intendency, China agrees to three. China, also, agrees to the article relating to the Hanyehping Company as revised by Japan.

It is hoped that the Japanese Government will appreciate the conciliatory spirit of the Chinese Government in making this final concession and forthwith give her assent thereto.

There is one more point. At the beginning of the present negotiations it was mutually agreed to observe secrecy, but unfortunately a few days after the presentation of the demands by Japan an Osaka newspaper published an "Extra" giving the text of the demands. The foreign and the Chinese press has since been paying considerable attention to this question and frequently publishing pro-Chinese or pro-Japanese comments in order to call forth the world's conjecture, a matter which the Chinese Government deeply regrets. The Chinese Government has never carried on any newspaper campaign and the Chinese Minister of Foreign Affairs has repeatedly declared it to the Japanese Minister.

In conclusion, the Chinese Government wishes to express its hope that the negotiations now pending between the two countries will soon come to an end and whatever misgivings foreign countries entertain toward the present situation may be quickly dispelled.

CHINA'S REPLY TO JAPAN'S REVISED DEMANDS

CHINA'S REPLY OF MAY 1, 1915, TO THE JAPANESE REVISED DEMANDS OF APRIL 26, 1915.

GROUP I

The Chinese Government and the Japanese Government, being desirous of maintaining the general peace in Eastern Asia and further strengthening the friendly relations and good neighborhood existing between the two nations, agree to the following articles:

ARTICLE 1. The Chinese Government declare that they will give full assent to all matters upon which the Japanese and German Governments may hereafter mutually agree, relating to the disposition of all interests which Germany, by virtue of treaties or recorded cases, possesses in relation to the Province of Shantung.

The Japanese Government declares that when the Chinese Government give their assent to the disposition of interests above referred to, Japan will restore the leased territory of Kiao-chou to China; and further recognize the right of the Chinese Government to participate in the negotiations referred to above between Japan and Germany.

ART. 2. The Japanese Government consent to be responsible for the indemnification of all losses occasioned by Japan's military operation around the leased territory of Kiao-chou. The customs, telegraphs and post offices within the leased territory of Kiao-chou shall, prior to the restoration of the said leased territory to China, be administered as heretofore, for the time being. The railways and telegraph lines erected by Japan for military purposes are to be removed forthwith. The Japanese troops now stationed outside the original leased territory of Kiao-chou are now to be withdrawn first, those within the original leased territory are to be withdrawn on the restoration of the said leased territory to China.

ART. 3. (Changed into an exchange of notes.)

The Chinese Government declare that within the Province of Shantung and along its coast no territory or island will be ceded or leased to any Power under any pretext.

Art. 4. The Chinese Government consent that as regards the railway to be built by China herself from Chefoo or Lungkow to connect with the Kiao-chou-Tsinanfu Railway, if Germany is willing to abandon the privilege of financing the Che-foo-Weihsien line, China will approach Japanese capitalists for a loan.

Art. 5. The Chinese Government engage, in the interest of trade and for the residence of foreigners, to open by herself as soon as possible certain suitable places in the Province of Shantung as Commercial Ports.

(Supplementary exchange of notes.)

The places which ought to be opened are to be chosen, and the regulations are to be drafted, by the Chinese Government, but the Japanese Minister must be consulted before making a decision.

Art. 6. If the Japanese and German Governments are not able to come to a definite agreement in future in their negotiations respecting transfer, etc., this provisional agreement contained in the foregoing articles shall be void.

GROUP II

The six articles which are found in Japan's Revised Demands of April 26, 1915, but omitted herein, are those already initialed by the Chinese Foreign Minister and the Japanese Minister.

The Chinese Government and the Japanese Government, with a view to developing their economic relations in South Manchuria, agree to the following articles:

Art. 2. Japanese subjects in South Manchuria may, by arrangement with the owners, lease land required for erecting suitable buildings for trade and manufacture or for agricultural enterprises.

Art. 3. Japanese subjects shall be free to reside and travel in South Manchuria and to engage in business and manufacture of any kind whatsoever.

Art. 3a. The Japanese subjects referred to in the preceding two articles, besides being required to register with the local authorities passports, which they must procure under the existing regulations, shall also observe police rules and regulations and pay taxes in the same manner as Chinese. Civil and criminal cases shall be tried and adjudicated by the authorities of the defendant's nationality and an officer can be deputed to attend the proceedings. But all cases purely between Japanese subjects, and mixed cases between Japanese and Chinese, relating to land or disputes arising from lease contracts, shall be tried and adjudicated by Chinese Authorities and the Japanese Consul may also depute an officer to attend the proceedings.

When the judicial system in the said Province is completely reformed, all the civil and criminal cases concerning Japanese subjects shall be tried entirely by Chinese law courts.

RELATING TO EASTERN INNER MONGOLIA

(To be exchanged by notes.)

ARTICLE 1. The Chinese Government declare that China will not in future pledge the taxes, other than customs and salt revenue, of that part of Eastern Inner Mongolia under the jurisdiction of South Manchuria and Jehol Intendency, as security for raising loans.

ART. 2. The Chinese Government declare that China will herself provide funds for building the railways in that part of Eastern Inner Mongolia under the jurisdiction of South Manchuria and the Jehol Intendency; if foreign capital is required, China will negotiate with Chinese capitalists first, provided this does not conflict with agreements already concluded with other Powers.

ART. 3. The Chinese Government agrees, in the interest of trade and for the residence of foreigners, to open by China herself certain suitable places in that part of Eastern Inner Mongolia under the jurisdiction of South Manchuria and the Jehol Intendency, as Commercial Marts.

The regulations for the said Commercial Marts will be made in accordance with those of other Commercial Marts opened by China herself.

GROUP III

The relations between Japan and the Hanyehping Company being very intimate, if the said Company comes to an agreement with the Japanese capitalists for coöperation, the Chinese Government shall forthwith give their consent thereto. The Chinese Government further declare that China will not convert the Company into a state enterprise, nor confiscate it nor cause it to borrow and use foreign capital other than Japanese.

LETTER TO BE ADDRESSED BY THE JAPANESE MINISTER TO THE CHINESE MINISTER OF FOREIGN AFFAIRS

Excellency:

I have the honor to state that a report has reached me that the Chinese Government have given permission to foreign nations to construct on the coast of Fukien Province dock-yards, coaling stations for military use, naval bases and other establishments for military purposes and further that the Chinese Government are borrowing foreign capital for putting up the above-mentioned construction or establishments. I shall be much obliged if the Chinese Government will inform me whether or not these reports are well founded in fact.

REPLY TO BE ADDRESSED BY THE CHINESE MINISTER OF FOREIGN AFFAIRS TO THE JAPANESE MINISTER

Excellency:

I have the honor to acknowledge the receipt of your Excellency's Note of ————————. In reply I beg to state that the Chinese Government have not given permission to foreign Powers to construct, on the coast of Fukien Province, dock-yards, coaling stations for military use, naval bases or other establishments for military purposes; nor do they contemplate borrowing foreign capital for putting up such constructions or establishments.

JAPAN'S ULTIMATUM

ULTIMATUM DELIVERED BY JAPANESE MINISTER TO MINISTER OF FOREIGN AFFAIRS AT 3 O'CLOCK P. M. ON MAY 7TH, 1915

The reason why the Imperial Government opened the present negotiations with the Chinese Government is first to endeavor to dispose of the complications arising out of the war between Japan and Germany, and secondly to attempt to solve various questions which are detrimental to the intimate relations of China and Japan with a view to solidifying the foundation of cordial friendship subsisting between the two countries to the end that the peace of the far East may be effectively and permanently preserved. With this object in view, definite proposals were presented to the Chinese Government in January of this year, and up to to-day as many as twenty-five conferences were held with the Chinese Government in perfect sincerity and frankness.

In the course of the negotiation the Imperial Government has consistently explained the aims and objects of the proposals in a conciliatory spirit, while on the other hand the proposals of the Chinese Government, whether important or unimportant, have been attended to without any reserve.

It may be stated with confidence that no effort has been spared to arrive at a satisfactory and amicable settlement of those questions.

The discussion of the entire corpus of the proposals was practically at an end at the twenty-fourth conference; that is, on 17th of the last month. The Imperial Government, taking a broad view of the negotiations and in consideration of the points raised by the Chinese Government, modified the original proposals with considerable concessions and presented to the Chinese Government on the 26th of the same month the revised proposals for agreement, and at the same time it was offered that, on the acceptance of the revised proposals, the Imperial Government would, at a suitable opportunity, restore with fair and proper conditions, to the Chinese Government the Kiao-chou territory, in the acquisition of which the Imperial Government had made a great sacrifice.

On the 1st of May, the Chinese Government delivered the reply to the revised proposals of the Japanese Government, which is contrary to the expectations of the Imperial Government. The Chinese Government not only did not give a careful consideration to the revised proposals, but even with regard to the offer of the Japanese Government, to restore Kiao-chou to the Chinese Government, the latter did not manifest the least appreciation of Japan's good will and difficulties.

From the commercial and military points of view Kiao-chou is an important place, in the acquisition of which the Japanese Empire sacrificed much blood and money, and, after the acquisition, the Empire incurs no obligation to restore it to China. But with the object of increasing the future friendly relations of the two countries, she went to the extent of proposing its restoration, yet to her great regret, the Chinese Government did not take into consideration the good intention of Japan and manifest appreciation of her difficulties. Furthermore, the Chinese Government not only ignored the friendly feelings of the Imperial Government offering the restoration of Kiao-chou Bay, but also in replying to the revised proposals they even demanded its unconditional restoration; and again China demanded that Japan should bear the responsibility of paying indemnity for all the unavoidable losses and damages resulting from Japan's military operations at Kiao-chou; and still further in connection with the territory of Kiao-chou China advanced other demands and declared that she has the right of participation at the future peace conference to be held between Japan and Germany. Although China is fully aware that the unconditional restoration of Kiao-chou and Japan's responsibility of indemnification for the unavoidable losses and damages can never be tolerated by Japan, yet she purposely advanced these demands and declared that this reply was final and decisive.

Since Japan could not tolerate such demands, the settlement of the other question, however compromising it may be, would not be to her interest. The consequence is that the present reply of the Chinese Government is, on the whole, vague and meaningless.

Furthermore, in the reply of the Chinese Government to the other proposals in the revised list of the Imperial Government, such as South Manchuria and Eastern Inner Mongolia, where Japan particularly has geographical, political, commercial, industrial and strategic relations, as recognized by all the nations, and made more remarkable in consequence of the two wars in which Japan was engaged, the Chinese Government overlooks these facts and does not respect Japan's position in that place. The Chinese Government even freely altered those articles which the Imperial Government, in a compromising spirit, have formulated in accordance with the statement of the Chinese Representatives thereby making the statements of the Representatives an empty talk; or on seeing them conceding with the one hand and withholding with the other, it is very difficult to attribute faithfulness and sincerity to the Chinese Authorities.

As regards the articles relating to the employment of advisers, the establishment of schools and hospitals, the supply of arms and ammunition and the establishment of arsenals, and railway concessions in South China in the revised proposals, they are either proposed with the proviso that the consent of the Power concerned must first be obtained, or they are merely to be recorded in the minutes in accordance with the statement of the Chinese delegates, and thus they are not in the least in conflict either with Chinese sovereignty or her treaties with the Foreign Powers. Yet the Chinese Government in their reply to the proposals, alleging that these proposals are incompatible with their sovereign rights and the Treaties with the Foreign Powers, defeat the expectations of the Imperial Government. In spite of such attitude of the Chinese Government, the Imperial Government, though regretting to see that there is no room for further negotiation, yet warmly attached to the preservation of the peace of the far East, is still hoping for a satisfactory settlement in order to avoid the disturbance of the relations.

So in spite of the circumstances which admitted no patience, they have reconsidered the feelings of the Government of their neighboring country and with the exception of the article relating to Fukien, which is to be the subject of an exchange of notes as has already been agreed upon by the Representatives of both nations, will undertake to detach the Group V from the present negotiations and discuss it separately in the future. Therefore the Chinese Government should appreciate the friendly feelings of the Imperial Government by immediately accepting without any alteration all the articles of Groups I, II, III and IV and the exchange of notes in connection with Fukien Province in Group V as contained in the revised proposals presented on the 26th of April.

The Imperial Government hereby again offer their advice and hope that the Chinese Government upon this advice will give a satisfactory reply by 6 o'clock p. m. on the 9th day of May. It is hereby declared that if no satisfactory reply is received before or at the designated time, the Imperial Government will take steps they may deem necessary.

JAPAN'S EXPLANATORY NOTE

EXPLANATORY NOTE ACCOMPANYING MEMORANDUM DELIVERED TO THE MINISTER OF FOREIGN AFFAIRS BY THE JAPANESE MINISTER THE SEVENTH DAY OF MAY, 1915

1. With the exception of the question of Fukien to be arranged by an exchange of notes, the five articles postponed for later negotiations refer to (a) the employment of advisers, (b) the establishment of schools and hospitals, (c) the railway concessions in South China, (d) the supply of arms and ammunition and the establishment of arsenals, (e) the propagation of Buddhism.

2. The acceptance by the Chinese Government of the article relating to Fukien may be either in the form as proposed by the Minister of Japan on the 26th of April or in that contained in the Reply of the Chinese Government of May 1st. Although the Ultimatum calls for the immediate acceptance by China of the modified proposals presented on April 26th, without alteration, but it should be noted that it merely states the principle and does not apply to this article and articles 4 and 5 of this note.

3. If the Chinese Government accept all the articles as demanded in the Ultimatum the offer of the Japanese Government to restore Kiao-chou to China made on the 26th of April, will still hold good.

4. Article 2 of Group II relating to the lease or purchase of land, the terms "lease" and "purchase" may be replaced by these terms, "temporary lease" and "perpetual lease" or "lease on consultations," which means a long-term lease with its unconditional renewal.

Article 4 of Group II relating to the approval of laws and ordinances and local taxes by the Chinese Consul may form the subject of a secret agreement.

5. The phrase "to consult with the Japanese Government" in connection with questions of pledging the local taxes for raising loans and the loans for construction of railways, in Eastern Inner Mongolia, which is similar to the agreement in Manchuria relating to the matters of the same kind, may be replaced by the phrase "to consult with the Japanese capitalists."

The article relating to the opening of trade marts in Eastern Inner

Mongolia in respect to location and regulations, may, following the precedent set in Shantung, be the subject of an exchange of notes.

6. From the phrase "those interested in the Company" in Group III of the revised list of demands, the words "those interested in" may be deleted.

7. The Japanese version of the Formal Agreement and its annexes shall be the official text or both the Chinese and Japanese shall be official texts.

CHINA'S REPLY TO THE ULTIMATUM

THE REPLY OF THE CHINESE GOVERNMENT TO THE ULTIMATUM OF THE JAPANESE GOVERNMENT, DELIVERED TO THE JAPANESE MINISTER OF FOREIGN AFFAIRS ON THE 8TH OF MAY, 1915

On the 7th of this month, at three o'clock p. m., the Chinese Government received an Ultimatum from the Japanese Government together with an Explanatory Note of seven articles. The Ultimatum concluded with the hope that the Chinese Government up to 6 o'clock p. m. on the 9th of May, will give a satisfactory reply, and it is hereby declared that if no satisfactory reply is received before or at the designated time, the Japanese Government will take steps she may deem necessary.

The Chinese Government with a view to preserving the peace of the far East, hereby accepts, with the exception of those five articles of Group V postponed for later negotiation, all the articles of Groups I, II, III and IV, and the exchange of Notes in connection with Fukien Province in Group V as contained in the revised proposals presented on the 26th of April and in accordance with the Explanatory Note of seven articles accompanying the Ultimatum of the Japanese Government with the hope that thereby all outstanding questions are settled, so that the cordial relationship between the two countries may be further consolidated. The Japanese Minister is hereby requested to appoint a day to call at the Ministry of Foreign Affairs to make the literary improvement of the text and sign the Agreement as soon as possible.

APPENDIX S

NEW TREATIES AND NOTES

BETWEEN

CHINA AND JAPAN

(Translated from the Chinese)

TREATY RESPECTING THE PROVINCE OF SHANTUNG

His Excellency the President of the Republic of China and His Majesty the Emperor of Japan, having resolved to conclude a Treaty with a view to the maintenance of general peace in the Extreme East and the further strengthening of the relations of friendship and good neighborhood now existing between the two nations, have for that purpose named as their Plenipotentiaries, that is to say:

His Excellency the President of the Republic of China, Lou Tseng-tsiang, *Chung-ching*, First Class *Chia Ho* Decoration, Minister of Foreign Affairs.

And His Majesty the Emperor of Japan, Hioki Eki, *Jushii*, Second Class of the Imperial Order of the Sacred Treasure, Minister Plenipotentiary, and Envoy Extraordinary:

Who, after having communicated to each other their full powers and found them to be in good and due form, have agreed upon and concluded the following Articles:—

ARTICLE 1. The Chinese Government agrees to give full assent to all matters upon which the Japanese Government may hereafter agree with the German Government relating to the disposition of all rights, interests and concessions which Germany, by virtue of treaties or otherwise, possesses in relation to the Province of Shantung.

ART. 2. The Chinese Government agrees that as regards the railway to be built by China herself from Chefoo or Lungkow to connect with the Kiao-chou-Tsinanfu railway, if Germany abandons the privilege of financing the Chefoo-Weihsien line, China will approach Japanese capitalists to negotiate for a loan.

ART 3. The Chinese Government agrees in the interest of trade and for the residence of foreigners, to open by China herself as soon as possible certain suitable places in the Province of Shantung as Commercial Ports.

ART. 4. The present treaty shall come into force on the day of its signature.

The present treaty shall be ratified by His Excellency the President of the Republic of China and His Majesty the Emperor of Japan, and the ratification therof shall be exchanged at Tokio as soon as possible.

In witness whereof the respective Plenipotentiaries of the High Contracting Parties have signed and sealed the present Treaty, two copies in the Chinese language and two in Japanese.

Done at Peking this twenty-fifth day of the fifth month of the fourth year of the Republic of China, corresponding to the same day of the same month of the fourth year of Taisho.

EXCHANGE OF NOTES RESPECTING SHANTUNG

Peking, the 25th day of the 5th month of the 4th year of the Republic of China.

Monsieur le Ministre,

In the name of the Chinese Government I have the honor to make the following declaration to your Government:—"Within the Province of Shantung or along its coast no territory or island will be leased or ceded to any foreign Power under any pretext."

I avail, etc.,

(Signed) LOU TSENG-TSIANG.

His Excellency,
Hioki Eki,
Japanese Minister.

REPLY

Peking, the 25th day of the 5th month of the 4th year of Taisho.

Excellency,

I have the honor to acknowledge the receipt of Your Excellency's note of this day's date in which you made the following declaration in the name of the Chinese Government:—"Within the Province of Shantung or along its coast no territory or island will be leased or ceded to any foreign Power under any pretext."

In reply I beg to state that I have taken note of this declaration.

I avail, etc.,

(Signed) HIOKI EKI.

His Excellency,
Lou Tseng-tsiang,
Minister Foreign Affairs.

EXCHANGE OF NOTES RESPECTING THE OPENING OF PORTS IN SHANTUNG

Peking, the 25th day of the 5th month of the
4th year of the Republic of China.

Monsieur le Ministre,

I have the honor to state that the places which ought to be opened as Commercial Ports by China herself, as provided in Article 3 of the Treaty respecting the Province of Shantung signed this day, will be selected and the regulations therefor will be drawn up, by the Chinese Government itself, a decision concerning which will be made after consulting the Minister of Japan.

I avail, etc.,

(Signed) LOU TSENG-TSIANG.

REPLY

Peking, the 25th day of the 5th month of the
4th year of Taisho.

Excellency,

I have the honor to acknowledge the receipt of Your Excellency's note of this day's date in which you stated "that the places which ought to be opened as Commercial Ports by China herself, as provided in Article 3 of the Treaty respecting the province of Shantung signed this day, will be selected and the regulations therefor will be drawn up, by the Chinese Government itself, a decision concerning which will be made after consulting the Minister of Japan."

In reply, I beg to state that I have taken note of the same.

I avail, etc.,

(Signed) HIOKI EKI.

His Excellency,
    Lou Tseng-tsiang,
        Minister of Foreign Affairs.

EXCHANGE OF NOTES RESPECTING THE RESTORATION OF THE LEASED TERRITORY OF KIAO-CHOU BAY

Peking, the 25th day of the 5th month of the
4th year of Taisho.

Excellency,

In the name of my Government I have the honor to make the following declaration to the Chinese Government:—

When, after the termination of the present war, the leased territory of Kiao-chou Bay is completely left to the free disposal of

Japan, the Japanese Government will restore the said leased territory to China under the following conditions:—

1. The whole of Kiao-chou Bay to be opened as a Commercial Port.

2. A concession under the exclusive jurisdiction of Japan to be established at a place designated by the Japanese Government.

3. If the foreign Powers desire it, an international concession may be established.

4. As regards the disposal to be made of the buildings and properties of Germany and the conditions and procedure relating thereto, the Japanese Government and the Chinese Government shall arrange the matter by mutual agreement before the restoration.

I avail, etc.,

(Signed) HIOKI EKI.

His Excellency,
   Lou Tseng-tsiang,
     Minister of Foreign Affairs.

REPLY

Peking, the 25th day of the 5th month of the 4th year of the Republic of China.

Monsieur le Ministre,

I have the honor to acknowledge the receipt of your Excellency's note of this day's date in which you made the following declaration in the name of your Government:—

"When, after the termination of the present war, the leased territory of Kiao-chou Bay is completely left to the free disposal of Japan, the Japanese Government will restore the said leased territory to China under the following conditions:—

"1. The whole of Kiao-chou Bay to be opened as a Commercial Port.

"2. A concession under the exclusive jurisdiction of Japan to be established at a place designated by the Japanese Government.

"3. If the foreign Powers desire it, an international concession may be established.

"4. As regards the disposal to be made of the buildings and properties of Germany and the conditions and procedure relating thereto, the Japanese Government and the Chinese Government shall arrange the matter by mutual agreement before the restoration."

In reply, I beg to state that I have taken note of this declaration.

I avail, etc.,

(Signed) LOU TSENG-TSIANG.

Treaty Respecting South Manchuria and Eastern Inner Mongolia

His Excellency the President of the Republic of China and His Majesty the Emperor of Japan, having resolved to conclude a Treaty with a view to developing their economic relations in South Manchuria and Eastern Inner Mongolia, have for that purpose named as their Plenipotentiaries, that is to say:

His Excellency the President of the Republic of China, Lou Tseng-tsiang, *Chung-ching*, First Class *Chia-ho* Decoration, and Minister of Foreign Affairs; and His Majesty the Emperor of Japan, Hioki Eki, *Jushii*, Second Class of the Imperial Order of the Sacred Treasure, Minister Plenipotentiary and Envoy Extraordinary;

Who, after having communicated to each other their full powers, and found them to be in good and due form, have agreed upon and concluded the following Articles:—

ARTICLE 1. The Two High Contracting Parties agree that the term of lease of Port Arthur and Dalny and the terms of the South Manchuria Railway and the Antung-Mukden Railway, shall be extended to 99 years.

ART. 2. Japanese subjects in South Manchuria may, by negotiation, lease land necessary for erecting suitable buildings for trade and manufacture or for prosecuting agricultural enterprises.

ART. 3. Japanese subjects shall be free to reside and travel in South Manchuria and to engage in business and manufacture of any kind whatsoever.

ART. 4. In the event of Japanese and Chinese desiring jointly to undertake agricultural enterprises and industries incidental thereto, the Chinese Government may give its permission.

ART. 5. The Japanese subjects referred to in the preceding three articles, besides being required to register with the local Authorities passports which they must procure under the existing regulations, shall also submit to the police laws and ordinances and taxation of China.

Civil and criminal cases in which the defendants are Japanese shall be tried and adjudicated by the Japanese Consul; those in which the defendants are Chinese shall be tried and adjudicated by Chinese Authorities. In either case an officer may be deputed to the court to attend the proceedings. But mixed civil cases between Chinese and Japanese relating to land shall be tried and adjudicated by delegates of both nations conjointly in accordance with Chinese law and local usage.

When, in future, the judicial system in the said region is completely reformed, all civil and criminal cases concerning Japanese subjects shall be tried and adjudicated entirely by Chinese law courts.

ART. 6. The Chinese Government agrees, in the interest of trade and for the residence of foreigners, to open by China herself, as soon as possible, certain suitable places in Eastern Inner Mongolia as Commercial Ports.

ART. 7. The Chinese Government agrees speedily to make a fundamental revision of the Kirin-Changchun Railway Loan-Agreement, taking as a standard the provisions in railway agreements made heretofore between China and foreign financiers.

When in future, more advantageous terms than those in existing railway loan agreements are granted to foreign financiers in connection with railway loans, the above agreement shall again be revised in accordance with Japan's wishes.

ART. 8. All existing treaties between China and Japan relating to Manchuria shall, except where otherwise provided for by this Treaty, remain in force.

ART. 9. The present Treaty shall come into force on the date of its signature. The present Treaty shall be ratified by His Excellency the President of the Republic of China and His Majesty the Emperor of Japan, and the ratifications thereof shall be exchanged at Tokio as soon as possible.

In witness whereof the respective Plenipotentiaries of the two High Contracting Parties have signed and sealed the present Treaty, two copies in the Chinese language and two in Japanese.

Done at Peking this twenty-fifth day of the fifth month of the fourth year of the Republic of China, corresponding to the same day of the same month of the fourth year of Taisho.

EXCHANGE OF NOTES RESPECTING THE TERMS OF LEASE OF PORT ARTHUR AND DALNY AND THE TERMS OF SOUTH MANCHURIAN AND ANTUNG-MUKDEN RAILWAYS

Peking, the 25th day of the 5th month of the 4th year of the Republic of China.

Monsieur le Ministre,

I have the honor to state that, respecting the provisions contained in Article 1 of the Treaty relating to South Manchuria and Eastern Inner Mongolia, signed this day, the term of lease of Port Arthur and Dalny shall expire in the 86th year of the Republic or 1997. The date for restoring the South Manchuria Railway to China shall fall due in the 91st year of the Republic or 2002. Article 21 in the Original South Manchurian Railway Agreement providing that it may be redeemed by China after 36 years from the day on which the traffic is opened is hereby canceled.   The term of the Antung-Mukden Railway shall expire in the 96th year of the Republic or 2007.

I avail, etc.,

His Excellency,   (Signed) Lou Tseng-tsiang.
  Hioki Eki,
    Japanese Minister.

REPLY

Peking, the 25th day of the 5th month of the
4th year of Taisho.

Excellency,

I have the honor to acknowledge the receipt of Your Excellency's note of this day's date in which you stated that "respecting the provisions contained in Article 1 of the Treaty relating to South Manchuria and Eastern Inner Mongolia, signed this day, the term of lease of Port Arthur and Dalny shall expire in the 86th year of the Republic or 1997.   The date for restoring the South Manchurian Railway to China shall fall due in the 91st year of the Republic or 2002.   Article 12 in the original South Manchurian Railway Agreement providing that it may be redeemed by China after 36 years from the day on which the traffic is opened, is hereby canceled.   The term of the Antung-Mukden Railway shall expire in the 96th year of the Republic or 2007."

In reply I beg to state that I have taken note of the same.

I avail, etc.,

His Excellency,   (Signed) Hioki Eki.
  Lou Tseng-tsiang,
    Minister of Foreign Affairs.

EXCHANGE OF NOTES RESPECTING THE OPENING OF PORTS IN EASTERN
INNER MONGOLIA

Peking, the 25th day of the 5th month of the
4th year of the Republic of China.

Monsieur le Ministre,

I have the honor to state that the places which ought to be opened as Commercial Ports by China herself, as provided in Article 6 of the Treaty respecting South Manchuria and Eastern Inner Mongolia signed this day, will be selected, and the regulations therefor will be drawn up, by the Chinese Government itself, a decision concerning which will be made after consulting the Minister of Japan.

I avail, etc.,

His Excellency,   (Signed) Lou Tseng-tsiang.
  Hioki Eki,
    Japanese Minister.

Reply

Peking, the 25th day of the 5th month of the 4th year of Taisho.

Excellency,

I have the honor to acknowledge the receipt of Your Excellency's note of this day's date in which you stated "that the places which ought to be opened as Commercial Ports by China herself, as provided in Article 6 of the Treaty respecting South Manchuria and Eastern Inner Mongolia signed this day, will be selected, and the regulations therefor, will be drawn up, by the Chinese Government itself, a decision concerning which will be made after consulting the Minister of Japan."

In reply, I beg to state that I have taken note of the same.

I avail, etc.,   (Signed) HIOKI EKI.

His Excellency, Lou Tseng-tsiang,
Minister of Foreign Affairs.

South Manchuria

Peking, the 25th day of the 5th month of the 4th year of the Republic of China.

Monsieur le Ministre,

I have the honor to state that Japanese subjects shall, as soon as possible, investigate and select mines in the mining areas in South Manchuria specified hereinunder, except those being prospected for or worked, and the Chinese Government will then permit them to prospect or work the same; but before the Mining regulations are definitely settled, the practice at present in force shall be followed.

Fengtien.

LOCALITY	DISTRICT	MINERAL
Niu Hsin T'ai	Pen-hsi	Coal
Tien Shih Fu Kou	"	"
Sha Sung Kang	Hai-lung	"
T'ieh Ch'ang	Tung-hua	"
Nuan Ti T'ang	Chin	"
An Shan Chan region	From Liaoyang to Pen-hsi	Iron

Kirin (Southern portion)

		Coal & Iron
Sha Sung Kang	Ho-lung	Coal
Kang Yao	Chi-lin (Kirin)	Gold
Chia P'i Kou	Hua-tien	

I avail, etc.,

His Excellency, Hioki Eki,   (Signed) LOU TSENG-TSIANG.
Japanese Minister.

REPLY

Peking, the 25th day of the 5th month of the 4th year of Taisho.

Excellency,

I have the honor to acknowledge the receipt of Your Excellency's note of this day respecting the opening of mines in South Manchuria, stating: "Japanese subjects shall, as soon as possible, investigate and select mines in the mining areas in South Manchuria specified hereinunder except those being prospected for or worked, and the Chinese Government will then permit them to prospect or work the same; but before the Mining regulations are definitely settled, the practice at present in force shall be followed."

Fengtien.

LOCALITY	DISTRICT	MINERAL
Niu Hsin T'ai	Pen-hsi	Coal
Tien Shih Fu Kou	"	"
Sha Sung Kang	Hai-lung	"
T'ieh Ch'ang	Tung-hua	"
Nuan Ti T'ang	Chin	"
An Shan Chan region	From Liaoyang to Pen-hsi	Iron

Kirin (Southern portion)

Sha Sung Kang	Ho-lung	Coal & Iron
Kang Yao	Chi-lin (Kirin)	Coal
Chia P'i Kou	Hua-tien	Gold

I avail, etc.,

His Excellency,   (Signed) HIOKI EKI.
    Lou Tseng-tsiang,
    Minister of Foreign Affairs of the Republic of China.

EXCHANGE OF NOTES RESPECTING RAILWAYS AND TAXES IN SOUTH MANCHURIA AND EASTERN INNER MONGOLIA

Peking, the 25th day of the 5th month of the 4th year of the Republic of China.

Monsieur le Ministre,

In the name of my Government,

I have the honor to make the following declaration to your Government:—

China will hereafter provide funds for building necessary railways in South Manchuria and Eastern Inner Mongolia; if foreign capital is required China may negotiate for a loan with Japanese capitalists first: and further, the Chinese Government, when making a loan in future on the security of the taxes in the above-mentioned places (excluding the salt and customs revenue which have already been pledged by the Chinese Central Government) may negotiate for it with Japanese capitalists first.

I avail, etc.,

His Excellency,   (Signed) LOU TSENG-TSIANG.
  Hioki Eki,
    Japanese Minister.

REPLY

Peking, the 25th day of the 5th month of the 4th year of Taisho.

Excellency,

I have the honor to acknowledge the receipt of Your Excellency's note of this day's date respecting railways and taxes in South Manchuria and Eastern Inner Mongolia in which you stated:

"China will hereafter provide funds for building necessary railways in South Manchuria and Eastern Inner Mongolia; if foreign capital is required China may negotiate for a loan with Japanese capitalists first; and further, the Chinese Government, when making a loan in future on the security of taxes in the above mentioned places (excluding the salt and customs revenue which have already been pledged by the Chinese Central Government) may negotiate for it with Japanese Capitalists first."

In reply I beg to state that I have taken note of the same.

I avail, etc.,

His Excellency,   (Signed) HIOKI EKI.
  Lou Tseng-tsiang,
    Minister of Foreign Affairs.

EXCHANGE OF NOTES RESPECTING THE EMPLOYMENT OF ADVISERS IN SOUTH MANCHURIA

Peking, the 25th day of the 5th month of the 4th year of the Republic of China.

Monsieur le Ministre,

In the name of the Chinese Government, I have the honor to make the following declaration to your Government:—

"Hereafter, if foreign advisers or instructors on political, financial, military or police matters are to be employed in South Manchuria, Japanese may be employed first."

I avail, etc.,

His Excellency,   (Signed) LOU TSENG-TSIANG.
  Hioki Eki,
    Japanese Minister.

REPLY

Peking, the 25th day of the 5th month of the 4th year of Taisho.

Excellency,

I have the honor to acknowledge the receipt of Your Excellency's note of this day's date in which you made the following declaration in the name of your Government:—

"Hereafter if foreign advisers or instructors in political, military or police matters are to be employed in South Manchuria, Japanese may be employed first."

In reply, I beg to state that I have taken note of the same.

I avail, etc.,

(Signed) HIOKI EKI.

His Excellency,
    Lou Tseng-tsiang,
        Minister of Foreign Affairs.

EXCHANGE OF NOTES RESPECTING THE EXPLANATION OF "LEASE BY NEGOTIATION" IN SOUTH MANCHURIA

Peking, the 25th day of the 5th month of the 4th year of Taisho.

Excellency,

I have the honor to state that the term "lease by negotiation" contained in Article 2 of the Treaty respecting South Manchuria and Eastern Inner Mongolia signed this day shall be understood to imply a long-term lease of not more than thirty years and also the possibility of its unconditional renewal.

I avail, etc.,

(Signed) HIOKI EKI.

His Excellency,
    Lou Tseng-tsiang,
        Minister of Foreign Affairs.

REPLY

Peking, the 25th day of the 5th month of the 4th year of the Republic of China.

Monsieur le Ministre,

I have the honor to acknowledge the receipt of Your Excellency's note of this day's date in which you state:

"The term 'lease by negotiation' contained in Article 2 of the Treaty respecting South Manchuria and Eastern Inner Mongolia signed this day shall be understood to imply a long-term lease of not more than thirty years and also the possibility of its unconditional renewal."

In reply I beg to state that I have taken note of the same.

I avail, etc.,

(Signed) LOU TSENG-TSIANG.

His Excellency,
    Hioki Eki,
        Japanese Minister.

EXCHANGE OF NOTES RESPECTING THE ARRANGEMENT FOR POLICE LAWS AND ORDINANCES AND TAXATION IN SOUTH MANCHURIA AND EASTERN INNER MONGOLIA

Peking, the 25th day of the 5th month of the 4th year of the Republic of China.

Monsieur le Ministre,

I have the honor to state that the Chinese Authorities will notify the Japanese Consul of the police laws and ordinances and the taxation to which Japanese subjects shall submit according to Article 5 of the Treaty respecting South Manchuria and Eastern Inner Mongolia signed this day so as to come to an understanding with him before their enforcement.

I avail, etc.,

His Excellency,   (Signed) LOU TSENG-TSIANG.
    Hioki Eki,
        Japanese Minister.

REPLY

Peking, the 25th day of the 5th month of the 4th year of Taisho.

Excellency,

I have the honor to acknowledge the receipt of Your Excellency's note of this day's date in which you state:

"The Chinese Authorities will notify the Japanese Consul of the police laws and ordinances and the taxation to which Japanese subjects shall submit according to Article 5 of the Treaty respecting South Manchuria and Eastern Inner Mongolia signed this day so as to come to an understanding with him before their enforcement."

In reply, I beg to state that I have taken note of the same.

I avail, etc.,

His Excellency,   (Signed) HIOKI EKI.
    Lou Tseng-tsiang,
        Minister of Foreign Affairs.

The Postponement of Articles 2, 3, 4 and 5 of the Treaty Respecting South Manchuria and Eastern Inner Mongolia

> Peking, the 25th day of the 5th month of the
> 4th year of the Republic of China.

Monsieur le Ministre,

I have the honor to state that, inasmuch as preparations have to be made regarding Articles 2, 3, 4 & 5 of the Treaty respecting South Manchuria and Eastern Inner Mongolia signed this day, the Chinese Government proposes that the operation of the said Articles be postponed for a period of three months beginning from the date of the signing of the said Treaty.

I hope your Government will agree to this proposal.

> I avail, etc.,
> (Signed) Lou Tseng-tsiang.

His Excellency,
　Hioki Eki,
　　Japanese Minister.

Reply

> Peking, the 25th day of the 5th month of the
> 4th year of Taisho.

Excellency,

I have the honor to acknowledge the receipt of Your Excellency's note of this day's date in which you stated that, "inasmuch as preparations have to be made regarding Articles 2, 3, 4 & 5 of the Treaty respecting South Manchuria and Eastern Inner Mongolia signed this day, the Chinese Government proposes that the operation of the said Articles be postponed for a period of three months beginning from the date of the signing of the said Treaty."

In reply, I beg to state that I have taken note of the same.

> I avail, etc.,
> (Signed) Hioki Eki.

His Excellency,
　Lou Tseng-tsiang,
　　Minister of Foreign Affairs.

Exchange of Notes Respecting the Matter of Hanyehping

> Peking, the 25th day of the 5th month of the
> 4th year of the Republic of China.

Monsieur le Ministre,

I have the honor to state that if in future the Hanyehping Company and the Japanese capitalists agree upon coöperation, the Chinese

Government, in view of the intimate relations subsisting between the Japanese capitalists and the said Company, will forthwith give its permission. The Chinese Government further agrees not to confiscate the said Company, nor without the consent of the Japanese capitalists to convert it into a state enterprise, nor cause it to borrow and use foreign capital other than Japanese.

I avail, etc.,

(Signed) LOU TSENG-TSIANG.

His Excellency,
   Hioki Eki,
      Japanese Minister.

REPLY

Peking, the 25th day of the 5th month of the 4th year of Taisho.

Excellency,

I have the honor to acknowledge the receipt of Your Excellency's note of this day's date in which you state:

"If in future the Hanyehping Company and the Japanese capitalists agree upon coöperation, the Chinese Government, in view of the intimate relations subsisting between the Japanese Capitalists and the said Company, will forthwith give its permission. The Chinese Government further agrees not to confiscate the said Company, nor, without the consent of the Japanese capitalists to convert it into a state enterprise, nor cause it to borrow and use foreign capital other than Japanese."

In reply, I beg to state that I have taken note of the same.

I avail, etc.,

(Signed) HIOKI EKI.

His Excellency,
   Lou Tseng-tsiang,
      Minister of Foreign Affairs.

EXCHANGE OF NOTES RESPECTING THE FUKIEN QUESTION

Peking, the 25th day of the 5th month of the 4th year of Taisho.

Excellency,

A report has reached me to the effect that the Chinese Government has the intention of permitting foreign nations to establish, on the coast of Fukien Province, dock-yards, coaling stations for military use, naval bases, or to set up other military establishments; and also of borrowing foreign capital for the purpose of setting up the above-mentioned establishments.

I have the honor to request that your Excellency will be good enough to give me a reply stating whether or not the Chinese Government really entertains such an intention.

I avail, etc.,

(Signed) Hioki Eki.

His Excellency,
    Lou Tseng-tsiang,
        Minister of Foreign Affairs.

Reply

Peking, the 25th day of the 5th month of the 4th year of the Republic of China.

Monsieur le Ministre,

I have the honor to acknowledge the receipt of Your Excellency's note of this day's date, which I have noted.

In reply I beg to inform you that the Chinese Government hereby declares that it has given no permission to foreign nations to construct, on the coast of Fukien Province, dock-yards, coaling stations for military use, naval bases, or to set up other military establishments; nor does it entertain an intention of borrowing foreign capital for the purpose of setting up the above-mentioned establishments.

I avail, etc.,

(Signed) Lou Tseng-tsiang.

His Excellency,
    Hioki Eki,
        Japanese Minister.

APPENDIX T

JAPAN IN SHANTUNG

LETTER FROM REV. E. W. THWING, SUPERINTENDENT OF THE INTERNATIONAL REFORM BUREAU, PUBLISHED IN THE "CHINA PRESS," NOVEMBER 25, 1914

Editor, the "China Press,"

Sir.—I have just received the following letter from a missionary in Shantung, which may be of interest.

Shantung, November 20, 1914.

Mr. E. W. Thwing,

Peking, China.

My dear Mr. Thwing:

I have just read with much interest your article in the "China Press" of November 11, relative to America and China in the Pacific. I am glad you said what you did about the outrageous conduct and mistreatment of Chinese by the Japanese in Shantung. The English have in some cases tried to deny the reports, and the Japanese have made a greater effort to do so, but they remain. I believe that if our British friends knew the facts as they are they would be strong in their condemnation. We here, were not willing to sit and see our Chinese friends so badly mistreated and not open our mouths, and I voiced the opinion of the whole station in giving what information I made public, but some members of our Mission thought this unwise —those outside of the area who did not realize how bad conditions were—but, as you say, *"the worst has not been told."*

I have received a clipping from the "New York World" giving a statement from the Japanese Ambassador Chinda (despatch from Washington), in which he denies all reports about conduct of Japanese in the Province of Shantung. I hope very much that you will send a copy of your letter, in the "China Press," to the "World," or ask that they copy it as published. As a prominent British friend in Shantung wrote me, the truth will *do good,* and it has done good, for the Japanese were more careful after receiving requests from the British at Tsingtau to be more considerate.

We are just now in the midst of a most encouraging revival and evangelistic meeting here inside the city.

This letter shows the real reason, for the article referred to, which is simply to give publicity to known facts, in the hope that conditions may be improved, or future evils prevented. As in the campaign against opium, the facts only need to be known widely enough to bring a remedy. We owe much to the "China Press" for so fairly stating facts on both sides of many questions and this does not indicate an unfriendly spirit towards any people, or any nation.

Yours truly,

E. W. THWING.

Peking, November 27.

APPENDIX U

IDENTIC NOTES EXCHANGED BETWEEN THE UNITED KINGDOM AND RUSSIA WITH REGARD TO THEIR RESPECTIVE RAILWAY INTERESTS IN CHINA

April 28, 1899.

Sir C. Scott to Count Mouravieff

The undersigned, British Ambassador, duly authorized to that effect, has the honor to make the following declaration to His Excellency Count Mouravieff, Russian Minister for Foreign Affairs.

Great Britain and Russia, animated by a sincere desire to avoid in China all cause of conflict on questions where their interests meet, and taking into consideration the economic and geographical gravitation of certain parts of that Empire, have agreed as follows:

1. Great Britain engages not to seek for her own account, or on behalf of British subjects or of others, any railway concessions to the north of the Great Wall of China, and not to obstruct, directly or indirectly, applications for railway concessions in that region supported by the Russian Government.

2. Russia, on her part, engages not to seek for her own account, or on behalf of Russian subjects or of others, any railway concessions in the basin of the Yangtze and not to obstruct, directly or indirectly, applications for railway concessions in that region supported by the British Government.

The two Contracting Parties, having nowise in view to infringe in any way the sovereign rights of China or existing Treaties, will not fail to communicate to the Chinese Government the present arrangement, which, by averting all cause of complications between them, is of a nature to consolidate peace in the far East, and to serve the primordial interests of China herself.

CHARLES S. SCOTT.

St. Petersburg, April 28, 1899.

Sir C. Scott to Count Mouravieff

In order to complete the notes exchanged this day respecting the partition of spheres for concessions for the construction and working of railways in China, it has been agreed to record in the present additional note the agreement arrived at with regard to the line Shanhaikwan-Newchwang, for the construction of which a loan has been already contracted by the Chinese Government with the Shanghai-Hongkong Bank, acting on behalf of the British and Chinese Corporation.

The general arrangement established by the above-mentioned notes is not to infringe in any way the rights acquired under the said Loan Contract, and the Chinese Government may appoint both an English engineer and an European accountant to supervise the construction of the line in question, and the expenditure of the money appropriated to it.

But it remains understood that this fact cannot be taken as constituting a right of property or foreign control, and that the line in question is to remain a Chinese line, under the control of the Chinese Government, and cannot be mortgaged or alienated to a non-Chinese Company.

As regards the branch line from Siaohieshan to Sinmintin, in addition to the aforesaid restrictions, it has been agreed that it is to be constructed by China herself, who may permit European—not necessarily British—engineers to periodically inspect it, and to verify and certify that the work is being properly executed.

The present special agreement is naturally not to interfere in any way with the right of the Russian Government to support, if it thinks fit, applications of Russian subjects or establishments for concessions for railways, which, starting from the main Manchurian line in a southwesterly direction, would traverse the region in which the Chinese line terminating at Sinmintin and Newchwang is to be constructed.

CHARLES S. SCOTT.

St. Petersburg, April 28, 1899.

The same, *mutatis mutandis,* was sent the same day by Count Mouravieff, Russian Minister for Foreign Affairs, to Sir Charles Scott.

APPENDIX V

DECLARATION BETWEEN GREAT BRITAIN AND FRANCE, WITH REGARD TO THE KINGDOM OF SIAM AND OTHER MATTERS (ADVANTAGES IN YUNNAN AND SZECHUEN; TERRITORIES TO THE WEST OF THE LOWER NIGER; COMMERCIAL ARRANGEMENTS IN TUNIS)

SIGNED AT LONDON, JANUARY 15, 1896.

The Undersigned, duly authorized by their respective Governments, have signed the following Declaration:

I. The Governments of Great Britain and France engage to one another that neither of them will, without the consent of the other, in any case, or under any pretext, advance their armed forces into the region which is comprised in the basins of the Petcha Bouri, Mieklong, Menam and Bang Pa Kong (Petriou) Rivers and their respective tributaries, together with the extent of coast from Muong Bang Tapan to Muong Pase, the basins of the rivers on which these two places are situated, and the basins of the other rivers, the estuaries of which are included in that coast; and including also the territory lying to the north of the basin of the Menam, and situated between the Anglo-Siamese frontier, the Mekong River, and the eastern watershed of the Me Ing. They further engage not to acquire within this region any special privilege or advantage which shall not be enjoyed in common by, or equally open to, Great Britain and France and their nationals and dependents. These stipulations, however, shall not be interpreted as derogating from the special clauses which, in virtue of the Treaty concluded on the 3rd October, 1893, between France and Siam, apply to a zone of 25 kilom. on the right bank of the Mekong and to the navigation of that river.

II. Nothing in the foregoing clause shall hinder any action on which the two Powers may agree, and which they shall think necessary in order to uphold the independence of the Kingdom of Siam. But they engage not to enter into any separate Agreement permitting a third Power to take any action from which they are bound by the present Declaration themselves to abstain.

III. From the mouth of the Nam Houk northwards as far as the

515

Chinese frontier the thalweg of the Mekong shall form the limit of the possessions or spheres of influence of Great Britain and France. It is agreed that the nationals and dependents of each of the two countries shall not exercise any jurisdiction or authority within the possessions or sphere of influence of the other.

The police of the islands in this part of the river which are separated from the British shore by a branch of the river shall, so long as they are thus separated, be entrusted to the French authorities. The fishery shall be open to the inhabitants of both banks.

IV. The two Governments agree that all commercial and other privileges and advantages conceded in the two Chinese provinces of Yunnan and Szechuen either to Great Britain or France, in virtue of their respective Conventions with China of the 1st March, 1894, and the 20th June, 1895, and all the privileges and advantages of any nature which may in the future be conceded in these two Chinese provinces, whether to Great Britain or France, shall, as far as rests with them, be extended and rendered common to both Powers and to their nationals and dependents, and they engage to use their influence and good offices with the Chinese Government for this purpose.

V. The two Governments agree to name Commissioners delegated by each of them, who shall be charged to fix by mutual agreement, after examination of the titles produced on either side, the most equitable delimitation between the British and French possessions in the region situated to the west of the Lower Niger.

VI. In conformity with the stipulations of Article XL of the General Convention concluded between Great Britain and the Regency of Tunis on the 19th July, 1875, which provides for a revision of that Treaty "in order that the two Contracting Parties may have the opportunity of hereafter treating and agreeing upon such other arrangements as may tend still further to the improvement of their mutual intercourse, and to the advancement of the interests of their respective people," the two Governments agree at once to commence negotiations for replacing the said General Convention by a new Convention, which shall correspond to the intentions proposed in the Article above referred to.

Done at London, the 15th January, 1896.

SALISBURY.
Alph. De Courcel.

APPENDIX W

THE PEKING PETITION

To the President of the United States, Washington:

We whose names are subscribed to this petition and to the accompanying Memorial do most urgently beg that the American Government, in compliance with the high mandate of the Christian civilization of the twentieth century, and in defense of the vital interests of the American as well as of the Chinese republic, and in furtherance of the sacred cause of world peace on the Pacific . . . . will immediately, in conjunction if possible with Great Britain and the other Powers, but if necessary alone, demand of the Chinese—not the Japanese—government representation, as parties in interest, in the conferences on the Twenty-one Demands now proceeding, which demands vitally affect American and world interests guaranteed under the Open Door Agreement. We further beg that, pending the arrival of such representatives of America and of Great Britain and other Powers, the Chinese and Japanese Governments shall be requested to suspend negotiations, in order that the interests of all nations may be effectively secured against infringement. And still further we beg that the Governments both of China and Japan may be notified that the presence of unusual bodies of Japanese troops on Chinese soil at this time not only embarrasses freedom of negotiations but constitutes an outrage on the rights, and a serious menace to the peace and safety, of Americans and of foreigners generally, and that pending the removal of such excessive contingents of Japanese troops all negotiations should be suspended. With all sentiments of profound respect we submit this Petition and accompanying Memorial, claiming no superior wisdom but only superior opportunities of acquaintance with the situation in its present serious aspect, and in its inevitable future consequences. We request that if not incompatible with the public interest this Petition and Memorial, with our names attached, may be communicated to the Associated Press for such further use as may serve the interests involved.

Peking, Easter, 1915.

CHARLES F. HUBBARD,
Minister of the Union Foreign Church.

W. A. P. MARTIN,
Ex-President of the Imperial University.

CHAUNCEY GOODRICH,
Chairman of the Mandarin Revision Committee.

H. H. LOWRY,
President Peking University.

JOHN WHORRY,
Chairman of the Union Wen-Li Bible Revision Committee.

COURTENEY H. FENN,
Principal Union Theological College.

EDWARD W. THWING,
Superintendent International Reform Bureau.

APPENDIX X

THE QUESTION OF JAPANESE IN THE UNITED STATES

SUMMARY OF THE AMERICAN POSITION
Aide-mémoire to the Japanese Embassy.

Viscount Chinda's aide-mémoire is presented apparently in pursuance of a telegram received on June 30 from the Imperial Minister for Foreign Affairs. In this telegram the statement is made that the larger part of the land actually owned by Japanese in California was acquired before July 17, 1911, the effective date of the existing treaty; and certain decisions of the Supreme Court of the United States in Chirac *vs.* Chirac, 2 Wheaton, 259, and other cases are invoked as guaranteeing rights of property which were acquired by Japanese subjects in the United States, while the treaty of 1894 was in operation.

The Department, following the example set in the aide-mémoire, refrains from entering on the present occasion into a minute analysis of each of the judicial decisions thus cited. The Department, however, accepts the enunciation of principle, quoted from the decision in Chirac *v.* Chirac, "that a right once vested does not require, for its preservation, the continued existence of the power by which it was acquired"; and that "if a treaty, or any other law, has performed its office by giving a right, the expiration of the treaty or law can not extinguish that right." The Department has already observed, in its reply to Viscount Chinda's note of the 4th of June, and now repeats, that it does not doubt that full protection will be extended by the courts to all vested rights of property.

So far as the aide-mémoire relates to rights secured by the existing treaty of 1911, the Department may again recur to the fact that, by Section 2 of the California statute, it is provided that aliens not eligible to citizenship under the laws of the United States "may acquire, possess, enjoy, and transfer real property or any interest therein in this State in the manner and to the extent and for the purposes prescribed by any treaty now existing between the Government of the United States and the nation or country of which such alien is a citizen or subject." As this clause in express terms requires the recognition of any rights secured by existing treaty, it is

519

not to be assumed that any right so secured would not be fully protected.

The aide-mémoire, however, appears to extend too far the theory that the ownership of property carries with it a vested right to dispose of such property in all the ways in which property may be transferred, by sale, by gift, by devise, or by descent, without future limitation or restriction. Such a theory would render it impossible for a country to alter its laws with regard to the transmission of property. So far as the Department is advised it has never been held that a right of ownership, vested either in a citizen or in an alien, would be impaired by a change in the law denying to any and all aliens the right to purchase lands. Such changes in the law have not been infrequent either in the United States or elsewhere, and it is believed that they have not been held to impair vested rights. If such rights are not impaired by forbidding alienation or transmission to all aliens, they are obviously not impaired by the prohibition of alienation or transmission to particular classes of aliens. Attention may in this relation be drawn to numerous treaties between the United States and other Powers by which it is provided that where, on the death of the owner, real estate in the territories of the one Power would descend upon a citizen of the other who is disqualified by alienage from taking, the latter shall be allowed a period, varying according to the stipulations of the treaties, to sell the land and withdraw the proceeds. These stipulations clearly recognize the fact that the right of ownership is not regarded as carrying with it an unlimited and unalterable right of disposition or descent.

The aide-mémoire, recurring to the "spirit and intent" of the existing treaty rather than to its particular stipulations, maintains that the provisions of the California statute discriminate against Japanese subjects "in a matter in which, internationally speaking, aliens are usually placed on national or most favored nation footing." The Department regrets that it is unable to admit that the assumption here made is well founded. Without entering minutely into an examination of conventional stipulations, the Department desires to point out that the alien ownership of land has seldom been treated in the practice of the United States as a matter of most favored nation treatment. The most favored nation clauses in the treaties of the United States have almost universally related to matters of commerce and navigation. In only a few cases, perhaps not more than two or three, has alien ownership been conceded by means of a most favored nation clause. With these exceptions the right of alien ownership has been secured only by special treaty stipulations, with the result that the citizens of countries not having such treaty with the United States were unable to enjoy the right of ownership.

In this relation the aide-mémoire quotes from Moore's Digest of International Law, volume 6, page 702, a summary to the effect that "a Mexican statute discriminating against citizens of the United States and other aliens in respect to the capacity to hold real estate in Mexico is in conflict with the treaty of 1831."

The Department desires to deal with the subject to which the foregoing summary relates, as it does with all other matters, with entire candor. The aide-mémoire correctly states that the treaty of 1831 contains no express provision on the subject of ownership of lands and that the most favored nation clause which it contains relates only to commerce and navigation and to certain other matters in which the holding of real estate is not included. Nevertheless, the Government of the United States then essayed to make the same argument which is now so strongly urged in behalf of the Imperial Government, but was in the end obliged practically to abandon it. The facts are as follows:

The remonstrance or protest of the United States related to certain Mexican laws restricting the right of alien ownership of lands, and particularly to the law of July 20, 1863, which contains the following article:

2. Any inhabitant of the Republic has the right to denounce up to two thousand five hundred hectares, and no more, of public lands, with the exception of the natural born and naturalized citizens of nations adjoining the Republic who, by no title whatever, can acquire public lands in the States bordering the said nations.

That this Department on the occasion in question went the full length of the present Japanese contention is conclusively shown by the text of its instruction dated June 23, 1879, which reads as follows:

The discrimination in this respect between those citizens and other foreigners is still believed to be invidious, unnecessary, at variance with the treaty, and quite incompatible with those friendly relations which the obvious interest of both countries requires should be maintained between them. . . .

The Mexican law of 1863 is specially invidious toward citizens of our border States, because it practically discriminates against them by name, and thereby stigmatizes them as unworthy to have the privilege of holding real estate. This stigma can not be acquiesced in by this

Government, which does not admit the right of any foreign Power to discriminate between citizens of different States of this Union, who can only be known abroad as citizens of the United States. It may be that the treaty of 1831 does not expressly confer upon citizens of the parties the right to hold real estate in their respective territories, nor does it provide for an equality of rights in that respect between Mexicans and our own citizens. Although the equality between citizens of the United States and other foreigners in Mexico is by the 2nd and 3rd Articles of the Treaty literally restricted to matters of commerce and navigation, it may also fairly be construed to include a like equality in the privilege of acquiring and holding real estate. It can not be doubted that if the construction now claimed had been anticipated, it would have been thwarted by an explicit provision. There is believed to be no such discrimination against Mexican citizens in any law in this country. There may be at least one effect of the Mexican Act of 1863, which may have escaped the attention of that Government. Both the Treaty of Guadalupe Hidalgo and the Gadsen treaty guarantee to those Mexican citizens in the ceded territories who might become citizens of the United States their full rights of property in those territories. It is understood that many of those persons were owners of real estate in the border Mexican States. The effect of the law adverted to may be to confiscate that property while the title to that of those in Texas or elsewhere who were formerly Mexicans is guaranteed to them by treaty. It is hoped, therefore, that the policy of the Mexican Government on this subject will be so changed as to free it from the serious objections which have been pointed out.

The position of the Mexican Government was set forth in a note of its Minister of Foreign Affairs to the minister of the United States in Mexico, dated May 26, 1879, which reads as follows:

Having informed the President of the Republic of the contents of this note, by his direction I have the honor to make the following reply:

The right which a sovereign State has to concede or refuse to foreigners the privilege of acquiring real estate in its territory is indisputable and universally recognized, as well as to establish a limit to this right when it has been conceded. In the use of that right, in exercise of its sovereignty, Mexico has issued different laws upon the subject, among them that of the 11th of March, 1842, which, on permitting foreigners established and resident in the Republic to acquire and possess city and rural property in the territory, made exceptions of those departments adjoining or fronting other nations, determining that in these foreigners could not acquire real estate without express permission from the Government, and that of the 20th of July, 1863, which prohibits native or naturalized citizens of the adjoining countries to acquire public lands in the States of the Republic bordering on those countries.

Mexico, upon issuing these laws, has not infringed the stipulations of article 3rd of the treaty of 1831 nor has it violated the spirit which prevails in that convention, because nothing is established in them which should be considered as contrary to the liberty, privileges, and security guaranteed to North American citizens in order that they may go with their vessels and cargoes to any market, port, or river of the Republic to which other foreigners are admitted, nor are said citizens prevented from renting houses and warehouses for the purposes of their commerce, nor are they prevented from dealing in all kinds of products, manufactures, and goods, nor are they obliged to pay higher duties, imposts, or emoluments than are paid by the citizens of the most favored nations, nor is there anything, in a word, conceded to the latter with respect to navigation and commerce which is denied to North American citizens.

On the other hand, the equality of privileges, exemptions and rights with the most favored nations, stipulated with the United States in Art. III of the treaty of 1831 refers to navigation and commerce; but although it should extend to another subject (capitulo), that equality should be understood to be under circumstances also equal, and with reference to the acquisition of lands in the frontier States, it can not be sustained that the United States which adjoin Mexico are in the same condition as the nations of Europe or of South America, for instance.

I should at the same time call the attention of Your Excellency to the exception contained in the law of July 20, 1863, which is the most peremptory disposition referred to by the clause of the contract which gave rise to this note, which should not be considered as referring exclusively to the citizens of the United States, as it also comprehends those of the neighboring Republic of Guatemala, having the same conditions of boundary with Mexico; hence there is not nor can there be any justifiable motive for the Government of the United States to consider the prohibition established by the aforesaid law as an exclusion injurious to its citizens, and which refers to the nations bordering on the Republic.

It was in reply to this exposition of the law by the Mexican Government, which has been called forth by previous representations on the part of the United States, that the instructions above quoted, of subsequent date, were sent. They were duly communicated to the Mexican Government. On August 20, 1879, the minister of the United States of Mexico wrote to the Department as follows:

On the 17th ultimo I communicated to the Mexican Foreign Office in a note of that date the substance of your despatch No. 646, of June

23rd, relating to the prohibition to citizens of the United States from acquiring real estate and public lands in the Mexican border States.

Up to this date I have received no acknowledgment of my note and I regard it as highly probable that no reply will be made thereto, neither have we any reason to expect that the policy of the Mexican Government on the subject will be changed, as a result of the protest you have directed me to make.

The forecast of the American minister proved to be correct and the remonstrance of June 23, 1879, remained unanswered. The law also remained unaltered.

The aide-mémoire expresses the belief that the present instance is the first one in which a Power, being a party to a reciprocal commercial treaty guaranteeing most favored nation treatment "in all that concerns commerce and navigation," has ever been placed by the other contracting party at a disadvantage, as compared with nontreaty countries, "in matters which, in the treaty, are made the subject of reciprocal concession." This passage seems to blend two questions which are by no means interdependent. As is observed in the Department's note of the 16th instant, if the contracting parties have dealt with a certain subject by means of an express reciprocal agreement, it is hardly open to either party to assert that the adjustment thus made is not fair and equal, or that it is open to objection because it falls short of most favored nation treatment.

In the animadversions of the aide-mémoire upon discriminatory legislation the Department desires to express a general concurrence. It must, however, be admitted that discriminations of one kind and another very widely prevail, and that it is often necessary to deal with them in a tolerant spirit in order that greater causes of irritation may be avoided. Perhaps in no case is it more essential to take this moderate view than in that of the ownership of lands.

The aide-mémoire quotes a resolution of the House of Representatives of the United States on December 13, 1911, calling for the termination of the then existing commercial treaty between the United States and Russia because of the refusal of the Russian Government, as the resolution declared, to admit American Jews generally to that country. This resolution, it may be observed, was never communicated to the Russian Government and never assumed an international character. The passage quoted in the aide-mémoire does not appear in the resolution adopted by Congress; and notice was, as the aide-mémoire correctly states, given to Russia of the intention to terminate the treaty on the ground that it was "no longer fully responsive, in various respects, to the needs of the political and material relations of the two countries." The treaty was subsequently terminated, but, with this exception, the previous conditions continue and the discrimination complained of remains unchanged.

The aide-mémoire refers to the California statute as discriminating against Japanese subjects "in the matter of ownership of lands and houses." The distinctions on this subject have been pointed out in the Department's note of the 16th instant, in which the meaning and effect of the clauses of the existing treaty are fully set forth. It may be repeated that the statute contains no discrimination against Japanese as such, but applies equally to all aliens not eligible to citizenship.

The Department, following the example of the aide-mémoire, has forborne to enter into the discussion of the various and sometimes intricate questions affecting corporations as compared with individuals. These are questions peculiarly appropriate for judicial examination; for, while it is held that a corporation is a "citizen" of, or has its "domicile" in, the State by which it was created, even though a majority of its stockholders may be citizens of other States or countries, yet these are matters more or less of legal regulation, and the rights, privileges, and immunities of corporations are by no means coextensive in all matters with those of natural persons.

The aide-mémoire refers to a suggestion that the question of alien ownership of land in the several States of the United States is beyond the reach of the treaty-making power. The Department desires only to say that such a suggestion has not come from the Government of the United States. The aide-mémoire is correct in its statement that this subject has been dealt with by the treaty-making power, and that the provisions of the treaties on the subject have been upheld by the courts.

The aide-mémoire quotes from an instruction of this Department of March 5, 1875, in which the Secretary of State of the United States declared, in a case arising in Brazil, that the Imperial Government at Rio de Janeiro must be held accountable for any injury to the person or property of a citizen of the United States committed by the authorities of a Province. The Department is not disposed to question the correctness of this view, but would call attention to the fact that, in the instruction referred to, the statement was made that, as the governors of the Provinces in Brazil were appointed by the Imperial Government, "the latter may be regarded as specially responsible for their acts in all cases where the law of nations may have been infringed, *and justice may be unobtainable through the courts.*"

As is stated in Department's note of the 16th instant, the subjects of His Imperial Majesty will find in the courts of the United States, in the manner provided by the Constitution of the United States, full protection for all their legal rights, held under treaty or otherwise, and this Government will stand ready at all times through its proper officials to use its good offices to secure the prompt and efficacious determination of such suits. Such appears to be the proper and feasible course in the present matter, in which questions of various kinds may arise, in respect of which it is scarcely possible to forecast the appropriate forms of action. The courts of the United States, as is well known, deal only with actual questions, with actual infractions of rights, and not with infractions merely mooted or apprehended.

The California School case and the Horcon Ranch case presented questions of a different order from those now under consideration. In the California School case a single and actual treaty question, not relating to a matter of property, had arisen and was ready for adjudication. In the Horcon Ranch case a suit in equity was brought by the Government of the United States against an irrigation company for the purpose of preserving an international boundary to which the United States was directly a party. The United States is no doubt interested in the maintenance of all its treaties; but, as the numerous adjudicated cases cited in the aide-mémoire clearly show, questions concerning private titles to land, whether such titles be assured by treaty or not, are adjudicated upon the suit of the parties in interest without any interposition on the part of the Government of the United States.

Not only is this the practice, but it is greatly to the advantage of individual suitors that it is so. As Governments not infrequently differ in the interpretation of treaties, the private individual, if dependent for judicial protection upon the motion of the Government within whose jurisdiction he asserts that his treaty rights are denied, might be deprived of an effective remedy altogether, in case that Government should hold that the treaty was not violated. Moreover, the individual suitor, in presenting his arguments and allegations, is not restrained by the responsibility which necessarily attaches to the declarations and contentions of an immediate party to the international compact. His dependence upon the action of such a party would hamper his efforts and diminish the opportunity for redress.

For these reasons the judicial defense of private rights, and particularly of rights of private property, even where they may have vested under a treaty, is left to the suit of the individuals concerned. In the present instance, however, this Government has offered to go beyond the usual practice and to use its good offices to facilitate the progress of the judicial procedure, out of deference to the susceptibilities of a friendly Power to whom this Government wishes ever to be bound by the closest ties of amity and respect.

DEPARTMENT OF STATE,
Washington, July 16, 1913.

THE JAPANESE MINISTER FOR FOREIGN AFFAIRS TO THE JAPANESE AMBASSADOR.

Received by the ambassador August 23, 1913, and received at the Department of State August 26, 1913.

(Telegram)

Imperial Japanese Embassy,
Washington.

The two communications addressed to you by the Honorable the Secretary of State on the 16th of July last, in further discussion of the question of the recently enacted alien land law of California, have been received and carefully considered by the Imperial Government.

That act, by depriving the Japanese subjects of the right of land ownership, while freely continuing the right, not only in favor of the subjects and citizens of all the other Powers with which the United States maintain reciprocal treaty relations, but in favor of many nontreaty aliens, has established a discrimination of the most marked and invidious character against Japan. The measure is, moreover, in the opinion of the Imperial Government, unjust and inequitable, and contrary to the letter and spirit of the Japanese-American treaty, as well as at variance with the accepted precepts governing and regulating the intercourse of good neighborhood, and being admittedly *ex industria* discriminatory against this Empire as compared with other States, it is also mortifying to the nation and disregardful of the national susceptibilities of the Japanese people.

This is the gravamen of Japan's complaint. The notes of the Honorable W. J. Bryan contain remarks in explanation and extenuation of the action of California, but nothing, in the estimation of the Imperial Government, which answers fundamentally to that complaint or which tends to shake their conviction regarding the main question. If, as is confidently believed, the existing treaty between Japan and the United States has been violated, there is but one remedy, and the Imperial Government are unable to escape the conclusion that the duty of applying that remedy devolves solely upon the Government of the United States, as the measure complained of has, despite the protest lodged by you, been permitted to go into operation.

The Imperial Government reserve for the present the further discussion of the question at issue. There are, however, some statements and conclusions advanced by Mr. Bryan which the Imperial Government feel it their duty forthwith to call in question. This instruction is designed to answer those observations.

I hasten, in the first place, to say that the Imperial Government do not for a moment imagine that the discrimination complained of was the outcome of a national policy. They regard, and have from the outset regarded, the action in question as of a local character. But, whatever causes may have been responsible for the measure, it can not be denied that, in its final manifestation, it is clearly indicative of racial antagonism. Nor, in the opinion of the Imperial Government, can any justification for such enactment be found in the assertion that it was "the emanation of economic conditions." It is the high office of modern treaties of commerce to prevent undue international discriminations, and the most favored nation principle, which finds a place in nearly all such compacts, has had the effect, in an international sense, of equalizing opportunities in all the various avenues of commercial and industrial life. It is true that special privileges are, in exceptional circumstances, sometimes granted by one nation in favor of another, but the present case stands out, it is believed, as the one single instance without historical parallel, in which a State maintaining, by treaty, the reciprocal most favored nation relations with another State, has ever, in a matter such as that under discussion, essayed to discriminate against such other State, as compared with third powers with which no such relations exist. The action of Mexico in 1863, which was so strongly condemned by the United States, furnishes no such parallel, since the law in that case was, it appears, based upon considerations of a geographic nature exclusively.

The Secretary of State denies the proposition advanced by you to the effect that the California statute discriminates against the Japanese subjects, and that in the matter of land ownership aliens are usually, internationally speaking, placed on national or most favored nation footing. In support of that denial he cites the practice which prevails in the United States on the subject of alien land ownership, and he adds "that the citizens of countries not having such treaty with the United States (*i. e.,* treaty granting, either expressly or by inference, under the most favored nation clause, the right of land ownership) were unable to enjoy the right of ownership." This statement has naturally caused surprise to the Imperial Government, and they confess their inability to understand it. It not only conflicts directly with the California law in question and is irreconcilable with the statutes of many States of the Union by which the right of alien ownership is accorded independently of treaty stipulations, but it declares, in effect, that the discrimination complained of, which has been repeatedly recognized as a fact, is without foundation. In these circumstances it is quite sufficient for the Imperial Government to repeat their contention that, by the California enactment, the Japanese subjects are denied the right of real estate ownership in localities in which that right is freely conceded to aliens belonging not only to the States which have no treaty engagements with the United States on the subject, but to the Powers which have no commercial treaties whatever with the United States.

Recurring to the subject of the Mexican incident, I desire to say that the Imperial Government are unable, upon the record in the case, to concur with Mr. Bryan in the view that the United States was, in the end, obliged practically to abandon its contention. Reading in natural sequence the correspondence exchanged between the United States and Mexico, the conviction is, it seems to me, irreprovable, that the quoted words of the Secretary of State on the occasion, instead of being regarded as an argument, must be accepted as the deliberate conclusion of the American Government on the subject.

It is unnecessary, it seems to me, to follow Mr. Bryan in his remarks concerning the negotiations connected with the conclusion of the treaty of 1911. It is sufficient to say that the reason, why no stipulation regarding land ownership was inserted in the treaty, is because neither contracting party desired at that time such a stipulation, the United States equally with Japan. The assurance contained in Viscount Uchida's note of February 21, 1911, on the subject of liberal interpretation of the Japanese land law, was given at the instance of the United States, because of the condition of reciprocity contained in that law. The assurance was given, as stated in the note, "In return for the rights of land ownership which are granted to Japanese by the laws of the various States of the United States."

The laws of Japan on the subject of alien land tenure are not illiberal, but, in any case, they contain no provisions discriminating, in any manner whatever, against the citizens of the United States. On the contrary, in all that relates to land ownership, as well as in the matter of all other civil rights, the American citizens, without distinctions and without conditions, are accorded in Japan full and complete most favored nation treatment, and there is no desire on the part of the Japanese administration to modify this state of things. What Japan claims is nothing more than fair and equal treatment.

The Secretary of State, it is observed, dwells at length upon the subject of labor immigration into the United States, and, in the same relation, he refers to the action of Japan in circumstances somewhat analogous to those existing in America. The reason or necessity for this exposition is not understood by the Imperial Government. The question of immigration has nothing whatever to do with the present controversy, and any reference to it only tends to obscure the real issue. This announcement I wish to make very categorical. More than four years ago, the Imperial Government willingly coöperated with the American Government in adopting suitable measures in regulation of labor movements from Japan to the United States. The steps thus taken were entirely efficacious, so that during the past three years considerably more Japanese laborers left the United States than have entered that country. The Government of the United States has recognized and frankly admitted the sufficiency of the measures enforced by the Imperial Government in the matter. The Japanese ambassador to the United States, at the time of the conclusion of the treaty of 1911, declared under the authority of his Government that the Imperial Government were fully prepared to maintain with equal effectiveness the limitation and control which were then exerted in regulation of the emigration of laborers to the United States. Accordingly, in order to correct and finally dispel the popular error, I wish to say that there is no question whatever between Japan and the United States on the subject of the Japanese labor immigration into the United States. The present controversy relates exclusively to the question of the treatment of the Japanese subjects who are lawfully in the United States or may hereafter lawfully become resident therein consistently with the existing regulations. So far as such subjects are concerned, the Imperial Government claim for them fair and equal treatment, and are unable either to acquiesce in the unjust and obnoxious discrimination complained of, or to regard the question as closed so long as the existing state of things is permitted to continue.

You are requested to explain the substance of this instruction to the Secretary of State and deliver a copy.

THE JAPANESE MINISTER FOR FOREIGN AFFAIRS TO THE JAPANESE AMBASSADOR.

Delivered at State Department June 10, 1914.

> Imperial Japanese Embassy,
> Washington.

Among the more important pending questions that confronted me when I assumed charge of this Department, was the issue resulting from the enactment last year of the legislature of California respecting alien real property ownership. The measure, as you are aware, undertook in effect to draw a distinction in the matter of such ownership between aliens belonging to different races. The avowed purpose of the law was, on the one hand, to annul the then existing right of ownership so far as Japanese subjects were concerned and, on the other, to continue the right in favor of aliens of the white and black races.

I have given the subject my most serious consideration and am consequently well satisfied that the enactment in question is not only in disregard of the letter and spirit of the existing treaty between Japan and the United States of America, but is essentially unfair and invidiously discriminatory against my countrymen and inconsistent as well with the sentiment of amity and good neighborhood which has always presided over the relations between the two countries. Nor can I escape the conviction that the said enactment which was intended to have international effect is also in excess of the authority of the State of California for the reason that the separate States of the United States are, internationally speaking, wholly unknown and entirely without responsibility. In any case, the Imperial Government are confident that such action as complained of stands without historical parallel, and they are happy to believe that the legislation in question forms no part of the general policy of the Federal Government, but is the outcome of unfortunate local conditions. I therefore fully concur in the views which you, in pursuance of instructions from my predecessor, presented to the Honorable the Secretary of State on the subject.

I also cordially appreciate the motives which in the interest of international conciliation and good will induced Baron Makino to give favorable consideration to the idea of concluding a convention regarding the matter. But the project, as it stands at the present time, instead of composing existing misunderstandings, would, I fear, tend to create new difficulties. Accordingly, you are instructed to inform Mr. Bryan that the Imperial Government are disinclined to continue the negotiations looking to the conclusion of a convention on the lines of the project which has been under discussion, but that they prefer to recur to the correspondences which were interrupted by the ineffective negotiations, and that they will now look for an answer to the note which you handed to Mr. Bryan on the 26th August last, hoping that in a renewal of the study of the case a fundamental solution of the question at issue may happily be found.

The negotiations looking to an adjustment of the matter in dispute by means of a convention having failed, the advantage of still withholding from the public the correspondences that have passed between the two Governments on the subject is no longer apparent. You are consequently also instructed to announce to the Secretary of State that the Imperial Government desire to make public the correspondences in question, believing that fuller and more accurate information regarding the matter will contribute to the final settlement of the controversy.

You are authorized in carrying out the above instructions to hand a copy of this note to Mr. Bryan.

APPENDIX Y

THE DISABILITIES OF ALIENS IN JAPAN
(From the "Japan Chronicle," March 16, 1916)

In the new book which Mr. J. E. De Becker has brought out, entitled "Pointers on Japanese Law," considerable interest is likely to be felt by foreigners residing in this country in the first two chapters, which are headed "Rights of Aliens" and "Disabilities of Aliens." It is noteworthy that the first chapter is longer than the second, but that may be merely because the explanation required is more voluminous. The principal rights expressly conceded to foreigners are the right of travel and residence and the enjoyment of full protection of their persons and property; access to courts of justice on the same terms as Japanese; religious freedom; no discrimination in taxation; exemption from military service, military contributions, and forced loans; the right to manufacture and trade; the right to enter into partnership with foreigners and Japanese, or to become shareholders in joint-stock companies; the right to come with ships or cargoes to ports open to foreign commerce, and not to pay higher duties than are paid by Japanese; exemption from transit duties, and equality of treatment with Japanese in regard to warehousing facilities, drawbacks, and exportation; the right to lease land and to acquire rights of superficies in land—*i. e.,* to erect buildings or plant trees—for the purposes of residence or trade; the right to take mortgages upon land and buildings.

It will be observed that these are practically all treaty stipulations, and suggest a time—never, it may be hoped, likely to recur—when it was necessary to negotiate for even elementary rights for aliens. So far as the Japanese law is concerned, the only reference to foreigners in the Civil Code is the declaration in Article 2 that foreigners enjoy private rights except so far as forbidden by treaty, law, or regulations. Mr. de Becker explains that private rights mean simply rights as between man and man, such as ownership and contract rights.

The chapter on the disabilities of aliens runs as follows (we omit certain paragraphs of explanation) :—

(*a*) Foreigners cannot own land as individuals, but can become superficiary holders for exceedingly long periods. While a superficies is by no means equal to ownership, if care be taken in drawing and recording, it is a fairly valuable class of holding; but it is still young and has weak and inconvenient points which are gradually being discovered, and is still somewhat of an unknown quantity. A company formed under the Japanese law by foreigners can own land, but not Perpetual Leases of lands in the former Settlements. . . .

(b) Foreigners cannot become owners of ships flying the Japanese national flag. Foreigners can be interested in (1) limited partnerships (Gōshi-Kwaisha), (2) joint-stock limited partnerships (Kabushiki Gōshi-Kwaisha), and (3) joint-stock limited companies (Kabushiki-Kwaisha) owning Japanese ships; but in the first case they cannot become partners with unlimited liability, in the second case the same rule applies, and in the third case they cannot become directors. In other words, the law is so arranged that all the executive power is vested in the hands of Japanese subjects.

(c) Foreigners cannot at present become shareholders in certain banks, such as the "Bank of Japan," the "Yokohama Specie Bank," or the "Agricultural and Industrial Banks." The Articles of a few private companies (e.g. The Nippon Yusen Kwaisha) exclude foreigners from membership.

(d) Foreigners cannot, as individuals, engage in mining, but a company formed under the Japanese law by foreigners can do so.

(e) Foreigners cannot become members, shareholders or brokers of the various Exchanges; and they cannot become members of Japanese Chambers of Commerce.

(f) Foreigners cannot engage in the Emigration business either as individuals or as shareholders in Emigration companies.

(g) Foreigners appearing as plaintiffs or as accessory intervenors on the side of plaintiffs must, on the demand of the defendants, furnish security for costs. This does not apply where by treaty, or by the laws of the State to which the plaintiff belongs, a Japanese in a similar case would not be bound to furnish security. The Japanese Courts will not enforce the judgments of foreign tribunals except in virtue of a Treaty or Convention guaranteeing reciprocity.

(h) A foreigner can only sue in forma pauperis so far as by treaty, or by the laws of his State, a Japanese could, in a similar case, claim such indulgence.

(i) Foreigners cannot hold any public offices and cannot become members of the Japanese Bar.

(j) Foreigners do not enjoy the franchise.

(k) Foreign commercial juridical persons are recognised by law; but private non-commercial corporate bodies are not, except in virtue of a special treaty or convention.

With regard to the ownership of land, Mr. de Becker points out that the measure passed some years ago, while the treaties were under negotiation, with the ostensible object of granting land ownership to foreigners, and which has never been promulgated, is a half-hearted piece of legislation which is quite worthless for the object with which it has been devised. It might also have been well to warn lease-holders that according to a decision of the Supreme Court in Japan the terms of a lease fixing the rent offer no protection against an in-crease of rent by the landlord, who may raise the rent if the value of the land is increased by improvements made by the tenant or by an increase in the value of surrounding property. We cannot say whether this decision applies to leases between Japanese because the only cases we know of are those brought by Japanese landlords against foreign leaseholders, and the only cases quoted in the Courts are those in which foreigners are concerned. The restriction of the ownership of ships to native subjects is one that prevails in most countries, the reason being that in a state of war a Government finds it necessary to commandeer ships, and foreign ownership under the flag might raise awkward complications. But an additional disability is that the coasting trade, including voyages between Japan and Formosa, is reserved to Japanese vessels, so that while Japanese ships may ply to and from any British port (Hongkong to Singa-pore, Singapore to Calcutta, Colombo, or Bombay), a British vessel is prohibited from carrying a pound of tea or a single passenger be-tween Nagasaki and Kobe or Yokohama. Again, the exclusion of resident foreigners from the holding of shares in certain banks, steamship, and development companies—and the list given by Mr. de Becker could be materially extended—is extremely unjust, seeing that these undertakings are subsidized or guaranteed by the Gov-ernment out of the taxes which foreigners equally with Japanese have to pay. It could be readily understood that the authorities may desire to keep the profits of subsidized undertakings within the country, but this could be done by making domicile the test, not nationality, for it is evidently most unfair that foreign resi-dents who in theory bear an equal burden of taxation—it is in practice heavier than that borne by Japanese, as we have pointed out on many occasions—should be excluded from the profits of en-terprises which are subsidized by those taxes.

So we might go through the list of disabilities. Why should for-eigners, as individuals, be prohibited from mining enterprises, but yet if formed into a company enjoy the right? Both individual and corporation are equally subject to Japanese law. Such a prohibition does not establish confidence in Japan, nor is it likely to cause for-eign capital to be invested in the country to develop Japan's mineral wealth. Why are foreigners excluded from becoming members, shareholders, or brokers of the various Exchanges? We do not know what the practice is in other countries, but in both England and America aliens are entitled to hold these positions on the Exchanges, so long as they obey the rules, while as Chambers of Commerce are not semi-Government institutions any one can belong to them who pays the fee and is elected after application. Foreigners are not likely to aspire to public office in Japan, but, seeing the many commercial questions affecting foreigners that come into the Japanese Courts, it is a distinct injustice that foreigners should be denied the right to become members of the Japanese Bar. The English Bar is open to any man of whatever nationality who qualifies according to the regulations, and several Japanese attorneys are proud to describe themselves as Barristers of the Inner Temple, &c., but we never heard of one of them advocating the throwing open of the Japanese Bar to Englishmen. There is no concern for reciprocity. With regard to the last item mentioned by Mr. de Becker, no foreigner is likely to complain because he is denied the franchise. Every country reserves the suffrage to its own citizens. But in Japan the exclusion goes further, even the municipal franchise being withheld. On the Pacific coast of America, where the Japanese complain of the injustice with which they are treated, they nevertheless possess the municipal franchise if in the position of ratepayers. On the other hand, in a town like Kobe, where foreigners contribute largely to the rates, they have no voice whatever in the manner in which the public revenue is spent. They cannot cast a vote for a member of the Assembly or become members. All they are permitted to do is to pay the taxes, and the local authorities are careful that in this respect there are no backsliders. Again, we hear from time to time a good deal concerning the injustice of the laws excluding Japanese laborers from America and the British Colonies, yet a regulation of exclusion is also in force in Japan against alien laborers, and for much the same reason as in America and Canada. Mr. de Becker points out that by Imperial Ordinance No. 352 of 1899 (the year in which the Revised Treaties came into force) laborers of alien nationality—including men employed in connection with agriculture, fishing, mining, civil engineering, architecture, manufacturing, transporting, carting, stevedoring, and other miscellaneous work—may not reside outside the former Foreign Settlements and the mixed residential districts except with the permission of the prefectural governor. We believe we are correct in saying that such permits are never given. Some years ago a Japanese contractor engaged a body of Chinese coolies for work on a railway, but was compelled to repatriate them by the authorities. On another occasion a foreign firm employing a couple of Chinese skilled artisans at some works outside the limits of the former Foreign Settlement was informed by the authorities that this was against the law, and, though every effort was made to obtain the permission of the prefectural governor, it was of no avail, the governor evidently receiving instructions from Tokyo that no exceptions were to be made. It may, of course, be necessary for the Japanese to protect their own people against an incursion of laborers from China, with a much lower standard of living, but in that case there ought not to be so much fuss made of similar precautions taken on the Pacific coast of America.

In the course of the discussion that has taken place over the Anglo-Japanese Alliance, Japanese newspapers and publicists have expressed much resentment at the opposition offered by Englishmen to the extension of Japanese influence or territory in the East. Putting aside the provisions of the Anglo-Japanese Alliance, can Japanese be surprised that the extension of Japanese dominion is not welcomed when it is seen that it is coincident with the imposition of so many disabilities on foreigners? Denial of landholding rights, exclusion from the coasting trade, prohibition from investing in companies which are subsidized out of taxation, exclusion from the Exchanges, the municipal franchise, the right to practice at the Bar. When it is seen that the Customs carefully register the nationality of exporters or importers, to supply figures to the "professors" of High Commercial Schools who desire to prove that the foreigner is gradually being driven out of trade in Japan; when the Agricultural and Commercial Department preaches (not merely in time of war, but always) the doctrine that imports must be checked and exports increased, and that Japanese must get the import as well as the export trade into their own hands; when there is a tariff that is almost prohibitive on foreign goods wherever Japan sets up her flag; when reciprocity in the diplomatic language employed by Japan means superior advantage,—can any Japanese possessed of impartiality be surprised that the extension of Japanese power and influence is not regarded by British and other residents in the far East with enthusiasm? We hold that the policy is a mistaken one, even from the point of view of Japan's interests. A little more liberality in theory and practice would make a great difference to Japan's welfare and prosperity.

APPENDIX Z

SINO-RUSSO MONGOLIAN AGREEMENT
(*Translation from the French*)

The President of the Republic of China, His Imperial Majesty the Emperor of all Russias, and His Holiness the Bogdo Djembzoun Damba Khoutoukhtou Khan of Outer Mongolia, animated by a sincere desire to settle by mutual agreement various questions created by a new state of things in Outer Mongolia, have named for that purpose their Plenipotentiary Delegates, that is to say:

The President of the Republic of China, General Py-Koue-Fang and Monsieur Tcheng-Loh, Envoy Extraordinary and Minister Plenipotentiary of China to Mexico;

His Imperial Majesty the Emperor of all Russias, His Councilor of State Alexandre Miller, Diplomatic Agent and Consul-General in Mongolia; and His Holiness the Bogdo Djembzoun Damba Khoutoukhtou Khan of Outer Mongolia, Erdeni Djonan Beise Shirnin Damdin, Vice-Chief of Justice, and Touchetou Tsing Wang Tchakdourjab, Chief of Finance, who having verified their respective full powers found in good and due form, have agreed upon the following:

ARTICLE I

Outer Mongolia recognizes the Sino-Russian Declaration and the Notes exchanged between China and Russia of the fifth day of the eleventh month of the second year of the Republic of China, 23rd October, 1913.

ARTICLE II

Outer Mongolia recognizes China's suzerainty. China and Russia recognize the autonomy of Outer Mongolia forming part of Chinese territory.

ARTICLE III

Autonomous Mongolia has no right to conclude international treaties with foreign powers respecting political and territorial questions.

As respects questions of a political and territorial nature in Outer

Mongolia, the Chinese Government engages to conform to Article II of the Note exchanged between China and Russia on the fifth day of the eleventh month of the second year of the Republic of China, 23rd October, 1913.

Article IV

The title: "Bogdo Djembzoun Damba Khoutoukhtou Khan of Outer Mongolia" is conferred by the President of the Republic of China. The calendar of the Republic as well as the Mongol calendar of cyclical signs are to be used in official documents.

Article V

China and Russia, conformably to Articles II and III of the Sino-Russian Declaration of the fifth day of the eleventh month of the second year of the Republic of China, 23rd October, 1913, recognize the exclusive right of the autonomous government of Outer Mongolia to attend to all the affairs of its internal administration and to conclude with foreign powers international treaties and agreements respecting questions of a commercial and industrial nature concerning autonomous Mongolia.

Article VI

Conformably to the same Article III of the Declaration, China and Russia engage not to interfere in the system of autonomous internal administration existing in Outer Mongolia.

Article VII

The military escort of the Chinese Dignitary at Urga provided for by Article III of the above-mentioned Declaration is not to exceed two hundred men. The military escorts of his assistants at Ouliassoutai, at Kobdo, and at Mongolian-Kiachta are not to exceed fifty men each. If, by agreement with the autonomous government of Outer Mongolia, assistants of the Chinese Dignitary are appointed in other localities of Outer Mongolia, their military escorts are not to exceed fifty men each.

Article VIII

The Imperial Government of Russia is not to send more than one hundred and fifty men as consular guard for its representative at Urga. The military escorts of the Imperial consulates and vice-consulates of Russia, which have already been established or which may be established by agreement with the autonomous government of Outer Mongolia, in other localities of Outer Mongolia, are not to exceed fifty men each.

ARTICLE IX

On all ceremonial or official occasions the first place of honor is due to the Chinese Dignitary. He has the right, if necessary, to present himself in private audience with His Holiness Bogdo Djembzoun Damba Khoutoukhtou Khan of Outer Mongolia. The Imperial Representative of Russia enjoys the same right of private audience.

ARTICLE X

The Chinese Dignitary at Urga and his assistants in the different localities of Outer Mongolia provided for by Article VII of this agreement are to exercise general control lest the acts of the autonomous government of Outer Mongolia and its subordinate authorities may impair the suzerain rights and the interests of China and her subjects in autonomous Mongolia.

ARTICLE XI

Conformably to Article IV of the Note exchanged between China and Russia on the fifth day of the eleventh month of the second year of the Republic of China (23rd October, 1915), the territory of autonomous Outer Mongolia comprises the regions which were under the jurisdiction of the Chinese Amban at Ourga, or the Tartar-General at Ouliassoutai and of the Chinese Amban at Kobdo; and connects with the boundary of China by the limits of the banners of the four aimaks of Khalkha and of the district of Kobdo, bounded by the district of Houloun-Bouire on the east, by Inner Mongolia on the south, by the Province of Sinkiang on the southwest, and by the districts of Altai on the west.

The formal delimitation between China and autonomous Mongolia is to be carried out by a special commission of delegates of China, Russia and autonomous Outer Mongolia, which shall set itself to the work of delimitation within a period of two years from the date of signature of the present Agreement.

ARTICLE XII

It is understood that customs duties are not to be established for goods of whatever origin they may be, imported by Chinese merchants into autonomous Outer Mongolia. Nevertheless, Chinese merchants shall pay all the taxes on internal trade which have been established in autonomous Outer Mongolia and which may be established therein in the future, payable by the Mongols of autonomous Outer Mongolia. Similarly the merchants of autonomous Outer Mongolia, when importing any kind of goods of local production into "Inner China," shall pay all the taxes on trade which have been established in "Inner China" and which may be established therein in the future, payable by Chinese merchants. Goods of foreign origin imported from autonomous Outer Mongolia into "Inner China" shall be subject to the customs duties stipulated in the regulations for land trade of the seventh year of the reign of Kouang-Hsu (1881).

ARTICLE XIII

Civil and criminal actions arising between Chinese subjects residing in autonomous Outer Mongolia are to be examined and adjudicated by the Chinese Dignitary at Urga and by his assistants in the other localities of autonomous Outer Mongolia.

ARTICLE XIV

Civil and criminal actions arising between Mongols of autonomous Outer Mongolia and Chinese subjects residing therein are to be examined and adjudicated conjointly by the Chinese Dignitary at Urga and his assistants in the other localities of autonomous Outer Mongolia, or their delegates, and the Mongolian authorities. If the defendant or accused is a Chinese subject and the claimant or the complainant is a Mongol of autonomous Outer Mongolia, the joint examination and decision of the case are to be held at the Chinese Dignitary's place at Niga and at that of his assistants in the other localities of autonomous Outer Mongolia; if the defendant or the accused is a Mongol of autonomous Outer Mongolia and the claimant or the complainant is a Chinese subject, the case is to be examined and decided in the same manner in the Mongolian yamen. The guilty are to be punished according to their own laws. The interested parties are free to arrange their disputes amicably by means of arbitrators chosen by themselves.

ARTICLE XV

Civil and criminal actions arising between Mongols of autonomous Outer Mongolia and Russian subjects residing therein are to be examined and decided conformably to the stipulations of Article XVI of the Russo-Mongolian Commercial Protocol of 21st October, 1912.

ARTICLE XVI

All civil and criminal actions arising between Chinese and Russian subjects in Autonomous Outer Mongolia are to be examined and decided in the following manner: in an action wherein the claimant or the complainant is a Russian subject and the defendant or accused is a Chinese subject, the Russian Consul personally or through his delegate participates in the judicial trial, enjoying the same rights as the Chinese Dignitary at Urga or his delegate or his assistants in the other localities of Autonomous Outer Mongolia. The Russian Consul or his delegate proceeds to the hearing of the claimant and the Russian witnesses in the court in session, and interrogates the defendant and the Chinese witnesses through the medium of the Chinese Dignitary at Urga or his delegate or of his assistants in the other localities of Autonomous Outer Mongolia; the Russian Consul or his delegate examines the evidence presented, demands security for "revindication" and has recourse to the opinion of experts, if he considers such expert opinion necessary for the elucidation of the rights of the parties, etc.; he takes part in deciding and in the drafting of the judgment, which he signs with the Chinese Dignitary at Urga or his delegate or his assistants in the other localities of Autonomous Outer Mongolia. The execution of the judgment constitutes a duty of the Chinese authorities.

The Chinese Dignitary at Urga and his Assistants in the other localities of Autonomous Outer Mongolia may likewise personally or through their delegates be present at the hearing of an action in the Consulates of Russia wherein the defendant or the accused is a Russian subject and the claimant or the complainant is a Chinese subject. The execution of the judgment constitutes a duty of the Russian authorities.

Article XVII

Since a section of the Kiachta-Urga-Kalgan telegraph line lies in the territory of Autonomous Outer Mongolia, it is agreed that the said section of the said telegraph line constitutes the complete property of the Autonomous Government of Outer Mongolia. The details respecting the establishment on the borders of that country and Inner Mongolia of a station to be administered by Chinese and Mongolian employees for the transmission of telegrams, as well as the questions of the tariff for telegrams transmitted and of the apportionment of the receipts, etc., are to be examined and settled by a special commission of technical delegates of China, Russia and Autonomous Outer Mongolia.

Article XVIII

The Chinese postal institutions at Urga and Mongolian Kiachta remain in force on the old basis.

Article XIX

The Autonomous Government of Outer Mongolia will place at the disposal of the Chinese Dignitary at Urga and of his Assistants at Ouliassoutai, Kobdo and Mongolian-Kiachta as well as of their staff, the necessary houses, which are to constitute the complete property of the Government of the Republic of China. Similarly, necessary grounds in the vicinity of the residences of the said staff are to be granted for their escorts.

Article XX

The Chinese Dignitary at Urga and his Assistants in the other localities of Autonomous Outer Mongolia and also their staff are to enjoy the right to use the courier stations of the Autonomous Mongolian Government conformably to the stipulations of Article XI of the Russo-Mongolian Protocol of 21st October, 1912.

Article XXI

The stipulations of the Sino-Russian declaration and the Notes exchanged between China and Russia of the 5th day of the 11th month of the 2nd Year of the Republic of China, 23rd October, 1913, as well as those of the Russo-Mongolian Commercial Protocol of the 21st October, 1912, remain in full force.

Article XXII

The present Agreement drawn up in triplicate in Chinese, Russian, Mongolian and French languages, comes into force from the day of its signature. Of the four texts which have been duly compared and found to agree, the French text shall be authoritative in the interpretation of the Present Agreement.

Done at Kiachta the 7th day of the Sixth Month of the Fourth Year of the Republic of China, corresponding to the Twenty-fifth of May, Seventh of June, One Thousand Nine Hundred Fifteen.

THE END.